D1352732

Assessment of Mental Capacity

FOURTH EDITION

REMOVED
FROM
STOCK

Other titles available from Law Society Publishing:

Advising Mentally Disordered Offenders: A Practical Guide (2nd edn)
Carolyn Taylor and Julia Krish, with Frank Farnham

Deprivation of Liberty: Collected Guidance
The Law Society

Elderly Client Handbook (5th edn)
General editor: Caroline Bielanska

Health and Social Care Handbook
Caroline Bielanska with Fiona Scolding

Lasting Powers of Attorney: A Practical Guide (2nd edn)
Craig Ward

Mental Capacity: A Guide to the New Law (2nd edn)
Nicola Greaney, Fenella Morris and Beverley Taylor

Probate Practitioner's Handbook (7th edn)
General editor: Lesley King

Law Society Wills and Inheritance Protocol
The Law Society

Titles from Law Society Publishing can be ordered from all good bookshops or direct (telephone 0370 850 1422, email **lawsociety@prolog.uk.com** or visit our online shop at **bookshop.lawsociety.org.uk**).

ASSESSMENT OF MENTAL CAPACITY

A Practical Guide for Doctors and Lawyers

FOURTH EDITION

The British Medical Association and the Law Society

General Editor: Alex Ruck Keene

The Law Society

ISBN-13: 978-1-78446-038-9

First published 1995
Second edition 2004
Third edition 2010
This fourth edition published in 2015 by the Law Society
113 Chancery Lane, London WC2A 1PL

Typeset by Columns Design XML Ltd, Reading
Printed by TJ International Ltd, Padstow, Cornwall

The paper used for the text pages of this book is FSC® certified. FSC (the Forest Stewardship Council®) is an international network to promote responsible management of the world's forests.

FSC
www.fsc.org
MIX
Paper from
responsible sources
FSC® C013056

Contents

Foreword	xi
Preface	xv
Acknowledgements	xvii
About the authors	xxi
Table of cases	xxv
Table of statutes	xxxi
Table of statutory instruments	xxxv
Table of international treaties and instruments	xxxix
Abbreviations	xli

PART I: INTRODUCTION

1	**The law, practice and this book**		**3**
	1.1	Mental capacity and the law	3
	1.2	How to use this book	6
	1.3	Scope of this book	8
	1.4	Further advice	10
2	**Professional and ethical issues**		**11**
	2.1	Capacity to instruct a solicitor	11
	2.2	Confidentiality	14
	2.3	Creating the right environment for assessing capacity	17
	2.4	Refusal to be assessed	19
	2.5	People assessed as lacking capacity	20
	2.6	Individuals at risk	21
	2.7	Summary of points for doctors	22
	2.8	Summary of points for lawyers	23

PART II: LEGAL PRINCIPLES

3	**The Mental Capacity Act 2005: capacity and best interests**		**27**
	3.1	The legal framework	27

3.2	The statutory principles	28
3.3	Definition of mental capacity	30
3.4	The test of capacity	31
3.5	Incapacity or vulnerability?	33
3.6	Who assesses capacity?	35
3.7	Best interests	36
3.8	Application and exclusions	38
3.9	The Convention on the Rights of Persons with Disabilities	42

4	**The legal principles: capacity and evidence**	**45**
4.1	Capacity and the role of the courts	45
4.2	Capacity and the law of evidence	46
4.3	Solicitors instructing doctors	52
4.4	Doctors receiving instructions from solicitors	53
4.5	Witnessing documents	54

PART III: LEGAL TESTS OF CAPACITY

5	**Capacity to deal with financial affairs**	**59**
5.1	Types of powers of attorney	59
5.2	Ordinary powers of attorney	60
5.3	Lasting powers of attorney	60
5.4	Enduring powers of attorney	68
5.5	Capacity to manage property and affairs	70
5.6	Capacity to claim and receive social security benefits	75
5.7	Protection from financial abuse	78

6	**Capacity to make a will**	**81**
6.1	Introduction	81
6.2	Testamentary capacity: the position at common law	82
6.3	The Mental Capacity Act 2005	85
6.4	Supervening incapacity	86
6.5	The needs for medical evidence: the golden rule	87
6.6	The duty of the draftsman to ascertain capacity	90
6.7	Checklist	91
6.8	Capacity to revoke a will	93
6.9	Statutory wills	94

7	**Capacity to make a gift**	**96**
7.1	Introduction	96
7.2	The test of capacity: the common law	97
7.3	The Mental Capacity Act 2005	98

7.4   Burden of proof   99
7.5   Checklist   100
7.6   Gifts made by attorneys   101
7.7   Gifts made by deputies   104
7.8   Risk of financial abuse   105

8   Capacity to litigate   106

8.1   Introduction   106
8.2   The test of capacity to litigate   108
8.3   Applying the test   110
8.4   Litigation friends   114
8.5   Implications of incapacity   114
8.6   The Court of Protection   115

9   Capacity to enter into a contract   117

9.1   Introduction   117
9.2   General rules   117
9.3   Voidable contracts   118
9.4   Necessaries   118
9.5   Contractual capacity: impact of the Mental Capacity Act
       2005   119
9.6   Deputies and attorneys   120
9.7   Checklist   120

10   Capacity to vote   122

10.1   'Capacity to vote'   122
10.2   Entitlement to vote   122
10.3   Legal incapacity to vote   123
10.4   Registration   124
10.5   At the polling station   127
10.6   Postal and proxy voting   128
10.7   Conclusion   129

11   Capacity and personal relationships   130

11.1   Right to form relationships   130
11.2   Family relationships   131
11.3   Sexual relationships   133
11.4   Capacity to consent to marriage or to enter into a civil
       partnership   135
11.5   Capacity to separate, divorce or dissolve a civil partnership   140
11.6   Conclusion   141

12 Capacity to consent: the criminal law and sexual offences   **142**

12.1 Introduction   142
12.2 The Sexual Offences Act 2003   142
12.3 Giving evidence in court   145
12.4 Conclusion   147

13 Capacity and medical treatment   **148**

13.1 Introduction   148
13.2 The need for patient consent   149
13.3 Treatment without consent   150
13.4 Capacity to consent to medical procedures   151
13.5 Care and treatment for adults who lack capacity to consent   155
13.6 Attorneys and deputies   159
13.7 Advance statements and decisions   162
13.8 Confidentiality and disclosure   169

14 Capacity to consent to research and innovative treatment   **173**

14.1 Introduction   173
14.2 Capacity to consent to research   174
14.3 Research governance: the ethical framework   175
14.4 Researching involving adults who lack capacity   175
14.5 Innovative treatment   181

15 Capacity and deprivation of liberty   **183**

15.1 Introduction   183
15.2 Deprivation of liberty: an overview   184
15.3 Authorising a deprivation of liberty   185
15.4 Capacity and the deprivation of liberty   186

16 Capacity and the Mental Health Act 1983   **190**

16.1 Introduction   190
16.2 Treatment for mental disorder: MCA 2005 or MHA 1983?   191
16.3 Admission under MHA 1983   192
16.4 Mental health treatment under MHA 1983: patients who are not detained in hospital   193
16.5 Mental health treatment under MHA 1983: patients detained in hospital   194
16.6 Patients detained under MHA 1983: other decisions   196

PART IV: PRACTICAL ASPECTS OF THE ASSESSMENT OF MENTAL CAPACITY

17 Practical guidance for doctors   201

17.1 Introduction   201
17.2 Balancing empowerment with protection   202
17.3 Mental capacity – a legal concept   203
17.4 Preparing for an assessment of capacity   208
17.5 The duty to 'enhance' mental capacity   209
17.6 Recording the assessment   211
17.7 A systematic approach to assessing capacity   212
17.8 The mental state in relation to capacity   213
17.9 Assessment tools   217
17.10 Retrospective assessment   218

18 Practical guidelines for lawyers   219

18.1 Introduction   219
18.2 Who should assess the person?   222
18.3 Psychiatric diagnoses   225
18.4 Medical assessment of mental conditions   230
18.5 General guidance   233

APPENDICES

A   Mental Capacity Act 2005, ss.1–6 (as amended by Mental
    Health Act 2007)   235
B   Mental Capacity Act 2005 Code of Practice, Chapters 2–4   240
C   Court of Protection   269
D   Court of Protection: Practice Direction 9E – Applications
    Relating to Serious Medical Treatment   274
E   The Official Solicitor   278
F   Certificate as to capacity to conduct proceedings (Official
    Solicitor)   280
G   COP3 Assessment of Capacity and Guidance Notes   289
H   Sample letter to a GP requesting evidence of testamentary
    capacity   304
I   Addresses   307
J   Further reading   309

Index   313

Foreword

The first edition of this book was launched on Friday 19 January 1996 at a conference at the headquarters of the British Medical Association in Tavistock Square, London WC1. The conference was chaired by my predecessor as Master of the Court of Protection, Mrs AB Macfarlane, who had just retired. I was the first speaker in the morning session and I spoke about the 'Legal tests of mental capacity'. The first presentation after lunch was by Dame Brenda Hale, who at that time was a High Court judge of the Family Division. She had previously been a Law Commissioner and had drafted the Report on Mental Incapacity, which was published on 28 February 1995. She discussed 'Proposals for law reform'. The conference was a sell-out. Over three hundred people attended.

The main message I tried to get over in my speech was that it is important that diagnostic screening tests, such as the mini-mental state examination (MMSE), should not be allowed to usurp the actual legal test for capacity to make a particular decision. For example, if someone is making a will, their capacity should be assessed according to the criteria laid down in *Banks* v. *Goodfellow* (1870) LR 5 QB 549, and not on the basis of whether they can count backwards from 100 by subtracting seven, five times, to reach 65, or whether they can draw two overlapping pentagons to create a parallelogram.

To illustrate this point I described an occasion a few years earlier when I had assessed whether a 90-year-old woman, who lived in a nursing home in Taunton, was capable of creating an enduring power of attorney (EPA). The legal test for capacity to create an EPA was, and still is, the test described by Lord Hoffmann (Mr Justice Hoffmann, as he then was) in *Re K, Re F* [1988] Ch 310. I asked her the date of her birth and she told me she was born in 1901. Now this was an interesting year in which to be born, because it marked the end of one era and the beginning of another: Queen Victoria died on 22 January 1901 and was succeeded by her eldest son, King Edward VII. I got rather carried away with this idea and asked her, 'Who was on the throne when you were born?' She replied, 'I don't know and – do you know what? – I don't f***ing care'. It was a sharp retort and it made me realise how impertinent my question had been. The identity of the monarch at the time of her birth had absolutely no bearing on her capacity to make an EPA ninety years later.

In many ways the publication of the Law Commission's Report on Mental Incapacity and the publication of the first edition of *Assessment of Mental*

Capacity: Guidance for Doctors and Lawyers also marked the beginning of a new era – even more than the enactment of the Mental Capacity Act (MCA) 10 years later in 2005 and its implementation in 2007. Both works were referred to with approval by the first instance judge in the landmark decision in *Masterman-Lister* v. *Brutton & Co.* [2002] EWCA Civ 1889, which hived off the capacity to litigate from the capacity to manage one's property and affairs generally. Subsequently, there was a series of cases which sought further to dissect the capacity to litigate into discrete decisions relating to the various steps that litigants reach during the course of personal injury proceedings. In *Bailey* v. *Warren* [2006] EWCA Civ 51 there was a difference of opinion in the Court of Appeal. Lady Justice Hallett considered that the specific issue in respect of which Mr Bailey's capacity needed to be assessed was simply whether to accept an offer of compromise, whereas Lady Justice Arden considered that the right approach was to ask whether the individual steps formed part of a larger sequence of events which should be seen as a whole, or whether they were in fact self-contained steps, which were not connected with each other. The most recent development in this line of authorities was the decision of the United Kingdom Supreme Court in *Dunhill* v. *Burgin* [2014] UKSC 18, in which Baroness Hale of Richmond held that the test for capacity to conduct proceedings for the purpose of Part 21 of the Civil Procedure Rules 1998 is the capacity to conduct the claim or cause of action which the claimant in fact has, rather than to conduct the claim as formulated by her lawyers.

Whereas in personal injury cases in the Queen's Bench Division, capacity issues have tended to focus on these themes, Chancery Division judges, who adjudicate on cases involving the validity of wills and lifetime gifts after the event, have been required to consider an individual's capacity retrospectively and have reinforced the common law tests in *Banks* v. *Goodfellow* and *Re Beaney (Deceased)* [1978] 1 WLR 770 respectively. They have held that the words in section 1(1) of MCA 2005 'for the purposes of this Act' indicate that the definition of incapacity in sections 2 and 3 of MCA 2005 applies only to matters arising specifically under that Act and these do not include a retrospective consideration of capacity to make a will or a substantial lifetime gift (*Kicks* v. *Leigh* [2014] EWHC 3926 (Ch); *Walker* v. *Badmin* [2015] WTLR 493).

In proceedings under MCA 2005 itself, almost all the reported decisions on capacity have been in health and welfare cases heard by High Court Judges of the Family Division, who are also nominated judges of the Court of Protection. They have come up with some valuable insights into the assessment of capacity. For example, and in no particular order:

1.   The opinions of professionals are, of course, important evidence, but it is the court alone that is in the position to weigh up all the evidence and it is the court that must make the ultimate decision (*CC* v. *KK and STC* [2012] EWHC 2136 (COP)).

2. There is a danger that if one considers section 2(1) before considering section 3(1) of MCA 2005, the strength of the causative nexus between mental impairment and inability to make a decision will be watered down (*PC* v. *City of York Council* [2013] EWCA Civ 478).
3. There is a risk that professionals, including judges, may conflate a capacity assessment with a best interests analysis (*CC* v. *KK and STC*).
4. Inconsistency is not necessarily a sign of confusion. Equally, confusion is not necessarily an indication of incapacity (*LBL* v. *RYJ and VJ* [2010] EWHC 2665 (COP)).
5. It is not necessary for someone to demonstrate a capacity to understand and weigh up every detail of the respective options, but merely the salient factors (*LBL* v. *RYJ and VJ* and *CC* v. *KK and STC*).
6. When using and weighing relevant information, different individuals give different weight to different factors (*LBL* v. *RYJ and VJ*).
7. Although it would be an over-simplification to describe it as a snapshot, it can sometimes be a disadvantage when an assessment of capacity is based on just a single visit (*PH* v. *A Local Authority* [2011] EWHC 1704 (COP)).
8. The court must guard against imposing too high a test of capacity to decide certain issues because to do so would run the risk of discriminating against persons suffering from mental disability (*PH* v. *A Local Authority*).
9. There is a space between an unwise decision and one which an individual does not have the mental capacity to make. It is important to respect that space and to ensure that it is preserved, because it is within that space that an individual's autonomy operates (*PC* v. *City of York Council*).

Over the last twenty years this book has grown exponentially with the development of the subject matter. The first edition in 1996 ran to 152 pages, the second (2004) 236 pages, the third (2009) 278 pages, with the dimensions of the book getting larger and the print getting smaller all the time.

In England and Wales we tend to revisit our mental capacity legislation about once in a generation; every 25 to 30 years, on average. Although the date of the MCA is 2005, it is, in fact, 10 years older than that. The original draft bill appeared in the Law Commission's Report on Mental Incapacity in 1995. In the normal course of events, we should be starting to think about law reform now, but there is an even greater sense of urgency because of the need to ensure that our legislation is compliant with the United Nations Convention on the Rights of Persons with Disabilities (CRPD), which the United Kingdom ratified in 2009. The CRPD requires us:

1. to amend section 2(1) of MCA 2005 to remove the discriminatory words 'because of an impairment of, or a disturbance in the functioning of, the mind or brain';
2. to amend the best interests decision-making framework in section 4 in order to accord complete respect for the rights, will and preferences of the person;

3. to provide for a detailed and viable framework for supported decision-making in the exercise of capacity; and
4. to ensure that measures relating to the exercise of capacity are free of conflict of interest and undue influence.

I predict that in a few years' time the BMA and the Law Society may need to consider the joint publication of a couple of companion volumes, *Assessment of Supported Decision-making Capacity: Guidance for Doctors and Lawyers* and *Assessment of Undue Influence: Guidance for Doctors and Lawyers*.

I contributed to the first edition of this book and am proud to mention it in my CV. I am delighted that later editions have gone from strength to strength and, in particular, must pay tribute to the work of Penny Letts OBE, who was my co-contributor on the Law Society side to the first edition and subsequently acted as the general editor of the second and third editions. She has now decided to retire from editing the book and has been replaced as general editor by Alex Ruck Keene, whom I know and greatly respect. I am glad that this marvellous publication remains in safe hands.

Denzil Lush
Senior Judge of the Court of Protection
1 September 2015

Preface

The first three editions of *Assessment of Mental Capacity* have established this book as an indispensable guide for professionals working with people who lack, or who may lack, the capacity to make some decisions or to take actions on their own behalf. Although initially written with a medical and legal audience in mind, the practical, jargon-free approach has helped the book to find a wider readership.

The introduction to the second edition published in 2004 raised the question of legal reform. At the time, decision-making in this area was governed by the common law, which was widely held to be fragmented, complex and out of date. That edition drew attention to the Law Commission's successive consultations on the legal framework for decision-making and raised the possibility of legal change. That change became a reality during 2007 when the Mental Capacity Act (MCA) 2005, which incorporates many of the common law's legal and ethical insights, came fully into force in England and Wales.

The third edition of *Assessment of Mental Capacity* from the BMA and the Law Society sought to address the impact of MCA 2005, and to that end sets out the main features and principles the Act, as well as the innovations that the Act introduced such as lasting powers of attorney in relation to health and welfare decisions. As it reflected the law as at the end of November 2009, the third edition contained a degree of speculation as to how the Act would affect the working practices of doctors and lawyers.

This fourth edition reflects the lessons learned from the first seven years of the Act's life, not all of which – sadly – have been positive. In particular, it has become clear that giving effect to the core principles contained in section 1 of the Act is not something that is easily or quickly done. It requires both a clear awareness of the legal framework and sufficient time to ensure a proper understanding of the individual in question. This book cannot assist with the latter, but written by experts from a variety of disciplines, and combining practical advice with a thorough grounding in the legal framework, it represents a vital guide to the former.

As Senior Judge Lush notes in his foreword, it is likely that the next edition of this work will look very different as we continue to come to terms with the implications of the Convention on the Rights of Persons with Disabilities. It is therefore particularly appropriate that we use this occasion to pay tribute to the work of Penny Letts, the moving force behind the three previous editions of the work, and also core aspects of the Mental Capacity Act 2005 Code of Practice. We will continue our quest for better recognition of the rights of those with disabilities from a very sound basis, a sound basis laid in significant part by Penny. We are grateful that she was in a position to provide comments upon the text of this edition, but sad that she felt that the time had come to lay down her editorial responsibilities.

The law is stated as at 1 September 2015.

Alex Ruck Keene and Julian Sheather
September 2015

Acknowledgements

FOURTH EDITION (2015)

The Law Society would like to thank Alex Ruck Keene for applying his knowledge, enthusiasm and attention to detail to the role of general editor. The Law Society would like to thank the British Medical Association for the opportunity to prepare and publish this fourth edition, particularly Dr Julian Sheather for his invaluable co-ordination, contribution, and review.

The Law Society is also greatly indebted to:

Contributors
Tracey Calvert
Victoria Butler-Cole
Dr Claudia Camden-Smith
Martyn Frost
Sheree Green
Lesley King
Nicola Kohn
Alex Ruck Keene
Dr Lucy Series
Dr Julian Sheather
Dr Ben Spencer
Fenella Morris QC
Beverley Taylor

Foreword
Senior Judge Denzil Lush

Reviewers
British Medical Association Medical Ethics Committee
Law Society's Mental Health and Disability Committee
Law Society's Wills and Equity Committee
Penny Letts OBE

ACKNOWLEDGEMENTS

Tim Spencer Lane
Dr Julian Sheather

THIRD EDITION (2009)

General Editor
Penny Letts

Contributors
Victoria Butler-Cole
Fenella Morris QC
Alex Ruck Keene
Alistair Pitblado
Dr Julian Sheather
Beverley Taylor

Reviewers
Gordon R Ashton
Dr JS Bamrah
Veronica English
Tim Spencer Lane
Denzil Lush
Dr Jan Wise

SECOND EDITION (2004)

Managing Editor
Penny Letts

Editorial staff
Veronica English
Jenny McCabe
Gillian Romano-Critchley
Ann Sommerville

Contributors
Gordon R Ashton
Penny Letts
Peter Rowlands

Edward Solomons
Jonathan Waite

Reviewers
Anthony Harbour
Denzil Lush
The British Medical Association's Medical Ethics Committee
The Law Society's Mental Health and Disability Committee

FIRST EDITION (1995)

Contributors
Nigel Eastman
Michael Hinchcliffe
Penny Letts
Denzil Lush
Steven Luttrell
Lydia Sinclair
Ann Sommerville

Membership of the Assessment of Mental Capacity Working Party for the first edition (1993–1995)
James Birley
Nigel Eastman
Stuart Horner
Penny Letts
Denzil Lush
Lydia Sinclair
Ann Sommerville
David Watts

About the authors

The following authors, editor and contributors have updated the text of this fourth edition of *Assessment of Mental Capacity*.

AUTHORS

The British Medical Association is a membership organisation that looks after the professional and personal needs of doctors practising in all branches of medicine in the UK. Its Medical Ethics Committee debates medical ethics, medical law, and the relationship between the medical profession, the public and the state. The BMA's Medical Ethics Department answers ethical enquiries from doctors and publishes guidance on a wide range of issues, including consent, confidentiality and treatment of incapacitated adults.

The Law Society is a membership organisation that represents solicitors qualified in England and Wales practising both at home and internationally. The Society protects and promotes the interests of the profession by providing advice, training, products and services to its members; developing new legal markets; and influencing law and policy through representation activities. The Society's Mental Health and Disability Committee reviews and promotes improvements in law, and practice and procedure affecting elderly people and those with mental or physical disabilities.

GENERAL EDITOR

Alex Ruck Keene is a barrister at 39 Essex Chambers and an honorary research lecturer at the University of Manchester. He has appeared in cases involving the Mental Capacity Act 2005 at all levels up to and including the Supreme Court. He also trains and writes extensively about mental capacity issues and is the creator of the website **www.mentalcapacitylawandpolicy.org.uk**.

CONTRIBUTORS

Victoria Butler-Cole is a barrister at 39 Essex Chambers who specialises in health and social care. She is frequently instructed by family members, local authorities and the Official Solicitor in cases concerning capacity and best interests in the Court of Protection. She is a contributing editor to the *Court of Protection Law Reports* (Jordan Publishing); *Heywood and Massey: Court of Protection Practice* (Sweet & Maxwell); and the 39 Essex mental capacity newsletter.

Tracey Calvert is a lawyer who has worked both in private practice and in an in-house capacity. She was employed by the Law Society and the Solicitors Regulation Authority for many years as a senior ethics adviser and, in her last role, as part of the policy team which drafted the SRA Handbook which was launched in October 2011. She now runs her own regulatory compliance consultancy (**www.oakallsconsultancy.co.uk**) and has written a number of compliance-related books and articles including *Compliance and Ethics in Law Firms* (Law Society, 2015).

Dr Claudia Camden-Smith is a consultant psychiatrist, currently working in Women's medium secure services at St Andrew's Hospital, Northampton. She completed her medical training at the University of Cape Town, South Africa, before completing specialist training in psychiatry of intellectual disability in Wessex. She has a first class Masters' degree in medical law and ethics from De Montfort University. She has published and spoken on MCA 2005 with a particular interest in mental capacity and end of life decision-making. She provides specialist expertise to both criminal and family courts.

Martyn Frost is a director of Trenfield Trust & Estate Consulting Ltd, having previously worked for a trust company and been a consultant with two law firms. He is a former deputy chair of STEP and a council member, as well as a former vice president of the Association of Corporate Trustees. He has written and lectured extensively on wills and trusts issues. He is an editor of the *Wills & Trusts Law Reports* (Legalese Ltd).

Sheree Green is the Court of Protection lead at Anthony Collins Solicitors in Birmingham. She has been appointed by the Office of the Public Guardian to their panel of professional deputies and is also an accredited mental health representative. She a member of the Law Society's Mental Health and Disability Committee and ad hoc Court of Protection Rules Committee.

Professor Lesley King is professional development consultant for the University of Law and member of the Law Society's Wills and Equity Committee as well as the Probate and Estates Committee of STEP. She is co-author of *Wills, Taxation* *and Administration: A Practical Guide*, 10th edn (Sweet & Maxwell, 2011); *A Modern Approach to Wills, Administration and Estate Planning (with Precedents)* (Jordan Publishing, 2015); *A Modern Approach to Lifetime Tax Planning for Private Clients (with Precedents)* (Jordan Publishing, 2014); *A Practitioner's Guide to Wills*, 3rd edn (STEP, 2011); and *Wills: A Practical Guide* (Wildy, Simmonds and Hill Publishing, 2011); and editor of the *Probate Practitioner's Handbook*, 7th edn (Law Society, 2015). Lesley is also a contributor to the Wills and Intestacy volume of *Halsbury's Laws of England*, and columnist for the *Law Society Gazette* on wills and probate matters. She lectures extensively on wills, taxation and related matters.

Nicola Kohn is a barrister at 39 Essex Street. She is regularly instructed by individuals, NHS bodies and local authorities before the High Court and the Court of Protection.

Fenella Morris QC is a barrister at 39 Essex Chambers. She is regularly instructed in cases concerning the health, welfare and finances of incapable adults and has appeared in a number of leading cases, including *P and Q* v. *Surrey County Council* [2011] EWCA Civ 190 in the Supreme Court. She is co-author of *Mental Capacity: A Guide to the New Law*, 2nd edn (Law Society, 2008).

Dr Lucy Series (PhD) is a research associate at Cardiff University. Her research focuses on legal capacity, adult social care and disability rights.

Dr Julian Sheather (PhD) is deputy head of ethics at the British Medical Association. His particular interests lie in public health ethics, mental health, consent and mental capacity. Julian is the BMA's lead on health and human rights. He is a co-author of *Medical Ethics Today* and is a regular contributor to the *British Medical Journal* and the *Journal of Medical Ethics*. Julian is a member of the British Medical Journal's Ethics Committee, and the Institute of Medical Ethics. He also lectures widely both nationally and internationally on a range of topics in medical ethics.

Dr Ben Spencer is a specialist registrar in psychiatry on the South London and Maudsley Training Scheme and an NIHR doctoral research fellow at the Department of Psychological Medicine, Institute of Psychiatry, Psychology and Neuroscience, King's College London. He has an LLM in mental health law, and he is currently investigating mental capacity for decisions around participation in research in people who are unwell in hospital with psychosis.

Beverley Taylor is a solicitor and barrister. She recently retired as Deputy Official Solicitor, having headed the office's healthcare and welfare team for a number of years. Prior to retirement she headed the office' s property and affairs team. She is co-author of *Mental Capacity: A Guide to the New Law*, 2nd edn (Law Society, 2008). She is currently a member of the Law Society's Mental Health and Disability Committee, the Camden and Kings Cross Research Ethics Committee and the St George's University Hospitals NHS Foundation Trust Clinical Ethics Committee.

Table of cases

A (Capacity: Refusal of Contraception), *Re, see* A Local Authority *v.* A (by the Official Solicitor)

A (Male Sterilisation), *Re* [2000] 1 FLR 549 .... App.B

A Local Authority *v.* A (by the Official Solicitor); *sub nom Re* A (Capacity: Refusal of Contraception) [2010] EWHC 1549 (Fam); [2011] Fam 61 .... 11.3.1

A Local Authority *v.* DL; *sub nom Re* L (Vulnerable Adults with Capacity: Court's Jurisdiction) (No. 2) [2012] EWCA Civ 253; [2013] Fam 1 .... 3.5, 13.4.4

A Local Authority *v.* AK (Capacity to Marry) [2013] COPLR 163... 11.4, 11.4.1, 11.4.2

A Local Authority *v.* E [2012] EWHC 1639 (COP); [2012] COPLR 441............ 13.7.4

A Local Authority *v.* K [2013] EWHC 242 (COP); [2013] COPLR 194............. 13.5.4

A Local Authority *v.* SY [2013] EWHC 3485 (COP); [2014] COPLR 1.............. 4.2.7

A Primary Care Trust *v.* LDV [2013] EWHC 272 (Fam); [2013] COPLR 204 .... 15.4.1, 15.4.2, 15.4.3

A *v.* A. *See* Simms *v.* Simms

A, B and C *v.* X and Z [2012] EWHC 2400 (COP); [2013] COPLR 1; [2013] WTLR 187 .... 4.2.2, 5.3.1, 5.6.2, 6.9, 8.3

ABC *v.* St George's Healthcare NHS Trust [2015] EWHC 1394 (QB) 13.8.3

Aintree University Hospitals NHS Foundation Trust *v.* James [2013] UKSC 67; [2014] AC 591 .... 3.6, 3.7, 13.5.1, 13.7.1

Airedale NHS Trust *v.* Bland [1993] AC 789; [1993] 1 All ER 821................... 13.7.4

AJ (Deprivation of Liberty Safeguards), *Re* [2015] EWCOP 5; [2015] COPLR 167 .... 15.3

AK (Adult Patient) (Medical Treatment: Consent), *Re* [2001] 1 FLR 129.......... App.B

Akerman-Livingstone *v.* Aster Communities Ltd [2015] UKSC 15; [2015] 2 WLR 721 .... 3.9

Allen, *Re* (unreported, COP, 21 July 2009) case no. 11661922009, Senior Judge Lush 3.7

An NHS Trust *v.* DE [2013] EWHC 2562 (Fam); [2013] COPLR 531............. 11.3.1

Ashkettle, *Re*; Ashkettle *v.* Gwinnett [2013] EWHC 2125 (Ch); [2013] WTLR 1331 .... 6.5

Aster Healthcare Ltd *v.* Estate of Shafi [2014] EWHC 77 (QB); [2014] 3 All ER 283 .... 9.4.2

B (A Local Authority) *v.* RM, MM and AM [2010] EWHC 3802 (Fam); [2010] COPLR Con Vol 247 .... 3.8.3

B (Adult: Refusal of Medical Treatment), *Re* [2002] EWHC 429 (Fam); [2002] 2 All ER 449 .... 13.2

B *v.* Croydon Health Authority [1995] 1 All ER 683...................................... 16.6

Bailey *v.* Warren [2006] EWCA Civ 51.. Foreword

Baker Tilly (A Firm) *v.* Makar [2013] EWHC 759 (QB); [2013] COPLR 245 .... 8.3

Banks v. Goodfellow (1870) LR 5 QB 549 .... Foreword, 6.2, 6.3, 6.7.3, 6.9, App.B, App.H

Battan Singh v. Armichand [1948] AC 161 .... 6.4

Beaney (Deceased), Re [1978] 1 WLR 770; [1978] 2 All ER 595 ..... 5.3.1, 7.2, 7.3, 9.2, App.B

Bedford (County) Case, Burgess' Case (1785) 2 Lud EC 381 .... 10.3

Bennett v. Bennett [1969] 1 WLR 430 .... 11.4.1

Bird v. Luckie (1850) 8 Hare 301 .... 3.2, 6.2

BKR, Re [2015] SGCA 26 .... 3.5

Blackman v. Man [2007] EWHC 3162 (Ch); [2008] WTLR 389 .... 6.7.3

Blankley v. Central Manchester and Manchester Children's University
    Hospitals NHS Trust [2015] EWCA Civ 18; [2015] 1 Costs LR 119 .... 2.1.2

Boughton v. Knight (1873) LR 3 P&D 64 .... 9.2, App.B

Bradbury v. Paterson [2014] EWHC 3992 (QB) 8.3

Bray v. Pearce (unreported, ChD, 6 March 2014) 6.3

Buckley, Re, see Public Guardian v. C

Burgess v. Hawes [2013] EWCA Civ 94; [2013] WTLR 453 .... 4.2.8, 6.5

C (Adult: Refusal of Medical Treatment), Re [1994] 1 WLR 290, [1994] 1 All
    ER 819 .... 13.4.2, 17.3.2

C v. V, see Re S and S (Protected Persons)

CAF, Re (unreported, QB, 23 March 1962) 5.6.1

Calvert (Litigation Guardian) v. Calvert (1997) 32 OR (3d) 281 .... 11.5

Carmarthenshire CC v. Lewis [2010] EWCA Civ 1567 .... 8.3

Cattermole v. Prisk [2006] 1 FLR 693; [2006] Fam Law 98 .... 6.5

CC v. KK and STCC [2012] EWHC 2136 (COP); [2012] COPLR 627 ... Foreword, 4.1, 4.2.6, 4.2.8, 8.3

Cheshire West and Chester Council v. P. See Surrey County Council v. P

City of Westminster Social and Community Services Dept v. C [2008] EWCA
    Civ 198; [2009] Fam 11 .... 11.4, 11.4.1

City of York Council v. C, see PC v. City of York Council

Clancy v. Clancy [2003] EWHC 1885 (Ch); [2003] WTLR 1097 .... 6.4

Cloutt, Re (unreported, COP, 7 November 2008) 5.4.2

Collis, Re (unreported, COP, 27 October 2010) 5.3.1

Connolly v. Croydon Health Services NHS Trust [2015] EWHC 1339 (QB) 13.3

D (Children), Re [2015] EWCA Civ 749 .... 8.2.2, 8.3

D v. An NHS Trust (Medical Treatment: Consent) [2003] EWHC 2793 (Fam);
    [2004] 1 FLR 1110 .... 13.5.4

D v. R (Deputy of S) [2010] EWHC 2405 (COP); [2010] COPLR Con Vol
    1112 .... 3.2

Davey (Deceased), Re [1980] 3 All ER 342 .... 11.4.3

De Louville De Toucy v. Bonhams 1793 Ltd [2011] EWHC 3809 (Ch); [2012]
    BPIR 793 .... 8.1, 8.2.3

DP, Re; Public Guardian v. JM [2014] EWCOP 7 .... 5.3.3

DT, Re [2015] EWCOP 10; [2015] COPLR 225 .... 5.4.2

Dunhill v. Burgin [2014] UKSC 18; [2014] 1 WLR 933 .... Foreword, 8.1, 8.2.2, 8.3

Durham v. Durham (1885) 10 PD 80 .... 6.8, 11.4

E (Mental Health Patient), Re [1984] 1 WLR 320 .... 8.4

F (Adult Patient: Sterilisation) [2001] Fam 15 .... App.B

F (Interim Declarations), Re [2009] EWHC B30 (Fam); [2009] COPLR Con
    Vol 390 .... App.C

F (Mental Patient: Sterilisation), *Re, see* F *v.* West Berkshire Health
   Authority
F *v.* West Berkshire Health Authority [1989] 2 All ER 545; *sub nom Re* F
   (Mental Patient: Sterilisation) [1990] 2 AC 1 .... 5.6.4, 13.2, 13.5.1
Feltham *v.* Freer Bouskell [2013] EWHC 1952 (Ch); [2013] WTLR 1363 . 2.1.1, 6.5, 6.6
Fischer *v.* Diffley [2013] EWHC 4567 (Ch); [2014] WTLR 757 .... 6.3
Folks *v.* Faizey [2006] EWCA Civ 381 .... 8.1
G *v.* E (By his Litigation Friend the Official Solicitor) [2010] EWCA Civ 822;
   [2010] COPLR Con Vol 431 .... 15.4.1.
Gillick *v.* West Norfolk and Wisbech Area Health Authority [1986] AC 112 .... 3.8.2,
   3.8.3
GM, *Re, see Re* MJ
Gregory *v.* Turner [2003] EWCA Civ 183; [2003] 1 WLR 1149 .... 8.4
GS, *Re* COP Case 11582024, Preston County Court, 10 July 2008 .... 8.5
Harbin *v.* Masterman [1896] 1 Ch 351 .... 8.3, App.E
Harcourt, *Re* (2012) MHLO 74 (LPA) 5.3.3
Harrison *v.* Rowan (1820) 3 Washington 585 .... 6.7.4
HE *v.* A Hospital NHS Trust [2003] EWHC 1017 (Fam); [2003] 2 FLR 408 .... 13.7.6
Heart of England NHS Foundation Trust *v.* JB [2014] EWHC 342 (COP);
   (2014) 137 BMLR 232 .... 13.4.2, 13.4.3
Hillingdon London Borough Council *v.* Neary [2011] EWHC 1377 (COP);
   [2011] COPLR Con Vol 632 .... 15.2
Hirst *v.* United Kingdom (No. 2) Application 74025/01, (2006) 42 EHRR 41 ...... 10.4.2
HL *v.* United Kingdom Application 45508/99, (2004) 40 EHRR 761; (2004)
   81 BMLR 131 .... 15.1
Hoff *v.* Atherton [2004] EWCA Civ 1554; [2005] WTLR 99 .... 6.3, 6.5
Hunt *v.* Fylde Borough Council [2008] BPIR 1368 .... 8.1, 8.2.3
IM *v.* LM, AB and Liverpool City Council (Capacity to Consent to Sexual
   Relations) [2014] EWCA Civ 37; [2015] Fam 61 .... 11.2.1, 11.3.1, 12.2.1
Imperial Loan Company *v.* Stone [1892] 1 QB 599 .... 9.3
ITW *v.* Z, *see Re* M
J (Enduring Power of Attorney), *Re* [2009] EWHC 436 (Ch), [2010] 1 WLR
   210 .... 5.4
Jeffrey *v.* Jeffrey [2013] EWHC 1942 (Ch); [2013] WTLR 1509 .... 6.5
Jones *v.* Parkin, *see Re* Meek
K, *Re*; *Re* F [1988] Ch 310; [1988] 1 All ER 358 .... Foreword, 5.3.1, 5.4.1
Kenward *v.* Adams (1975) The Times, 29 November .... 5.3.1, 6.5, 18.1, App.B
Kerr *v.* Badran [2004] NSWSC 735 .... 6.7.3
Key *v.* Key, *see Re* Key
Key, *Re*; Key *v.* Key [2010] EWHC 408 (Ch); [2010] WTLR 623 .... 6.2, 6.3, 6.5
Kicks *v.* Leigh [2014] EWHC 3926 (Ch); [2015] WTLR 579 ..... Foreword, 6.3, 7.3, 7.4
Kiss *v.* Hungary (2013) 56 EHRR 38 .... 10.2
Knox *v.* Till [1999] 2 NZLR 753; [2000] Lloyd's RE PN 49 .... 6.6
L (Vulnerable Adults with Capacity: Court's Jurisdiction), *Re* (No. 2). *See* A
   Local Authority v DL
LBL *v.* RYJ and VJ [2010] EWHC 2665 .... Foreword
Leger *v.* Poirier [1944] 3 DLR 1 .... 6.2
Lindsay *v.* Wood [2006] EWHC 2895 (QB) 5.6.3
Local Authority X *v.* MM (An Adult), *see Re* MM
M, *Re*; *sub nom* ITW *v.* Z [2009] EWHC 2525 (Fam); [2010] 3 All ER 682 .... 3.7
McDonnell *v.* Loosemore [2007] EWCA Civ 1531 .... 5.8
Marshall *v.* Whateley, *see Re* Marshall
Marshall, *Re*; Marshall *v.* Whateley [1920] 1 Ch 284 .... 9.6

Masterman-Lister v. Brutton & Co; Masterman-Lister v. Jewell [2002] EWCA
    Civ 1889; [2003] 1 WLR 1511 .... Foreword, 2.1.1, 4.1, 4.2.5, 4.2.7, 5.6.1, 5.6.2,
                                         5.6.3, 8.2.1, 8.2.2, 8.3, 17.3.3, 18.1, App.B
Masterman-Lister v. Jewell; Masterman-Lister v. Brutton & Co [2002] EWHC
    417 (QB) .... 4.1, 4.2.5, 5.6.1, 8.2.1, 8.2.2, 8.3, 17.3.3, 18.1, App.B
MB (Medical Treatment), Re [1997] 2 FLR 426; (1997) 38 BMLR 175... 13.4.2, 13.4.3,
                                                                            App.B
McClintock v. Calderwood [2005] EWHC 836 (Ch)....................................... 6.1
Meek, Re; Jones v. Parkin [2014] EWCOP 1; [2014] WTLR 1155..................... 7.7
Milroy v. British Telecommunications plc [2015] EWHC 532 (QB)................... 8.3
Mitchell v. Alasia [2005] EWHC 11 (QB)... 5.6.3
MJ, Re; sub nom Re GM [2013] EWHC 2966 (COP); [2013] WTLR 835........... 7.6.1
MM, Re; Local Authority X v. MM (An Adult) [2007] EWHC 2003 (Fam);
    [2009] 1 FLR 443 .... 3.8, 6.3
MN (Adult), Re [2015] EWCA Civ 411... 3.7
Montgomery v. Lanarkshire Health Board [2015] UKSC 11; [2015] 2 WLR
    768 .... 13.4.1, 13.4.2
NCC v. PB and TB [2014] EWCOP 14; [2015] COPLR 118............................ 3.4
NHS Trust 1 and NHS Trust 2 v. FG [2014] EWCOP 30; [2015] 1 WLR
    1984 .... 13.5.4
NHS Trust v. Dr A [2013] EWHC 2442 (COP); [2013] COPLR 605............ 15.3, 16.6
NHS Trust v. T (Adult Patient: Refusal of Medical Treatment) [2004] EWHC
    1279 (Fam); [2005] 1 All ER 387 .... 8.3
Nottinghamshire Healthcare NHS Trust v. RC [2014] EWCOP 1317; [2014]
    COPLR 468 .... 13.7.8, 16.5
Okehampton Case, Robin's Case (1791) 1 Fras 29, 162............................... 10.3
P (Abortion), Re [2013] EWHC 50 (COP); [2013] COPLR 405...................... 13.5.4
P, Re [2009] EWHC 163 (Ch); [2009] WTLR 651....................................... 6.9
PA v. JA. See A v. A
Park's Estate, Re; Park v. Park [1954] P 112; [1953] 3 WLR 1012.... 11.4, 11.5, 17.3.2,
                                                                            18.1
Parker v. Felgate (1883) 8 PD 171... 6.4
PC v. City of York Council; sub nom City of York Council v. C [2013] EWCA
    Civ 478; [2014] Fam 10 .... Foreword, 3.4, 3.4.3, 11.2.1, 11.4, 11.5
Pearce v. Beverley [2013] EWHC 2627 (Ch); [2014] WTLR 85......................... 6.3
Perrins v. Holland [2009] EWHC 1945 (Ch); [2009] WTLR 1387; affirmed
    [2010] EWCA Civ 840; [2011] Ch 270 .... 6.3, 6.4
PH v. A Local Authority [2011] EWHC 1704 (COP); [2012] COPLR 128..... Foreword,
                                                                            4.2.7, 4.4
Public Guardian v. Lutz, see Re Treadwell (Deceased)
Public Guardian v. C; sub nom Re Buckley [2013] EWHC 2965 (COP);
    [2013] WTLR 373 .... 7.6.1
Public Guardian v. JM, see Re DP
R (A Minor) (Wardship: Consent to Medical Treatment), Re [1992] Fam 11;
    [1992] 1 FLR 190 .... 3.8.2
R (on the application of Chester) v. Secretary of State for Justice [2013]
    UKSC 63; [2014] AC 271 .... 10.4.2
R (on the application of Munjaz) v. Mersey Care NHS Trust [2005] UKHL
    58; [2006] 2 AC 148 .... 2.5.2
R (on the application of Stevens) v. Plymouth City Council [2002] EWCA Civ
    388; [2002] LGR 565 .... 2.2, App.B
R (on the application of Tracey) v. Cambridge University Hospitals NHS
    Foundation Trust [2014] EWCA Civ 822; [2014] 3 WLR1054 .... 13.4.2

R v. A (G) [2014] EWCA Crim 299; [2014] 1 WLR 2469 .... 12.2.1
R v. C [2009] UKHL 42; [2009] 1 WLR 1786 .... 12.2.1, 12.2.2
R v. Collins, ex p Brady (2000) 58 BMLR 173 .... 17.8.1, App.B
R v. NW [2015] EWCA Crim 559 .... 12.2.2
R v. Olugboja [1981] 3 WLR 585 .... 12.2.2
RB v. Brighton and Hove City Council [2014] EWCA Civ 561; [2014]
    COPLR 629 .... 1.1.2
Redbridge London Borough Council v. G (By Her Litigation Friend the
    Official Solicitor) [2014] EWHC 485 (COP); [2014] COPLR 292 .... 3.5
RGB v. Cwm Taf Health Board [2013] EWHC B23 (COP); [2014] COPLR
    83 .... 13.7.1
Richmond v. Richmond (1914) 58 Sol Jo 784; 111 LT 273 .... 4.1
Royal Bank of Scotland v. Etridge [2001] UKHL 44; [2002] 2 AC 773 .... App.B
RP v. United Kingdom Application 38245/08 [2013] 1 FLR 744; (2012) 130
    BMLR 1 .... 8.4
S and S (Protected Persons), Re; C v. V [2010] 1 WLR 1082; [2009] WTLR
    315 .... 3.7
S, Re (unreported, COP, 13 March 1997) 5.3.3
S (Sterilisation: Patient's Best Interests) [2000] 2 FLR 389 .... App.B
Sabatini, Re (1970) 114 Sol Jo 35 .... 6.8
Saulle v. Nouvet [2007] EWHC 2902 (QB); [2008] WTLR 729 ..... 4.2.5, 6.3, 8.2.2, 8.3,
                                                                                  17.3.3
SB (A Patient: Capacity to Consent to Termination), Re [2013] EWHC 1417
    (COP); [2013] COPLR 445 .... 4.2.6, 8.3, 16.1
SBC v. PBA [2011] EWHC 2580 (Fam); [2011] COPLR Con Vol 1095 .... 2.5.2
Scammell v. Farmer [2008] EWHC 1100 (Ch); [2008] WTLR 1261 .. 6.3, 6.5, 6.7.3, 7.3
Sharp v. Adam [2006] EWCA Civ 449; 10 ITELR 419 .... 6.2
Sheffield City Council v. E (An Alleged Patient) [2004] EWHC 2808 (Fam);
    [2005] Fam 326 .... 6.8, 8.3, 11.4, App.B
Sidaway v. Board of Governors of the Bethlem Royal Hospital and Maudsley
    Hospital [1985] AC 871 .... 13.4.3
Simms v. Simms; PA v. JA; sub nom A v. A [2002] EWHC 2734 (Fam);
    [2003] 1 All ER 669 .... 14.5
Simon v. Byford [2014] EWCA Civ 280; [2014] WTLR 1097 .... 6.2, 6.7.2
Simpson, Re (1977) 121 Sol Jo 224 .... 6.5
Social Security Commissioners' Decision R(A) 1/95 .... 5.7.1
Social Security Commissioners' Decision R(IS) 14/96 .... 5.7.1
Social Security Commissioners' Decision R(IS) 5/00 .... 5.7.1
Stowe v. Joliffe (1874) LR 9 CP 734 .... 10.3
Surrey County Council v. P; Cheshire West and Chester Council v. P [2014]
    UKSC 19; [2014] AC 896 .... 3.9, 15.2, 15.3, 15.4.1, 16.3
Sutton v. Sutton [2009] EWHC 2576 (Ch); [2010] WTLR 115 .... 7.2
T (Adult: Refusal of Treatment), Re [1993] Fam 35; [1992] 4 All ER 649 .... 13.4.3,
                                                                            13.4.4, App.B
Tameside v. Glossop Acute Services Health Trust v. CH [1996] 1 FLR 762;
    (1996) 31 BMLR 93 .... 16.6
Tchilingirian v. Ouzounian [2003] EWHC 1220 (Ch); [2003] WTLR 709 .... 6.1
Thorpe v. Fellowes Solicitors LLP [2011] EWHC 61 (QB); [2011] PNLR 13 .... 2.1.1
Tower Hamlets London Borough Council v. TB and SA [2014] EWCOP 53;
    [2015] COPLR 87 .... 11.3.1
Treadwell (Deceased), Re; Public Guardian v. Lutz [2013] EWHC 2409
    (COP); [2013] COPLR 587 .... 7.7
W (EEM), Re [1971] 1 Ch 123 .... 5.6.4

W (Enduring Power of Attorney) [2001] Ch 609; [2001] 1 FLR 832.................. 5.3.1
W *v.* Egdell [1990] Ch 359; [1989] 1 All ER 1089............................... 2.2, App.B
Walker, *Re* [1905] 1 Ch 160.. 9.6
Walker v. Badmin [2015] WTLR 493.. Foreword, 6.3
Wallace' Estate, *Re*; Solicitor of the Duchy of Cornwall *v.* Batten [1952] 2
    TLR 925 .... 6.4
Wharton *v.* Bancroft [2011] EWHC 3250 (Ch); [2012] WTLR 693...................... 6.5
White *v.* Jones [1995] 1 All ER 691.. 6.5, 6.6
Winterwerp *v.* Netherlands Application 6301/73, (1979) 2 EHRR 387............... 15.4.1
X (Court of Protection Practice), *Re* [2015] EWCA Civ 599..................... 8.4, 15.4.1
X (Deprivation of Liberty), *Re* (No. 2) [2014] EWCOP 37; [2015] 2 All ER
    1165 .... 8.4
X (Deprivation of Liberty), *Re* [2014] EWCOP 25; [2014] COPLR 674............ 15.4.1
X Primary Care Trust *v.* XB [2012] EWHC 1390 (Fam); [2012] COPLR 577
    3.4.2, 13.7.7
XCC *v.* AA [2012] EWHC 2183 (COP); [2012] COPLR 730................ 11.4.1, 11.4.2
XZ *v.* Public Guardian [2015] EWCOP 35.. 5.3
Zsolt Bujdosó and five others *v.* Hungary Communication 4/2011, Committee
    on the Rights of Persons with Disabilities, 14 September 2011, adopted
    2-13 September 2013 .... 10.2

Table of statutes

Abortion Act 1967................ 5.1, 13.5.4
Adults with Incapacity
  (Scotland) Act 2000 .... 1.3.2, App.J
Anti-social Behaviour, Crime
  and Policing Act 2014
    s.121(2) 11.4.1
    s.121(5) 11.4.1
Care Act 2014............ 3.5, 13.8.1, 14.4.2
    s.32 .... 1.3.2
    s.42 .... 3.5
    s.45 .... 13.8.1
Children Act 1989....... 3.8.1, 3.8.2, 11.2,
                       11.4.2
    s.1 .... 11.2
    s.8 .... 11.2
Civil Partnership Act 2004
    s.50(1)(a) 6.8
Criminal Justice Act 2003
    s.116(1) 12.3.2
       (2)(b) 12.3.2
       (e) 12.3.2
       (4) 12.3.2
Data Protection Act 1998 ...... 2.2, 13.8.5,
                    14.4.1, App.J
Electoral Administration Act
  2006
    s.73 .... 10.3, 10.4.1, 10.5
Electoral Registration and
  Administration Act 2013 .... 10.4.1
Enduring Powers of Attorney
  Act 1985 .... 5.2, 5.4, App.C, App.J
Family Law Act 1996
    Part IVA 11.4.1
Family Law Reform Act 1969
    s.8(1) 3.8.3
Health and Social Care Act
  2001 .... App.J
Health and Social Care Act
  2008 .... App.J
House of Lords Act 1999.............. 10.3

Human Fertilisation and
  Embryology Act 1990 ...... 3.8.4, 11.2,
                           App.J
Human Rights Act 1998... 4.1, 8.2.1, 11.1,
                           App.J
Human Tissue Act 2004 ..... 14.4.1, App.J
Inheritance (Provision for
  Family and Dependants) Act
  1975 .... 6.2, 6.7.4
Inheritance Tax Act 1984
    s.19 .... 7.1
Legal Aid, Sentencing and
  Punishment of Offenders Act
  2012 .... 13.7.4
    Sch.1, Part 1, para. 5(3)
Matrimonial Causes Act 1973 .... 11.4.1
    s.11 .... 11.4.1
    s.12 .... 11.4.1
       (c) 6.8
    s.13 .... 11.4.1
    s.16 .... 6.8
Mental Capacity Act 2005
  Part 1 .... 1.1.2
    s.1 .... 2.5.1, 3.1, 3.2, 5.3, 5.3.1,
          5.6.2, 7.3, 8.3, 9.5, 13.4.2,
          13.6.2, 14.1, App.A, App.B,
                           App.C
     (1) 2.1.1
     (2) 4.2.1, 6.6, 7.3, 13.4.1,
                 17.3.1, App.B, App.F
     (3) ... 6.3, 11.3.1, 13.4.1, 17.3.2,
               17.5, App.B, App.F
     (4) .... 7.3, 17.3.1, App.B, App.F
     (5) .... 13.5.1, App.B
     (6) .... App.B
    s.2 ... 3.1, 5.3.1, 5.6.2, 6.9, 7.3, 8.6,
         9.5, 13.4.2, 13.6.2, 14.1,
         14.2, 15.4.2, 15.4.3, 16.3,
         16.5, 18.1, App.A, App.C,
                          App.F

Mental Capacity Act 2005 – *continued*
s.2(1) ..... Foreword, 3.3, 3.4, 3.4.1,
     4.2.2, 4.2.6, 7.3, 8.3, 11.4.2,
     17.3.2, 18.2, 18.3.1, App.B
  (2) .... 18.3.1, App.B
  (3) ...... 3.3, 17.5, 18.3.1, App.B
  (4) .... 3.2, App.B
s.3 .... 3.1, 3.4.2, 5.3.1, 5.6.2,
     7.3, 9.5, 13.4.2, 13.6.2,
     14.1, 14.2, 18.1, App.A,
     App.B, App.C, App.F
  (1) ...... Foreword, 3.4.2, 17.3.2,
     App.B
    (d) .... App.B
  (2) .... App.B
  (3) .... App.B
  (4) .... 5.3.1, 17.5.2, App.B
s.4 .... 3.1, 3.2, 3.7, 11.4.1, 13.3,
     13.7, 15.4.2, App.A, App.C
  (5) 3.7
  (6)(a) 13.7.1
  (7) 13.5.1
  (7)(c) 13.6.1
  (10) 3.7, 13.7.4
s.4A .... App.A
s.4B .... 15.3, App.A
s.5 .... 3.1, 13.5.2, 13.5.3, 13.7.4,
     15.2, App.A
  (1) .... 3.6, 13.5.2, App.B
  (4) 13.5.2
s.6 .... 3.1, 13.5.3, 15.2, App.A
  (1)–(3) 13.5.3
s.6(4) 13.5.3
s.7 .... 9.4.2
  (1)–(2) 9.4.2
s.9(2)(b) 5.3
s.10(4) 5.3
s.12 .... 7.6.1, 7.7
  (2)(b) 7.6.1
  (3)(b) 7.6.1
s.13(2) 5.3.3
s.15 .... 11.2
  (1)(a) 3.6
s.16 .... 11.2
  (1)(b) 5.5
  (2) 15.3, 15.4.1
    (a) .... App.A
    (b) 5.5
  (4) .... App.C
s.18(1)(i) 6.9
  (3) .... 3.8.2, App.A, App.F
s.19(9)(a) 7.7
s.20(5) 13.6.4

s.21 .... 3.8.3
s.21A 15.3
s.22(2)(b) 5.3.3
  (4)(b) 5.3.3
s.23 .... 7.6.1
  (3) 5.4.2
  (4) 5.4.2
s.24 .... 13.7, 13.7.5, App.A
  (1) 13.7.2
s.25 .... 13.7, 13.7.5, App.A
  (5)–(6) 13.7.4
s.26 .... 13.7, App.A
  (1) 13.7.8
  (3) 13.7.8
s.27 .... 3.8.4, 11.2
  (1)(a) 11.4
  (c)–(d) 11.5
s.28 .... 3.8.4
s.29 .... 3.8.4, 10.5
  (1) 10.4.1
s.30 .... 14.4.2
  (1)–(2) 14.4.2
s.31 .... 14.4.2
  (2)–(7) 14.4.2
s.32 .... 14.4.2
  (4) 14.4.2
  (6) 14.4.2
  (9) 14.4.2
s.33 .... 14.4.2
s.34 .... 14.4.2
ss.35–41 .... 3.7, 13.5.1
s.42 .... App.F
s.42(4)–(5) 2.5.2
s.43 .... App.F
s.44 .... 3.8.2
s.45(1) .... App.C
s.46(2)(a)–(c) .... App.D
s.48 .... App.C
s.58 .... 5.6
  (1)(h) 5.8
s.61 .... App.C
s.62 .... 3.8.4, 13.7.2
s.64(1) 15.3
s.64(5) 15.2
Sched.A1 .... 13.5.3, 15.1, 15.3,
     15.4.2, 16.2, App.A
   para. 10 .... 15.4.2
   para. 15 .... 15.4.2
   para. 180 .... 15.3
Sched.1 .... 5.3
   para. 2(1)(e) 5.3
Sched.2, paras. 2–3 .... 6.9
   para. 4 .... 6.9

Sched.4 .... 5.4
    para. 23(1)
    para. 3(3) 7.6.2
    para. 4(1)–(2) 5.4
    para. 6 .... 5.4
    para 23(1) 5.6.4
Sched.6, para. 20 .... App.B
Mental Health Act 1983 .... 1.1.2, 1.2,
    1.3.2, 2.2, 2.4, 3.8.3, 3.8.4,
    5.6.4, 10.4.2, 13.5.3, 13.6.3,
    13.7.8, 15.2, 15.3, 15.4.1,
    15.4.2, 16.1–16.6, App.B,
    App.F, App.G
s.1 .... 5.6.4
    (2) 11.4.1, 12.3.1
s.2 .... 16.3
s.3 .... 16.3
s.4 .... 16.5
s.5 .... 16.3, 16.6
s.6 .... 16.6
s.12 .... 15.4.2
ss.17A–17G 16.4
s.28 .... 16.5
Part III 10.4.2
Part IV 3.8.4, 16.3, 16.5
s.57 .... 16.5
s.58 .... 16.5
s.58A 16.5
s.62 .... 16.5
s.62A 16.4
s.63 .... 16.5, 16.6
Part 4A 16.4
s.64C(2)(b) 16.14
s.64D 16.4
    (4) 16.4
s.64G 16.4
Part VII ...... 5.6, 5.7.1, 8.3, App.C,
    App.J
s.117 .... 7.6.1
s.131 .... 16.3
s.135 .... App.B
s.136 .... 16.5
Mental Capacity Act
(Singapore) 3.5
Mental Health Act 2007 5.6.4, 12.3.1, 16.4
Powers of Attorney Act 1971 .... App.J
s.4 .... 5.2
Representation of the People
Act 1983 .... 10.2, App.J
    s.1 .... 10.2
    s.2 .... 10.2
    s.3 .... 10.4.2
    s.3(1) 3.4.1

s.3A 10.3, 10.4.2
s.4(6) 10.4.2
s.7 .... 10.4.2
    (6) 10.4.2
s.7B(4)(b) 10.4.2
s.160(4)(a)(i) 10.3
Sched.1 .... 10.5
Representation of the People
Act 2000 .... 10.4.2, 10.5, 10.6
    s.1(1) 10.2
    (2) 10.4.2
    s.2 .... 10.4.2
    s.4 .... 10.4.2
    s.12 .... 10.5
    s.13 .... 10.5
Sale of Goods Act 1979 .... 9.4.1
    s.3(3) 9.4.2
    s.8(3) 9.4.2
Senior Courts Act 1981
    s.90 .... App.E
Sexual Offences (Amendment)
Act 2000
    s.1 .... 11.3
Sexual Offences Act 2003 ...... 12.1, 12.2,
    12.2.1–12.2.4, App.J
    s.1(1) 12.2.2
    s.2(1) 12.2.3
    s.3(1) 12.2.3
    s.4(1) 12.2.3
    s.6(1) 12.2.3
    s.7(1) 12.2.3
    s.8(1) 12.2.3
    s.30(1) 12.2.2, 12.2.4
    (2)(a) 12.2.1
    s.31(1) 12.2.4
    s.32(1) 12.2.4
    s.33(1) 12.2.4
    s.34 .... 12.2.4
    s.34(1) 12.2.2
    ss.35–42 .... 12.2.4
    ss.74–76 .... 12.2.1
Social Security Acts 5.7
Social Services and Well-being
(Wales) Act 2014 .... 2.4
    s.127 .... 2.4
Wills Act 1837
    s.9(a) 6.4
    s.18 .... 6.8
    s.18B 6.8
    s.20 .... 6.8
Youth Justice and Criminal
Evidence Act 1999 .... 2.3.1
    s.16(1)(b) 12.3.1

Youth Justice and Criminal Evidence Act
  1999 – *continued*
    s.16(2) 12.3.1
       (5) 12.3.1

s.24 .... 12.3.1
s.27 .... 12.3.1
s.29(2) 12.3.1

Table of statutory instruments

Abortion Regulations 1991, SI 1999/499 .... 13.8.1
    reg.4 .... 13.8.1
Civil Legal Aid (Procedure) Regulations 2012, SI 2012/3098 .... 2.1.2
    reg.22 .... 2.1.2
Civil Procedure Rules 1998, SI 1998/3132 .... 8.2.2, 8.3, App.F, App.J
    Part 3
        rule 3.9(7) 12.3.1
    Part 5
        rule 5(2)(b)(iii) .... App.D
    Part 19 .... App.E
    Part 21 .... Foreword, 5.5, 8.1, 8.2.1, 8.2.2, 8.2.3
        rule 21(2) 5.5
        rule 21.1 .... App.B
        rule 21.4(3) 8.4
        rule 21.5 .... 8.4
    Part 35 .... 18.1
        PD 35 .... 18.1
Criminal Procedure (Amendment) Rules 2007, SI 2007/2204 .... 5.5
Court of Protection (Amendment) Rules 2009, SI 2009/582 .... App.J
Court of Protection (Amendment) Rules 2015, SI 1548/548 .... 4.2.6, App.C
Court of Protection Fees (Amendment) Order 2009, SI 2009/513 .... App.J
Court of Protection Fees Order 2007, SI 2007/1745 .... App.J
Court of Protection Rules 2007, SI 2007/1744 .... 4.2.6, 13.5.4, App.C, App.J
    rule 3A 8.6
        (4) 8.6
    PD 4A .... App.J
    PD 4B .... App.J
    PD 6A .... App.J
    PD 7A .... App.J
    PD 8A .... App.J
    PD 9A .... App.J
    PD 9B .... App.J
    PD 9C .... App.J
    PD 9D .... 7.6.1, 7.6.2, 7.7, App.J
    PD 9E .... 13.5.4, 16.6, App.D, **App.E**, App.J
    PD 9F .... 6.9, App.J
    PD 9G .... App.J
    PD 9H .... App.J
    PD 10A .... App.J
    PD 10B .... App.J
    PD 12A .... App.J

Court of Protection Rules 2007, SI 2007/1744 – *continued*
    PD 13A .... App.J
    PD 14B .... App.J
    PD 14C .... App.J
    PD 14E .... App.J
    Part 17 .... 8.1
    PD 19A .... App.J
    PD 20A .... App.J
    PD 21A .... App.J
    PD 22A .... App.J
    PD 22B .... App.J
    PD 22C .... App.J
    PD 23A .... App.J
    PD 23B .... App.J
    rule 71 .... App.D
    rule 73(1) .... App.B
    rule 74(2)(a) 8.6
    rule 75 .... App.D
    rule 95(e) 4.2.6
    rule 85(2) .... App.D
    rule 92 .... App.D
    rule 141(4) 8.6
    rule 142(3) 8.6
    rule 143 .... 8.6
    rule 156 .... App.E
Family Proceedings Rules 1991, SI 1991/1247 .... App.J
Family Procedure Rules 2010, SI 2010/2955 .... 8.2.2, App.F
    Part 15 .... 8.1
        rule 15.4 .... 8.4
        rule 15.5 .... 8.4
    Part 16 .... 8.1
        rule 16.10 .... 8.4
        rule 16.9(2)(c) 8.4
    Part 23
        rule 23(1) 8.2.2
Family Procedure (Adoption) Rules 2005, SI 2005/2795
    Part 7 .... 8.1, 8.2.2
Human Medicines Regulations 2012, SI 2012/1916 .... 14.1
Human Tissue Act 2004 (Persons who Lack Capacity to Consent and
    Transplants) Regulations 2006, SI 2006/1659 .... App.J
Insolvency Rules 1986, SI 1986/1925 .... 8.1, 8.2.3, App.J
    rule 7.43(1), (2) 8.2.3
Lasting Powers of Attorney, Enduring Powers of Attorney and Public
    Guardian Regulations 2007, SI 2007/1253 .... 5.3, App.J
    reg.15 .... 5.3.2
Lasting Powers of Attorney, Enduring Powers of Attorney and Public
    Guardian (Amendment) Regulations 2009, SI 2009/1884 .... 5.3, 13.6.2, App.J
Lasting Powers of Attorney, Enduring Powers of Attorney and Public
    Guardian (Amendment) Regulations 2013, SI 2013/506 .... 5.3, 13.6.2, App.J
    reg.2(2) 5.32
Lasting Powers of Attorney, Enduring Powers of Attorney and Public
    Guardian (Amendment) Regulations 2015, SI 2015/899 .... 5.3, App.J

Local Elections (Principal Areas) (England and Wales) Rules 2006, SI
2006/3304 .... 10.5
Medicines for Human Use (Clinical Trials) (Amendment) (No. 2) Regulations
2006, SI 2006/2984 .... 14.4.4, App.J
Medicines for Human Use (Clinical Trials) (Amendment) Regulations 2006,
SI 2006/1928 .... App.J
reg.27 .... 14.4.3
Medicines for Human Use (Clinical Trials) Regulations 2004, SI 2004/1031
14.1, 14.3, 14.4.1, 14.4.3, App.J
reg.2 .... 14.4.3
Part 3 .... 14.2
Sched.1, Part 2 .... 14.4.3
para.2 .... 14.4.3
para. 6 .... 14.3
Mental Capacity (Deprivation of Liberty: Appointment of Relevant Person's
Representative) (Amendment) Regulations 2008, 2008/2368 .... App.J
Mental Capacity (Deprivation of Liberty: Appointment of Relevant Research
Person's Representative) Regulations 2008, SI 2008/1315 .... App.J
Mental Capacity (Deprivation of Liberty: Standard Authorisations,
Assessments and Ordinary Residence) Regulations 2008, SI 2008/1858 .... App.J
Mental Capacity Act (Independent Mental Capacity Advocates) (General)
Regulations 2006, SI 2006/1832
reg.4 .... 13.5.4
Mental Capacity Act 2005 (Appropriate Body) (England) Regulations 2006,
SI 2006/2810 .... App.J
reg.2 .... 14.4.2
Mental Capacity Act 2005 (Appropriate Body) (Wales) Regulations 2007, SI
2007/883 .... App.J
Mental Capacity Act 2005 (Commencement No.2) Order 2007, SI
2007/1031 .... App.J
Mental Capacity Act 2005 (Independent Mental Capacity Advocate) (General)
Regulations 2006, SI 2006/1832 .... App.J
Mental Capacity Act 2005 (Independent Mental Capacity Advocate) (Wales)
Regulations 2006, SI 2007/852 .... App.J
Mental Capacity Act 2005 (Independent Mental Capacity Advocates)
(Expansion of Role) Regulations 2006, SI 2006/2883 .... App.J
Mental Capacity Act 2005 (Loss of Capacity During Research) (England)
Regulations 2007, SI 2007/679 .... App.J
Mental Capacity Act 2005 (Loss of Capacity During Research) (Wales)
Regulations 2007, SI 2007/837 .... App.J
Mental Capacity Act 2005 (Transfer of Proceedings) Order 2007, SI
2007/1899 .... 3.8.3, App.J
Mental Capacity Act 2005 (Transitional and Consequential Provisions) Order
2007, SI 2007/1898 .... App.J
Mental Health Act 2007 (Commencement No.10 and Transitional Provisions)
Order 2009, SI 2009/139 .... App.J
Public Guardian (Fees etc) (Amendment) Regulations 2007 (SI 2007/2616)
Public Guardian (Fees etc) Regulations 2007, SI 2007/2051 .... App.J
Public Guardian Board Regulations 2007, SI 2007/1770 .... App.J
Representation of the People (England and Wales) (Description of Electoral
Registers and Amendment) Regulations 2013, SI 2013/3198
reg.10 .... 10.4.1

Representation of the People (England and Wales) Regulations 2001, SI
2001/341
reg.12 .... 10.5
reg.26(1)(j) 10.4.1
Social Security (Claims and Payments) Regulations 1987, SI 1987/1968
reg.33 .... 5.7.1

Table of international treaties and instruments

European Convention for the Protection of Human Rights and Dignity of the
  Human Being with regard to the Application of Biology and Medicine:
  Convention on Human Rights and Biomedicine (Oviedo Convention) .... App.J
European Convention for the Protection of Human Rights and Fundamental
  Freedoms 1950 .... 3.9, 4.1, 4.2.6, 10.4.2, 11.1, App.J
    art.5 .... 15.1, 15.2
      (1) 15.2, 16.3
        (e) 15.4.1
    art.6(1) 8.2.1
    art.8 .... 2.2, 11.1, 12.2.1
    art.12 .... 11.1
    art.14 .... 3.9
EU Directive 2001/20/EC 14.1
EU Regulation 536/2014 (Clinical Trial Regulations) 14.1, 14.3, 14.4.1, 14.4.3
    art.2 .... 14.3
Hague Convention on the International Protection of Adults .... App.J
UN Convention on the Rights of Persons with Disabilities 1991.... 1.1.2, 3.7, 3.9, 4.2.6,
                                                                    5.7.1, 10.2, 11.1
    art.12.4 .... 5.7.1
    art.23 .... 11.1
    art.29 .... 10.2
    Optional Protocol 2006 .... 3.9, 5.7.1
UN Declaration on Human Rights 1948.. 11.1, 11.6

Table of international treaties and instruments

Abbreviations

ACO	Authorised Court Officer
BMA	British Medical Association
CAFCASS	Children and Family Court Advisory and Support Service
CAMHS	children and adolescent mental health services
CJD	Creutzfeldt Jakob disease
COPR	Court of Protection Rules
CPR	Civil Procedure Rules
CRPD	Convention on the Rights of Persons with Disabilities
CTO	Community Treatment Order
DoLS	Deprivation of Liberty Safeguards
DPA 1998	Data Protection Act 1998
DSM-5	American Psychiatric Association, Diagnostic and Statistical Manual
DWP	Department for Work and Pensions
ECHR	European Convention for the Protection of Human Rights and Fundamental Freedoms
ECT	electro-convulsive therapy
EPA	enduring power of attorney
ERO	Electoral Registration Officer
FP(A)R	Family Procedure (Adoption) Rules
FPR	Family Procedure Rules
GP	general practitioner
HMCTS	HM Courts and Tribunals Service
ICD-10	International Classification of Disease (10th edition)
IHT	inheritance tax
IMCA	Independent Mental Capacity Advocate
IB	indicative behaviour
IR	Insolvency Rules
LPA	lasting power of attorney
MacCAT-T	MacArthur Competence Assessment Tool for Treatment
MCA 2005	Mental Capacity Act 2005
MHA	Mental Health Act
OPG	Office of the Public Guardian

P	the person said to lack capacity in proceedings before the Court of Protection
PTSD	post-traumatic stress disorder
RPA	Representation of the People Act
SRA	Solicitors Regulation Authority
WHO	World Health Organization

PART I

Introduction

CHAPTER 1

The law, practice and this book

1.1   Mental capacity and the law   1.3   Scope of this book
1.2   How to use this book   1.4   Further advice

1.1 MENTAL CAPACITY AND THE LAW

Capacity is the ability to do something. In a legal context it refers to a person's ability to do something, including making a decision, which may have legal consequences for that person, or for other people. Mental capacity can be the pivotal issue in balancing the right to autonomy in decision-making and the right to protection from harm.

Doctors and lawyers have common responsibilities to ensure the protection of people who lack capacity to decide specific matters for themselves and to promote the autonomy and choices of those who can regulate their own lives. The careful assessment of whether individuals have or lack capacity to make particular decisions is essential to the protection of their rights. Doctors, lawyers and other professionals will be responsible for carrying out assessments of capacity. Effective communication, both between any professionals involved and with the person being assessed, is vital. This book sets out to aid communication, in particular between doctors and lawyers, and to clarify the legal framework within which assessment of capacity takes place.

1.1.1 Background

The issue of capacity took on increased importance in England and Wales in the lead up to, and coming into effect of, the Mental Capacity Act 2005. As indicated in previous editions of this book, reform of the law relating to mental capacity was a long and protracted process, starting in 1989 with a five-year inquiry by the Law Commission which published its final report, including a draft Bill, in 1995.[1] The

---

[1]   Law Commission (1995) *Mental Incapacity* (Law Com No 231), TSO.

government undertook further consultation,[2] leading to a policy statement[3] and eventual publication in 2003 of a second draft Mental Incapacity Bill.[4] The draft Bill was subject to pre-legislative scrutiny by a Joint Parliamentary Select Committee which made a number of recommendations for improvements.[5] The Joint Committee gave the following reasons why new legislation was necessary:

- the inadequacies of the (then) common law to safeguard those who lack capacity;
- the need to promote awareness and good practice in dealing with those lacking capacity;
- the government's duty to fulfil human rights obligations towards those lacking capacity;
- the government's commitment to promote non-discrimination in respect of people lacking capacity; and
- the need to achieve a better balance between autonomy and protection for those who are unable to make decisions.

This process of consultation and scrutiny finally resulted in the Mental Capacity Act (MCA) 2005 which came fully into effect on 1 October 2007. The Act gave statutory provision to clarify and govern the making of decisions by and on behalf of people who may lack capacity to make specific decisions for themselves. In the words of the House of Lords Select Committee convened to conduct post-legislation scrutiny of the Act in 2013–14, the Act:

> was a visionary piece of legislation for its time, which marked a turning point in the statutory rights of people who may lack capacity – whether for reasons of learning disability, autism spectrum disorders, senile dementia, brain injury or temporary impairment. The Mental Capacity Act placed the individual at the heart of decision-making. Capacity was to be presumed unless proven otherwise. Decision-making was to be supported to enable the individual as far as possible to take their own decisions. Unwise decisions were not to be used as indicators of a lack of capacity – like others, those with impairments were entitled to take risks and to make poor decisions. When a person was found to lack capacity for a specific decision, the 'best interests' process ensured that their wishes and feelings were central to the decision being made and, importantly, provided protection from harm to vulnerable adults. The Act signified a step change in the legal rights afforded to those who may lack capacity, with the potential to transform the lives of many.[6]

---

[2] Lord Chancellor's Department (1997) *Who Decides? Making Decisions on Behalf of Mentally Incapacitated Adults* (Cm 3803), TSO.
[3] Lord Chancellor's Department (1999) *Making Decisions: The Government's Proposals for Making Decisions on Behalf of Mentally Incapacitated Adults* (Cm 4465), TSO.
[4] Draft Mental Incapacity Bill 2003 (Cm 5859-I), TSO.
[5] Joint Committee on the Draft Mental Capacity Bill (2003) *Report of the Joint Committee on the Draft Mental Incapacity Bill*, Vol I (HL Paper 198-I, HC 1083-I), TSO.
[6] House of Lords Select Committee on the Mental Capacity Act 2005 (2014) *Mental Capacity Act 2005: Post-legislative Scrutiny*, HL Paper 139, available at **www.publications.parliament.uk/pa/ld201314/ldselect/ldmentalcap/139/139.pdf**.

The third edition of this book (published in 2010) was written at a time when MCA 2005 was still in its relative infancy, and to some extent had to include a degree of speculation as to how the changes introduced by the Act would take effect, and as to the impact of MCA 2005 on other areas of decision-making outside the scope of the Act.

We are now a decade from the enactment of MCA 2005, and eight years from its coming into force. It is, unfortunately, all too clear that while the Act, in the main, continues to be held in high regard (and indeed has had a significant impact in other jurisdictions):

> its implementation has not met the expectations that it rightly raised. The Act has suffered from a lack of awareness and a lack of understanding. For many who are expected to comply with the Act it appears to be an optional add-on, far from being central to their working lives. [...] In [the health and social care] sectors the prevailing cultures of paternalism (in health) and risk-aversion (in social care) have prevented the Act from becoming widely known or embedded. The empowering ethos has not been delivered. The rights conferred by the Act have not been widely realised. The duties imposed by the Act are not widely followed.[7]

In our experience, one of the most important barriers to proper implementation of the Act remains misunderstandings among professionals as to how the Act is intended to work (and not to work). As in the previous edition of the book, our primary aim remains to assist in breaking down that barrier by seeking to help doctors and lawyers reach a common understanding of the requirements of the law in all areas where an assessment of capacity may be needed. It is important that both professions work within their own areas of professional expertise and cooperate with each other in the interests of those they seek to serve.

1.1.2 Changes to the previous edition

Readers will note that we have excised much of the pre-MCA case law that was discussed in the previous edition. This is primarily because there is now a significant body of practice and case law from the Court of Protection (and other courts) in which MCA 2005 has been considered and applied.[8] We further consider that at

---

[7] House of Lords Select Committee on the Mental Capacity Act 2005 (2014) *Mental Capacity Act 2005: Post-legislative Scrutiny*, HL Paper 139, available at **www.publications.parliament.uk/pa/ld201314/ldselect/ldmentalcap/139/139.pdf**.

[8] The Court of Appeal in *RB* v. *Brighton and Hove City Council* [2014] EWCA 561; [2014] COPLR 629 noted (in relation to the Court of Protection) that '[t]he cases which arise for decision under Part 1 of MCA 2005 (including the present case) tend to be acutely difficult, not admitting of any obviously right answer. The task of the court is to apply the statutory provisions, paying close heed to the language of the statute. Nevertheless, as judges tread their way through this treacherous terrain, it is helpful to look sideways and see how the courts have applied those statutory provisions to other factual scenarios. This has nothing to do with either the doctrine of precedent or the principles of statutory interpretation. The purpose is simply to see how other judicial decisions have exposed the issues or attempted to reconcile the irreconcilable' (para.40), per Jackson LJ.

least some of the pre-MCA case law placed an insufficient emphasis upon the empowerment of the individual whose capacity is in doubt.

The importance of both:

(a)   supporting the individual to make the decision(s) in question; and
(b)   (where, despite those efforts, the individual lacks that capacity) ensuring that their voice is heard in the decision-making process

has been highlighted by the rising prominence of the United Nations Convention on the Rights of Persons with Disabilities,[9] which challenges the two fundamental building blocks of the legal framework established by MCA 2005: the very concept of mental capacity and substitute decision-making based upon best interests (see further **3.9**). We anticipate, by the time of the next edition of this book, MCA 2005 may well have been amended in consequence of the Convention. We do not address it in detail, however, because the Convention has not yet been incorporated into English law.

The other substantive change to the book is the addition of a new chapter (**Chapter 16**) highlighting issues relating to capacity that arise in the context of admission, assessment, and treatment under the Mental Health Act (MHA) 1983. This addition has been prompted by the 2015 edition of the Mental Health Act Code of Practice (MHA Code of Practice),[10] which rightly emphasises the importance of the proper assessment of mental capacity in the context of MHA 1983.

1.2   HOW TO USE THIS BOOK

This book sets out to provide a useful resource and tool for the health and legal professions. It is intended to be a source of information appropriate to the assessment of mental capacity in a variety of contexts. Some repetition in the text is unavoidable and indeed desirable since it is expected that health and legal professionals will refer to the sections which are relevant to a particular patient or client rather than read the book from cover to cover.

Part I begins with a description of the purpose of the book and an explanation of the limits of its coverage. It continues with an outline of the important professional and ethical issues for health and legal professionals that arise from a consideration of mental capacity.

Part II outlines the key principles and concepts underpinning the legal framework of MCA 2005, examines the statutory definition and test of capacity and considers how decisions should be made on behalf of people lacking capacity. It also considers the overlapping legislation affecting children and young people and

---

[9]   The United Kingdom had ratified the Convention by the time of the previous edition of this book but, tellingly, it was not mentioned in the body of the text.
[10]   Department of Health (2015) *Mental Health Act 1983 Code of Practice*, available at **www.gov.uk/government/publications/code-of-practice-mental-health-act-1983**.

some specific decisions excluded from MCA 2005. Other legal principles relevant to the assessment of capacity are also described.

Part III examines the legal tests of capacity which apply to various decisions or activities that an individual may wish to undertake (e.g. making a will or getting married). Different requirements apply to different types of decisions. Lawyers often seek a medical opinion when they are asked to advise, or act on behalf of, a client whose mental capacity to make specific decisions is in doubt. Lawyers who ask doctors to assess a person's capacity should always make clear the activity or transaction in which the person intends to engage or the decision that the person expects to make, as well as the legal requirements in this respect. **Part III**, by clarifying the legal requirements for a number of activities or decisions, is primarily intended as a reminder to lawyers and to help doctors who have been asked to conduct an assessment of a person's capacity. References to statute and case law are given where appropriate.

Medical practitioners also have to assess an individual's mental capacity to clarify whether medical treatment can proceed without the patient's consent. Whether an apparent consent or refusal of treatment is legally valid is discussed in **Chapter 13** and specific safeguards relating to medical research are considered in **Chapter 14**, both aimed primarily at health professionals.

Chapter 15 and **Chapter 16** take a slightly different form. They do not address particular decisions, but rather how questions of capacity arise in two related contexts. **Chapter 15** highlights how questions of capacity are important in the context of deprivation of liberty for purposes of providing care or treatment in hospital or care homes. **Chapter 16** identifies the key issues relating to capacity in relation to those who may be receiving treatment under MHA 1983 and those admitted to hospital for assessment and treatment for mental disorder.

Part IV deals with the medical practicalities of assessing capacity. **Chapter 17** sets out the accepted practice for carrying out assessments of capacity and will be familiar to practitioners who regularly work in the mental health field. It is primarily intended to assist health professionals who only occasionally encounter a request for an assessment of capacity to be carried out. **Chapter 18** aims to help lawyers direct their requests for a medical opinion appropriately and to be aware of the steps involved in a medical assessment.

Please note that when referring to the person lacking capacity we have chosen to adopt the plural 'they/them/their' to avoid using either just the masculine or feminine or, potentially more confusing, a combination of both. Note also that we use, on occasion, the term 'incapacitated' in respect of a person who lacks capacity in one or more domains. This is a shorthand, used solely to avoid undue repetition. As set out in more detail in **Chapter 3**, strictly speaking a person can never be said simply to be incapacitated: they must always be said to lack capacity to make one (or more) decisions. The term 'vulnerable client' or 'vulnerable person' is used in places. There is a strong move away from the use of the word 'vulnerable' in social care because of its potentially discriminatory connotations. It is therefore no longer used in the safeguarding context. It is, however, a term that remains familiar to many doctors and lawyers, and is also used by the High Court in connection with the exercise of its inherent jurisdiction (see **3.5**). It is therefore used – sparingly – in this book. Finally, the initial 'P' is used in a number of chapters to refer to the subject of proceedings before the Court of Protection.

1.3 SCOPE OF THIS BOOK

1.3.1 What is covered?

Law and medical practice in England and Wales

This book deals with the legal position in England and Wales regarding the legal rights and treatment of adults (defined in MCA 2005 as people aged 16 years and over) who may lack mental capacity to make specific decisions for themselves. The focus is on MCA 2005 itself and other areas of the civil law affecting the private rights of citizens. It also indicates the relationship between the law and accepted medical practice and looks in particular at the impact of MCA 2005 on relevant areas of practice. It should be noted that, as devolution gathers pace, there is the potential for increasing divergence between the relevant statutory provisions and Codes of Practice that apply in England and those that apply in Wales. Key differences that already exist are highlighted in the book.

Information for doctors and lawyers

The book brings together information for health and legal professionals on the interpretation of the law as it affects the concept of capacity to make decisions in various situations and the role of both professions in the assessment of capacity. Pointers are also given for good practice in the assessment of mental capacity.

1.3.2 Outside the scope of this book

Children

The legal position of children under 16 years is different and is beyond the scope of this book. The BMA has published separate guidance for doctors on all aspects of healthcare for children and young people.[11] The Law Society manages a Children Law Accreditation Scheme, which accredits practitioners who have been assessed as competent to represent children in legal proceedings.[12]

However, apart from a few exceptions (indicated where relevant) the main provisions of MCA 2005 described in this book also apply to young people aged

---

[11] BMA (2001) *Consent, Rights and Choices in Health Care for Children and Young People*, Wiley Blackwell.
[12] See **www.lawsociety.org.uk/support-services/accreditation/children-law/**.

16–17 as they apply to adults aged 18 years and over. The key ways in which MCA 2005 applies to children and young people are described in **Chapter 3**, including the complexities that arise in relation to the assessment of capacity.

Jurisdictions outside England and Wales

The book deals with the law in England and Wales. It does not deal with other parts of the UK.

In Scotland, statutory guidance has been published on the Adults with Incapacity (Scotland) Act 2000, which became law in April 2001 and introduced a statutory framework for decision-making for people with impaired capacity.[13] The BMA has issued separate guidance for doctors on the requirements in Scotland for the assessment of capacity and the treatment of adults who lack capacity to consent.[14]

In Northern Ireland, decision-making in this area is covered by common law and the Mental Health (Northern Ireland) Order 1986, although as at autumn 2015 the Northern Ireland Assembly was engaged in the passage of an innovative Mental Capacity Bill which will (if enacted) represent a model for the rest of the United Kingdom.[15]

The criminal law

The book sets out the legal provisions relating to the civil law (those areas of law concerning the private rights of citizens). It does not cover aspects of the criminal law, except for one specific area. **Chapter 12** deals with the provisions in the criminal law relating to protection of adults at risk of sexual abuse, which may arise in the context of consent to sexual relationships. Other issues such as a defendant's 'fitness to plead' or the need for an 'appropriate adult' to be present during police questioning are not considered. Further information for lawyers advising and representing mentally disordered people who are the subject of criminal investigation or proceedings is available from the Law Society.[16]

Physical incapacity

This book does not consider specific issues arising from a person's physical incapacity. Separating issues arising from a person's lack of physical or mental capacity is not always straightforward – for example, when considering the fitness

---

[13] The Scottish Executive has published codes of practice and other information about the operation of the Act. See **www.gov.scot/Topics/Justice/law/awi**.

[14] BMA (2009) *Medical Treatment for Adults with Incapacity: Guidance on Ethical and Medico-legal Issues in Scotland*, BMA. See **http://bma.org.uk/practical-support-at-work/ethics/mental-capacity/mental-capacity-scotland**.

[15] See **www.niassembly.gov.uk/assembly-business/legislation/primary-legislation-current-bills/mental-capacity-bill/**.

[16] C Taylor, J Krish and F Farnham (2009) *Advising Mentally Disordered Offenders: A Practical Guide* (2nd edn), Law Society Publishing.

to drive of a person with dementia, both physical and mental impairment may be present. Also, severe physical disabilities may affect a person's ability to communicate their wishes or decisions. Where physical incapacity inhibits communication, every effort should be made to assist the person to communicate, but where this is not possible, the same considerations in assessing capacity will apply as to those with mental disabilities. MCA 2005 makes it clear that when an individual is unable to communicate a decision by any means they will be treated as if they lack capacity to make that decision (see **3.4**).

Mental Health Act 1983

The interface between MHA 1983 and MCA 2005 is addressed in outline terms in **Chapter 16**, with a focus on the areas where a person's capacity is of particular significance. The detail of mental health legislation is beyond the scope of this book.

1.4 FURTHER ADVICE

Assessing, advising or treating people who may lack capacity to make relevant decisions are complex matters, often giving rise to professional or ethical dilemmas in both medical and legal practice. Some key issues affecting both professions are discussed in **Chapter 2**, but further advice may be needed when considering an individual case. The British Medical Association (BMA) and the Law Society offer guidance on ethical issues to their members. Doctors can contact the Ethics Department of the BMA and solicitors can telephone the Ethics Helpline (0370 606 2577) operated by the Solicitors Regulation Authority. Guidance is also available from bodies such as the Ministry of Justice, the Office of the Official Solicitor, the Office of the Public Guardian, the Department of Health and the General Medical Council (see **Appendix I** and **Appendix J**).

CHAPTER 2

Professional and ethical issues

2.1   Capacity to instruct a solicitor
2.2   Confidentiality
2.3   Creating the right environment for assessing capacity
2.4   Refusal to be assessed
2.5   People assessed as lacking capacity
2.6   Individuals at risk
2.7   Summary of points for doctors
2.8   Summary of points for lawyers

2.1   CAPACITY TO INSTRUCT A SOLICITOR

2.1.1   The importance of capacity

If a client has capacity to give a solicitor instructions on a matter, then, as a general rule, the solicitor must act upon those instructions unless there are proper reasons for them not to do so.[1] Conversely, if a client does not have capacity to give instructions, a solicitor will not be able to act without steps being taken to ensure that a person is identified with authority to give instructions on the client's behalf.[2] To do otherwise may place the solicitor at risk of a range of both professional sanctions and/or civil claims.[3]

Therefore a key question for any solicitor is whether they are satisfied that their client has capacity to give them instructions on the matter in question.

There is a presumption of capacity under MCA 2005, s.1(1) (see **3.2**). It is also clear that, merely because a potential client is elderly, there is no duty upon a solicitor to obtain medical evidence as to their capacity to give them instructions:

---

[1]   SRA Code of Conduct 2011, outcomes 1.1–1.3 and IBs 1.7 and 1.12.
[2]   See (in the context of wills), *Feltham* v. *Freer Bouskell* [2013] EWHC 1952 (Ch); [2013] WTLR 1363 at para.53: '[w]here a solicitor is instructed to prepare and execute a will for a client, if the client does not have mental capacity, he has no client and cannot accept instructions.' See further **Chapter 6**.
[3]   Those risks are summarised at paras.1.4.1 and 1.4.2 of Law Society Practice Note: Meeting the Needs of Vulnerable Clients (2 July 2015), available at **www.lawsociety.org.uk/support-services/ advice/practice-notes/meeting-the-needs-of-vulnerable-clients-july-2015/**. See also, in the context of wills, **Chapter 6** and Law Society (2013) *Wills and Inheritance Protocol*, para.2.7.6.

such would be 'insulting and unnecessary'.[4] A solicitor is, in general, only required to make inquiries as to capacity 'if there are circumstances such as to raise doubt as to this in the mind of a reasonably competent practitioner'.[5] However, if a solicitor has any doubt as to whether a client has capacity to provide an instruction or instructions in relation to the relevant matters, they should undertake an assessment of capacity (or seek a formal assessment of capacity from an appropriately qualified expert) before any instructions are acted upon so as to secure both their interests and those of the client.[6]

Different levels of capacity are required for different transactions, for example, different considerations apply to making a will than in conducting personal injury litigation. A solicitor must therefore assess the client's understanding in the context of the relevant legal test of capacity (as set out in **Part III**) and then consider whether the client is able to convey in general terms what they wish the solicitor to do.

This does not mean that the client must be able to understand all the details of the law – it is the role of the lawyer to provide legal advice. It is also possible that the client may be clear about some aspects of a legal transaction or proceedings while lacking capacity to deal with others. The Court of Appeal has stressed the importance of 'the issue-specific nature' of the test of capacity:

> that is to say the requirement to consider the question of capacity in relation to the particular transaction (its nature and complexity) in respect of which the decisions as to capacity fall to be made. It is not difficult to envisage claimants in personal injury actions with capacity to deal with all matters and take all 'lay client' decisions related to their actions up to and including a decision whether or not to settle, but lacking capacity to decide (even with advice) how to administer a large award.[7]

This 'issue-specific' approach has been given statutory codification by MCA 2005, which stresses that an assessment of capacity must be made in relation to the specific decision in question at the particular time the decision needs to be made.

In the same way, lawyers must consider the client's capacity to give instructions in respect of each particular transaction at the time a decision needs to be made. If there are grounds to doubt a client's capacity, it will often be advisable for the lawyer to seek a medical opinion (see further **3.6**). It will be necessary to explain to the doctor the relevant legal test of capacity and ask for an opinion as to how the client's medical condition may affect their ability to make the decision in question. However, it is for the solicitor ultimately to decide whether they are satisfied that the client has the required level of capacity, using the medical opinion and other relevant evidence to inform the assessment.

---

[4] *Thorpe* v. *Fellowes Solicitors LLP* [2011] EWHC 61 (QB); [2011] PNLR 13 at para.77.

[5] *Ibid.* at para.75.

[6] See footnote 3.

[7] *Masterman-Lister* v. *Brutton & Co and Jewell & Home Counties Dairies* [2002] EWCA Civ 1889; [2003] 1 WLR 1511 at para.27, per Kennedy LJ. These *dicta* remain of equal force since the coming into force of MCA 2005.

Useful and detailed guidance as to how solicitors can meet the needs of vulnerable clients including those who may lack capacity can be found in the Law Society Practice Note: Meeting the Needs of Vulnerable Clients (Vulnerable Clients Practice Note), issued in 2015.[8]

2.1.2 Incapacity and its consequences

If a solicitor considers that a *potential* client lacks capacity to give them instructions, they are entitled to decline to act on their behalf.[9] If the solicitor wishes to act for them, the solicitor must first make sure that they are able to identify a person who has the requisite authority to give them instructions. It is important to note that this will also include a situation where an existing client of a solicitor wishes to instruct them on a new matter if the solicitor has (or should have) grounds to consider that the client may not have capacity to give instructions in relation to it.

If a solicitor considers that an *existing* client has lost the capacity to continue to give them instructions, then the following considerations apply:

- generally a retainer terminates by operation of law when a client loses the capacity to give or confirm instructions. However, there may be exceptions to this rule (in particular where the retainer has provided for the potential loss of such capacity);[10]
- Where an existing client loses capacity to instruct the solicitor, they should as far as practicable act fairly and take action to protect their client's interests.[11] However, if the solicitor is to *continue to act*, they need to make sure that they have identified a person who is able to give them instructions.

Depending on the circumstances, the solicitor may be able to act (or to continue to act) on behalf of a client lacking capacity to instruct them by obtaining their instructions from a litigation friend, attorney or court appointed deputy. For example:[12]

- A solicitor may act under the instructions of an attorney (such as a family member) appointed under a registered enduring power of attorney (EPA) or lasting power of attorney (LPA), provided the decision in question is within the scope of their authority. A solicitor may act under the instructions of a court appointed deputy (depending upon the scope of the deputy's authority) (see further **Chapter 5**).

---

[8] Law Society Practice Note: Meeting the Needs of Vulnerable Clients (2 July 2015), available at **www.lawsociety.org.uk/support-services/advice/practice-notes/meeting-the-needs-of-vulnerable-clients-july-2015/**.

[9] *Ibid.* at 4.7.

[10] *Blankley* v. *Central Manchester and Manchester Children's University Hospitals NHS Trust* [2015] EWCA Civ 18; [2015] 1 Costs LR 119.

[11] SRA Code of Conduct 2011, outcomes 1.1–1.3.

[12] See also Law Society Practice Note: Meeting the Needs of Vulnerable Clients (2 July 2015) at 4.7.1 and 5.3, available at **www.lawsociety.org.uk/support-services/advice/practice-notes/meeting-the-needs-of-vulnerable-clients-july-2015/**.

- Where there are no current proceedings, but where proceedings are contemplated, the solicitor may be able to identify a third party who can give instructions on the client's behalf, as a proposed litigation friend[13] (see further **Chapter 8**).

A solicitor must always be careful when taking instructions from someone other than the client, in particular to be astute to consider whether: (1) the instructions are in the client's best interests; and (2) whether they reveal any conflict of interest between the client and the person giving the instructions: see further section 5 of the Vulnerable Clients Practice Note.

2.2 CONFIDENTIALITY

Carrying out an assessment of capacity may require doctors and lawyers to share information about the personal circumstances of the person being assessed. Yet doctors, lawyers and other professionals are bound by a duty of confidentiality towards their clients, imposed through their professional ethical codes and reinforced by law.[14]

The Data Protection Act (DPA) 1998 also regulates practice in this area. DPA 1998 provides individuals with a number of important rights to ensure that personal information and in particular, sensitive personal information (such as health information) is processed fairly and lawfully. Processing includes holding, recording, using and disclosing information. The Act applies to all forms of media, including paper and images. It requires that all data processing must be 'fair' and 'lawful'. This means that all patients including those who lack capacity must know when and what information about them is being processed. The processing itself must be lawful and this includes meeting common law confidentiality obligations, which are likely to require patient consent (or the consent of a nominated proxy) to be obtained. DPA 1998 also requires organisations that wish to process identifying information to use the minimum of information necessary and to retain it for only as long as it is needed for the purpose for which it was originally collected.

---

[13] Where relevant, the proposed litigation friend is able to sign an application for legal aid on behalf of the client: see the Civil Legal Aid (Procedure) Regulations 2012, SI 2012/3098, reg.22 and para.3.12 of the Standard Civil Contract 2014, available at **www.gov.uk/government/publications/standard-civil-contract-2014**.

[14] European Convention on Human Rights, art.8; Data Protection Act 1998. See, in relation to doctors, Department of Health (2003) *Confidentiality: NHS Code of Practice*, available at **www.gov.uk/government/publications/confidentiality-nhs-code-of-practice**; Health and Social Care Information Centre (2014) *Code of Practice on Confidential Information*, available at **http://systems.hscic.gov.uk/infogov/codes/cop/code.pdf**; and (2013) *A Guide to Confidentiality in Health and Social Care: Treating Confidential Information with Respect* (version 1.1), available at **www.hscic.gov.uk/media/12822/Guide-to-confidentiality-in-health-and-social-care/pdf/HSCIC-guide-to-confidentiality.pdf**.

As a general principle, personal information may only be disclosed with the client's consent, even to close relatives or 'next of kin'. However, the courts have confirmed there are circumstances when disclosure is necessary in the absence of consent:

> The decided cases very clearly establish: (i) that the law recognises an important public interest in maintaining professional duties of confidence; but (ii) that the law treats such duties not as absolute but as liable to be overridden where there is held to be a stronger public interest in disclosure.[15]

In relation to people who lack capacity to consent to (or refuse) disclosure, a balance must be struck between the public and private interests in maintaining confidentiality and the public and private interests in permitting, and occasionally requiring, disclosure for certain purposes. Some guidance has been offered in the case of *R (on the application of Stevens)* v. *Plymouth City Council*, which concerned an application for disclosure of social services records to the mother (and nearest relative) of a young adult with learning disabilities who was subject to local authority guardianship under MHA 1983. In allowing limited disclosure to the mother, Lady Justice Hale (as she then was) said:

> [The young adult's] interest in protecting the confidentiality of personal information about himself must not be underestimated. It is all too easy for professionals and parents to regard children and incapacitated adults as having no independent interests of their own: as objects rather than subjects. But we are not concerned here with the publication of information to the whole wide world. There is a clear distinction between disclosure to the media with a view to publication to all and sundry and disclosure in confidence to those with a proper interest in having the information in question.[16]

A similar balancing act must be carried out by professionals seeking or undertaking assessments of capacity. It is essential that information concerning the person being assessed, which is directly relevant to the decision in question, is made available to ensure that an accurate and focused assessment can take place. Every effort must first be made to obtain the person's consent to disclosure by providing a full explanation as to why this is necessary and the risks and consequences involved. If the person is unable to consent or refuse, relevant disclosure (of the minimum necessary to achieve the objective of assessing capacity) may be permitted where this is in the person's best interests. However, this does not mean that everyone has to know everything.

Chapter 16 of the MCA Code of Practice[17] provides advice on access to information about individuals lacking capacity to consent to disclosure. The Code states at para.16.8 the relevant factors as to whether someone else might be able to see information relating to an individual who lacks capacity, which include:

---

[15]   *W* v. *Egdell* [1990] Ch 359 at 419e.
[16]   *R (on the application of Stevens)* v. *Plymouth City Council* [2002] EWCA Civ 388; [2002] LGR 565 at para.49.
[17]   Office of the Public Guardian (2007) *Mental Capacity Act 2005 Code of Practice*, available at **www.gov.uk/government/publications/mental-capacity-act-code-of-practice**.

- whether the person requesting the information is acting as an agent, such as a court appointed deputy or attorney for the person who lacks capacity;
- whether disclosure is in the best interests of the person who lacks capacity; and
- what type of information has been requested.

Specific guidance for lawyers and doctors is given in the following sections.

2.2.1 Lawyers

There is a general principle, enshrined in outcome 4.1 of the SRA Code of Conduct 2011, that a solicitor (and the solicitor's firm) is under a duty to:

> keep the affairs of clients confidential unless disclosure is required or permitted by law or the client consents.

The reference to clients in this outcome includes former clients. The duty of confidentiality extends to all confidential information about a client's affairs, irrespective of the source of the information, and subject only to limited exceptions in the absence of the client's specific consent. There is no specific exception which permits informing a doctor about the contents of a client's will, for example, or the extent of the client's property and affairs, without first having obtained express consent from the client.

However, there have been decisions in cases involving wills in which disclosure (with the client's approval) may be expected. In *Kenward* v. *Adams* the judge stated that there is a 'golden if tactless rule' that:

> when a solicitor is drawing up a will for an aged testator or one who has been seriously ill, it should be witnessed and approved by a medical practitioner, who ought to record his examination of the testator and his findings … (and) that if there was an earlier will it should be examined and any proposed alterations should be discussed with the testator.[18]

The so-called 'golden rule' is discussed further at **6.5**.

Any solicitor who cannot obtain from the client consent to the disclosure of confidential information, or has not obtained consent in advance in anticipation of the need for disclosure, would be advised to discuss the matter with their internal Compliance Office for Legal Practice and any compliance and risk colleagues and also seek the advice of the Solicitors Regulation Authority (see **Appendix I**).

2.2.2 Doctors

Doctors are bound by a professional duty to maintain the confidentiality of personal health information unless the patient gives valid consent to disclosure, or, if the patient is incapable of giving consent, the doctor believes disclosure to be in that person's best interests. Exceptionally, confidential information can be disclosed

---

[18] *Kenward* v. *Adams* (1975) *The Times*, 29 November.

without consent where the public interest outweighs the interest in maintaining confidentiality. Difficult decisions may arise if relatives, carers or the patient's lawyer approach the doctor for a medical report on an individual whose capacity to consent is in doubt, but the patient refuses to be assessed (this is discussed in **2.4**) or else agrees to assessment but not to disclosure of the results. The General Medical Council recognises that there are some exceptional circumstances when disclosure of confidential information can be made without consent in the best interests of a person lacking capacity to consent.

As mentioned above, general guidance on sharing information about a person who lacks capacity can be found in Chapter 16 of the MCA Code of Practice. More detailed ethical guidance on confidentiality and disclosure of health information, which draws together guidance from professional and regulatory bodies, is available from the BMA,[19] and the questions of confidentiality are discussed further at **13.8**.

2.3 CREATING THE RIGHT ENVIRONMENT FOR ASSESSING CAPACITY

Detailed guidance on the practical aspects of assessing capacity is given in **Part IV** and further advice is given in the MCA Code of Practice, in particular Chapters 3 and 4 (see **Appendix B**). The following pointers may be helpful to both doctors and lawyers when trying to create the right environment and optimise the conditions for assessing capacity:[20]

- Try to minimise anxiety or stress by making the person feel at ease.
- If the cause of the incapacity can be treated, the doctor should, in so far as possible, treat it before the assessment of capacity is made.
- If the person's capacity is likely to improve, wait until it has improved. Obviously, if the assessment is urgent it may not be possible to wait.
- Be aware of any medication which could affect capacity (e.g. medication which causes drowsiness). Consider delaying the assessment until any negative effects of medication have subsided.
- If there are communication or language problems, consider enlisting the services of a speech therapist or a translator, or consult family members on the best methods of communication.
- Be aware of any cultural, ethnic or religious factors which may have a bearing on the person's way of thinking, behaviour or communication.

---

[19] See the BMA's *Confidentiality and Disclosure of Health Records Tool Kit* (**http://bma.org.uk/ practical-support-at-work/ethics/confidentiality-and-health-records**) which includes 16 'cards' covering specific areas which raise particularly difficult issues. The GNC is revising its guidance, with a view to publishing a further iteration in the summer of 2016.

[20] This list was originally devised by Denzil Lush, a contributor to the first edition of this book and now Senior Judge of the Court of Protection. It was influential in framing the guidance in the MCA Code of Practice (see **Appendix B**). See also para.4.6 of the Law Society Practice Note: Meeting the Needs of Vulnerable Clients (2 July 2015), available at **www.lawsociety.org.uk/support-services/ advice/practice-notes/meeting-the-needs-of-vulnerable-clients-july-2015/**.

- Choose the best time of day for the examination. Some people are better in the morning; others are more alert in the afternoon or early evening.
- Be thorough, but complete the assessment within a reasonable time to avoid tiring or confusing the client.
- Avoid obtrusive time-checking. It should be possible, without too much discernible eye movement, to keep a check on the time.
- If more than one test of capacity has to be applied, try to do each assessment on a different day, if possible.
- Choose the best location. Usually, someone will feel more comfortable in their own home than in, say, a doctor's surgery or a lawyer's office.
- Try and ensure that there are no obstructions between you and the client which could hinder the development of a relationship of equals: for example consider the height and positioning of the chairs.
- So far as it is within your control, make sure that the temperature in the room is comfortable and that the lighting is soft and indirect, but sufficiently bright for easy eye contact and interpretation of expression and to allow you to study any relevant documentation.
- Consider whether or not a third party should be present. In some cases the presence of a relative, friend or other person (such as an advocate or attorney) could reduce anxiety. In others, their presence might actually increase anxiety. In some cases a third party might be a useful interpreter. In others, they could be intrusive.
- Try and eliminate any background noise or distractions, such as the television or radio, or people talking.
- If possible, make sure that other people cannot overhear you and that others will not interrupt you either from within or outside the room: for example, by telephone.
- Be sensitive towards other disabilities, such as impaired hearing or eyesight, which could mislead you into assuming that a person lacks capacity.
- Speak at a volume and speed that can be easily understood. Try to use short sentences with familiar words. If necessary, accompany your speech with slightly exaggerated gestures or facial expressions and other means of non-verbal communication.
- If necessary, provide verbal or visual aids to stimulate and improve the person's memory.
- If carrying out more than one test of cognitive functioning, allow a reasonable time for general relaxed conversation between each test so as to avoid any sense of disappointment at failing a particular test.
- If possible, try to avoid subjecting the client to an increasingly demoralising sequence of 'I don't know' answers.
- Take one decision at a time – be careful to avoid making the client tired or confused.
- Don't rush – allow the client time to think things over or ask for clarification where that is possible and appropriate.

- Some organisations (e.g. BILD, Mencap and Sense) have produced specialised material to support decision-making and decision-makers should consider whether it is appropriate to use it (see **Appendix J**).
- It may be appropriate to provide access to relevant supportive technology.

2.4 REFUSAL TO BE ASSESSED

There may be circumstances in which a person whose capacity is in doubt refuses to undergo an assessment of capacity or refuses to be examined by a doctor. It will usually be possible to persuade someone to agree to an assessment if the consequences of refusal are carefully explained. For example, it should be explained to people wishing to make a will (see **Chapter 6**) that the will could possibly be challenged and held to be invalid after their death, while evidence of their capacity to make a will would prevent this from happening. Similarly, a lasting power of attorney (see **5.3**) could be challenged without evidence of the donor's capacity, with the result that the attorney chosen by the donor may be unable to act. Or it may not be possible to pursue legal proceedings unless the court is satisfied that a party to the proceedings has capacity (see **Chapter 8**). The solicitor may also have to decline to act directly or at all on the person's behalf if there are doubts about the person's capacity to give instructions, indicating the need for special arrangements to be made (see **2.1**).

If the person appears to lack capacity to consent to or refuse assessment, it will normally be possible for an assessment to proceed so long as the person is compliant and this is considered to be in the person's best interests (see **2.5** and **Chapter 3**). In some circumstances, if the person is, or is likely to be, the subject of an application to the Court of Protection, it may be possible for the Court of Protection Special Visitor to carry out the assessment (see **Appendix C**). However, in the face of an outright refusal, no one can be forced to undergo an assessment of capacity. Entry to a person's home cannot be forced in such cases and a refusal to open the door to the doctor may be the end of the matter, and other evidence of capacity (or lack of it) may need to be used, such as letters written by them or witness evidence of their actions or behaviour. It should be noted, however, that:

- If there are proper grounds to believe that the person's refusal to undergo the assessment is due to the influence of a third party, then it may be possible to invoke the inherent jurisdiction of the High Court (see **3.5**) to seek injunctions requiring that third party to allow access to the person.[21] However, if, upon

---

[21] In Wales, upon the coming into force of the Social Services and Well-being (Wales) Act 2014, s.127, an authorised officer may apply to a justice of the peace for an adult protection and support order in relation to a person living in any premises within a local authority's area to enable the authorised officer and any other person accompanying the officer to speak in private with a person suspected of being an adult at risk; to enable the authorised officer to ascertain whether that person is making decisions freely; and to enable the authorised officer properly to assess whether the person is an adult at risk and to make a decision on what, if any, action should be taken.

achieving that unfettered access, the person still refuses to cooperate with the assessment, then there is nothing that can be done.

- Where there are serious concerns about the person's mental health, an assessment under MHA 1983 may be warranted but only where it is believed that detention in hospital for assessment or treatment for mental disorder may be necessary.

2.5 PEOPLE ASSESSED AS LACKING CAPACITY

2.5.1 The 'best interests' principle

Both lawyers and doctors need to appreciate that if an individual is judged to lack capacity to make the decision in question, any act or decision taken on that person's behalf must be in that person's best interests. The principle of best interests was firmly established under the common law and is now enshrined in statute in MCA 2005, which includes a checklist of factors which must be taken into account when determining someone's best interests. The principles in MCA 2005, s.1 must also be considered (see **Chapter 3** for details).

2.5.2 The Mental Capacity Act Code of Practice

MCA 2005 is accompanied by a statutory Code of Practice[22] providing guidance to anyone using the Act's provisions, including anyone involved in assessing capacity, as well as those involved in caring for or working with people who may lack capacity to make particular decisions.

MCA 2005 imposes a duty on certain people to 'have regard to' any relevant guidance in the MCA Code of Practice when acting in relation to a person lacking capacity.[23] The specified people are those acting in one or more of the following ways (as described in other chapters of this book):

- as an attorney acting under a lasting power of attorney (see **Chapter 5**);
- as a deputy appointed by the court (see **Appendix C**);
- as a person carrying out research under MCA 2005 (see **Chapter 14**);
- as an Independent Mental Capacity Advocate (see **Chapter 3**);
- in applying the deprivation of liberty safeguards (see **Chapter 15**);
- in a professional capacity; and/or
- for remuneration.

The statutory duty to have regard to the MCA Code of Practice therefore applies to those exercising formal powers or duties under MCA 2005 (attorneys and deputies),

---

[22] Office of the Public Guardian (2007) *Mental Capacity Act 2005 Code of Practice*, and see also Ministry of Justice (2008) *Mental Capacity Act 2005: Deprivation of Liberty Safeguards – Code of Practice to Supplement the Main Mental Capacity Act 2005 Code of Practice*, both available at **www.scie.org.uk/mca-directory/keygovernmentdocuments.asp**.
[23] MCA 2005, s.42(4).

and to professionals (including lawyers, doctors, health and social care profession-als) and others acting for remuneration (such as paid carers). Such people must be able to demonstrate that they are familiar with the Code, and if they have not followed relevant guidance contained in it, they will be expected to give cogent reasons why they have departed from it.[24]

MCA 2005 also confirms that a provision of the Code, or a failure to comply with the guidance set out in the Code, can be taken into account by a court or tribunal where it appears relevant to a question arising in any criminal or civil proceedings.[25] There is no liability for breach of the Code itself, but compliance or non-compliance may be a factor in deciding the issue of liability for breach of some other statutory or common law duty. This may apply to anyone using the provisions of the Act, since they are obliged to act in accordance with the principles of MCA 2005, which includes acting in the best interests of a person lacking capacity, as described in **Chapter 3**.

2.6   INDIVIDUALS AT RISK

This chapter (and indeed this book) focuses primarily upon those who may lack capacity to give instructions or to take specific decisions. It is important to remember, however, that both solicitors and doctors are, by the nature of their professions, very likely often to be engaged with individuals with physical and/or mental disabilities. The consequences of these disabilities may mean:

- they require enhanced support to engage the services of solicitors or to participate fully in the process of the provision of medical treatment; and
- they are more susceptible to undue influence or duress at the hands of third parties.

The risks of undue influence and duress are addressed in the SRA Code of Conduct 2011 at Chapter 1 (client care), which states that the following indicative behav-iours may tend to show that a solicitor is not acting in accordance with the principles and outcomes of the SRA Handbook:

IB(1.25) acting for a *client* when instructions are given by someone else, or by only one *client* when you act jointly for others unless you are satisfied that the *person* providing the instructions has the authority to do so on behalf of all of the *clients* ...

IB(1.28) acting for a *client* when there are reasonable grounds for believing that the instructions are affected by duress or undue influence without satisfying yourself that they represent the *client's* wishes.

---

[24]   This is based on the House of Lords judgment in *R (on the application of Munjaz)* v. *Mersey Care NHS Trust* [2005] UKHL 58; [2006] 2 AC 148. See also *SBC* v. *PBA* [2011] EWHC 2580 (Fam); [2011] COPLR Con Vol 1095.
[25]   MCA 2005, s.42(5).

Guidance for solicitors as to how to identify (and to meet the needs of) vulnerable clients, looking at, but beyond, the issues of capacity can be found in the Law Society's Vulnerable Clients Practice Note.[26]

Guidance for general practitioners (but of wider application) in relation to vulnerable patients can be found on the BMA website.[27]

2.7 SUMMARY OF POINTS FOR DOCTORS

The following paragraphs give a brief summary of the issues doctors should be aware of when carrying out an assessment of capacity.

In many situations where a judgment about capacity has to be made a doctor's opinion will be obtained. A general practitioner (GP), consultant, other hospital doctor or prison or police doctor may be approached to provide this. If the medical practitioner is not routinely involved in assessing capacity, the practical steps outlined in **Part IV** may provide a helpful guide. Assessment requires some knowledge of the person, including their ethnicity, cultural or religious values and social situation. There is a legal presumption of capacity unless the contrary is shown and assumptions about capacity should not be made merely on the basis of the person's age, appearance, condition or behaviour. In most cases, more than a brief interview and reading of other medical reports is necessary.

Capacity is ultimately a legal concept (see **Part II**). The doctor must assess the person's capacity in relation to whatever activity that person is attempting to carry out. The understanding required for each decision will depend on the complexity of the information relevant to the decision and the legal test to be applied. Doctors who are asked to give an assessment of an individual's capacity must be clear about the relevant legal test (see **Part III**) and should ask a lawyer to explain it, if necessary. For decisions covered by MCA 2005 (financial, healthcare and personal welfare decisions) anyone involved in assessing capacity must have regard to the guidance given in the MCA Code of Practice (see **Appendix B**).

Every person is entitled to privacy and confidentiality (see **2.2**) but if the doctor does not know the individual it may be necessary to seek views from others with professional and personal knowledge of that person and knowledge of the specific decision in question. For example, assessment of whether someone has capacity to make financial decisions in managing their property and financial affairs depends partly on the decisions which need to be made and the amounts and complexity of

---

[26] Law Society Practice Note: Meeting the Needs of Vulnerable Clients (2 July 2015), available at **www.lawsociety.org.uk/support-services/advice/practice-notes/meeting-the-needs-of-vulnerable-clients-july-2015/**. The term 'vulnerable client' was used in this Practice Note, although it is no longer used in the safeguarding context, because it remains a familiar term to legal practitioners.

[27] BMA (2011) *Safeguarding Vulnerable Adults – a Tool Kit for General Practitioners*, available at **www.bma.org.uk/-/media/files/pdfs/practical%20advice%20at%20work/ethics/safeguarding vulnerableadults.pdf**.

the assets involved. A doctor who is asked to provide a medical report in such a case needs some knowledge of the person's assets and the skills required to administer them.

When asked to assess a person with a learning disability, doctors should not rely solely on prior reports giving an estimated 'mental age' but must ensure that a current assessment is made. Statements of a person's mental age may be misleading if they do not reflect the person's experience and the context for the particular decision. Assessments of capacity should be regularly reviewed to take account of changing circumstances or fluctuations in the person's condition.

In some circumstances, health professionals may be asked to witness a patient's signature to a legal document. By witnessing the document, it may be inferred that the doctor or nurse is confirming the patient's capacity to enter into the legal transaction effected by the document, rather than merely indicating that the witness has seen the patient sign the document. Doctors and nurses should be clear as to what they are being asked to do. (See **4.5** on witnessing documents.)

2.8 SUMMARY OF POINTS FOR LAWYERS

The following paragraphs provide a summary of useful points for solicitors to consider when acting for a person who may lack capacity to make specific decisions.

If a solicitor has any doubt as to whether a client has capacity to provide an instruction or instructions in relation to the relevant matters, they should undertake a capacity assessment (or seek a formal capacity assessment from an appropriately qualified expert) before any instructions are acted upon (see **2.1**).

There is a legal presumption of capacity unless the contrary is shown. Whether a client has capacity to make a particular decision is a matter of law, to be determined by applying the correct legal test. Different levels of capacity are required for different activities. If there is doubt about a client's mental capacity, it is advisable for the lawyer to seek a medical opinion. Medical practitioners should be asked to give an opinion as to the client's capacity in relation to the particular activity or decision in question, rather than a general assessment of the client's mental condition. In order to do this, the solicitor has a responsibility to explain to the doctor the relevant legal test of capacity (see **Part III**).

It is important to choose a doctor who has the skills and experience to carry out the particular assessment. This may be the person's GP in situations where familiarity with and personal knowledge of the patient may be helpful. In some cases, a specialist with expertise in the patient's particular medical condition may be preferable. **Chapter 17** provides further information.

A doctor's assessment assumes more weight in borderline cases or those at risk of challenge, which together form the majority of cases upon which doctors and lawyers need to liaise. The most obvious cases of incapacity, such as when a person is unconscious or has very severe learning disabilities, are less likely to require detailed medical confirmation. Similarly, where the person is demonstrably capable of dealing with the matter in hand, medical assessment is superfluous. Fluctuating capacity presents particular difficulties and medical evidence is likely to be essential to demonstrate a person's capacity to take action during a lucid interval (see **4.2.2**).

Capacity can be enhanced by the way explanations are given, by the timing of them or by other simple measures discussed in this book. It can be impaired by fatigue, pain, anxiety or unfamiliar surroundings. Yet doctors are constantly working under constraints of time or location and other limitations, including perhaps their own preconceptions or prior reports from others about the extent of a person's capacity. Their training also emphasises the concept of promoting the patient's health interests in all circumstances. It is therefore important to ask doctors to assess what the person is actually capable of deciding at the time when the decision needs to be made, not whether the decision is sensible or wise.

PART II

Legal principles

CHAPTER 3

The Mental Capacity Act 2005: capacity and best interests

3.1   The legal framework
3.2   The statutory principles
3.3   Definition of mental capacity
3.4   The test of capacity
3.5   Incapacity or vulnerability?

3.6   Who assesses capacity?
3.7   Best interests
3.8   Application and exclusions
3.9   The Convention on the Rights of Persons with Disabilities

3.1   THE LEGAL FRAMEWORK

In England and Wales, the law in relation to adults who lack the capacity to make decisions on their own behalf is laid down in MCA 2005. The Act, supported by the accompanying MCA Code of Practice[1] issued by the Lord Chancellor, provides a comprehensive legal framework for the making of decisions on behalf of adults who may lack capacity to make specific decisions for themselves. The legal framework set out in MCA 2005 is based on two fundamental concepts: lack of capacity and best interests. This chapter describes how MCA 2005 defines and applies those concepts.

MCA 2005 applies to all personal welfare decisions, healthcare decisions and financial decisions taken on behalf of people who permanently or temporarily lack capacity to make those decisions for themselves. All professionals working with adults who lack, or who may lack, capacity to make such decisions need to be familiar with the underlying principles and main provisions of the Act and must also have regard to the MCA Code of Practice.

MCA 2005 confirms the previous common law position that capacity is function-specific, relating to each particular decision at the time the decision needs to be

---

[1]   Office of the Public Guardian (2007) *Mental Capacity Act 2005 Code of Practice* and Ministry of Justice (2008) *Mental Capacity Act 2005: Deprivation of Liberty Safeguards – Code of Practice to supplement the main Mental Capacity Act 2005 Code of Practice*, both available at **www.scie.org.uk/ mca-directory/keygovernmentdocuments.asp**.

made, and many of the provisions of MCA 2005 are based on relevant principles and procedures previously established by the common law.

In particular, MCA 2005 has established the common law principle of 'best interests' as the legal basis for anyone (family member, carer or professional) who is acting or making decisions on behalf of a person who lacks capacity to make those decisions for themselves. The Act sets out a checklist of factors which must always be taken into account when determining someone's best interests (see **3.7**).

While MCA 2005 enshrined in statute existing best practice (as described in earlier editions of this book) and former common law principles, it also introduced into the law several provisions, including:

- the ability to nominate substitute decision-makers in relation to health and welfare decisions (in addition to financial decisions) under an LPA;
- the development of a new Court of Protection with extended powers;
- safeguards when adults who lack capacity to consent to their participation are enrolled in certain forms of research; and
- (with effect from 1 April 2009) the deprivation of liberty safeguards.

These provisions are described in the following chapters, so far as they are relevant to the assessment of capacity. The sections of MCA 2005 that contain the principles and preliminary matters (ss.1–6) are reproduced in **Appendix A** of this book. The chapters of the MCA Code of Practice most relevant to making an assessment of capacity (Chapters 2, 3 and 4) are reproduced in **Appendix B**.

The last section of this chapter (**3.9**) sets out the key provisions of the United Nations Convention on the Rights of Persons with Disabilities (CRPD). The CRPD does not yet form part of the law of England and Wales in the sense that the rights it enshrines can be relied upon directly by individuals. However, it is increasingly being referred to by courts in the context with which this book is concerned, and presents a significant challenge to how questions of capacity and best interests are addressed in MCA 2005.

3.2 THE STATUTORY PRINCIPLES

MCA 2005 starts with a statement of guiding principles setting out the values that underpin the legal requirements in the Act and govern all decisions made and actions taken under its powers. Where confusion arises about how aspects of MCA 2005 should be implemented, it will be helpful to refer to these statutory principles. Actions or decisions that clearly conflict with the principles are unlikely to be lawful, although there may be occasions on which the principles are in tension with each other, and some balancing will be required.

The five statutory principles, as set out MCA 2005, s.1, are:

1. **A person must be assumed to have capacity unless it is established that he lacks capacity.** The starting point for assessing a person's capacity to make a

particular decision is always the presumption that the individual has capacity. Where there is doubt, the burden of proof is generally on the person who is seeking to establish a lack of capacity and the matter is decided according to the usual civil standard, the balance of probabilities.[2]

2. **A person is not to be treated as unable to make a decision unless all practicable steps to help him to do so have been taken without success.** People must be supported and encouraged to make their own decisions wherever possible. Chapter 3 of the MCA Code of Practice (see **Appendix B**) gives detailed guidance on a range of practicable steps which may assist in maximising a person's decision-making capacity, although the relevance of the various steps suggested will vary depending on the particular circumstances.

3. **A person is not to be treated as unable to make a decision merely because he makes an unwise decision.** This principle confirms the common law right of a person to make decisions which others may consider to be unwise.[3] Some caution may need to be applied in operating this principle in practice. While an unwise decision should not, by itself, be sufficient to indicate lack of capacity, it may be sufficient to raise doubts as to the person's capacity, for example if the decision is out of character.[4] The critical point, however, is what matters is the ability to *make the decision*, not the *outcome* of that decision.

4. **An act done, or decision made, under this Act for or on behalf of a person who lacks capacity must be done, or made, in his best interests.** This establishes 'best interests' as the single criterion to govern all actions or decision-making affecting people who lack capacity to make specific decisions for themselves. Further details on the meaning and determination of best interests are set out in MCA 2005, s.4 (see **3.7**).

5. **Before the act is done, or the decision is made, regard must be had to whether the purpose for which it is needed can be as effectively achieved in a way that is less restrictive of the person's rights and freedom of action.** Where there is more than one course of action or a choice of decisions to be made, all possible options or alternatives should be considered (including whether there is a need for any action or decision at all). Other options need only be considered so long as the desired purpose of the action or decision can still be achieved. Since the decision-maker is only required to 'have regard to' this principle, an option which is not the least restrictive alternative may be chosen if this is in the best interests of the person lacking capacity.

In assessing capacity, the first three of these principles are particularly important. A decision that someone lacks capacity is not to be made lightly. The starting point is

---

[2]   MCA 2005, s.2(4).
[3]   *Bird* v. *Luckie* (1850) 8 Hare 301.
[4]   See *D* v. *R (Deputy of S)* [2010] EWHC 2405 (COP); [2010] COPLR Con Vol 1112.

the presumption that people do not lack capacity, even when they make unwise choices, and all practicable steps must first be taken to help them make the decision in question before they are assessed as lacking capacity. Chapter 3 of the MCA Code of Practice contains many suggestions to facilitate decision-making (see also the checklist at **2.3**). The Code also sets out a list of questions that should be asked before carrying out an assessment of capacity:[5]

- Does the person have all the relevant information they need to make the decision?
- If they are making a decision that involves choosing between alternatives, do they have information on all the different options?
- Would the person have a better understanding if information was explained or presented in another way?
- Are there times of day when the person's understanding is better?
- Are there locations where they may feel more at ease?
- Can the decision be put off until the circumstances are different and the person concerned may be able to make the decision?
- Can anyone else help the person to make choices or express a view (for example, a family member or carer, an advocate or someone to help with communication)?

The need to ensure that steps are taken to support an individual to take their own decisions was given even greater emphasis after MCA 2005 was enacted by the ratification of the CRPD, discussed further at **3.9**.

3.3 DEFINITION OF MENTAL CAPACITY

Capacity refers to the ability that a person possesses to make specific decisions or to take actions that influence their life, ranging from a simple decision about what to have for breakfast, to far-reaching decisions about investments or serious medical treatment. It is a concept that has legal consequences, but is founded in the actual abilities of the individual in question.

MCA 2005 stipulates that people should not be labelled 'incapable' simply on the basis that they have been diagnosed with a particular condition, or because of any preconceived ideas or assumptions about their abilities due, for example, to their age, appearance, condition or any aspect of their behaviour.[6] Rather it must be shown that they lack capacity for each specific decision at the time the decision needs to be made. Individuals retain the legal right to make those decisions for which they continue to have capacity.

MCA 2005, s.2(1) states that:

> a person lacks capacity in relation to a matter if at the material time he is unable to make a decision for himself in relation to the matter because of an impairment of, or a disturbance in the functioning of, the mind or brain.

---

[5] Office of the Public Guardian (2007) *Mental Capacity Act 2005 Code of Practice*, para.4.36, available at **www.gov.uk/government/publications/mental-capacity-act-code-of-practice**.
[6] MCA 2005, s.2(3).

Capacity is therefore decision-specific and time-specific and the inability to make the decision in question must be because of 'an impairment of, or a disturbance in the functioning of, the mind or brain'. Loss of capacity can be partial or temporary and capacity may fluctuate. It is essential that an assessment of capacity is based on the individual's ability to make a specific decision at the time it needs to be made, and not their ability to make decisions in general. It is both logically and legally wrong to say that someone 'lacks capacity' as a general statement; rather, the person may lack capacity to make a particular decision at a particular time.

3.4 THE TEST OF CAPACITY

For the purposes of the Act, the test as to whether a person lacks capacity to take a decision is contained in MCA 2005, s.2(1) (set out in **3.3**).[7] The MCA Code of Practice suggests that this test is broken down into two parts: the 'diagnostic' and the 'functional' elements.[8]

In practice, however, experience has taught that it is better to break the test down into three questions:[9]

1. Does the individual have an impairment of, or a disturbance in the functioning of, their mind or brain (for example, a disability, condition or trauma that affects the way their mind or brain works)?
2. Is the person unable to make a specific decision at the time it needs to be made for one (or more) of the specific reasons given in MCA 2005?
3. Is the person's inability to make the specific decision at the time when it needs to be made *because of* the impairment of, or disturbance in the functioning of, their mind or brain?

The ordering of the first and second questions above reflects the ordering in the MCA Code of Practice. However, as the Court of Appeal noted in the *City of York Council* case,[10] this ordering in fact represents a reversal of the test as set out in MCA 2005, s.2(1). The Court of Appeal did not specifically determine which order the questions needed to be asked in,[11] and there are policy arguments to support either order.

It is likely that the best answer is that it will depend upon the context. For instance, in a psychiatric setting, it is more likely than not that an impairment or disturbance will be present, and greater focus will be required upon the person's

---

[7]   This point was emphasised by the Court of Appeal in *PC* v. *City of York Council; sub nom City of York Council* v. *C* [2013] EWCA Civ 478; [2014] Fam 10.
[8]   See paras.4.11–4.13.
[9]   This approach also reflects the concerns expressed by the Court of Appeal in *City of York Council* v. *C* [2013] EWCA Civ 478; [2014] Fam 10.
[10]   *City of York Council* v. *C* [2013] EWCA Civ 478; [2014] Fam 10 at para.58, per McFarlane LJ.
[11]   Parker J in *NCC* v. *PB and TB* [2014] EWCOP 14; [2015] COPLR 118 doubted the Court of Appeal had intended to require questions to be asked in the reverse of the traditionally accepted order.

functional inability to take a decision. Conversely, in the community setting where a person has had no previous involvement with social or healthcare services but appears to be unable to take a decision (or the decision that the person is taking appears to the professionals to be concerning), more focus may well be required upon whether any impairment or disturbance is present.

In any event, no matter which order the first and second questions are asked in, the third question must always be specifically addressed because it is the question which decides whether the person lacks capacity to take the decision in question for purposes of MCA 2005.[12] As set out at **3.5**, there are situations in which a person may not be able to make the decision in question, but where that inability does not bring them within the scope of MCA 2005.

Assessing capacity will not always be straightforward, particularly if a person has fluctuating capacity or where some capacity is demonstrable but its extent is uncertain. Detailed practical advice about the assessment of mental capacity is given in **Part IV** of this book.

3.4.1 Impairment or disturbance

To be relevant for purposes of MCA 2005, s.2(1), the impairment or disturbance does not need to be permanent. It can include (but is not limited to) conditions associated with some forms of mental illness, dementia, significant learning disabilities, the long-term effects of brain damage, physical or medical conditions that cause confusion, drowsiness or loss of consciousness, concussion following a head injury, and the symptoms of alcohol or drug use.

3.4.2 Inability to take a decision

MCA 2005, s.3 defines what it means to be unable to make a decision. Four factors must be considered:[13]

1. **Does the person understand the information relevant to the decision to be made?** The information relevant to a decision includes information about the reasonably foreseeable consequences of deciding one way or another, or of failing to make the decision. An explanation of all relevant information must have been given to the person using the means of communication that is most appropriate for their particular circumstances.

2. **Can the person retain that information in their mind?** Retaining information for even a short time may be adequate in the context of some decisions – it will depend on what is necessary for the decision in question. Aids to recollection such as notes, pictures, photographs and voice recorders may be helpful.

---

[12] Emphasised strongly by the Court of Appeal in *City of York Council* v. *C* [2013] EWCA Civ 478; [2014] Fam 10.
[13] MCA 2005, s.3(1).

3.   **Can the person use or weigh that information as part of the decision-making process?** An apparently irrational or unwise decision is not necessarily proof that an individual has failed to use or weigh relevant information, but it may trigger the need for a more detailed assessment, particularly if the decision is out of character. The focus must be on the process of decision-making (for example, whether the person can weigh up any risks involved) not the outcome. The person may be assisted in that process by professional advice or support from family or friends.

4.   **Can the person communicate the decision?** Where an individual cannot communicate their decision in any way, by talking, using sign language or any other means, the Act states that the individual is unable to make a decision for themselves. Examples include people who are unconscious or in a coma, or in the later stages of motor neurone disease, who may very well be conscious yet totally unable to communicate.[14]

3.4.3   The link between the impairment or disturbance and the inability to take a decision

If an impairment or disturbance in the person's mind or brain is causing them to be unable to do any of the four things set out above, then they do not have capacity to make the decision in question. In any assessment of capacity, an explanation will always be required as to how the 'causative nexus' is satisfied.[15] In other words, the person conducting the assessment will have to be able to explain *how* the impairment or disturbance has caused the inability to take the decision. Pro forma capacity assessment forms that only provide boxes for the 'diagnostic' and 'functional' elements of the capacity test are therefore dangerous because they do not draw the assessor's attention sufficiently to the need for this link to be explained, and therefore are likely to lead them to incorrect conclusions.

3.5   INCAPACITY OR VULNERABILITY?

Case law decided since MCA 2005 was brought into force has made clear there is a significant class of people who are unable to take their own decisions but whose inability to do so stems from the influence exercised over them by others (for instance family members), rather than from any impairment or disturbance of their mind or brain. The law treats such individuals very differently to those considered to lack capacity for purposes of MCA 2005. Crucially, professionals (or indeed anyone else) cannot take decisions on their behalf. It is, however, possible for any person or body concerned as to whether the individual is under duress to seek the

---

14   See, e.g., *X Primary Care Trust* v. *XB* [2012] EWHC 1390 (Fam); [2012] COPLR 577.
15   The term 'causative nexus' was used in *City of York Council* v. *C* [2013] EWCA Civ 478; [2014] Fam 10 at para.58, per McFarlane LJ.

assistance of the High Court to provide protection under its inherent jurisdiction.[16] The inherent jurisdiction of the High Court – which exists to fill gaps in the statutory law – has been described in that case as the 'great safety net' which could be deployed to protect such individuals, categorised for these purposes as 'vulnerable'. The jurisdiction exists as a facilitative, rather than a dictatorial jurisdiction, to be deployed to enable the individual in question to take their own decisions free from the influence of others.

In law, the distinction between a person who lacks capacity to take a decision (or decisions) for purposes of MCA 2005 and a person who has capacity but is vulnerable turns on whether that inability is caused by an impairment of, or disturbance in the functioning of, the mind or brain. The case law does not speak entirely with one voice as to whether the impairment or disturbance must be the *main* or simply *a* cause of the inability to take a decision.[17] However, if the primary cause is the influence of a third party, then it is suggested that, in law, that person should be considered to have capacity to make the decision, and, if they require protection, that such protection must be obtained from the High Court.

In practice, the situation where the person in question has (for instance) a learning disability and is also in a social situation that causes professionals concern, disentangling whether the individual in question lacks capacity to take material decisions or requires the protection of the High Court under its inherent jurisdiction can be a difficult question.[18] Medical professionals should always consider whether to seek legal advice in such circumstances. Such a situation may trigger the duty on a local authority to make inquiries under the safeguarding provisions of the Care Act 2014 (in England),[19] and require multi-disciplinary input from both clinical and social work professionals.[20]

---

[16] See *Re L (Vulnerable Adults with Capacity: Court's Jurisdiction)* (No.2) [2012] EWCA Civ 253; [2013] Fam 1.

[17] See *Re L (Vulnerable Adults with Capacity: Court's Jurisdiction)* (No.2) [2012] EWCA Civ 253; [2013] Fam 1; *Redbridge London Borough Council* v. *G (By Her Litigation Friend the Official Solicitor)* [2014] EWHC 485 (COP); [2014] COPLR 292; *NCC* v. *PB and TB* [2014] EWCOP 14 and also – by analogy – the decision of the Singapore Court of Appeal in *Re BKR* [2015] SGCA 26 (the Singaporean Mental Capacity Act being modelled on the English MCA and the Court of Appeal specifically in that case considering the English case law.

[18] For a good example, requiring the assistance of two experts, see *Redbridge London Borough Council* v. *G (By Her Litigation Friend the Official Solicitor)* [2014] EWHC 485 (COP); [2014] COPLR 292.

[19] Care Act 2014, s.42. The equivalent duty in Wales willl in due course be found in Social Services and Well-Being Act (Wales) Act 2014, s.126.

[20] For more details on the inherent jurisdiction of the High Court and its functions in this context see Chapter 11 of G Ashton, ed. (2015) *Court of Protection Practice* (published annually), Jordan Publishing. Statutory guidance upon safeguarding is contained in Chapter 14 of Department of Health (2014) *Care and Support Statutory Guidance*, available at **www.gov.uk/government/ publications/care-act-2014-statutory-guidance-for-implementation**. For more in relation to the obligations upon solicitors in this context, see Law Society Practice Note: Meeting the Needs of Vulnerable Clients (2 July 2015), available at **www.lawsociety.org.uk/support-services/advice/ practice-notes/meeting-the-needs-of-vulnerable-clients-july-2015/**.

3.6 WHO ASSESSES CAPACITY?

MCA 2005 does not specify who should assess capacity. However, the following general rules apply:

1. a person who wishes to carry out an act in connection with the care or treatment of another on the basis that they lack capacity to that act will only be protected from liability if (as a first step) they are reasonably satisfied that the person concerned lacks capacity in relation to the matter(s) in question;[21] and
2. a person who wishes to make a decision on behalf of another on the basis that they lack capacity to make it needs to be satisfied that they lack capacity in relation to the matter(s) in question.

In all informal contexts, MCA 2005 requires that any assessment that a person lacks capacity must be based on a 'reasonable belief' that the person lacks the capacity to consent to the care or treatment being proposed, backed by objective reasons.[22] This requires taking reasonable steps to establish that the person lacks capacity to make the decision in question.[23] What will be reasonable steps for a decision-maker in either of the cases set out above will depend on the circumstances. The more serious the decision, the more formal the assessment of capacity is likely to be necessary.

In a healthcare setting, the doctor or healthcare professional proposing the particular treatment or medical procedure is responsible for ensuring that the patient's capacity is assessed. For legal transactions, solicitors are responsible for ensuring that – where appropriate – their client's capacity to instruct them is assessed. In both cases, the doctor/healthcare professional or solicitor may carry out the capacity assessment themselves, or consider that they cannot do so without the assistance of a specialist (for instance a psychiatrist or a psychologist). For more on the specific legal tests that need to be applied to particular categories of decisions, see **Part IV**.

It is important to understand, however, that enlisting specialist advice *does not* amount to placing the responsibility on the specialist adviser to determine whether the decision-maker should act. In other words, a treating doctor seeking expert input from a psychiatrist as to whether their patient lacks capacity to consent to a proposed medical procedure is not thereby placing the responsibility upon the psychiatrist to decide whether the medical procedure should go ahead. Rather, it is ultimately for the doctor to consider (with the benefit of the assistance of the psychiatrist) whether they have reasonable grounds to believe that the patient lacks capacity to consent to the procedure and hence whether they are in a position to proceed on a 'best interests' basis. Similarly, a solicitor deciding whether or not a

---

[21]   MCA 2005, s.5(1).

[22]   If the Court of Protection concludes that an individual lacks capacity and makes a declaration to that effect under MCA 2005, s.15(1)(a), that constitutes a judicial finding of fact.

[23]   MCA 2005, s.15(1)(a) and Office of the Public Guardian (2007) *Mental Capacity Act 2005 Code of Practice*, available at **www.gov.uk/government/publications/mental-capacity-act-code-of-practice**. Paragraphs 4.44–4.45 of the Code provide guidance on 'reasonable belief' and the possible steps to take to establish a lack of capacity (see **Appendix B**).

client has capacity to instruct them remains ultimately responsible for that assessment, even if they receive expert assistance from a medical professional. See further for practical pointers in this regard **Chapters 17** and **18** and also, in relation to wills, where retrospective questions are most often asked as to the steps taken, see **6.7**.

Where there are disputes about whether a person lacks capacity and these cannot be resolved using more informal methods, the Court of Protection can be asked for a declaration about the person's capacity (see **Appendix C**).

3.7 BEST INTERESTS

Where someone lacks capacity to make a particular decision, MCA 2005 establishes 'best interests' as the criterion for any action taken or decision made on that person's behalf. In view of the wide range of decisions and actions covered by the Act and the varied circumstances of the people affected by its provisions, the concept of best interests is not defined in MCA 2005. Instead a 'checklist' of common factors which must be considered when determining what is in a person's best interests is set out in MCA 2005, s.4. That checklist should be applied in relation to the options that are actually available to the person (or realistically likely to be available in the future).[24]

The checklist can be summarised as follows:

1. **Equal consideration and non-discrimination.** The person determining best interests must not make assumptions about someone's best interests merely on the basis of their age or appearance, condition or an aspect of their behaviour.
2. **All relevant circumstances.** Try to identify all the issues and circumstances relating to the decision in question which are most relevant to the person who lacks capacity to make that decision.
3. **Regaining capacity.** Consider whether the person is likely to regain capacity (e.g. after receiving medical treatment). If so, can the decision wait until then?
4. **Permitting and encouraging participation.** Do whatever is reasonably practicable to permit and encourage the person to participate, or to improve their ability to participate, as fully as possible in any act done or any decision affecting them.
5. **The person's wishes, feelings, beliefs and values.** Try to find out the views of the person lacking capacity, including:

    • the person's past and present wishes and feelings – both current views

---

[24] *Re MN (Adult)* [2015] EWCA Civ 411; [2015] Med LR 287. This is particularly important where the availability of options (for instance in relation to residence or care arrangements) is dependent upon decisions made by public bodies as to how to meet the care or treatment needs of those for whom they have responsibility. Those decisions are very often not best interests decisions at all. See further A Ruck Keene *et al.* (2014) *Court of Protection Handbook: A User's Guide*, Legal Action Group, Chapter 25.

and whether any relevant views have been expressed in the past, either verbally, in writing or through behaviour or habits;

- any beliefs and values (e.g. religious, cultural, moral or political) that would be likely to influence the decision in question;
- any other factors the person would be likely to consider if able to do so (this could include the impact of the decision on others).

6.   **The views of other people.** Consult other people, if it is practicable and appropriate to do so, for their views about the person's best interests and, in particular, to see if they have any information about the person's wishes, feelings, beliefs or values.[25] But be aware of the person's right to confidentiality – not everyone needs to know everything. In particular, it is important to consult:

- anyone previously named by the person as someone to be consulted on the decision in question or matters of a similar kind;
- anyone engaged in caring for the person, or close relatives, friends or others who take an interest in the person's welfare;
- any attorney of a lasting or enduring power of attorney made by the person;
- any deputy appointed by the Court of Protection to make decisions for the person.

For decisions about serious medical treatment or a change of residence and where there is no one who fits into any of the above categories, the NHS body or the local authority involved has a duty to appoint an Independent Mental Capacity Advocate (IMCA), who must be consulted before any decision is made.[26]

As the purpose of consultation is to enable a best interests decision to be made on behalf of the person, consultation is not necessary where it would be likely to be unduly onerous, contentious, futile or serve no useful purpose.[27] Clear reasons should always be given identifying why – for instance – a spouse is not to be consulted on one of these grounds.

7.   **Life sustaining treatment.** Where the decision concerns the provision or withdrawal of life-sustaining treatment (defined in MCA 2005 as being treatment which a person providing healthcare regards as necessary to sustain life[28]), the person determining whether the treatment is in the best interests of

---

[25]   See *Aintree University Hospitals NHS Foundation Trust* v. *James* [2013] UKSC 67; [2014] AC 591 at para.39.

[26]   See MCA 2005, ss.35–41 and the SCIE Mental Capacity Act Directory at **www.scie.org.uk/mca-directory/keygovernmentdocuments.asp**.

[27]   *Re Allen*, 2009 (unreported, COP, 21 July 2009), decision of Senior Judge Lush (case number 11661992).

[28]   MCA 2005, s.4(10).

someone who lacks capacity to consent must not be motivated by a desire to bring about the individual's death.[29]

Not all the factors in the best interests 'checklist' will be relevant to all types of decisions or actions, but they must still be considered if only to be disregarded as irrelevant to that particular situation. Any option which is less restrictive of the person's rights or freedom of action must also be considered, so long it is in the person's best interests.

Different judges have expressed different views as to the weight to be placed upon the person's own views (past and present),[30] and it is likely that the case law will evolve in this area, not least under the influence of the CRPD (see further **3.9**). It is, however, clear that the purpose of undertaking the best interests determination is to enable the decision to be taken that is right for the person as an individual human being, rather than the decision that suits either the professionals or family members concerned.[31] This may, on occasion, mean that the decision that is in the person's best interests is a decision that the professionals would themselves regard as unwise.

Detailed guidance on determining best interests is given in Chapter 5 of the MCA Code of Practice.

3.8 APPLICATION AND EXCLUSIONS

The core principles of MCA 2005 and the test set out at **3.4** apply to the assessment of capacity in the situations covered by MCA 2005: financial, healthcare and welfare decisions which may need to be made for an individual by someone else. The Code states that the common law may continue to apply in other situations where capacity may need to be assessed, for example: making a will, making a gift, entering into a contract, carrying out litigation and marrying.[32]

In *Local Authority X* v. *MM (Adult)*[33] Munby J considered when it would be appropriate to adopt the then new statutory test. In his view judges sitting elsewhere than in the Court of Protection and deciding cases where what is in issue is, for

---

[29] MCA 2005, s.4(5).
[30] There is a tension between decisions such as *Re S and S (Protected Persons); C* v. *V* [2010] 1 WLR 1082; [2009] WTLR 315, in which HHJ Marshall QC held that, if the person in question expresses a view that is not irrational, impracticable or irresponsible, 'then that situation carries great weight and effectively gives rise to a presumption in favour of implementing those wishes, unless there is some potential sufficiently detrimental effect for P of doing so which outweighs this', and decisions such as *Re M*; sub nom *ITW* v. *Z* [2009] EWHC 2525 (Fam); [2010] 3 All ER 682, in which wishes and feelings were identified as being but one of the factors that are to be taken into account. For more detail, see the article by A Ruck Keene and C Auckland 'More presumptions please, wishes, feelings and best interests decision-making' (2015) *Elder Law Journal* 293.
[31] *Aintree University Hospitals NHS Foundation Trust* v. *James* [2013] UKSC 67; [2014] AC 591 at para.45.
[32] Office of the Public Guardian (2007) *Mental Capacity Act 2005 Code of Practice*, available at **www.gov.uk/government/publications/mental-capacity-act-code-of-practice**, paras.4.32 and 4.33.
[33] *Local Authority X* v. *MM (Adult)* [2007] EWHC 2003 (Fam); [2009] 1 FLR 443.

example, capacity to make a will or capacity to make a gift, could only adopt the new definition, if it was appropriate having regard to the existing principles of the common law.[34]

Cases decided since MCA 2005 came into force have made clear that some common law tests of capacity continue to be relevant (as described in **Part III**). There is a high degree of overlap between the MCA test and the common law tests that apply. However, the tests are not always identical (a good example being the test that is applied to decide whether a person has or had the capacity to make a will, discussed in **Chapter 6** or to make a lifetime gift, discussed in **Chapter 7**). It is therefore important to be clear precisely which test to apply – which means, as a first step, being clear as to the nature and context of the decision in question.

3.8.1 Children and young people

MCA 2005 applies to those aged 16 years and over who may lack capacity to make specific decisions, leaving matters concerned with the care and welfare of children and young people to be resolved under other legislation (most notably the Children Act 1989) and the common law. However, some overlap is inevitable, particularly for young people aged 16–17. Some complexities also arise in relation to the assessment of capacity (or competence) of children and young people to make specific decisions affecting them.

3.8.2 Children aged under 16

MCA 2005 does not generally apply to children aged under 16, except in two specific circumstances:

- MCA 2005 allows the Court of Protection to make decisions about the manage-ment of property and financial affairs of children under 16 who are likely still to lack the capacity to make such decisions after they turn 18;[35] and
- the criminal offences of ill-treatment or wilful neglect of a person lacking capacity apply regardless of the victim's age.[36]

In these cases, capacity will have to be assessed with reference to MCA 2005, as in the case of adults.

Where welfare or healthcare decisions are required of a child aged under 16, any disputes may be resolved by the family courts under the Children Act 1989. In such cases, the common law test of *Gillick* competence applies: i.e. whether the child has sufficient maturity and intelligence to understand the nature and implications of the proposed treatment.[37] *Gillick* competence is a 'developmental concept' reflecting

---

[34] See *Local Authority X* v. *MM (Adult)* [2007] EWHC 2003 (Fam); [2009] 1 FLR 443 at paras.77–80.
[35] MCA 2005, s.18(3).
[36] MCA 2005, s.44.
[37] *Gillick* v. *West Norfolk and Wisbech Area Health Authority* [1986] AC 112.

the child's increasing development to maturity, so that a child will not lose or acquire competence on a day-to-day or week-by-week basis.[38] The understanding required for different treatments or decisions may vary, depending on the nature of the decision in question.

3.8.3 Young people aged 16 or 17

The main provisions of MCA 2005 apply to young people aged 16 or 17. The starting point for assessing whether a young person aged 16 or 17 has capacity to make a specific decision is therefore the test of capacity in MCA 2005, having regard to MCA principles. However, there may be circumstances where 16–17-year-olds who are unable to make a decision for themselves will not be covered by the provisions of MCA 2005.

A young person may be unable to make a decision either:

- because of an impairment of, or disturbance in the functioning of, their mind or brain (they lack capacity within the meaning of MCA 2005); or
- for reasons of immaturity (due to the person's age, they are unable to make the decision in question).

Young people aged 16 and 17 are presumed to have capacity to consent to surgical, medical or dental treatment.[39] If a young person suffers from an impairment of, or a disturbance in the functioning of, the mind or brain which may affect their ability to make a particular healthcare decision, an assessment of capacity under MCA 2005 will be required, notwithstanding the presumption that the young person has capacity.

However, if there is no such impairment or disturbance, MCA 2005 will not apply if it can be established that the young person's inability to make a decision is because:

- they do not have the maturity to understand fully what is involved in making the decision (i.e. they lack *Gillick* competence); or
- the lack of maturity means that they feel unable to make the decision for themselves (for example, where particularly complex or risky treatment is proposed, they may be overwhelmed by the implications of the decision).[40]

In cases where MCA 2005 applies, decisions about a young person's care or treatment may be made under the provisions of the Act in the person's best interests (see **Chapters 11** and **13**), without the need to obtain parental consent (although those with parental responsibility should generally be consulted).

The Court of Protection may become involved in decisions about medical treatment where there is a disagreement between the young person and the treating

---

[38] *Re R (A Minor) (Wardship: Consent to Medical Treatment)* [1992] 1 FLR 190 at 200.

[39] Family Law Reform Act 1969, s.8(1).

[40] Office of the Public Guardian (2007) *Mental Capacity Act 2005 Code of Practice*, para.12.13, available at **www.gov.uk/government/publications/mental-capacity-act-code-of-practice**.

health professionals, or in decisions about welfare matters, for example if the young person's parents do not appear to be acting in the best interests of the young person. MCA 2005 makes provision for the transfer of cases affecting anyone under 18 from the Court of Protection to the family courts and vice versa. The choice of court will depend on the particular circumstances and what is the most appropriate way of dealing with the matter in question.[41]

Particular complexities may arise concerning the care and treatment of children and young people with mental disorder, involving some interaction between MHA 1983, MCA 2005 and legislation relating to children. The Department of Health issued specific guidance for professionals working with children, young people and families in children and adolescent mental health services (CAMHS), adult mental health services and children's services.[42] The Mental Health Act Code of Practice also provides guidance on the treatment of children under MHA 1983.[43]

3.8.4 Decisions excluded from MCA 2005

The MCA Code of Practice states that there 'are certain decisions which can never be made on behalf of a person who lacks capacity to make those specific decisions. This is because they are either so personal to the individual concerned, or governed by other legislation'.[44] These excluded decisions are set out in MCA 2005,[45] and are summarised under the sub-headings below.

Family relationships

Nothing in MCA 2005 permits a decision to be made on someone's behalf on the following:

- consent to marriage or a civil partnership;
- consent to have sexual relations;
- consent to a decree of divorce on the basis of two years' separation;
- consent to the dissolution of a civil partnership;
- consent to a child being placed for adoption or the making of an adoption order;

---

[41] MCA 2005, s.21; and Mental Capacity Act 2005 (Transfer of Proceedings) Order 2007, SI 2007/1899. Guidance as to when it is more appropriate for the Court of Protection to hear the application was given by Hedley J in *B (A Local Authority)* v. *RM, MM and AM* [2010] EWHC 3802 (Fam); [2010] COPLR Con Vol 247.

[42] National Institute for Mental Health in England (2009) *The Legal Aspects of the Care and Treatment of Children and Young People with Mental Disorder: A Guide for Professionals*, available at **www.iris-initiative.org.uk/silo/files/children-and-young-people-mh-legal-guide.pdf**. In particular, Chapter 2 deals with the principles and concepts involved in assessing the ability of children and young people to make decisions for themselves.

[43] Department of Health (2015) *Mental Health Act 1983 Code of Practice*, available at **www.gov.uk/government/publications/code-of-practice-mental-health-act-1983**. See **Chapter 16**.

[44] Office of the Public Guardian (2007) *Mental Capacity Act 2005 Code of Practice*, para.1.9, available at **www.gov.uk/government/publications/mental-capacity-act-code-of-practice**.

[45] MCA 2005, ss.27–29.

- discharge of parental responsibility for a child in matters not relating to the child's property; or
- consent under the Human Fertilisation and Embryology Act 1990.

Mental Health Act matters

Where a person who lacks capacity to consent is detained in hospital under MHA 1983 and is being given medical treatment under the provisions of Part 4 of that Act, nothing in MCA 2005 authorises anyone to:

- give the person treatment for mental disorder; or
- consent to the person being given treatment for mental disorder.[46]

In other words, the consent to treatment provisions and safeguards in Part 4 of MHA 1983 will in principle 'trump' the provisions of MCA 2005 in relation to treatment for mental disorder of patients liable to be detained under the 1983 Act.

The key aspects of the interface between mental health and mental capacity legislation is given in **Chapter 16**.

Voting rights

MCA 2005 does not permit a decision on voting (at an election for any public office or at a referendum) to be made on behalf of a person who lacks capacity to vote (see **Chapter 10** on questions relating to voting).

Unlawful killing or assisting suicide

For the avoidance of doubt, it is made clear in MCA 2005 that the Act does not affect the law relating to unlawful killing such as euthanasia, murder, manslaughter or assisted suicide.[47]

3.9 THE CONVENTION ON THE RIGHTS OF PERSONS WITH DISABILITIES

The Convention on the Rights of Persons with Disabilities (CRPD), concluded in 2006, seeks to bring about a radical change in the approach adopted in the social, political and legal arenas to those with disabilities (and, indeed, to the very concept of disability). Among other provisions, it seeks to bring about a fundamental shift away from the taking of decisions on behalf of individuals on the basis of an asserted lack of capacity. The CRPD has been very widely ratified, the United Kingdom ratifying the Convention in 2009. The United Kingdom also ratified the Optional Protocol, enabling individuals or groups to take complaints to the Committee on the

---

[46] MCA 2005, s.28.
[47] MCA 2005, s.62.

Rights of Persons with Disabilities (the oversight body for the CRPD) (the Committee). The Committee can request information from and make recommendations to states which are party to the Convention.

The CRPD is not yet incorporated into English law, such that it is not possible to rely upon rights enshrined therein in the same fashion as (for instance) rights contained in the European Convention on Human Rights (ECHR). However, the CRPD has increasingly been referred to the English courts, both as an aid to interpretation of the ECHR and also more broadly as an aid to construction of statutes.[48]

Most important of the rights guaranteed in the CRPD for present purposes is art.12, which provides for equal recognition before the law. Giving full effect to art.12 (especially as interpreted by the Committee) poses very substantial challenges for any legal framework that provides for either the total or partial removal of an individual's capacity to make their own decisions and for others to make those decisions on their behalf. MCA 2005 is precisely such a framework.

There are substantial grounds to doubt whether MCA 2005 is compatible with art.12 in at least two regards:

- The diagnostic element of the capacity test arguably discriminates against those with disabilities because it is more likely that a person with a disability will be found to satisfy this limb of the test.
- (More controversially) the approach in MCA 2005 to substitute decision-making is predicated upon an objective analysis of what is believed to be in the best interests of the individual concerned, rather than being based upon the person's own will and preferences.[49]

It is understood that the Committee will be undertaking an examination of the compliance by (all jurisdictions of) the United Kingdom in 2016–17, and it may very well be that in due course substantial legislative change will be required. In the interim, it is suggested that – at a minimum – compliance with the principles of the Convention requires significantly greater emphasis to be placed upon:

- supporting those whose capacity may be in doubt to take their own decisions; and

---

[48] See, e.g., the references by the Supreme Court to the CRPD in *Surrey County Council* v. *P; Cheshire West and Chester Council* v. *P* [2014] UKSC 19; [2014] AC 896 and *Akerman-Livingstone* v. *Aster Communities* [2015] UKSC 15; [2015] 2 WLR 721.

[49] See Committee on the Rights of Persons with Disabilities, 'General comment on Article 12: Equal recognition before the law', available at **www.ohchr.org/EN/HRBodies/CRPD/Pages/ GC.aspx**. The compatibility of MCA 2005 with the CPRD is discussed in detail in the Position Paper prepared by Essex Autonomy Project for the Ministry of Justice in 2014 entitled *Achieving CRPD Compliance: Is the Mental Capacity Act of England and Wales compatible with the United Nations Convention on the Rights of Persons with Disabilities? If Not, What Next?*, available at **http:// autonomy.essex.ac.uk/uncrpd-report**. A useful introduction to the requirements of the CRPD can be found in the article by Dr Lucy Series entitled 'Comparing old and new paradigms of legal capacity' (2014) *Elder Law Journal* 62.

- identifying the wishes and feelings of those who (despite such support) are unable to take their own decisions, where it is possible to identify such wishes and feelings, complying with them as far as possible or alternatively giving sufficiently compelling reasons for departing from them in any best interests decision taken on their behalf.

CHAPTER 4

The legal principles: capacity and evidence

4.1	Capacity and the role of the courts	4.4	Doctors receiving instructions from
4.2	Capacity and the law of evidence		solicitors
4.3	Solicitors instructing doctors	4.5	Witnessing documents

4.1 CAPACITY AND THE ROLE OF THE COURTS

Whether a person has or lacks capacity to do something is a question that must generally be decided by reference to the framework set out in MCA 2005 (see **Chapter 3**). Some common law tests of capacity may require additional or different considerations, for example in relation to testamentary capacity (see **Chapter 6**). In some cases, it may ultimately be a question for a court to answer. Where a court becomes involved, the final decision rests with the judge, although evidence from a wide range of sources (including the views of family members, of care home staff, a solicitor, health or social care professionals or other expert witnesses) may be of assistance in enabling a court to arrive at its conclusions.[1]

In practice doctors, solicitors, social workers and carers make decisions about capacity every day of the week and very few cases ever get as far as a court. Nevertheless, the courts retain their overall jurisdiction in these matters (which court will depend upon the nature of the decision, and whether it is governed by the common law or MCA 2005).

By making a decision on capacity, anyone with authority over an individual can deprive that person of some civil rights and liberties enjoyed by most adults and (in

---

[1] See (under the common law) *Richmond* v. *Richmond* (1914) 111 LT 273; *Masterman-Lister* v. *Jewell; Masterman-Lister* v. *Brutton & Co* [2002] EWHC 417 (QB); and *Masterman-Lister* v. *Brutton & Co; Masterman-Lister* v. *Jewell* [2002] EWCA Civ 1889; [2003] 1 WLR 1511. The same principle applies in relation to the Court of Protection: see *CC* v. *KK and STCC* [2012] EWHC 2136 (COP); [2012] COPLR 627.

some cases) safeguarded by the Human Rights Act 1998[2] (see also **3.9**). Alternatively, such a decision could permit the person lacking capacity to do something, or carry on doing something, whereby harm or serious prejudice could result either to the person lacking capacity or to others.

Doctors and lawyers should always bear in mind that if they conclude someone has or lacks capacity to make a decision or enter into a transaction, they might have to justify to a court their reasons for that conclusion. It is helpful therefore to know what effect an opinion as to someone's capacity could have on the individual concerned. For example, it could restrict, protect, or empower them.

If a case does go to court, the judge has to:

- decide what the background facts are;
- apply the law to those facts; and
- come to a decision as to the person's capacity to make the decision in question.

Others involved in making decisions about capacity might find it useful to follow the same steps.

4.2 CAPACITY AND THE LAW OF EVIDENCE

4.2.1 Presumption of capacity

To keep any investigation of the facts within manageable bounds, courts apply various rules of evidence. These are based on conclusions (presumptions) which must, or may, be drawn from particular facts. Presumptions are either irrebuttable or rebuttable:

- If a presumption is irrebuttable, it is not open to challenge and the court must arrive at a particular conclusion, regardless of any evidence to the contrary.
- If a presumption is rebuttable, the court has to assume that certain facts are true until the contrary is proved. The most well-known rebuttable presumption is the presumption of innocence: that anyone charged with a criminal offence is presumed to be innocent until proved to be guilty.

One important rebuttable presumption that applies to mental capacity is the presumption of capacity, now enshrined as one of the statutory principles of MCA 2005.[3] An adult is presumed to have the mental capacity to make a particular decision, until the contrary is proved. The burden of proof rests on those asserting that the individual does not have the capacity to take the particular decision in question.

Since capacity must always be assessed in relation to a specific task at a particular time, it may need to be reviewed frequently. The Code explains that it is important to

---

[2] The Human Rights Act 1998, which came into effect in October 2000, incorporates into UK law the bulk of the substantive rights set out in the European Convention on Human Rights (ECHR).
[3] MCA 2005, s.1(2).

review capacity from time to time, as people can improve their decision-making capabilities. Someone with an ongoing condition may become able to make some, if not all, decisions. The Code states that:

capacity should always be reviewed:
- whenever a care plan is being developed or reviewed,
- at other relevant stages of the care planning process, and
- as particular decisions need to be made.[4]

Prior to the implementation of MCA 2005 it was considered that there was also a presumption of continuance, i.e. once it has been proved that someone lacks capacity, this state of affairs is presumed to continue until the contrary is proved. While there has yet to be a definitive ruling upon this point by the courts, it is doubtful whether this presumption would now be upheld by them, because it is difficult to square with the time- and issue-specific nature of capacity enshrined in MCA 2005. That having been said, the courts are likely to conclude that when an individual has been assessed as lacking capacity in relation to a particular decision at a particular time, it may be easier to show that the individual lacks capacity in relation to the same or a similar decision at another time.

4.2.2 Lucid intervals or fluctuating capacity

The presumptions of capacity and continuance tend to suggest that a person is either constantly capable or constantly incapable. Capacity can fluctuate, however, and an intermittent state of capacity is known at law as a 'lucid interval' or 'fluctuating capacity'. Generally speaking, a deed or document signed by someone who lacks capacity is void and of no effect. But if it is signed during a lucid interval it may be valid. This will almost certainly need to be confirmed by medical evidence, and the courts have emphasised the importance of obtaining contemporaneous evidence in such cases so as to avoid (expensive and time-consuming) disputes after the event.[5]

When dealing with someone who has fluctuating capacity, it is important to remember that it may be possible to put off the decision until the person has the capacity to make it. Indeed, failing to do so represents a breach of the second principle in MCA 2005, because it represents a failure to give the individual the practically available support that they need to take their own decisions. Whether it is possible to defer the decision will depend upon the urgency of the situation, but whether or not to defer the decision is a matter that should always be considered by reference to the needs of the individual in question, not the administrative (or other) convenience of others.

---

[4] Office of the Public Guardian (2007) *Mental Capacity Act 2005 Code of Practice*, para.4.29, available at **www.gov.uk/government/publications/mental-capacity-act-code-of-practice**.

[5] See, in particular, *A, B and C v. X and Z* [2012] EWHC 2400 (COP); [2013] COPLR 1 (the making of a will and the granting of lasting power of attorney).

In this regard, it is, finally, important to remember that the test is whether the person is unable to take the decision 'at the material time'.[6] There may be some cases in which that material time is extended over a significant period. A good example is in relation to managing property and affairs where, as one judge has described it:

> the general concept is an ongoing act and, therefore, quite unlike the specific act of making a will or making an enduring power of attorney. The management of affairs relates to a continuous state of affairs whose demands may be unpredictable and may occasionally be urgent.[7]

A similar approach has also been adopted in relation to the capacity of the subject of proceedings before the Court of Protection to conduct proceedings before that court (see further **8.3**).[8]

4.2.3 The burden of proof

Generally, if someone alleges something, that person has to prove it. In cases involving mental capacity the burden of proof is affected by the operation of the presumption of capacity. So the burden of proof is on the person who alleges that someone lacks capacity (because capacity is presumed until the contrary is proved). As noted above, where someone has been shown to lack capacity in relation to a particular decision, it may be easier to discharge the burden of proof in relation to a subsequent similar decision.

4.2.4 The standard of proof

Those on whom the burden of proof rests must prove their case to a particular standard. There are two standards of proof:

- 'beyond reasonable doubt', which only applies in criminal proceedings; and
- 'the balance of probabilities', which applies in civil proceedings.

In deciding whether or not someone has capacity to enter into a particular transaction or make a particular decision, the standard of proof is the civil standard, the balance of probabilities (confirmed by MCA 2005, in cases to which that Act applies).[9] In practical terms this is the most important rule of evidence in assessing capacity. Having decided what the facts are, and having applied the law to those facts, the assessor must then decide whether on balance the individual is more likely to have capacity, or more likely to lack capacity to do something.

---

6 MCA 2005, s.2(1).
7 Hedley J in *A, B and C* v. *X and Z* [2012] EWHC 2400 (COP); [2013] COPLR 1 at para.41.
8 *A, B and C* v. *X and Z* [2012] EWHC 2400 (COP); [2013] COPLR 1 at para.43.
9 MCA 2005, s.2(4).

4.2.5 Character evidence and similar fact evidence

In criminal cases, evidence about a person's character or past events which are similar to those under consideration may only be admitted in certain circumstances, in an effort to avoid unfair prejudice to a defendant. In civil cases, however, a person's psychiatric history is usually highly relevant to the question of capacity and is therefore almost always admissible.

The court may also take into account other witness or documentary evidence which is relevant to the person's capacity to take the decision in question. For example, in the *Masterman-Lister* case[10] (see also **5.5.1**) the court gave detailed consideration to Mr Masterman-Lister's diaries, letters and computer documents. In *Saulle* v. *Nouvet*[11] the court took into account witness statements and oral evidence from family members as well as home videos of Mr Saulle. The court must, however, be 'alive to the fact that [it is] … investigating … capacity not outcomes, although of course outcomes can often cast a flood of light on capacity'.[12]

4.2.6 The evidence of the person themselves

In layman's terms the evidence of the person themselves as to their own abilities would appear logically to be the most important evidence as to their capacity to take a particular decision or decisions. However, 'evidence' has a particular legal definition, and whether the person who is the subject of proceedings before the Court of Protection (the most likely forum in which capacity will fall to be determined) is capable of giving evidence as to their own capacity is a question that has yet conclusively to be determined by the courts.

There are a number of legal complexities that arise, including as to whether P – as the subject of Court of Protection proceedings is known – is in any given case competent to give evidence (see further **Chapter 8**). Some of these legal complexities have now been removed by amendments to the Court of Protection Rules (COPR), which provide much greater formal latitude to the Court of Protection to admit and act upon 'information' from P whether or not P is capable of giving evidence on oath.[13] That information could include information as to factual matters (for instance, the circumstances under which P was living in their home environment). However, there remains a question as to whether P's assertions about their own abilities can be said to be 'evidence' as to their capacity.

---

[10]   *Masterman-Lister* v. *Brutton & Co; Masterman-Lister* v. *Jewell* [2002] EWCA Civ 1889; [2003] 1 WLR 1511.

[11]   *Saulle* v. *Nouvet* [2007] EWHC 2902 (QB); [2008] WTLR 729.

[12]   *Masterman-Lister* v. *Brutton & Co; Masterman-Lister* v. *Jewell* [2002] EWCA Civ 1889; [2003] 1 WLR 1511 at para.54.

[13]   See COPR rule 95(e), as amended by the Court of Protection (Amendment) Rules 2015, SI 1548/548, which provides that the court may 'admit, accept and act upon such information, whether oral or written, from P, … as the court considers sufficient, although not given on oath and whether or not it would be admissible in a court of law apart from this rule'.

Judges of the Court of Protection, in particular, have shown an increasing willingness to hear from P and it is clear that they have taken what they have heard into account in their decision as to whether P has or lacks the material decision-making capacity.[14] Encouraging the participation of P in the proceedings to determine their capacity in material regards is also entirely in line with the principles of MCA 2005, the ECHR[15] and the Convention on the Rights of Persons with Disabilities (as to which, see **3.9**).

The courts have yet to pronounce definitely, however, upon precisely what a judge is doing when they are hearing from P in this context, nor is there any guidance to be found in the relevant procedural rules or associated Practice Directions. Are they conducting their *own* capacity assessment when they do so? Or is the information that they gain from the person simply part of the information that they are required to take into account when reaching the decision as to whether the person has or lacks the material capacity for purposes of MCA 2005, s.2(1)? It is likely that it is the latter, but it is also likely that this issue will be the subject of further judicial scrutiny (and, most likely, guidelines from the higher courts) in due course as judges more regularly meet and hear from the person concerned in contested capacity cases.

4.2.7 Opinion evidence and expert evidence

In court proceedings witnesses are usually confined to stating the facts – what they have seen or heard – and are not permitted to express their own opinions. An exception is made in the case of expert witnesses who are entitled not only to say what they have seen and heard but also to express the opinion they formed as a result.

There is no formal definition as to what constitutes expertise. In general, people will be treated as experts if they have devoted time and attention to the particular branch of knowledge involved, or if they have had practical experience of it and, in some cases, if they have acquired a reputation for being skilled in it.

The law has traditionally regarded registered medical practitioners in relevant fields as de facto experts on mental capacity, and therefore considered them entitled to express an opinion as to whether a person is or was capable of understanding the nature and effects of a particular transaction. Prior to the coming into force of MCA 2005, the Court of Appeal had confirmed that in almost every civil case where a

---

[14] Particularly clear examples being the decisions of Baker J in *CC* v. *KK and STCC* [2012] EWHC 2136 (COP); [2012] COPLR 627 and Holman J in *Re SB (A Patient: Capacity to Consent to Termination)* [2013] EWHC 1417 (COP); [2013] COPLR 445.

[15] See, in particular, the Strasbourg cases analysed by Dr Lucy Series in *The Participation of the Relevant Person in Proceedings in the Court of Protection: A Briefing Paper on International Human Rights Requirements*, available at **http://sites.cardiff.ac.uk/wccop/the-rule-of-personal-presence/**.

court is required to make a decision as to capacity, it would need medical evidence to guide it, although this would not necessarily be given greater weight than other relevant evidence.[16]

In the majority of contested capacity cases (whether before the Court of Protection or otherwise), it remains the case that it is likely that the court will call upon medical expertise. However, it should not be assumed that this will always be the case, and Court of Protection judges in particular have increasingly emphasised the extent to which other professionals – especially social workers – are capable of giving evidence as to capacity.[17] They have also, on more than one occasion, preferred the evidence of professionals with familiarity with the individual concerned over the evidence of a medical expert who is (on paper) better qualified to give evidence as to capacity.[18]

A doctor should therefore not necessarily assume that a court will accept their evidence as to an individual's capacity *merely because* they are medically qualified. In giving an opinion on capacity, it is therefore important that they should set out their particular qualifications and experience which may have a bearing on their expertise in assessing capacity and on applying MCA 2005 and the MCA Code of Practice. The BMA issues guidance for doctors who act or are considering acting as expert witnesses.[19]

4.2.8 The weight of evidence

Whether or not the burden of proof is discharged depends on the weight and value which the judge attaches to the various strands of evidence. This involves weighing up the credibility or reliability of the evidence, and ultimately comes down to deciding which version of the relevant matters is more likely to be correct. Although the courts attach a great deal of weight to medical evidence, one doctor's opinion may not be shared by another, and it is not unprecedented for a judge to favour the evidence of someone who is not even medically qualified. In *Burgess* v. *Hawes*,[20] the Court of Appeal made clear that the courts should place considerable weight upon a contemporaneous record of an assessment of capacity (in that case to enter into a will) by an experienced solicitor, and should 'be cautious about acting on the

---

[16]   *Masterman-Lister* v. *Brutton & Co; Masterman-Lister* v. *Jewell* [2002] EWCA Civ 1889; [2003] 1 WLR 1511 at para.29.

[17]   See, in particular, *A Local Authority* v. *SY* [2013] EWHC 3485 (COP); [2014] COPLR 1 at para.22. See also COP3 (and accompanying guidance notes) at **Appendix G**, required for any application to the Court of Protection so as to establish that the person in question lacks the necessary decision-making capacity. That form was revised in 2013 to make clear that such evidence can be provided not just by doctors, but also by social workers or nurses.

[18]   See, e.g., *PH* v. *A Local Authority* [2011] EWHC 1704 (Fam); [2012] COPLR 128 where Baker J emphasised the apparently superficial nature of the assessment and the report of the (highly qualified) expert psychiatrist.

[19]   BMA (2007) *Expert Witness Guidance* and BMA (2005) *Guidance for Doctors Preparing Professional Reports and Giving Evidence in Court*, British Medical Association, both available at **www.bma.org.uk**.

[20]   *Burgess* v. *Hawes* [2013] EWCA Civ 94; [2013] WTLR 453 at para.60.

basis of evidence of lack of capacity given by a medical expert after the event, particularly when that expert has neither met nor medically examined the [individual]'.[21] In the Court of Protection context, by way of example, in *CC* v. *KK and STCC*,[22] the judge found the individual to have capacity to decide whether to live in a care home or in her own home in the face of evidence to the contrary from a number of health and social care professionals and an independently instructed expert psychiatrist.

4.3   SOLICITORS INSTRUCTING DOCTORS

Solicitors asking a doctor to provide medical evidence as to whether or not a client has capacity to make a particular decision should bear in mind the following points:

- It cannot automatically be assumed that all doctors are experts in these matters (see **Chapter 17**).
- The quality of the doctor's evidence depends heavily on the quality of the instructions given to the doctor.
- Be clear about the specific capacity that needs to be assessed, for example: capacity to enter into a contract; capacity to marry; capacity to create a lasting power of attorney; or capacity to make a decision about finances or property (see **Part III**).
- Inform the doctor about the legal test to be applied.
- Explain the legal test in simple language that an ordinary intelligent person, but someone who is not a qualified lawyer, will be able to understand.
- Let the doctor have all the relevant information needed to reach an informed opinion. For example, if an application is being made to the Court of Protection for the appointment of a financial deputy, the doctor needs to know something about the client's property and affairs in order to assess whether or not that client lacks capacity to make decisions about such property and affairs (but see **2.2** on confidentiality).
- Make sure that the doctor is aware that the standard of proof is the balance of probabilities, rather than beyond reasonable doubt.
- Remind the doctor that their opinion on the client's capacity may be open to challenge (and as a courtesy the doctor should be informed if the matter is likely to be contentious, without giving the impression that a lower standard of care will suffice in a non-contentious case).
- Wherever possible avoid asking for simultaneous assessments of a client's capacity for a variety of different transactions. For example, where a client is in the early stages of dementia it would be unreasonable to expect the doctor to assess in one examination whether the client is capable of making a will,

---

[21] *Burgess* v. *Hawes* [2013] EWCA Civ 94; [2013] WTLR 453 at para.60, per Mummery LJ; see also para.69, per Sir Scott Baker.
[22] [2012] EWHC 2136 (COP); [2012] COPLR 627

creating a lasting power of attorney, making a lifetime gift, and consenting to medical treatment, since the assessment must be made in relation to each decision at the time the decision needs to be made.

A sample letter of instruction to a doctor requesting a report upon testamentary capacity can be found in **Appendix H**. This letter can be adapted for other situations, so long as the correct legal test is clearly set out.

4.4 DOCTORS RECEIVING INSTRUCTIONS FROM SOLICITORS

Doctors assessing capacity at the request of a solicitor should bear the following points in mind:

- Guidance for doctors who have limited experience in assessing capacity is given in **Chapter 17**, but doctors should decline instructions from solicitors if they feel that they have insufficient knowledge or practical experience to make a proper assessment of capacity.
- If necessary, more information should be requested from the solicitor. Do not automatically assume that the solicitor is an expert in these matters or has passed on all relevant details.
- If necessary, further information should be requested regarding:
  - details of the test of capacity that the law requires, with an explanation of that test in simple language that an ordinary intelligent person who is not legally qualified can understand;
  - why a medical opinion is being sought and what effect the opinion might have on the patient or client;
  - the person's property, affairs or family background if they are relevant to the particular type of capacity to be assessed;
  - whether the matter is likely to be contentious or disputed (but doctors should not be pressurised into making a decision merely because it will please the solicitor or the person's family or one faction of the person's family).
- Wherever possible, keep reports specific, rather than general. Remember that:
  - a laconic opinion lacking detail, diagnosis and reasons is likely to be of little value in terms of evidence. By way of example, in the (Court of Protection) case of *PH* v. *A Local Authority*,[23] Baker J effectively discounted the weight of the independently – and jointly instructed – psychiatric expert. While he 'acknowledge[d] the expertise of [the expert] and [found] his approach to his assessment to have been appropriately objective and professional', Baker J 'was struck by the fact that his report, and

---

[23]   *PH* v. *A Local Authority* [2011] EWHC 1704 (Fam); [2012] COPLR 128.

the answers to the supplementary questions posed by the other parties, seemed somewhat superficial'.[24]

- the opinion could deprive the individual of the autonomy that most adults enjoy to make decisions about their own affairs;
- the opinion could allow the individual to do something or to carry on doing something which could be extremely prejudicial to the individual or somebody else;
- the opinion could affect the availability of certain financial benefits or services;
- doctors can be called on by a court to give an account of the reasons for arriving at a particular opinion.

4.5 WITNESSING DOCUMENTS

Medical professionals, especially those working in hospitals, are often reluctant to witness a patient's signature on a document. This is understandable because, more often than not, the professional status of a doctor or nurse is being invoked in order to lend authority to a transaction.

In the section on capacity and the law of evidence (see **4.2**) a distinction was drawn between ordinary witnesses and expert witnesses:

- Ordinary witnesses are expected merely to state what they have seen or heard. When it comes to witnessing a signature on a document, an ordinary witness simply states that the document was signed by a person in their presence.
- Expert witnesses are in a different position, because they are invited not only to say what they have seen or heard but also to express an opinion.

As was mentioned earlier, the law tends to regard medical practitioners as de facto experts on mental capacity. So when a doctor witnesses someone's signature on a document, there is an inference that the doctor considered the patient to have the requisite capacity to enter into the transaction effected by the document. If doctors are not confident about the person's capacity, or have not assessed it formally, they should decline to act as witnesses. They must also decline to act as witnesses if they are likely to benefit personally.

It is recommended that, in cases where there is any doubt about a patient's capacity to enter into a particular transaction, a medical professional should only witness the patient's signature on a document when:

- they have formally assessed the patient's capacity;
- they are satisfied that, on the balance of probabilities, the patient has the requisite capacity to enter into the transaction effected by the document; and
- they make a formal record of their examination and findings.

---

[24]   *PH* v. *A Local Authority* [2011] EWHC 1704 (Fam); [2012] COPLR 128 at para.56.

Some NHS Trusts have policies which in effect prohibit their staff from witnessing legal documents. In such cases, the health professional should take advice from the Trust before acting as a witness.

4.5.1   When medical evidence should be obtained

Obtaining medical evidence about a person's capacity is sometimes required by the law, while in other cases, it is merely desirable or a matter of good practice. The so-called 'golden rule' that has been said to apply in the context of an instruction to a solicitor to draw up a will for an elderly person or for someone who is seriously ill is discussed at **6.5**, but for present purposes the important points to emphasise in relation to this 'golden rule' are that:

- The onus is always on the solicitor taking the client's instructions to satisfy themselves as to the person's capacity and understanding of the decision in question, and to keep a proper record and attendance notes of the steps taken and the evidence on which they base their conclusions.
- Those steps may require – in some cases – enlisting the assistance of a medical practitioner.
- Where a medical professional has been asked by a solicitor (or another professional) for such assistance, they need to be clear about what they are being asked to do, and why they are being asked to do it.

Legal tests of capacity

PART III

Legal tests of capacity

CHAPTER 5

Capacity to deal with financial affairs

5.1	Types of powers of attorney	5.6	Capacity to claim and receive social security benefits
5.2	Ordinary powers of attorney		
5.3	Lasting powers of attorney	5.7	Protection from financial abuse
5.4	Enduring powers of attorney		
5.5	Capacity to manage property and affairs		

5.1 TYPES OF POWERS OF ATTORNEY

A power of attorney is a deed by which one person (the donor) gives another person (the attorney) the authority to act in the donor's name and on their behalf. Historically that power could only be exercised in respect of the donor's property and financial affairs. However, following the coming into force of MCA 2005, an attorney can be granted the power to make decisions concerning the health and/or welfare of the donor (see **Chapter 13**).

A power of attorney can be specific or general. If it is specific, the attorney only has the authority to do the things specified by the donor in the power. If it is general, the attorney has the authority to do anything that the donor can lawfully do by an attorney. The law imposes certain restrictions on what actions a donor can delegate to an attorney. For example, an attorney cannot execute a will on the donor's behalf, nor act in situations which require the personal knowledge of the donor (such as acting as a witness in court). Therefore under a general power of attorney, the attorney only has the authority to do what the donor can lawfully delegate to someone else.

There are three types of powers of attorney:

- an ordinary power of attorney, which ceases to have effect if the donor becomes mentally incapable;
- a lasting power of attorney (LPA), which continues to operate after a donor has become mentally incapable (but must be registered with the Office of the Public Guardian (the OPG) before use);

- an enduring power of attorney (EPA), which is similar in broad terms to an LPA for property and financial affairs. Following implementation of MCA 2005, an EPA can no longer be created but, as discussed below, those made before 1 October 2007 will continue to be valid and will therefore be of relevance for practitioners for some years to come.

5.2 ORDINARY POWERS OF ATTORNEY

The test of capacity which a person must satisfy in order to make an ordinary power of attorney is that the donor understands the nature and effect of what they are doing. As a general rule, ordinary powers of attorney are automatically revoked when the donor loses mental capacity.[1] If there is any doubt as to the donor's capacity to do the act in question, it would be advisable for the donor to create a lasting power rather than an ordinary power, so long as the donor has the requisite capacity to do so.

Ordinary powers of attorney fell out of popular use when the Enduring Powers of Attorney Act 1985 came into force, as private client solicitors more routinely prepared EPAs for their clients. Ordinary powers of attorney then tended to be used as a temporary expedient only (for example, where the donor was going abroad for several months and needed someone to look after various legal or financial transactions during their absence). The historic view is that the capacity required to create an ordinary power of attorney is coexistent with the donor's capacity to do the act which the attorney is authorised to do.

Following the implementation of MCA 2005, there has been a resurgence in the making and use of ordinary powers of attorney, often alongside LPAs, particularly where the donor wants to empower their attorney to make decisions, pending the registration of the LPA (which can take several weeks).

5.3 LASTING POWERS OF ATTORNEY

Lasting powers of attorney (LPAs) became available in England and Wales on 1 October 2007, when MCA 2005 came into force. They replace EPAs, and while there are many similarities between EPAs and LPAs, there are also significant differences:

- LPAs can cover health and welfare decisions (see **Chapter 13**), unlike EPAs which are restricted to property and financial affairs.
- LPAs can be registered at any time and must be registered before they are used, (unlike EPAs, which must be registered when the donor is or is becoming incapable of managing their property and affairs) (see **5.5**).

---

[1] There is one exception to this as provided for in the Powers of Attorney Act 1971, s.4, where a power of attorney is expressed to be 'irrevocable'.

- Attorneys acting under an LPA (referred to as 'donees' in MCA 2005) have a legal duty to act in accordance with the principles set out in MCA 2005[2] and to have regard to the MCA Code of Practice. Apart from those who are acting in a professional capacity, EPA attorneys have no such statutory duties, though they may have a duty at common law to act in the donor's best interests.
- LPAs allow donors to appoint replacement attorneys if their chosen attorney is unable to act, whereas EPAs do not.

MCA 2005 provides that donors can choose more than one person to make different kinds of decisions. For instance, a donor may wish to grant an LPA in favour of one person for the purposes of managing the donor's property and financial affairs, and a separate LPA in favour of another person for purposes of making decisions affecting the donor's welfare.[3] MCA 2005 also allows the donor to appoint two or more attorneys and to specify whether they should act:

- jointly (i.e. always act together);
- jointly and severally (either together or independently); or
- jointly in respect of some matters and jointly and severally in respect of others.

Only adults aged 18 or over can make an LPA. The relevant prescribed form must be used.[4] There are separate forms for health and welfare LPAs and those dealing with property and affairs. MCA 2005 and associated regulations[5] set down a number of requirements that must be satisfied before an LPA can be validly acted upon, including:

- The donor must sign a statement saying that they have read (or had read to them) the LPA, including section 8 of the LPA form, 'Your legal rights and responsibilities'.
- The donor has to decide whether anyone should be 'notified' when an application is made to the OPG for the registration of the LPA. For LPAs made before 1 July 2015, the document had to include the name of one or more people (not any of the attorneys) whom the donor wished to be told about any application to register the LPA. This notification requirement does not exist in relation to LPAs made after that date.

---

[2] MCA 2005, s.1. See **Appendix A**.
[3] MCA 2005, s.10(4).
[4] Available from the Office of the Public Guardian (see **www.gov.uk/government/organisations/office-of-the-public-guardian**). The initial prescribed LPA forms were in use from 1 October 2007 until 31 March 2011. They were then first revised in 2009 and the new forms prescribed in the Lasting Powers of Attorney, Enduring Powers of Attorney and Public Guardian (Amendment) Regulations 2009, SI 2009/1884 were available from 1 October 2009 (the 2009 forms). The 2009 forms were then further revised in 2013 under the Lasting Powers of Attorney, Enduring Powers of Attorney and Public Guardian (Amendment) Regulations 2013, SI 2013/506. Subsequently the Lasting Powers of Attorney, Enduring Powers of Attorney and Public Guardian (Amendment) Regulations 2015, SI 2015/899 introduced new forms for use from 1 July 2015.
[5] Lasting Powers of Attorney, Enduring Powers of Attorney and Public Guardian Regulations 2007, SI 2007/1253, as amended by SI 2009/1884, and further amended by SI 2015/899.

- The attorney(s) must sign a statement saying that they have read (or had read to them) the LPA, including section 8 of the LPA form, 'Your legal rights and responsibilities', that they understand they must act in accordance with the principles of MCA 2005 and the MCA Code of Practice, and that they understand their duties (in particular the duty to make decisions and act in the donor's best interests).
- The document must include a certificate completed by an independent third party (called the 'certificate provider'), confirming that:[6]

    - as far as they are aware, the donor understands the LPA's purpose and the scope of the authority under it;
    - nobody has used fraud or undue pressure to trick or force the donor into making the LPA; and
    - there is nothing to stop the LPA being created.

A certificate provider can either be someone chosen by the donor who has known the donor personally for at least two years, or someone chosen by the donor as a person with relevant professional skills and expertise.

Unless the LPA is registered with the OPG, it does not take effect[7] and the attorney will have no authority under the power. Once the LPA has been registered by the donor or the attorney, the authority of the attorney will depend on the wording of the LPA.

Unless expressed to the contrary, the attorney under a financial LPA will have the authority to make all decisions about the donor's financial and property affairs, whether or not the donor has capacity. If, however, even after registration the donor has capacity to perform some tasks, such as running a bank account or shopping, then the fact that the power has been registered should not as matter of practice prevent the donor from carrying out these activities.

In the LPA for property and financial affairs (prescribed form LP1F), the donor has opportunity in section 5 of the LPA to specify when the attorneys can make decisions. There are two options within the form:

- 'as soon as my LPA has been registered (and also when I don't have mental capacity)'; or
- 'only when I don't have mental capacity'.

There is a note of caution alongside the second option, warning donors that this option may result in their LPA becoming less useful, as the attorney(s) may have to establish the donor's lack of capacity each time they try to use the LPA.

The MCA Code of Practice (para.7.33) makes clear that it is the donor's responsibility to decide how their capacity should be assessed in these circumstances, and the donor can specify, for instance, that the LPA can only be used if

---

[6] MCA 2005, Sched.1, para.2(1)(e), as amended.
[7] MCA 2005, s.9(2)(b) and Sched.1.

their GP or another doctor confirms in writing that they lack capacity to make specific decisions about property or finances.

That a donor can take steps to ensure that an attorney (or attorneys) can only act in very specific circumstances was confirmed in *XZ* v. *Public Guardian*.[8] In this case, the Public Guardian refused to register an LPA because he considered that complex conditions for the assessment of the donor's mental capacity 'imposed an unreasonable fetter on the attorneys' power to act, and were therefore, ineffective as part of an LPA' (para.11). XZ only wanted his attorneys to act when he lacked capacity to make a specific decision for himself, and so required two psychiatrists' opinions to be sought, with the approval of a non-medically trained 'Protector'.

The court ordered the Public Guardian to register the LPA as drafted. Senior Judge Lush held that XZ's LPA did not contain any provisions which would be ineffective as part of an LPA; or would prevent the instrument from operating as a valid power of attorney.

Senior Judge Lush noted that although XZ acknowledged that his LPA would potentially be less effective as a result of the provisions in question, nevertheless he wished the provisions to remain as an integral part of the registered instrument. Senior Judge Lush confirmed that, while the inclusion of the detailed provisions might be viewed as unwise or impractical by the Public Guardian, then so long as they complied with the statutory provisions, the decision to include them was for XZ alone to make.

There is no parallel provision in the LPA for health and welfare (prescribed form LP1H), as a health and welfare LPA can only be used to make a decision for a donor if the donor lacks the mental capacity to make the specific decision for themselves.

5.3.1   Capacity to make a lasting power of attorney

Certificate to confirm understanding

The certificate provider (see above) has an important role to play in safeguarding against abuse. The certificate provider must state that, 'as far as I am aware', the donor understands what the LPA is, its contents, and the powers it gives to the attorney. The guidance provided by the OPG[9] suggests that the certificate provider should discuss with the donor the following topics to establish the donor's capacity and understanding:

- What is your understanding of what an LPA is?
- What are your reasons for making an LPA?
- Why have you chosen me to be your certificate provider?
- Who have you chosen to be your attorneys?
- Why them?

---

[8]   *XZ* v. *The Public Guardian* [2015] EWCOP 35.
[9]   Office of the Public Guardian (2015) *Make, Register or End a Lasting Power of Attorney*, available at **www.gov.uk/power-of-attorney**.

- What powers are you giving them?
- In what circumstances should the power be used by your attorneys?
- What types of decision would you like them to make, and what (if any) should they not take?
- If there are any restrictions in the LPA, what do you believe they achieve?
- What is the difference between any restrictions and any guidance made in the LPA?
- Have the chosen attorneys provided you with answers to any of these questions?
- Do you have any reason to think they could be untrustworthy?
- Do you know when you could cancel the LPA?
- Are there any other reasons why the LPA should not be created?

A certificate provider is advised to make (and retain) a contemporaneous note of the donor's responses to the questions posed.

Certificate providers should also have in mind the functional and diagnostic tests of capacity set down in MCA 2005.[10] But the questions the certificate provider is asked to confirm are limited to the donor's understanding of the purpose and scope of the LPA, while other tests of capacity to perform a legal act refer to the nature and effect of the act in question, which arguably require a greater degree of understanding. In practice, it is unlikely the two tests will differ to any significant extent.

The test for capacity to make a lasting power of attorney

When assessing a client's capacity to create an LPA reference should be made to MCA 2005, ss. 2–3, having regard to the principles in s.1. The case law in relation to the making of an EPA has some relevance to the capacity test for the making of an LPA. In *Re K, Re F*,[11] having stated that the test of capacity to create an enduring power of attorney was that the donor understood the nature and effect of the document, the judge set out four pieces of information which any person creating an enduring power of attorney should understand:[12]

- if such be the terms of the power, that the attorney will be able to assume complete authority over the donor's affairs;
- if such be the terms of the power, that the attorney will be able to do anything with the donor's property which the donor could have done;
- that the authority will continue if the donor should be, or should become, mentally incapable;
- that if the donor should be, or should become, mentally incapable, the power will be irrevocable without confirmation by the Court of Protection.

---

10   The statutory test of capacity in MCA 2005, ss.2 and 3, having regard to the principles in s.1. (See also **Chapter 3**.)
11   *Re K, Re F* [1988] 1 All ER 358.
12   *Re K, Re F* [1988] 1 All ER 358 at 363d–f.

The decision in *Re K, Re F* has been criticised for imposing too simple a test of capacity to create an EPA but the simplicity or complexity of the test depends largely on the questions asked by the person assessing the donor's capacity. For example, if the four pieces of basic relevant information described by the judge in *Re K, Re F* were mentioned to the donor, and if the donor was asked 'do you understand this?' in such a way as to encourage an affirmative reply, the donor would probably pass the test with flying colours and, indeed, the test would be too simple. If, on the other hand, the assessor were specifically to ask the donor 'what will your attorney be able to do?' and 'what will happen if you become mentally incapable?' the test would be substantially harder. That such questions susceptible to the answers 'yes' or 'no' may be inadequate for the purpose of assessing capacity to make a power of attorney can also be inferred from the decision in *Re Beaney (Deceased),*[13] confirmed by the Court of Appeal in *Re W (Enduring Power of Attorney).*[14]

The decision of Senior Judge Lush in *Re Collis*[15] highlighted how the test for capacity to make an EPA would need to be adapted to take account of the differences between EPAs and LPAs. He identified the following distinguishing factors between the two tests:

- the donor needs to understand that an LPA cannot be used until it has been successfully registered at the OPG;
- for a health and welfare LPA, the donor needs to understand that the attorney can only make a decision if at the material time the donor lacks the capacity to make that specific decision for himself;
- a donor should understand he can revoke an LPA at any time, provided he has the mental capacity to do so;
- the donor should understand the authority conferred by an LPA is subject to the provisions of MCA 2005 (particularly the s.1 principles and the s.4 best interests checklist);
- in determining the issue of capacity to make an LPA, MCA 2005, s.3(4) specifically requires the donor to be mindful of the foreseeable consequences of making or not making the LPA.

It is important to note that the test for capacity to make an LPA is not the same as the test for managing property and affairs generally (see **5.5**). This means that a person may have the necessary capacity to make an LPA, yet lack the capacity to make the very decisions that he will be calling upon his attorney to make under the terms of the LPA.

Although the legislation does not require that a certificate be completed by a medical practitioner, where the donor is of borderline capacity it is advisable that the certificate be completed by a doctor or other relevant professional, who should

---

[13] *Re Beaney (Deceased)* [1978] All ER 595.
[14] *Re W (Enduring Power of Attorney)* [2001] 1 FLR 832, paras.23 and 25.
[15] *Re Collis* (unreported, COP, 27 October 2010).

record their findings. Alternatively the certificate provider should obtain the views of a medical practitioner or other expert and record their findings.[16]

In *Re Collis*, Senior Judge Lush preferred the evidence of the solicitor acting as certificate provider to that of an experienced medical practitioner in their role as Court of Protection Special Visitor on the question of capacity. This decision was not a reflection of the respective quality of the evidence, but took account of the contemporaneous nature of the solicitor's evidence, compared to the retrospective view of the Special Visitor. In *A, B and C* v. *X and Z*, Hedley J emphasised that as a consequence of the fluctuating (and deteriorating) nature of X's condition, the making of an LPA, 'unless accompanied by contemporaneous medical evidence of capacity, would give rise to a serious risk of challenge or refusal to register'.[17] (Guidance for medical practitioners on the procedures to be followed in such circumstances is provided at **4.4**.)

Solicitors instructed to draw up an LPA on behalf of a client must first be satisfied that the client has the required capacity, assisted by a medical opinion where necessary. A Practice Note on this topic has been issued by the Law Society.[18]

5.3.2 Registration of a lasting power of attorney

Unless the LPA is registered with the OPG, it does not take effect. The application for registration can be made either by the donor or the attorney(s). Unless the Court of Protection provides otherwise, notification must first be given to the donor or attorney(s) (whoever is not the applicant for registration) and to the named person(s) (if any) included by the donor in the LPA instrument as 'a person to notify'.

The prescribed form for notification[19] makes it clear that the donor and any person notified have a right to object to registration (within three weeks of the date of the notice[20]). There are no specified grounds for objection by donors. Named persons or attorneys may either object to the Public Guardian on factual grounds (for example, because either the donor or an attorney is bankrupt or has died) or to the Court of Protection on the following grounds prescribed in the Regulations:[21]

- one or more of the requirements for the creation of an LPA have not been met;
- the power has been revoked or has otherwise come to an end;
- fraud or undue pressure was used to induce the donor to create the power;
- the donee has behaved, is behaving, or proposes to behave in a way that:

---

[16] *Kenward* v. *Adams* (1975) *The Times*, 29 November.

[17] *A, B and C* v. *X and Z* [2012] EWHC 2400 (COP); [2013] COPLR 1 at para.38.

[18] Law Society Practice Note: Lasting Powers of Attorney (8 December 2011), available at **www.lawsociety.org.uk/support-services/advice/practice-notes/lasting-powers-attorney/**.

[19] Form LPA3 (or LP3 as referred to in LP1F) Notice of Intention to Apply for Registration of a Lasting Power of Attorney. Available at **www.gov.uk/power-of-attorney**.

[20] Lasting Powers of Attorney, Enduring Powers of Attorney and Public Guardian (Amendment) Regulations 2013, SI 2013/506, reg.2(2).

[21] Lasting Powers of Attorney, Enduring Powers of Attorney and Public Guardian Regulations 2007, SI 2007/1253, reg.15.

- contravenes or would contravene his authority; or
- is not or would not be in the donor's best interests.

5.3.3 Capacity to revoke a lasting power of attorney

Until an application for registration has been made, the donor may revoke a power of attorney at any time. If the donor does so, but the attorney believes the donor lacks the capacity to revoke the power, the attorney can apply for registration of the power. The donor may then object to the registration on the ground that the power is no longer valid, and the court must decide whether this ground for objection is established. However, if the donor has destroyed the LPA document, it is not possible to apply for registration.

Even where the LPA has been registered, it can be revoked at any time when the donor has capacity to do so.[22] Unlike the position that prevailed in respect of an EPA, the Court of Protection no longer has to confirm the revocation, the relevant notice needing to be given to the Public Guardian. However, in cases of doubt an application may be made to the Court of Protection for a declaration as to whether the LPA has in fact been revoked by the donor.[23] The court will need to consider whether the donor has (or had) capacity to revoke the LPA at the relevant time.

The Court of Protection has authority under MCA 2005, s.22(4)(b) to revoke an LPA if the donor lacks capacity to do so. In *Re Harcourt*[24] Senior Judge Lush made clear that the Court of Protection can only exercise its powers to revoke an LPA if the donor lacks the requisite capacity to revoke the LPA themselves. Evidence will therefore be required of that lack of capacity before the court's jurisdiction is engaged. The cases decided since MCA 2005 came into force have not identified specifically what is required in order to have capacity to revoke an LPA, but it is likely that they are the same elements as were identified previously by Senior Judge Lush in *Re S*[25] in relation to the capacity to revoke an EPA.[26] In other words, the donor must know:

- who the attorney(s) are;
- what authority the attorney(s) have;
- why it is necessary or expedient to revoke the LPA; and
- what are the foreseeable consequences of revoking the power.

In *Re Harcourt*, Senior Judge Lush also held that the donor lacked capacity to give directions to the attorney with regard to the production of reports, accounts, records and any other information relating to the management of her property and financial affairs, to examine those reports and records, or to instruct a third party, such as a

---

[22] MCA 2005, s.13(2).
[23] MCA 2005, s.22(2)(b).
[24] *Re Harcourt* (2012) MHLO 74 (LPA).
[25] *Re S* (unreported, COP, 13 March 1997).
[26] This approach appears to have underpinned the decision both in *Re Harcourt* and also the decision in *Re DP, Public Guardian* v. *JM* [2014] EWCOP 7.

book keeper or accountant to examine the reports on her behalf and raise appropriate requisitions. This finding afforded the court the discretion to intervene on her behalf and to require the attorney to provide necessary accounts and supporting documentation.

5.4 ENDURING POWERS OF ATTORNEY

Enduring Powers of Attorney (EPAs) became available in England and Wales in March 1986, when the Enduring Powers of Attorney Act 1985 came into force. After the coming into force of MCA 2005 on 1 October 2007, an EPA can no longer be created, but EPAs made prior to that date remain valid.[27]

Unless the EPA specifically states that it will not come into force until the donor is mentally incapacitated (which is rare), the power is 'live' from the moment it is executed (i.e. signed and witnessed) by the donor and attorney. In other words, the attorney could act under it straight away and can continue to act, even though the donor may still be perfectly capable of looking after their own property and affairs. If the EPA is not registered with the OPG, the donor and the attorney have what is known as concurrent authority. Both of them can manage and administer the donor's property and affairs.

An attorney acting under an EPA must apply to the OPG for the registration of the power if the attorney has reason to believe that the donor is, or is becoming mentally incapable of managing and administering their property and affairs[28] (see **5.5**).

The donor and the donor's closest relatives must be informed of the attorney's intention to register the power. There is a statutory list of relatives who must be notified.[29] Both the donor and any of the relatives have the right to object to the registration of the power, for example, if they believe that the donor is not yet incapable of managing their own affairs, or that the power may be invalid because it has been revoked by the donor. Once the power has been registered by the OPG, the donor and the attorney no longer have concurrent authority. Only the attorney has the authority to manage and administer the donor's property and affairs. If, however, even after registration the donor has capacity to perform some tasks, such as running a bank account or shopping, the fact that the power has been registered should not as matter of practice prevent the donor from carrying out these activities.

---

[27] The Enduring Powers of Attorney Act 1985 was repealed by MCA 2005, but in respect of EPAs which remain valid after 1 October 2007 the relevant provisions were largely re-enacted in MCA 2005, Sched.45. The court will have regard to the principles of MCA 2005 when determining questions arising under pre-existing EPAs. See *Re J (Enduring Power of Attorney)* [2009] EWHC 436 (Ch); [2010] 1 WLR 210, in which the principle of encouraging autonomy enshrined in MCA 2005 was expressly cited in determining the validity of an EPA.

[28] MCA 2005, Sched.4, para.4(1) and (2).

[29] MCA 2005, Sched.4, para.6.

5.4.1 Capacity to make an enduring power of attorney

Since EPAs can no longer be made, the question of capacity to make an EPA is only relevant where someone is retrospectively challenging the validity of an EPA. The issues are similar, but not identical, to those applicable to determining capacity to make an LPA (see **5.3**). In particular the criteria set out in *Re K, Re F* (see **5.3.1**) must be satisfied to confirm the donor's understanding of the nature and effect of the EPA.

5.4.2 Capacity to revoke an enduring power of attorney

Until an application for registration has been made, the donor may revoke an EPA at any time. If the donor does so, but the attorney believes the donor lacks the capacity to revoke the power, the attorney can apply for registration of the power. The donor may then object to the registration on the ground that the power is no longer valid, and the court must decide whether this ground for objection is established. However, if the donor has destroyed the EPA documents, it cannot be registered. After registration, no revocation of an EPA by the donor is valid unless and until the Court of Protection confirms the revocation.

There have been no reported decisions on the capacity to revoke an EPA. According to *Cretney and Lush*,[30] the evidence which the court requires in order to be satisfied that the donor has the necessary capacity to revoke the power is as follows, whereby the donor should know:

- who the attorney(s) are;
- what authority the attorney(s) have;
- why it is necessary or expedient to revoke the power;
- what the foreseeable consequences of revoking the power are.

It is important that the evidence provided in support of an assertion that the donor lacks capacity to revoke an EPA is specifically directed to that transaction. In *Re Cloutt*,[31] Senior Judge Lush held that, because revocation of an EPA is a different transaction to the creation of an LPA, a doctor's certification of an LPA was not of itself sufficient proof of capacity to revoke an EPA.

In practice, where the donor of a registered EPA wishes to revoke it, the attorney often disclaims (that is, gives notice to the Public Guardian) that they wish to cease acting as attorney. The Court of Protection must then decide whether the donor has capacity to resume management of their own affairs, or whether a deputyship order or some other order should be made in respect of the donor.

In *Re DT*,[32] Senior Judge Lush highlighted the different criteria that the Court of Protection will apply if invited to revoke an EPA as opposed to an LPA (i.e. where

---

[30]   D Lush (2015) *Cretney and Lush on Lasting Powers of Lasting and Enduring Powers of Attorney*, Jordan Publishing, at 20.16, drawing upon the decision in *Re S* (unreported, COP, 13 March 1997).

[31]   *Re Cloutt* (unreported, COP, 7 November 2008), discussed in D Lush (2015) *Cretney and Lush on Lasting Powers of Lasting and Enduring Powers of Attorney*, Jordan Publishing, at 20.18.

[32]   *Re DT* [2015] EWCOP 10; [2015] COPLR 225.

steps are taken by someone other than the donor or attorney to obtain revocation). In relation to an EPA, MCA 2005, s.22(3) and (4) provide that the court may revoke an LPA if (a) the donor lacks the capacity to revoke the LPA, *and* (b) the attorney has behaved or is behaving in a way that contravenes his authority or is not in the donor's best interest, or proposes to behave in such a way. However, in the case of an EPA, the court does not need to be satisfied that the donor lacks the capacity to revoke it himself. It merely needs to be satisfied that, having regard to all the circumstances, and in particular the attorney's relationship to or connection with the donor, the attorney is unsuitable to be the donor's attorney.

5.5   CAPACITY TO MANAGE PROPERTY AND AFFAIRS

The question as to the capacity of a person to manage property and affairs will arise in three subtly different contexts:

- Where a judge sitting other than as a judge in the Court of Protection is considering whether a person has capacity to manage their property and affairs. In the context of civil litigation, the Civil Procedure (Amendment) Rules 2007[33] came into force at the same time as MCA 2005, introducing a new Part 21 and new rule 21(2) to the Civil Procedure Rules 1998 (CPR)[34]. Under these provisions, an adult litigant who lacks the mental capacity to conduct proceedings is a 'protected party' and may also be a 'protected beneficiary' if they lack mental capacity to manage any property received in the proceedings on their behalf. In both cases, the question is considered by reference to the statutory test set down in MCA 2005 (see **Chapter 8** for further and more detailed discussion).

- Where a person who has not previously made an LPA or an EPA lacks the capacity (within the meaning of MCA 2005) to manage and administer their property and affairs. In these circumstances, it may be necessary for someone to apply to the Court of Protection for an order setting out how the person's affairs may be dealt with.[35] Where long-term management of property and affairs is required it is likely that the court will appoint a deputy with authority to deal with the day-to-day management of the person's affairs. Deputies are, in broad terms, the equivalent to receivers previously appointed under Part VII of MHA 1983. Receivers appointed before MCA 2005 came into effect are treated under the new regime as property and affairs deputies appointed by the Court of Protection. An outline of the powers and procedures of the Court of Protection and the role of deputies is to be found at **Appendix C**.

---

33   Civil Procedure (Amendment) Rules 2007, SI 2007/2204.
34   Civil Procedure Rules 1998, SI 1998/3132.
35   MCA 2005, s.16(1)(b) and (2)(b).

- Where a person who made a valid EPA before 1 October 2007 now ceases to be capable of managing and administering their property and affairs. This will trigger the attorney's duty to register the EPA with the OPG.

5.5.1 The common law test for incapacity to manage property and affairs

The leading common law case remains that of *Masterman-Lister* v. *Jewell; Masterman-Lister v Brutton & Co*[36] and *Masterman-Lister* v. *Brutton & Co; Masterman-Lister* v. *Jewell* (in the Court of Appeal).[37] This confirmed the 'issue-specific nature' of the test of capacity, which must be considered in relation to the particular transaction under consideration. A distinction was drawn between capacity to manage day-to-day affairs, capacity to deal with the complexities of personal injury litigation, and capacity to manage a large award of damages.

In *Re CAF*[38] it was concluded:

the degree of incapacity of managing and administering a patient's property and affairs must be related to all the circumstances, including the state in which the alleged patient lives and the complexity and importance of the property and affairs which he has to manage and administer.

In personal injury actions, however, it is necessary to focus first on the person's ability to participate in the litigation rather than the whole of their affairs (see **Chapter 8**) and then to consider separately the person's capacity to manage any award of damages:

It is not difficult to envisage claimants ... with capacity to deal with all matters and take all 'lay client' decisions related to their actions up to and including a decision whether or not to settle, but lacking capacity to decide (even with advice) how to administer a large award.[39]

5.5.2 Capacity to manage property and affairs under MCA 2005

The test of capacity to be applied is that set out in MCA 2005, ss.2 and 3,[40] with regard to the principles within s.1 of the Act (see **Chapter 3**). MCA 2005 provides that capacity is time-specific and decision-specific, and must be assessed in relation to each decision, at the time that decision needs to be made (rather than as an assessment of capacity to manage financial affairs generally). The test requires the presence of an impairment of, or disturbance in the functioning of, the mind or brain that causes the person to be unable to understand information relevant to the

---

[36] *Masterman-Lister* v. *Jewell; Masterman-Lister v Brutton & Co* [2002] EWHC 417 (QB).

[37] *Masterman-Lister* v. *Brutton & Co; Masterman-Lister* v. *Jewell* [2002] EWCA Civ 1889; [2003] 1 WLR 1511.

[38] *Re CAF* (unreported, QB, 23 March 1962).

[39] *Re CAF* (unreported, QB, 23 March 1962) at 27.

[40] The statutory test of capacity in MCA 2005, ss.2 and 3, taking account of the principles in s.1. (See also **Chapter 3**.)

decision, retain it and use or weigh the information as part of the process of making the decision in question. However, the MCA Code of Practice suggests that where the impairment or disturbance is ongoing or long term, this may be relevant to an assessment of the person's capacity to manage their property and affairs generally.[41] This approach was recognised by Hedley J in the Court of Protection case of *A, B and C* v. *X and Z*,[42] where account was taken of the common law test in determining that X lacked the necessary mental capacity to manage his affairs, and Hedley J noted that:

> the general concept of managing affairs is an ongoing act and, therefore, quite unlike the specific act of making a will or making an enduring power of attorney. The management of affairs related to a continuous state of affairs whose demands may be unpredictable and may occasionally be urgent.[43]

Where an application is made to the Court of Protection for authority to make financial decisions on a person's behalf, the court will require evidence that the person lacks capacity to make the decision (or decisions) in question. Such evidence, in applying the test in MCA 2005,[44] is provided on Court of Protection Form COP3 'Assessment of Capacity' (see **Appendix G**). This form may be helpful when applying the statutory test of capacity in other situations.

Given the absence of specific provisions in the MCA Code of Practice governing the assessment of capacity to manage property and affairs, it is suggested the following checklist should be adopted (this checklist was set out in the first edition of this book in the common law context and was endorsed by Wright J in the High Court decision in *Masterman-Lister*).[45]

5.5.3 Checklist

The checklist is not intended to be exhaustive or authoritative, but gives some indication of the wide range of information which may be needed in order to make a proper assessment of a person's understanding of that information and hence, their capacity to manage their property and affairs.

The extent of the person's property and affairs

The extent of the person's property and affairs would include an examination of:

---

[41] Office of the Public Guardian (2007) *Mental Capacity Act 2005 Code of Practice*, available at **www.gov.uk/government/publications/mental-capacity-act-code-of-practice**, paras.4.28–4.30.

[42] *A, B and C* v. *X and Z* [2012] EWHC 2400 (COP); [2013] COPLR 1.

[43] *A, B and C* v. *X and Z* [2012] EWHC 2400 (COP); [2013] COPLR 1 at para.41.

[44] The statutory test of capacity in MCA 2005, ss.2 and 3, taking account of the principles in MCA 2005, s.1. (See also **Chapter 3**.)

[45] *Masterman-Lister* v. *Jewell; Masterman-Lister* v *Brutton & Co* [2002] EWHC 417 (QB) at para.25.

- income and capital (including savings and the value of the home), expenditure, and liabilities;
- financial needs and responsibilities;
- whether there are likely to be any changes in the person's financial circumstances in the foreseeable future;
- the skill, specialised knowledge, and time it takes to manage the affairs properly and whether the impairment of, or disturbance in the functioning of, the person's mind or brain is affecting the management of the assets;
- whether the person would be likely to seek, understand and act on appropriate advice where needed in view of the complexity of the affairs.

Personal information

Personal information about the person might include:

- age;
- life expectancy;
- psychiatric history;
- prospects of recovery or deterioration;
- the extent to which capacity could fluctuate;
- the condition in which the person lives;
- family background;
- family and social responsibilities;
- any cultural, ethnic or religious considerations;
- the degree of backup and support the person receives or could expect to receive from others.

A person's vulnerability

Other issues should be considered with the following questions:

- Could inability to manage the property and affairs lead to the person making rash or irresponsible decisions?
- Could inability to manage lead to exploitation by others – perhaps even by family members?
- Could inability to manage lead to the position of other people being compromised or jeopardised?

In *Masterman-Lister* Wright J held that 'while [the above questions] are plainly proper and appropriate questions to ask, they have to be answered, in my view, in the light of the other guidance set out in the checklist'. Subsequent cases have indicated that such questions may indeed be relevant (while decided under the common law, it is suggested that they remain relevant when considering the application of the statutory test). In *Mitchell* v. *Alasia*,[46] Cox J relied on qualities such as impulsiveness and volatility when deciding that the claimant was, by reason of his mental disorder, incapable of managing and administering his own affairs. And in *Lindsay* v. *Wood*, Stanley Burnton J observed that:

> When considering the question of capacity, psychiatrists and psychologists will normally wish to take into account all aspects of the personality and behaviour of the person in question, including vulnerability to exploitation.[47]

Empowerment Matters[48] has published free guidance focused primarily on how to assess an individual's capacity in relation to financial decision-making and gives practical suggestions about how to support someone to manage their money and financial decisions in a way that maintains their independence for as long as possible.

5.5.4 Capacity to manage property and affairs in the context of enduring powers of attorney

As part of the legacy of the old EPA regime, it is necessary to note that the old test of capacity to manage property and affairs survives in part in the regime of MCA 2005, falling for consideration only where:

(a)   a person has made a valid EPA; and
(b)   that EPA has not been registered.

Attorneys acting under an EPA must register it with the Public Guardian when they have reason to believe that the donor is or is becoming mentally incapable (see **5.4**). In this context, 'mentally incapable' means that the donor 'is incapable by reason of mental disorder within the meaning of MHA 1983, of managing and administering his property and affairs'.[49] (Note that this definition of mental disorder is the definition under MHA 1983 before it was amended by the Mental Health Act 2007 (MHA 2007).)

Therefore, for the purposes of registering an EPA, 'mental disorder' is defined as 'mental illness, arrested or incomplete development of the mind, psychopathic disorder and any other disorder or disability of the mind'.[50] It is also important to note that 'mental illness' is not defined in MHA 1983 and, as it is no longer a category of mental disorder in MHA 2007, no recent guidance is available on the meaning of this term.

---

[46]   *Mitchell* v. *Alasia* [2005] EWHC 11 (QB).
[47]   *Lindsay* v. *Wood* [2006] EWHC 2895 (QB) at para.18.
[48]   Empowerment Matters (2014) *Making Financial Decisions: Guidance for Assessing, Supporting and Empowering Specific Decision Making*, published online at **www.empowermentmatters.co.uk**. The guidance was commissioned by the Department of Health.
[49]   MCA 2005, Sched.4, para.23(1).
[50]   MHA 1983, s.1, as it stood prior to its amendment by MHA 2007.

It is perhaps worth noting that almost anyone satisfying the test for mental incapability in this context would also satisfy the test for lack of capacity under MCA 2005.

As we have already noted, a person's capacity to 'manage their property and affairs' depends largely on the value and complexity of their property and affairs and the extent to which that person may be vulnerable to exploitation. It has been held that property and affairs 'means business matters, legal transactions, and other dealings of a similar kind'.[51] It does not include personal matters such as where to live or decisions about medical treatment. However, in practical terms, 'power over the purse' can lead to an element of 'power over the person'.[52]

5.6 CAPACITY TO CLAIM AND RECEIVE SOCIAL SECURITY BENEFITS

There is a statutory mechanism through which social security benefits may be claimed on behalf of people lacking capacity to manage their own affairs. This procedure, called appointeeship, is normally used when an incapacitated person has limited assets and income only from benefits or pensions, and there is no need for more formal procedures.

5.6.1 Appointeeship

If a person is entitled to social security benefits, but is considered to be incapable of claiming and managing them, the Secretary of State for Work and Pensions can appoint an individual aged 18 or over (known as an 'appointee') to:

- exercise any rights and duties the claimant has under the Social Security Acts and Regulations, for example: claiming benefits; informing the relevant agency of the Department for Work and Pensions (DWP) of any change in the claimant's circumstances; and appealing against the decision of a decision-maker in a DWP agency;
- receive any benefits payable to the claimant;
- deal with the money received on the claimant's behalf in the interests of the claimant and their dependants.

An appointee may be appointed by the Secretary of State where:

- a person is, or is alleged to be, entitled to benefit, whether or not a claim for benefit has been made by him or on his behalf;
- that person is unable for the time being to act;

---

[51] *F* v. *West Berkshire Health Authority* [1989] 2 All ER 545 at 554d.
[52] *Re W (EEM)* [1971] 1 Ch 123.

- no deputy has been appointed by the Court of Protection (or receiver appointed under MHA 1983, Part VII but treated as being a deputy appointed by the Court of Protection) with power to claim or, as the case may be, receive benefit on the person's behalf.[53]

The test of capacity is therefore that the person is 'for the time being unable to act'. The phrase is not defined in regulations, but internal guidance for decision-makers published by the DWP suggests that people may be unable to act 'for example, because of senility or mental illness'.[54] Appointeeship should only be authorised when the person is incapable of managing their affairs, usually as a consequence of lack of mental capacity, although, exceptionally, an appointee 'may also be appropriate when the customer is physically disabled, e.g. if they have suffered a severe stroke'.[55] The DWP agency will usually arrange for a visiting officer to visit the person to make an independent assessment of their ability to manage their financial affairs and, more specifically, their ability to understand how to make and manage a claim to benefit. Further guidance states that: 'the visiting officer must assess whether the customer shows comprehension of the rights and responsibilities of making the claim.'[56]

Some decisions of the former Social Security Commissioners (now judges of the Upper Tribunal) have considered questions of whether the claimant has the relevant capacity, mainly in relation to the level of the claimant's understanding when making a claim which resulted in overpayment, but there are no formal legal criteria which specify the capacity required.[57] It has been suggested that in order to have the capacity to claim, receive and deal with benefits, an individual should be able to:

- understand the basis of possible entitlement (presumably with advice where necessary);
- understand and complete the claim form;
- respond to correspondence relating to social security benefits;
- collect or receive the benefits;
- manage the benefits in the sense of knowing what the money is for;
- choose whether to use it for that purpose and if so, how.[58]

---

[53] Social Security (Claims and Payments) Regulations 1987, SI 1987/1968, reg.33.
[54] Department for Work and Pensions (2013) *Decision Makers' Guide*, para.02440. This guidance is updated regularly and available at **www.gov.uk/government/collections/decision-makers-guide-staff-guide**.
[55] Department for Work and Pensions (2013) *Agents, Appointees, Attorneys, Deputies and Third Parties: Staff Guide*, available at **www.gov.uk/government/publications/procedures-for-dealing-with-agents-appointees-attorneys-deputies-and-third-parties**.
[56] Department for Work and Pensions (2013) *Agents, Appointees, Attorneys, Deputies and Third Parties: Staff Guide*, para.5171, available at **www.gov.uk/government/publications/procedures-for-dealing-with-agents-appointees-attorneys-deputies-and-third-parties**.
[57] See for example the following reported decisions of the Social Security Commissioners: R(A) 1/95 **www.osscsc.gov.uk/aspx/view.aspx?id=460**; R(IS) 14/96 **www.osscsc.gov.uk/aspx/view.aspx?id=684**; and R(IS) 5/00 **www.osscsc.gov.uk/aspx/view.aspx?id=361**.
[58] R Lavery and L Lundy (1994) 'The social security appointee system', *Journal of Social Welfare Law* 16:313–27:316.

The application for the appointment of an appointee, which is usually completed by the person applying to be appointed to this role, states: 'You may be asked to produce medical evidence of the claimant's inability to manage his own affairs.'[59] There is no standard form of medical certificate, however, and in the majority of cases, medical evidence is not required.

The DWP's own guidance on assessing a person's capacity advises:[60]

- assume they are capable until they demonstrate otherwise
- focus on the customer's abilities to understand and function in making particular decisions, e.g.:
  - can they pay bills?
  - do they know what income they have?
- do they have a general understanding of their benefits and what is involved in managing them – claiming, reporting changes, methods of payment?
- do they have a general understanding of the consequences of not claiming, reporting a change, not having a bank account?
- do they have an ability to understand and weigh up the information relevant to managing their decisions
- it may be helpful to have an independent person who is familiar with the customer present at the interview, e.g. a family member or social worker
- if the customer lives in a [Registered Care Home] or [Nursing Home], do not assume they are incapable – they may be quite capable of managing their affairs
- if the customer has lost the ability to communicate, e.g. because of a stroke, do not assume they are incapable. Make every effort to find out their views and wishes by all possible means
- record the details of the visit and the assessment of the customer's ability to act in their own right.

The Secretary of State can revoke an appointment at any time, and there is no right of appeal to a tribunal against the Secretary of State's refusal to appoint a particular individual as appointee or against the revocation of such an appointment. The DWP was required to develop a system for monitoring appointeeships, in order to comply with its obligations under the UN Convention on the Rights of Persons with Disabilities (see **3.9**).[61] An Appointee Review process was therefore introduced

---

[59] Department for Work and Pensions Form BF56 'Application for appointment to act on behalf of someone else'. See **www.gov.uk/become-appointee-for-someone-claiming-benefits**.

[60] Department for Work and Pensions (2013) *Agents, Appointees, Attorneys, Deputies and Third Parties: Staff Guide*, para.5180, available at **www.gov.uk/government/publications/procedures-for-dealing-with-agents-appointees-attorneys-deputies-and-third-parties**.

[61] Explanatory Memorandum on the United Nations Convention on the Rights of Persons with Disabilities and its Optional Protocol 2006: art.12.4 concerns safeguards for the exercise of substituted decision-making and includes a requirement for 'regular review' by a competent, independent and impartial authority or judicial body. (There was historically no review system for DWP appointees.) 'The United Kingdom's arrangements, whereby the Secretary of State may appoint a person to exercise rights in relation to social security claims and payments on behalf of an individual who is for the time being unable to act, are not at present subject to the safeguard of regular review, as required by Article 12.4 of the Convention and the UK reserves the right to apply those arrangements. The UK is therefore working towards a proportionate system of review.' See **www.un.org/disabilities**.

whereby the Secretary of State carries out a post-appointment check to ensure that an appointee is still needed. Thereafter there is provision for a limited case check every three years. The DWP's own guidance for potential appointees advises:[62]

> Your appointment can be stopped if:
>
> - you don't act properly under the terms of the appointment
> - the claimant is clearly able to manage their own benefits
> - you become incapable yourself

In reality, the DWP lacks the resources to visit the claimant and their appointee on a regular basis, following any appointment of an appointee and so will instead rely heavily on third parties (for example social workers, doctors, solicitors) to alert the DWP to any potential abuse or mismanagement by an appointee.

Appointees have no authority to deal with the claimant's capital. If the claimant has savings or capital which needs to be applied or invested, an application should be made to the Court of Protection for directions as to how to proceed.

5.7 PROTECTION FROM FINANCIAL ABUSE

People who are, or are becoming, incapable of dealing with their own financial affairs are particularly vulnerable to abuse, which can range from outright fraud to inadvertent mishandling of money by attorneys or appointees who are not fully aware of their duties and responsibilities.

Professional advisers have an important role to play in identifying any risk of abuse, particularly at the time of assessing capacity. The Law Society has published a Practice Note to support practitioners in identifying and acting on behalf of potentially vulnerable clients.[63]

When carrying out an assessment of capacity to make a financial decision or to manage property and affairs, professionals must act in accordance with MCA 2005 and the guidance in the MCA Code of Practice (see **Chapter 3** and **Appendix B**). The following checklist may also be helpful to professional advisers in assessing risk and guarding against possible abuse:[64]

- Never express an opinion on a person's capacity to make a decision without first seeing the person for that purpose.
- Make sure the correct test of capacity is applied in relation to the particular transaction being considered, taking account of the individual circumstances and, in particular, the vulnerability of the person being assessed.

---

[62] See **www.gov.uk/become-appointee-for-someone-claiming-benefits**.
[63] Law Society Practice Note: Meeting the Needs of Vulnerable Clients (2 July 2015), available at **www.lawsociety.org.uk/support-services/advice/practice-notes/meeting-the-needs-of-vulnerable-clients-july-2015/**.
[64] This checklist has been adapted from: D Lush 'Managing the financial affairs of mentally incapacitated persons in the United Kingdom and Ireland' in R Jacoby and C Oppenheimer (2002) *Psychiatry in the Elderly* (3rd edn), Oxford University Press.

- Be careful of mistaking the person's ability to express a choice (such as who should be the attorney) for the ability to understand the nature and effect of a particular transaction (such as making an LPA).
- In assessing the ability to understand information relevant to a decision, make sure the person is aware of and able to appreciate not only the benefits, but also the risks involved in the particular transaction.
- Always give reasons for deciding why a person has or does not have the required degree of understanding.

Solicitors authorised and regulated by the Solicitors Regulation Authority (SRA) must comply with the SRA Handbook 2011, updated online.[65] The SRA Handbook contains ten mandatory principles which apply to all those the SRA regulates and to all aspects of practice. SRA Principle 10 provides that a solicitor 'must not accept instructions where he or she suspects that they may have been given by a client under duress or undue influence'.

For some clients, although they may have the necessary mental capacity to give instructions in relation to the transaction (in accordance with the principles of MCA 2005), they may not be able to make the gift 'freely', as a consequence of experiencing an element of coercion or pressure (undue influence).

A solicitor's duty to assess any possibility of undue influence is set out in the indicative behaviours (IBs) found in Chapter 1 of the SRA Code of Conduct 2011:

IB(1.6) in taking instructions and during the course of the retainer, [have] proper regard to your client's mental capacity or other vulnerability, such as incapacity or duress.

Conversely:

IB(1.28) acting for a client when there are reasonable grounds for believing that the instructions are affected by duress or undue influence without satisfying yourself that they represent the client's wishes

would demonstrate a failure on the part of the lawyer to comply with the SRA Code of Conduct 2011.

If a solicitor suspects their client's instructions are the result of undue influence, they need to proceed with great care, and establish whether they can continue to act on their client's behalf. It is important to make detailed enquiries if the client proposes an unusual or suspicious transaction. If the client decides to proceed, against the advice of the solicitor, it is crucial to record the advice given, with the analysis of the risks involved.[66]

The Law Society Practice Note: Financial Abuse provides further guidance on the identification of adults at risk of financial abuse.[67]

---

[65] See **www.sra.org.uk/handbook/**.
[66] See *McDonnell* v. *Loosemore* [2007] EWCA Civ 1531.
[67] Law Society Practice Note: Financial Abuse (13 June 2013), available at **www.lawsociety.org.uk/support-services/advice/practice-notes/financial-abuse/**.

In addition, the Public Guardian has a statutory duty to deal with representations (including complaints) made about the actions of an attorney acting under a registered EPA or LPA, or a deputy appointed by the Court of Protection.[68] Anyone wishing to raise concerns should contact the unit of the OPG. There is a dedicated phone number for reporting concerns (0300 456 0300), and email address (opg.safeguardingunit@publicguardian.gsi.gov.uk). The OPG can investigate the actions of a deputy or attorney and can also refer concerns to other relevant agencies. The OPG can also make an application to the Court of Protection if it believes that action needs to be taken against an attorney (under a registered EPA or LPA) or deputy.

In addition to this specific duty, the OPG has a general responsibility for safeguarding adults at risk of abuse and has issued guidance on possible indicators of causal factors of abuse.[69] Where concerns are raised that are outside the Public Guardian's jurisdiction (e.g. in relation to unregistered EPAs or appointeeships) the OPG must refer them to the correct agency so that the concern is addressed.

---

[68]   MCA 2005, s.58(1)(h).
[69]   Office of the Public Guardian (2013) *Safeguarding Policy: Protecting Vulnerable Adults*, section 10, available at **www.gov.uk/government/publications/safeguarding-policy-protecting-vulnerable-adults**.

CHAPTER 6

Capacity to make a will

6.1   Introduction
6.2   Testamentary capacity: the position at common law
6.3   The Mental Capacity Act 2005
6.4   Supervening incapacity
6.5   The need for medical evidence: the golden rule

6.6   The duty of the draftsman to ascertain capacity
6.7   Checklist
6.8   Capacity to revoke a will
6.9   Statutory wills

6.1   INTRODUCTION

A will is a document in which the maker (called the 'testator' if he is a man; and the 'testatrix' if she is a woman) appoints an executor to settle their affairs when the person dies, and sets out how the person's estate is to be distributed after death. The maker of a will must be aged 18 or over. A will comes into operation only on the maker's death. Until then the maker can revoke the will, or make a new one at any time, provided that they still have the capacity to do so. The making of a new will normally revokes any previous will, provided the person making the will had the capacity to do so (see **6.8** on capacity to revoke a will) and directs in the new will that it revokes the previous will.

Someone who dies without leaving a valid will is said to die intestate.

About 10 per cent of the wills made in England and Wales are home-made, i.e. handwritten or typed by the person making it, usually on a pre-printed form bought or downloaded commercially. In most cases, however, people ask a solicitor, or other professional involved in will preparation, to prepare a will for them. This chapter is directed to the duties upon solicitors; equivalent duties should also rest upon other professional will-drafters.

Anyone instructed professionally to prepare a will must first be satisfied that the client has the required capacity (see **6.2** and **6.6**), assisted by a medical opinion where necessary (see **6.5**). The draftsman will discuss the client's circumstances; advise them of the various options; prepare a draft will based on the discussion and send a copy of the draft to the client for approval. The draft is then approved, or amended, and the will prepared in readiness for executing (signing) in the presence of two witnesses.

The degree of understanding that the law requires a testator to have is called testamentary capacity. A testator should have testamentary capacity both when the instructions are given to a solicitor or other draftsman for the preparation of the will (or, in the case of a home-made will, when they write or type it), and when it is executed (for an important exception to the latter, see **6.4**). The capacity to make a will is assessed on the individual concerned in the light of the complexity of the task being undertaken. This means the assessment is of the particular individual and their circumstances. The person with a straightforward estate and simple family circumstances, who requires a will in simple terms, may need a lower level of capacity to understand than would be the case were the assets, family circumstances and will to be of greater complexity.[1]

It is not the existence of any mental impairment *per se* that prevents a person making a valid will, but the degree of the impairment. Thus a diagnosis of dementia does not prevent a person making a will; it is the extent to which that illness diminishes their testamentary capacity that would prevent it.

6.2   TESTAMENTARY CAPACITY: THE POSITION AT COMMON LAW

The leading case on testamentary capacity is *Banks* v. *Goodfellow*.[2] In this case the testator, John Banks, was a bachelor in his 50s who, together with his teenaged niece, Margaret Goodfellow, lodged in a small village in north Cumberland. He suffered from paranoid schizophrenia. He was convinced that a local grocer was pursuing and persecuting him (and this continued even after the grocer had died). The grocer was accompanied in this task by various devils and demons (who were, on occasion, visibly present to John Banks). In 1863, with his solicitor's assistance, he made a short will leaving his entire estate (15 houses) to Margaret. He died in 1865 and Margaret inherited the estate.

There was no challenge to the will until Margaret died in 1867. She died under age and unmarried and her uncle's 15 properties passed, as a consequence of her death, to her half-brother, Edward Goodfellow. Edward, who was not related by blood to John Banks, inherited as the closest relative to Margaret when she died intestate. The will was contested by John's nephew (the son of John's half-brother) on the ground that John lacked testamentary capacity because of his paranoid delusions. The court held that partial unsoundness of mind, which has no influence

---

[1]   *McClintock* v. *Calderwood* [2005] EWHC 836 (Ch); *Tchilingirian* v. *Ouzounian* [2003] EWHC 1220 (Ch); [2003] WTLR 709.
[2]   *Banks* v. *Goodfellow* (1869–70) LR 5 QB 549.

on the way in which a testator disposed of his property, did not make a person incapable of validly disposing of his property by will[3] and therefore John Banks's will was valid.

Chief Justice Cockburn set out the following test for testamentary capacity (with numbering added for clarity):

> It is essential ... that a testator
>
> [1]   shall understand the nature of the act and its effects;
> [2]   shall understand the extent of the property of which he is disposing;
> [3]   shall be able to comprehend and appreciate the claims to which he ought to give effect;
> [4]   and, with a view to the latter object, that no disorder of mind shall poison his affections, pervert his sense of right, or prevent the exercise of his natural faculties – that no insane delusion shall influence his will in disposing of his property and bring about a disposal of it which, if the mind had been sound, would not have been made.[4]

Although the above text reads as though there are three elements with [4] being a rider attached to [3], the Court of Appeal has made clear that these are four distinct tests each of which must be passed in order to have testamentary capacity.[5]

A literal approach to the words used in the first three limbs of the test would indicate that they require different understanding for [1] and [2] on the one hand and [3] on the other. The requirement 'shall understand' for limbs [1] and [2] indicates actual understanding, whereas [3] indicates the ability to understand only. These words were considered by the Court of Appeal in *Hoff* v. *Atherton*,[6] where the suggestion that 'shall understand' required actual understanding was described as 'an over-literal approach to a judicial statement'. Therefore, the approach that should be taken is that the words 'shall understand' mean no more than a capacity to understand and this then aligns [1] and [2] with [3]. This construction of the test in this way provides a real practical hurdle for the draftsman, and any medical adviser, in differentiating between a client who has forgotten something, but is capable of remembering it, and a client who is not capable of remembering.[7] It is suggested that most who take will instructions will do so on the basis of establishing actual understanding as that gives a more certain understanding of the client's capacity to understand.

Limb [4] of the test above deals with the position that arose in *Banks* v. *Goodfellow*. In other words, it confirms that a disorder of the mind that does not affect the testator's dispositions in his will should not of itself lead to a will being invalid for want of capacity.

---

[3]   For an example of this, see *Hoff* v. *Atherton*, in which the testator suffered from mild to moderate dementia but the court was still satisfied that he had testamentary capacity.
[4]   *Banks* v. *Goodfellow* (1870) LR 5 QB 549 at 565.
[5]   *Sharp* v. *Adam* [2006] EWCA Civ 449; (2007) 10 ITELR 419.
[6]   [2004] EWCA Civ 1554; see also *Simon* v. *Byford* [2014] EWCA Civ 280; [2014] WTLR 1097.
[7]   *Simon* v. *Byford* [2014] EWCA Civ 280; [2014] WTLR 1097 at para.41.

As the *Banks* v. *Goodfellow* test is a common law test (i.e. one that is developed by judges, as opposed to being legislated by Parliament), it is capable of being developed further by judges as circumstances require. In *Re Key*,[8] the first modern extension of the test, the court took the view that the test should cover an inability to take decisions:

> I have been persuaded ... that [the testator] was simply unable during the week following his wife's death to exercise the decision-making powers of a testator ... I consider that [this view] is necessitated by the greater understanding of the mind now available from modern psychiatric medicine, in particular in relation to affective disorder.[9]

In considering a question of capacity, it must be remembered that everyone has the right to be capricious, foolish, biased or prejudiced, in making their will. Therefore, when a person's capacity is being assessed it is the ability to understand that is being considered, not whether or not it produces a sensible or wise decision. In *Bird* v. *Luckie* it was remarked that although the law requires a person to be capable of understanding the nature and effect of an action, it does not insist that the person behaves 'in such a manner as to deserve approbation from the prudent, the wise, or the good'.[10] There will be occasions when the capricious, irrational or eccentric nature of the will may be indicative of a lack of capacity.

The solicitor can assist the client, to a degree, in providing some information to the client. An explanation in broad terms, and simple language, of relevant basic information about the nature and effect of the will or the characteristics of joint property will be helpful. Few clients really understand these matters without them being explained. A lack of understanding after an explanation will be a warning sign for the draftsman.

Within reason, it may also be appropriate to discuss with the person making the will the characteristics of their assets and the implications of control of the assets, particularly in the context of the continuation of businesses. The court generally does not require an exact understanding of the assets or of the wider consequences of disposing of assets.[11]

But the third test, being able to comprehend and appreciate the claims to which they ought to give effect, is one that generally the person must pass unaided: 'a disposing mind and memory is one able to comprehend, of its own initiative and volition, the essential elements of will-making ... merely to be able to make rational responses is not enough, nor to repeat a tutored formula of simple terms.'[12]

---

[8]   *Re Key, Key* v. *Key* [2010] EWHC 408 (Ch); [2010] WTLR 623.

[9]   In this instance brought on by a severe reaction to bereavement. As well as an inability to make decisions, there was also a suggestion that the condition could lead to increased influence of the suggestions of others.

[10]   *Bird* v. *Luckie* (1850) 8 Hare 301.

[11]   *Simon* v. *Byford* [2014] EWCA Civ 280; [2014] WTLR 1097 at para.45.

[12]   *Leger* v. *Poirier* [1944] 3 DLR 1 at 11–12.

However, in the modern context the implications of the family provision legislation[13] are not generally understood and the solicitor, where necessary and required by the client, will provide advice on its implications for the client's intended will.

6.3 THE MENTAL CAPACITY ACT 2005

There was a prolonged period of uncertainty after October 2007 as to whether MCA 2005 replaced or modified the common law test in *Banks* v. *Goodfellow*. The point was considered fully in late 2014 in *Walker* v. *Badmin*,[14] where it was found that the Act had not replaced the common law test for testamentary capacity. This was the first time that the court had to consider this point fully.[15] Although it is possible that the Court of Appeal or the Supreme Court may reach a different decision in due course, it is suggested that practitioners can and should properly proceed on the basis that the test to apply remains the common law test.

The continued application of the common law test has relevance for the burden of proof in establishing the validity of the will where capacity is an issue. MCA 2005 would place the burden of proof on the person alleging lack of capacity, while at common law the position is different. The common law starts with a presumption that a will is valid, where it is rational and duly executed, and the burden is then on the challenger to show that there is a real doubt as to its validity. Once this is shown, the burden of proof is placed on the propounder of the will to show that the testator had capacity at the material time.[16]

The modern approach to the common law test was usefully summarised in *Perrins* v. *Holland*,[17] where Lewison J commented:

> there are six points that I should make. First, since the test is a common law test it is capable of being influenced by contemporary attitudes. Second, our general understanding of impaired mental capacity of adults has increased enormously since 1870. Third, we now recognise that an adult with impaired mental capacity is capable of making some decisions for himself, given help. Thus fourth, we recognise that the test of mental capacity is not monolithic, but is tailored to the task in hand: *Hoff* v. *Atherton* [2005] WTLR 99, 109. Fifth, contemporary attitudes toward adults with impaired capacity are more respectful of adult autonomy. Sixth, even the traditional test must be applied in the context of the particular testator and the particular estate. A testator with a complex estate

---

13 Inheritance (Provision for Family and Dependants) Act 1975.
14 *Walker* v. *Badmin* [2015] WTLR 493.
15 This decision is in line with earlier views expressed in *Re MM, Local Authority X* v. *MM (An Adult)* [2007] EWHC 2003 (Fam); [2009] 1 FLR 443; *Saulle* v. *Nouvet* [2007] EWHC 2902 (QB); [2008] WTLR 729; *Scammell* v. *Farmer* [2008] EWHC 1100 (Ch); [2008] WTLR 1261, *Pearce* v. *Beverley* [2013] EWHC 2627 (Ch); [2014] WTLR 85. It is also in line with the approach to gifts discussed in *Kicks* v. *Leigh* [2014] EWHC 3926 (Ch); [2015] WTLR 579, see **7.3.** The suggestion in *Perrins* v. *Holland* [2009] EWHC 1945 (Ch); [2009] WTLR 1387 to the contrary – i.e. that MCA 2005 replaced the common law test – was *obiter* without reasons given. Both *Fischer* v. *Diffley* [2013] EWHC 4567 (Ch); [2014] WTLR 757 and *Bray* v. *Pearce* (unreported, ChD, 6 March 2014) applied MCA 2005 in preference to the common law test without argument or reasons being given.
16 *Re Key, Key* v. *Key* [2010] EWHC 408 (Ch); [2010] WTLR 623.
17 *Perrins* v. *Holland* [2009] EWHC 1945 (Ch); [2009] WTLR 1387.

and many potential beneficiaries may need a greater degree of cognitive capability than one with a simple estate and few claimants.[18]

This offers a useful guide as to the areas that may well be developed further in future, and it may be that the common law evolves over time to reflect the principles of MCA 2005. In this regard, it is of note that the third of the points noted by Lewison J in *Perrins* v. *Holland* above is one that chimes with the principle in MCA 2005, s.1(3), namely that a person is 'not to be treated as unable to make a decision unless all practicable steps to enable him to do so have been taken without success'. Both before and after MCA 2005 came into force, the competent draftsman would seek to follow as far as possible this principle as a matter of good practice.

6.4 SUPERVENING INCAPACITY

A person may become ill, or their condition may deteriorate, between giving instructions for the preparation of a will and it being presented for execution, such that they do not have testamentary capacity when asked to execute their will. In these circumstances, if the will has been prepared strictly in accordance with the instructions given personally by the testator,[19] it may still be validly executed, if the testator recalls giving instructions to the solicitor and believes that the will being executed complies with those instructions. This is known as the rule in *Parker* v. *Felgate*.[20]

This case concerned a 28-year-old widow, Mrs Compton, who suffered from glomerulonephritis, or Bright's disease. In July 1882 she consulted her solicitor about making a new will. She wanted to leave some pecuniary legacies and the residue to Great Ormond Street Hospital. During August she experienced extreme renal failure. The will was drawn up on the basis of the earlier instructions, and it was signed by someone else in her presence and at her direction.[21] Four days later Mrs Compton died. Her father and brother, who would have benefited on her intestacy, contested the will on the ground that she lacked testamentary capacity when the will was executed.

The judge held that in a case of this nature, three questions must be asked:

1.   When the will was executed, did she remember and understand the instructions she had given to her solicitor?
2.   If it had been thought advisable to stimulate her, could she have understood each clause of the will when it was explained to her?

---

[18]   *Perrins* v. *Holland* [2009] EWHC 1945 (Ch); [2009] WTLR 1387 at para.40
[19]   *Battan Singh* v. *Armichand* [1948] AC 161.
[20]   *Parker* v. *Felgate* (1883) 8 PD 171; a recent application of this rule is *Clancy* v. *Clancy* [2003] EWHC 1885 (Ch); [2003] WTLR 1097.
[21]   Wills Act 1837, s.9(a).

3.   Was she capable of understanding, and did she understand, that she was executing a will for which she had previously given instructions to her solicitor?

These questions should be asked in the order of priority listed above, and if the answer to any one of them is 'yes' the will shall be valid. On the evidence in this particular case the jury answered 'no' to the first two questions, and 'yes' to the third, and accordingly Mrs Compton's will was valid.

The *Parker* v. *Feigate* rule was reviewed, and upheld, by the Court of Appeal in *Perrins* v. *Holland*.[22] The principle can also apply when the testator has written or typed it and his condition deteriorates between preparing the will and executing it.[23]

6.5   THE NEED FOR MEDICAL EVIDENCE: THE GOLDEN RULE

The so-called 'golden rule' identified by Templeman J[24] requires that a solicitor, when drawing up a will for an elderly person or someone who is seriously ill, should ensure that the will is witnessed or approved by a medical practitioner (see **4.5**). It has been held that this rule 'provides clear guidance as to how, in relevant cases, disputes can be avoided, or minimised (with the material relevant to the determination of the dispute contemporaneously recorded and preserved)'.[25]

On the other hand, the courts have repeatedly made the point that the views expressed by Templeman J do not amount to a rule, but simply a statement of best practice.[26] Alternatively, it may better be seen as an aspect of the draftsman's duty to ascertain that their client has the capacity to make the necessary decisions (see **6.6**).

It is also a feature of recent decisions that no criticism has been made of a solicitor's failure to follow the rule in cases of urgency[27] or where the solicitor was satisfied, after reasonable discussion and observation of the testator, that it was unnecessary to apply the rule.[28] However, where the solicitor acts in ignorance of the golden rule and the manner in which the will was dealt with falls short of that which the court expects, the solicitor may receive personal criticism from the court.[29]

On questions of capacity, the Court of Appeal has stressed that great value is to be placed on the evidence of the will draftsman:

---

22   *Perrins* v. *Holland* [2010] EWCA Civ 840; [2011] Ch 270 at para.52.
23   *Re Wallace' Estate; Solicitor of the Duchy of Cornwall* v. *Batten* [1952] 2 TLR 925.
24   See *Re Simpson* (1977) 121 Sol Jo 224; see also *Kenward* v. *Adams* (1975) *The Times*, 29 November, where Templeman J described this as 'the golden if tactless rule'.
25   *Cattermole* v. *Prisk* [2006] 1 FLR 693 at 699.
26   *Hoff* v. *Atherton* [2004] EWCA Civ 1554; [2005] WTLR 99; *Re Key, Key* v. *Key* [2010] EWHC 408 (Ch); [2010] WTLR 623.
27   *Wharton* v. *Bancroft* [2011] EWHC 3250 (Ch); [2012] WTLR 693: 'His job was to take the will of a dying man. A solicitor so placed cannot simply conjure up a medical attendant.'
28   *Scammell* v. *Farmer* [2008] EWHC 1100 (Ch); [2008] WTLR 1261.
29   *Re Key, Key* v. *Key* [2010] EWHC 408 (Ch); [2010] WTLR 623.

My concern is that the courts should not too readily upset, on the grounds of mental capacity, a will that has been drafted by an experienced independent lawyer. If, as here, an experienced lawyer has been instructed and has formed the opinion from a meeting or meetings that the testatrix understands what she is doing, the will so drafted and executed should only be set aside on the clearest evidence of lack of mental capacity.[30]

When this was considered later, it was noted that:

I accept the wisdom of [these] comments though I observe that they do not go so far as to suggest that, in every case, the evidence of an experienced and independent solicitor will, without more, be conclusive. Any view the solicitor may have formed as to the testator's capacity must be shown to be based on a proper assessment and accurate information or it is worthless ...[31]

When a medical practitioner witnesses a will, there is a strong inference that the doctor has made a formal assessment and reached the conclusion that the person has the requisite capacity to make a will (see **4.5**). To support this, the assessment made should be recorded and preserved.

Doctors should not be involved in an assessment of capacity to make a will, or act as witness to a will, in which they are named as a beneficiary. Where medical opinion is sought on an assessment as to testamentary capacity, this is best achieved by careful instructions to the doctor. There is a sample letter of instruction in **Appendix H**, setting out the relevant issues.

The circumstances usually faced by the solicitor are:[32]

1. **The client is unable to give coherent or satisfactory instructions.** The draftsman simply cannot proceed with a will. However the meeting should still be written up recording clearly as to what was observed and the conclusions reached, with reasons, as to why he could not proceed.

2. **The client can give instructions, but the draftsman is sure that the client does not have testamentary capacity.** As for 1. above, but with the additional recording of the will instructions. The draftsman also needs to consider carefully whether or not the meeting falls under description 3. below and further action is needed. It may be the case that the client is anxious to proceed and is willing to undergo a medical assessment,[33] notwithstanding the draftsman's conclusion. The draftsman would be justified in not proceeding with the will, given his own conclusion, but if the medical report finds that the client has capacity, the draftsman could be acting reasonably in proceeding notwithstanding his doubts. If, despite the medical practitioner's views, the

---

[30] *Burgess* v. *Hawes* [2013] EWCA Civ 94; [2013] WTLR 453 at para.60.

[31] *Re Ashkettle* [2013] EWHC 2125 (Ch); [2013] WTLR 1331; see also *Jeffrey* v. *Jeffrey* [2013] EWHC 1942 (Ch); [2013] WTLR 1509 on the need for supporting notes.

[32] This section is taken from M Frost, S Lawson and R Jacoby (2015) *Testamentary Capacity: Law, Practice and Medicine*, Oxford University Press, Chapter 4.

[33] Agreeing to a medical assessment will not require the same level of capacity as for a will and will therefore require a similarly lower level to retain a solicitor for this purpose.

draftsman still believed his own judgment was correct he could be justified in not proceeding. The testator then could try to engage another draftsman.

Time is critical during this process. If the client's capacity is borderline, it is most unlikely to improve with time and if the client is elderly the court would expect instructions to be dealt with swiftly because of the risk of death or loss of capacity.

3. **The client can give instructions, but the draftsman is uncertain whether or not the client has capacity.** The issue for the draftsman is can he proceed with the instructions? If he cannot form a conclusion as to capacity, the involvement of a qualified medical practitioner is justified in order to assist and not proceeding with the will until a positive medical report. The comments in [2] above apply as to time. The draftsman should have recorded carefully his observations and conclusions in order to be able to provide evidence as to why he reached the conclusion that he did.

4. **The client can give instructions, and on balance, but recognising that there may be some factors against capacity, the draftsman is satisfied that the client has capacity.** Given the draftsman's conclusion, he would be justified in proceeding with the will immediately. Introducing delay to comply with the golden rule seems unjustified if the draftsman has concluded that the client has capacity. The draftsman should have recorded carefully his observations and conclusions in order to be able to provide evidence as to why he reached the conclusion that he did. (See further the case of *Feltham* v. *Freer Bouskell* discussed in **6.6**.)

A medical report may assist in the event that the draftsman's judgment might be challenged, but it seems to contradict the draftsman's view of capacity to delay the will for this. Should the client die where there was a delay waiting for a medical report, where the draftsman had concluded for himself there was capacity, this can cause difficulties for the draftsman if there is a *White* v. *Jones* claim[34] (i.e. a claim that the failure to carry out the necessary tasks led to loss to an intended beneficiary or beneficiaries). A medical report shortly after the will is prepared and executed could substantially assist in supporting the draftsman's view.

5. **The client can give instructions and the draftsman is satisfied that the client has capacity.** This will cover most clients, but where the client is old or ill it should not be the case that the draftsman omits to write up his observations relevant to capacity. A later challenge to the will may well require him to give evidence as to his conclusions.

---

[34] *White* v. *Jones* [1995] 1 All ER 691.

6.6 THE DUTY OF THE DRAFTSMAN TO ASCERTAIN CAPACITY

When considering a client's capacity to make a will, it should not be overlooked that that the process starts with the client's engagement of the solicitor. Therefore, initially the solicitor should consider whether or not the client has the capacity to do this (see **2.1**). It is suggested that the capacity to retain a solicitor to prepare a will must be at the same level of understanding as that for giving the instructions for the will. If this was not the case, there would be the unreal position of a person being able to contract validly with a solicitor to prepare a will that the person was neither capable of giving instructions for nor executing. The solicitor will be assessing the person as to both the ability to engage him to prepare a will and his testamentary capacity.

In *Feltham* v. *Freer Bouskell*, the court held that: '[w]here a solicitor is instructed to prepare and execute a will for a client, if the client does not have capacity, he has no client and cannot accept instructions. If he has concerns as to mental capacity, he must either refuse the instructions and make the position clear to the client, or take steps to satisfy himself as to his client's mental capacity promptly.'[35] The emphasis on promptness here is of great importance in the light of the draftsman's duty of care when preparing a will.[36]

In *Feltham* v. *Freer Bouskell* the court also made the clearest statement yet that the English court considers that the draftsman *must* satisfy himself of his client's testamentary capacity: '[the solicitor] accepted instructions to act for [the testatrix] in relation to her desire to change her will. He did so subject to the requirement to satisfy himself that she was of sufficient mental capacity to alter her will.'[37]

In the light of this, it is unwise for any draftsman to:

- proceed without properly forming an opinion as to the client's capacity, or
- fail to take steps to assess their client's capacity in any case where there are grounds to doubt that capacity.

Although there is a presumption of capacity both at common law and under MCA 2005,[38] it would be most unwise to rely upon this presumption in any case where there are grounds to consider that it may be displaced, and where taking steps *at the time* could resolve that doubt. This is particularly so where the client may have fluctuating testamentary capacity (see further **4.2.2**).

---

[35] *Feltham* v. *Freer Bouskell* [2013] EWHC 1952 (Ch); [2013] WTLR 1363 at para.52.
[36] *White* v. *Jones* [1995] 1 All ER 691.
[37] *Feltham* v. *Freer Bouskell* [2013] EWHC 1952 (Ch); [2013] WTLR 1363 at para.64; decisions of the Canadian court have expressed this point often and clearly, as has the Australian court. Opposed to this, the New Zealand court in *Knox* v. *Till* [1999] 2 NZLR 753; [2000] Lloyd's RE PN 49 expressed the rather startling view that there was no duty to refuse to act in preparing a will where a client lacked capacity.
[38] MCA 2005, s.1(2).

6.7 CHECKLIST

The following checklist covers what is meant by 'understanding the nature of the act and its effects', 'understanding the extent of the property being disposed of' and being 'able to comprehend and appreciate the claims to which a person making a will ought to give effect'. It is not intended to be either authoritative or exhaustive, but to give an indication of the issues which the testator must be able to understand, depending on their individual circumstances. For the first three elements considered below the test of capacity involves the person's ability to understand issues that are central to the will. Information may be communicated by the solicitor to aid understanding. The final element of the test concerns the person's ability to exercise choice between those with claims on the person's bounty.

6.7.1 The nature of the act of making a will

People making a will should be able to understand that:

- they will die;
- the will shall come into operation on their death, but not before;
- they can change or revoke the will at any time before their death, provided they have the capacity to do so.

6.7.2 The effects of making a will

A testator should be able to understand (and where necessary, be able to make decisions regarding):

- who should be appointed as executor(s) (and perhaps why they should be appointed);
- who is bequeathed what in the will;
- if a beneficiary's gift is to be outright or conditional (for example, where the beneficiary is only entitled to the income from a lump sum during their lifetime, or is allowed to occupy residential property for the rest of the beneficiary's life);
- that if the testator spends money or gives away or sells assets during their lifetime, the beneficiaries' interests will be diminished or extinguished;
- that a beneficiary might die before the testator;
- if the testator has already made a will and, if so, how and why the new will differs from the old one;[39]
- the reasonably foreseeable consequences of making or not making a will at this time.

---

[39] The Court of Appeal in *Simon* v. *Byford* [2014] EWCA Civ 280; [2014] WTLR 1097 at para.41 has cast considerable doubt on this point but, in practical terms, looking for the client's ability or inability to understand this point can be of considerable significance in forming an opinion as to their capacity.

6.7.3 The extent of the property

It is important to note that the judgment in *Banks* v. *Goodfellow*[40] contains the word 'extent', rather than value. Practical difficulties can arise when the investments of the person making the will are managed by somebody else and there are no recent statements or valuations. In these cases solicitors should apply a reasonableness test to any estimate the person making the will gives about the extent of their wealth.[41]

A testator should be able to understand:

- the extent of all the property owned solely;
- the devolution of jointly owned property on death, and those joint interests that will devolve under the terms of the will;
- whether there are benefits payable on death which might not pass under the terms of the will (e.g. insurance policies and pension rights);
- that the extent of their property could change during their lifetime;
- whether they have any debts and how these are to be paid.

6.7.4 The claims of others

Testators should be able to comprehend and appreciate the claims to which they ought to give effect. The 'claims to which they ought to give effect' will usually mean those individuals connected to a testator by:

- blood, adoption, marriage, or civil partnership;
- cohabitation;
- dependency;
- nurturing and upbringing;
- close friendship.

In some circumstances this might include philanthropic institutions with which the testator is closely connected.

While a testator has the right to ignore these claims, even to the extent of being prejudiced or capricious towards them,[42] he must be capable of understanding his reasons for preferring some beneficiaries or excluding others. For example, possible beneficiaries may:

- already have received adequate provision from the testator;
- be financially better off than others being considered;
- have been more attentive or caring than others being considered;
- have completely estranged from the testator;
- have behaved criminally towards the testator;

---

[40] *Banks* v. *Goodfellow* (1870) LR 5 QB.

[41] *Scammell* v. *Farmer* [2008] EWHC 1100 (Ch); [2008] WTLR 1261 at para.97; *Blackman* v. *Man* [2007] EWHC 3162 (Ch); [2008] WTLR 389 at paras.118–119. See also the Australian case of *Kerr* v. *Badran* [2004] NSWSC 735 at para.49.

[42] That right is not unlimited: see the provisions of the Inheritance (Provision for Family and Dependants) Act 1975.

- be in greater need of assistance than others because of their age, or physical or mental disabilities.

None of the above requires a testator to have a lawyer's understanding of the terms of a will, merely that its dispositions are understood in their simplest terms.[43]

6.8 CAPACITY TO REVOKE A WILL

When a will is revoked it will be of no effect on the testator's death. A will can be revoked in one of three ways:

- If the testator subsequently gets married or enters into a civil partnership, the existing will is automatically revoked by operation of law,[44] unless it was specifically made in contemplation of that marriage or civil partnership (capacity to marry or enter into a civil partnership is discussed in **11.4**). If a testator who lacks testamentary capacity marries, any previous will is revoked if the testator has the requisite capacity to marry (which is a lower level of understanding than that required for a valid will).[45] A marriage which is voidable because one party lacked the capacity to understand the nature of the marriage contract[46] will revoke a will previously made by that person.[47]
- Validly executing a will which expressly states that the earlier will is revoked. In this case the usual rules on testamentary capacity apply to the later will.
- With the intention of revoking the will, the testator personally burns, tears or destroys it, or authorises somebody else to burn, tear or destroy it in the testator's presence.[48] This requires the capacity to revoke a will on the part of the testator (see below).

The capacity required to revoke a will by destruction was considered in *Re Sabatini*.[49] The argument was put forward that a lower standard of capacity was acceptable when a will is revoked by destruction. A person who was incapable of making a new will might understand that a beneficiary had become unworthy of their inheritance and wished to deprive them of it by tearing up the will and dying intestate. The judge rejected this argument, and said that as a general rule an individual must have the same degree of understanding when destroying a will as when making one. *Re Sabatini* established that a person who intends to revoke their will must be capable of:

- understanding the nature of the act of revoking a will;

---

43 *Harrison* v. *Rowan* (1820) 3 Washington 585.
44 Wills Act 1837, ss.18 and 18B.
45 *Durham* v. *Durham* (1885) 10 PD 80; *Sheffield City Council* v. *E (An Alleged Patient)* [2004] EWHC 2808 (Fam); [2005] Fam 326 at para.68.
46 Matrimonial Causes Act 1973, s.12(c) and Civil Partnership Act 2004, s.50(1)(a).
47 Matrimonial Causes Act 1973, s.16.
48 Wills Act 1837, s.20.
49 *Re Sabatini* (1970) 114 Sol Jo 35.

- understanding the effect of revoking the will (this might even involve a greater understanding of the operation of the intestacy rules than is necessary for the purpose of making a will, although there is no direct authority on the point and it would be extremely difficult to prove retrospectively);
- understanding the extent of their property;
- comprehending and appreciating the claims to which they ought to give effect.

6.9 STATUTORY WILLS

If a person either loses or never had testamentary capacity, an application can be made to the Court of Protection for a statutory will (or statutory codicil) to be drawn up and executed on that person's behalf.[50] The will, once executed, has the same effect as if that person had executed the will personally.[51]

The Court of Protection will require evidence of lack of testamentary capacity. The Court of Protection is required to apply the statutory test set down in MCA 2005, s.2. However, it appears, in practice, that the Court of Protection will apply the common law test of testamentary capacity[52] (see **6.2**). This was the test applied in *A, B and C* v. *X and Z*[53] by Hedley J. Although the point was fairly briefly dealt with,[54] Hedley J found, by implication, that the Court of Protection's jurisdiction to make a will could not arise without finding that the would-be testator failed the common law test of capacity.

In addition to information about the extent of the person's property and affairs, the court will require information as to the person's state of mind and health, their current and future care needs, their wishes and feelings (including, in particular, any wishes and feelings expressed in writing prior to the loss of testamentary capacity), their life expectancy and so forth.[55] The terms of an existing will and/or codicils will be relevant – as can previous wills.

In *Re (P)*,[56] Lewison J held that the aim of the court's inquiry when making a statutory will is to establish what is in the person's best interests, rather than (as previously) what the person might be expected to have done. In order to make that determination, it is necessary to adopt the same structured approach to determining the person's best interests as the court would adopt in other circumstances. Other cases subsequently have placed greater emphasis upon the individual's wishes and feelings (see **3.9**), but the ultimate decision must be the one that the court considers to be in the person's best interests.

---

[50] MCA 2005, s.18(1)(i) and Sched.2, paras.2 and 3.
[51] MCA 2005, Sched.2, para.4.
[52] *Banks* v. *Goodfellow* [1870] LR 5 QB 549.
[53] *A, B and C* v. *X and Z* [2012] EWHC 2400 (COP); [2013] WTLR 187.
[54] Permission to appeal the decision was granted, but the appeal was subsequently withdrawn.
[55] The information required by the court, and the procedures to be followed in are set out in Practice Direction 9F to the Court of Protection Rules: Applications Relating to Statutory Wills, Codicils, Settlements and Other Dealings with P's Property.
[56] *Re P* [2009] EWHC 163 (Ch); [2009] WTLR 651.

In the majority of cases, applications for a statutory will are likely to be made by an attorney appointed under an LPA with authority to deal with the person's property and affairs, or by a deputy appointed by the Court of Protection to make financial decisions for the person. The fact that a person is under the jurisdiction of the Court of Protection (either in relation to their property and affairs or their welfare), or has an attorney or deputy acting on their behalf, does not necessarily mean that the person lacks testamentary capacity.[57] If the person has testamentary capacity a solicitor can be instructed and the will drawn up in the normal way.

---

[57]   *A, B and C* v. *X and Z* [2012] EWHC 2400 (COP); [2013] WTLR 187.

CHAPTER 7

Capacity to make a gift

7.1 Introduction
7.2 The test of capacity: the common law
7.3 The Mental Capacity Act 2005
7.4 Burden of proof

7.5 Checklist
7.6 Gifts made by attorneys
7.7 Gifts made by deputies
7.8 Risk of financial abuse

7.1 INTRODUCTION

It is not uncommon for people (especially older people) to give away some or most of their assets to others, usually to their children or grandchildren.

The motivation for lifetime giving is often saving inheritance tax that may become payable on the person's death. A lifetime gift is completely exempt from inheritance tax under the Inheritance Tax Act 1984, s.19 as to the first £3,000 per tax year (an unused exemption can be carried forward one year). To the extent that it is not exempt, it is treated as potentially exempt; no tax is charged at the date the gift is made and it will become completely exempt if the transferor survives seven years from the date of the gift. Specific anti-avoidance provisions exist to prevent a taxpayer making a gift and then continuing to benefit from the gifted property. Provided the anti-avoidance provisions do not apply, giving away assets is an effective way of reducing tax on death, but professional advisers should counsel caution. People are living much longer and may have unforeseen financial needs.

Sometimes a gift is made for other reasons: perhaps to prevent assets falling into the hands of creditors on bankruptcy, or to enable the giver to claim social security benefits, or to be funded by a local authority if the person has to go into a care home. Parliament has anticipated most of these schemes and the relevant legislation usually contains lengthy anti-avoidance provisions which could render such gifts ineffective. The Law Society has also published a Practice Note on the subject of gifts of assets.[1]

---

[1] Law Society Practice Note: Making Gifts of Assets (6 October 2011), available at **www.lawsociety.org.uk/support-services/advice/practice-notes/gifts-of-assets/**. This Practice Note

Anyone who is asked to assess whether a person has capacity to make a gift should:

(a) not let the underlying purpose or motive affect the assessment, unless it is so perverse as to cast doubt on capacity; and

(b) be satisfied that the giver is acting freely and voluntarily, and that no one is pressurising the person into making a gift.

A professional who is the likely recipient should not be involved in an assessment of capacity to make a gift.

7.2   THE TEST OF CAPACITY: THE COMMON LAW

The most important case on capacity to make a gift is *Re Beaney (Deceased)*.[2] In this case a 64-year-old widow with three grown up children owned and lived in a three-bedroom semi-detached house. Her elder daughter lived with her. In May 1973, a few days after being admitted to hospital suffering from advanced dementia, the widow signed a deed of gift transferring the house to her elder daughter. The widow died intestate the following year. Her son and younger daughter applied successfully to the court for a declaration that the transfer of the house was invalid.

The rival contentions as to the test of capacity were:

• a narrow view which was that it was only necessary for Mrs Beaney to understand (1) that she was making a gift, (2) that the subject-matter of the gift was the house, and (3) that the person to whom she was giving it was her daughter; or

• a wider view that Mrs Beaney must also understand that she was giving away her only asset of value, and was thus depriving her other two children of any real interest in her estate.

The wider view was essentially an argument that the degree of understanding required for a lifetime gift is the same as that required for the making of a valid will, where it is necessary to show an understanding of the claims of all potential beneficiaries and the extent of the property to be disposed of (see **6.2**).

The judge in the case set out the following criteria for capacity to make a lifetime gift:

> The degree or extent of understanding required in respect of any instrument is relative to the particular transaction which it is to effect ... Thus, at one extreme, if the subject-matter and value of a gift are trivial in relation to the donor's other assets, a low degree of understanding will suffice. But, at the other, if its effect is to dispose of the donor's only asset of value and thus, for practical purposes, to preempt the devolution of his estate under [the donor's] will or ... intestacy, then the degree of understanding required is as

---

replaces previous guidance: *Gifts of Property: Implications for Future Liability to Pay for Long-term Care* (Law Society, 2000).

[2] *Re Beaney (Deceased)* [1978] 2 All ER 595.

high as that required for a will, and the donor must understand the claims of all potential donees and the extent of the property to be disposed of.[3]

The judge added that, even where the degree of understanding in making a gift of lesser value is not as high as that required for a will, the donor must be capable of understanding that they are making an outright gift and not, for example, merely transferring property to someone else so that it can be sold.

When someone wishes to make a substantial gift it is prudent to consider whether the donor understands the effect that disposing of the asset could have on the rest of their life or on the life of their dependants. In *Sutton* v. *Sutton*[4] a gift of the family home by a father to his son was set aside as invalid. There was substantial evidence of mental confusion. The judge held that Mr Sutton needed to be capable not only of understanding that he was giving away his house to his son, but also that the effect of the gift would be to deprive himself and his wife (in the event of her surviving him) of any entitlement to the house or legal right to stay there.

7.3 THE MENTAL CAPACITY ACT 2005

The MCA Code of Practice[5] makes specific reference to the common law tests of capacity and, at para.4.32, refers to *Re Beaney* in relation to capacity to make lifetime gifts. It states at para.4.33 that the Act is in line with the common law tests and does not replace them. It continues: '[w]hen cases come before the court on the above issues, judges can adopt the new definition if they think that it is appropriate.'

In *Kicks* v. *Leigh*[6] (decided in late 2014) the question of whether MCA 2005 should be adopted in relation to the test for capacity to make lifetime gifts was subject to detailed consideration for the first time. Stephen Morris QC, sitting as a Deputy High Court Judge, said that there was 'some uncertainty as to the potential interplay between' MCA 2005 and the common law, and noted that decisions made since MCA 2005 came into force were conflicting. The judge reviewed all the relevant decisions in order to decide whether he should apply the common law test, the MCA test or a combination of the two.

The judge said that he had not found it easy to decide but concluded that the correct approach to a post-MCA lifetime gift is to apply the common law principles in *Re Beaney* rather than those set out in MCA 2005, ss.2 and 3. He was particularly persuaded by the fact that MCA 2005, s.1 states that its principles apply 'for the purposes of this Act'. The Act is concerned with the powers of the Court of Protection to make decisions about the personal welfare (such as residence, medical treatment) and property and affairs (such as control, sale or acquisition of property) on behalf of a living person who lacks capacity. This, the judge considered, was a

---

[3]   *Re Beaney (Deceased)* [1978] 2 All ER 595 at 601f–h.
[4]   *Sutton* v. *Sutton* [2009] EWHC 2576 (Ch); [2010] WTLR 115.
[5]   Office of the Public Guardian (2007) *Mental Capacity Act 2005 Code of Practice*, available at **www.gov.uk/government/publications/mental-capacity-act-code-of-practice**.
[6]   *Kicks* v. *Leigh* [2014] EWHC 3926 (Ch); [2015] WTLR 579.

different task to that imposed upon a court in civil proceedings deciding – retrospectively – whether a person had the capacity to make a lifetime gift.

The judge said it was not appropriate to adopt the statutory test as it did more than merely encapsulate the common law principles. He thought the statutory test contained in MCA 2005, s.2(1) expanded upon common law principles, for example by identifying a number of specific sub-categories of capacity, and by dealing expressly with short-term memory retention. Furthermore, the approach to the burden of proof in MCA 2005, s.1(2) differs from that applied under the common law (see also **7.4**).

In light of the differences between MCA 2005 and the common law, one difficulty for those assessing capacity is what view to take of an unwise decision. MCA 2005 specifically states[7] that a person is not to be treated as unable to make a decision merely because they make an unwise decision. At common law the assessor will need to be satisfied that the donor understands the consequences of the gift. If the decision is 'obviously irrational or out of character'[8] it may trigger the need for a more thorough assessment of capacity. It may be that this question is revisited in due course in another case.

In respect of gifts made before the coming into force of MCA 2005 on 1 October 2007, it should be emphasised that the courts will, in any event, approach the question of capacity without reference to MCA 2005, but rather by the common law test set out above.[9]

7.4   BURDEN OF PROOF

Under MCA 2005 a person must be assumed to have capacity unless it is established that he lacks capacity. This suggests that the burden of proof starts with and remains throughout with the person alleging lack of capacity.

At common law, the burden of proving lack of mental capacity lies on the person alleging it. However, the evidential burden may shift from a claimant to the defendant if a prima facie case of lack of capacity is established. In *Kicks* v. *Leigh*[10] the judge, having reviewed the relevant cases, confirmed that while the legal burden is on the party asserting incapacity, if that party adduces evidence to raise a sufficient doubt from which incapacity can be inferred, then the evidential burden shifts to the opposing party.

---

[7]   MCA 2005, s.1(4).

[8]   Office of the Public Guardian (2007) *Mental Capacity Act 2005 Code of Practice*, available at **www.gov.uk/government/publications/mental-capacity-act-code-of-practice**, para.2.11.

[9]   See by analogy to the position in respect of testamentary capacity, *Scammell* v. *Farmer* [2008] EWHC 1100 (Ch); [2008] WTLR 1261, paras.25–29.

[10]   *Kicks* v. *Leigh* [2014] EWHC 3926 (Ch); [2015] WTLR 579.

7.5 CHECKLIST

This checklist includes some of the points that may need to be considered in order to establish whether someone has the capacity to make a lifetime gift of a substantial asset. Some elements may involve assessing the person's ability to receive and evaluate information which may possibly be communicated by others, such as a solicitor or other adviser. Others involve the person's ability to exercise personal choice. A lower level of capacity is sufficient where the gift is insignificant in the context of the person's assets as a whole.

7.5.1 The nature of the transaction

People making a gift should understand the following about the nature of the transaction:

- that it is a gift (rather than, say, a loan or a mortgage advance or the acquisition of a stake or share in the recipient's business or property);
- whether they expect to receive anything in return;
- whether they intend the gift to take effect immediately or at some later date (perhaps on death);
- who the recipient is;
- whether they have already made substantial gifts to the recipient or others;
- whether the gift is a one-off, or part of a larger transaction or series of transactions;
- the fact that if the gift is outright they will not be able to ask for the asset to be returned;
- the underlying purpose of the transaction.

7.5.2 The effect of the transaction

People who make a gift should understand the possible effects of the transaction, such as:

- the effect that making the gift will have on their own standard of living in the future, having regard to all the circumstances including their age, life expectancy, income, financial resources, financial responsibilities and financial needs;
- the effect that receiving the gift may have on the recipient;
- the effect that the making of the gift will have on their dependants.

7.5.3 The extent of the property

People who make a gift should understand the following about the extent of the property:

100

- that the subject-matter of the gift belongs to them, and that they are entitled to dispose of it;
- the extent (and possibly the value) of the gift in relation to all the circumstances and, in particular, in the context of their other assets.

7.5.4   The claims to which the giver ought to give effect

People who make a gift should be able to comprehend and appreciate the claims of the potential beneficiaries under their will or intestacy. For instance, they must appreciate:

- the effect the gift could have on other beneficiaries;
- why the recipient is more deserving than others (for example, the recipient may be less well-off financially, may have devoted more time and attention to caring for the person, or may be in need of greater assistance because of age or disability);
- whether it is necessary to compensate others, perhaps by making a new will;
- whether there was any bias or favouritism towards the recipient before making the gift.

7.6   GIFTS MADE BY ATTORNEYS

The provisions allowing attorneys to make gifts will vary depending on whether they are acting under lasting powers of attorney (LPAs) (see **5.3**) or enduring powers of attorney (EPAs) (see **5.4**).

7.6.1   Lasting powers of attorney

An attorney under a property and affairs LPA can only make gifts of the donor's money or belongings to:

- people who are related to or connected with the donor (including the attorney) on:

    - births or birthdays;
    - weddings or wedding anniversaries;
    - civil partnership ceremonies or anniversaries; or
    - any other occasion when families, friends or associates usually give presents.[11]

- any charity to whom the donor made or might have been expected to make gifts.[12]

---

[11]   MCA 2005, s.12(3)(b).
[12]   MCA 2005, s.12(2)(b).

The value of any gift or donation must be reasonable and take into account the size of the donor's estate.

The MCA Code of Practice states:

> The Donor cannot use the LPA to make more extensive gifts than those allowed under section 12 of the Act. But they can impose stricter conditions or restrictions on the attorney's powers to make gifts. They should state these restrictions clearly in the LPA document when they are creating it. When deciding on appropriate gifts, the attorney should consider the donor's wishes and feelings to work out what would be in the donor's best interests. The attorney can apply to the Court of Protection for permission to make gifts that are not included in the LPA.[13]

There is a simplified procedure for making gifts not specified in the LPA which may be used provided the gifts are not disproportionately large and the applicant knows or reasonably believes that there are unlikely to be any objections.[14]

In *Re Buckley*[15] Senior Judge Lush said that, subject to a sensible *de minimis* exception, where the potential infringement is so minor that it would be disproportionate to make a formal application to the court, an application *must* be made to the court for an order[16] in any of the following cases:

(a) gifts that exceed the limited scope of the authority conferred on attorneys by MCA 2005, s.12;

(b) loans to the attorney or to members of the attorney's family;

(c) any investment in the attorney's own business;

(d) sales or purchases at an undervalue; and

(e) any other transactions in which there is a conflict between the interests of the donor and the interests of the attorney.

Senior Judge Lush did not give any guidance in that case as to what a sensible *de minimis* exception would be but in *Re GM*[17] he gave further guidance. To be both proportionate and pragmatic, and to prevent the court from being overwhelmed with applications, with which it does not have the resources to cope, this *de minimis* exception can be construed as covering the annual inheritance tax (IHT) exemption of £3,000 and the annual small gifts exemption of £250 per person, up to a maximum of, say, 10 people in the following circumstances:

(a) where P has a life expectancy of less than five years;

(b) their estate exceeds the nil rate band for IHT purposes, currently £325,000;

---

[13] Office of the Public Guardian (2007) *Mental Capacity Act 2005 Code of Practice*, para.7.42, available at **www.gov.uk/government/publications/mental-capacity-act-code-of-practice**. See also the guidance issued to property and affairs attorneys, available at **www.gov.uk/government/ publications/getting-started-as-an-attorney-property-and-financial-affairs**.

[14] Court of Protection (23 June 2015) Practice Direction 9D: Applications by Currently Appointed Deputies, Attorneys and Donees in Relation to P's Property and Affairs, available at **www.judiciary.gov.uk/publications**.

[15] *Re Buckley* [2013] EWHC 2965 (COP); [2013] WTLR 373.

[16] Under MCA 2005, s.23.

[17] *Re GM* [2013] EWHC 2966 (COP); [2013] WTLR 835.

(c)   the gifts are affordable having regard to P's care costs and will not adversely affect P's standard of care and quality of life; and

(d)   there is no evidence that P would be opposed to gifts of this magnitude being made on their behalf.

He also said that the first and paramount consideration must be whether the gift is in P's best interests, and other circumstances to which regard should be given, in addition to the size of P's estate, include, but are not limited to, the following:

- the extent to which P was in the habit of making gifts or loans of a particular size or nature before the onset of incapacity;
- P's anticipated life expectancy;
- the possibility that P may require residential or nursing care and the projected cost of such care;
- whether P is in receipt of aftercare pursuant to MHA 1983, s.117 or NHS Continuing Healthcare;
- the extent to which any gifts may interfere with the devolution of P's estate under their will or intestacy; and
- the impact of inheritance tax on P's death.

7.6.2   Enduring powers of attorney

An attorney acting on behalf of the donor of an EPA (see **5.4**) has limited authority to make gifts provided that there is nothing in the power itself which prohibits the attorney from making gifts, and 'the value of each gift is not unreasonable having regard to all the circumstances and in particular the size of the donor's estate'.[18]

Attorneys can only make gifts to:

- a charity to which the donor has made gifts, or might be expected to make gifts if they were not mentally disordered;
- any person (including the attorney) who is related to or connected with the donor, provided that the gift is of a seasonal nature, or made on the occasion of a birth or marriage, or on the anniversary of a birth or marriage.

These rules apply regardless of whether the EPA is registered or unregistered, but an attorney cannot make gifts (unless authorised to do so by the Court of Protection) while the power is in the course of being registered. If the EPA is registered and the attorney wishes to make more substantial gifts, or gifts to people who are not related to or connected with the donor, or on an occasion other than a birth or marriage or birthday or wedding anniversary, the attorney should apply for an order of the Court of Protection (see **5.5** and **7.7**).

---

[18]   MCA 2005, Sched.4, para.3(3).

There is a simplified process for making such gifts provided they are not disproportionately large and the applicant knows or reasonably believes that there are unlikely to be any objections.[19]

7.7 GIFTS MADE BY DEPUTIES

There are no specific provisions in MCA 2005 governing the powers of deputies to make gifts or loans or enter into financial transactions in which a gift element is proposed on behalf of the person on whose behalf they are appointed to make financial decisions. The court order appointing the deputy will set out the extent, if any, of the deputy's powers to make gifts or loans (see **Appendix C**). It will commonly replicate the powers contained in MCA 2005, s.12 for attorneys acting under a lasting power of appointment to make gifts.

If the deputy considers that those powers are insufficient, there is a simplified mechanism by which applications to the Court of Protection can be made for approval of such gifts or transactions, so long as they are not disproportionately large and the applicant knows or reasonably believes that there are unlikely to be any objections.[20]

Most deputies are required to provide some sort of security (for example, a guarantee bond) to the Public Guardian to cover any loss as a result of the deputy's actions, including making unauthorised gifts of the person's money or property.[21] In cases of abuse the court can call in the bond which allows the estate of the incapacitous person to receive funds quickly to compensate for losses that have been incurred through the default of his deputy. It avoids the delay and expense which would otherwise be incurred bringing proceedings and enforcing any judgment obtained against a defaulting deputy. The defaulting deputy will usually face proceedings brought by the bond provider.[22]

Deputies should also have regard to the guidance issued by the Office of the Public Guardian as to how they are to discharge their duties.[23]

---

[19] Court of Protection (23 June 2015) Practice Direction 9D: Applications by Currently Appointed Deputies, Attorneys and Donees in Relation to P's Property and Affairs, available at **www.judiciary.gov.uk/publications**.

[20] Court of Protection (23 June 2015) Practice Direction 9D: Applications by Currently Appointed Deputies, Attorneys and Donees in Relation to P's Property and Affairs, available at **www.judiciary.gov.uk/publications**.

[21] MCA 2005, s.19(9)(a).

[22] For examples of bonds being called in, see *Re Joan Treadwell (Deceased), Public Guardian & Lutz* [2013] EWHC 2409 (COP); [2013] COPLR 587 and *Re Meek* [2014] EWCOP 1; [2014] WTLR 1155.

[23] Available at **www.gov.uk/government/publications/deputy-guidance-how-to-carry-out-your-duties**.

7.8   RISK OF FINANCIAL ABUSE

People who are (or are becoming) incapable of looking after their own affairs are at particular risk of financial abuse and one of the easiest forms of abuse is the improper gifting of their money or other assets. This may be where vulnerable people are persuaded to give away money or property without being fully aware of the circumstances, or having the capacity to do so, or when people appointed to act on their behalf (such as attorneys, deputies or appointees) abuse their position of trust (see **5.7**). The careful assessment of capacity to make a gift is therefore an important safeguard against financial abuse.

CHAPTER 8

Capacity to litigate

8.1 Introduction
8.2 The test of capacity to litigate
8.3 Applying the test

8.4 Litigation friends
8.5 Implications of incapacity
8.6 The Court of Protection

8.1 INTRODUCTION

People who lack capacity to conduct legal proceedings may become parties to proceedings in the High Court of Justice, the County Court and the Family Court, as well as in the Court of Protection (see **Appendix C**). Such individuals are traditionally said to lack 'litigation capacity' or 'capacity to litigate'; while such descriptions are not, in fact, entirely accurate, they are so well entrenched that they are used in this chapter.[1]

When an adult who lacks litigation capacity or a child is involved in legal proceedings (see also **2.1**), a procedure is needed to enable the proceedings to continue by appointing someone else to give instructions and otherwise conduct the proceedings on their behalf. These procedures are to be found in the relevant rules for the type of proceedings, which are:

- Civil Procedure Rules 1998 (CPR), Part 21.
- Family Procedure Rules 2010 (FPR), Part 15 (adults) and Part 16 (children).
- Family Procedure (Adoption) Rules 2005 (FP(A)R), Part 7.
- Insolvency Rules 1986 (IR), Part 7, Chapter 7.
- Court of Protection Rules 2007 (COPR), Part 17.

The majority of this chapter is concerned with adults who lack capacity to litigate in civil proceedings other than in the Court of Protection. The position of the subject of proceedings before the Court of Protection is addressed at **8.6**.

---

[1] The test now contained in the material rules (save for the anomalous Insolvency Rules 1986) is whether the individual lacks the capacity to conduct proceedings.

The adult litigant who lacks litigation capacity is referred to in civil, family and adoption proceedings as a 'protected party', and in insolvency proceedings as an 'incapacitated person' (see **8.2**). A child may also in some circumstances be a protected party (for example, in the case of a claim for damages on behalf of a brain injured child who will not be capable of handling the award after reaching the age of 18).

The litigant may also be a 'protected beneficiary' if they will lack capacity to manage any money recovered in the proceedings. The representative in civil and family proceedings is known as a 'litigation friend'.

The purpose of the various rules is to ensure that:

- adults who lack litigation capacity or children are represented by a suitable adult (a litigation friend);
- compromises and settlements agreed on their behalf are approved by the court;
- if an individual is also deemed to be a 'protected beneficiary', there is supervision of any money recovered in the proceedings.

Substantive decisions which determine how any significant funds recovered or damages awarded will be administered will be taken by the Court of Protection on the basis of its own determinations of capacity at times when they are necessary and in respect of particular decisions. Such decisions may also be made by a deputy appointed by the Court of Protection with the appropriate authority (see **5.5** and **Appendix C**).

Any proceedings involving a child or protected person conducted without such a representative will be invalid and any settlement set aside, unless the court retrospectively gives its approval.[2]

Solicitors asked to act on behalf of a protected person should ensure that a suitable person is put forward for appointment as litigation friend (see **8.4**). The appointment is generally made by the court that will hear the proceedings, but it is possible for a person in some cases to become a litigation friend without a court order.[3] Care should be taken to select a litigation friend who has no actual or potential conflict of interest with the person who lacks capacity. In most cases, a relative, friend or someone with a close connection with the protected party will act as litigation friend. A deputy already appointed by the Court of Protection may also be appointed to act as litigation friend, and will be entitled to do so in proceedings if the Court of Protection has specifically authorised them to conduct legal proceedings on behalf of the protected person. Where there is no suitable person willing and able to act as litigation friend, the Official Solicitor to the Senior Courts will consider accepting appointment, but should first be consulted and his consent

---

[2] *Dunhill* v. *Burgin* [2014] UKSC 18; [2014] 1 WLR 933. This case was decided in relation to CPR 1998, but it is suggested would be followed in relation to the other courts identified above. See, in regard to the Insolvency Rules 1986 *Hunt* v. *Fylde Borough Council* [2008] BPIR 1368 (which is not, strictly, a precedent, as it is a decision of a District Judge, but has been referred to with approval subsequently: see *De Louville De Toucy* v. *Bonhams 1793 Ltd* [2011] EWHC 3809 (Ch); [2012] BPIR 793).

[3] This will depend upon the specific rules that apply to the court in question.

obtained (which will only be forthcoming if, inter alia, security for his costs is given). Further information on the role of the Official Solicitor is given in **Appendix E.**

The courts have sought to discourage satellite litigation as to whether a litigation friend is required. Where an application to appoint a litigation friend is made with good reason and is supported by responsible evidence in accordance with the relevant procedural rules, there should be no need for the other party to the litigation to become involved except where that party has a financial interest (e.g. a claim for damages following a brain injury where the amount of damages may be increased if the Court of Protection becomes involved).[4]

8.2 THE TEST OF CAPACITY TO LITIGATE

8.2.1 The common law

The capacity to litigate was considered for the first time in detail in an English court by Wright J, and subsequently by the Court of Appeal, in *Masterman-Lister* v. *Brutton & Co*,[5] from which the following principles emerged:

1. Although there is no requirement in CPR Part 21 that a judge should consider medical evidence or be satisfied as to incapacity before a party to civil proceedings is to be treated as a patient (now a protected person), since the implementation of the Human Rights Act 1998 (and in particular art.6(1) of the European Convention on Human Rights), the court should always, as a matter of practice, at the first convenient opportunity, investigate the question of capacity whenever there is any reason to suspect that it might be absent. This means that, even where the issue does not seem to be contentious, a judge who is responsible for case management will almost certainly require the assistance of a medical report before being able to be satisfied that incapacity exists.

2. The test to be applied to determine a person's capacity is issue-specific. In relation to capacity to litigate, what has to be considered is whether a party to legal proceedings is capable of understanding, with the assistance of such proper explanation (in broad terms and simple language) from legal advisers and other experts as the case may require, the matters on which their consent or decision is likely to be necessary in the course of those proceedings.[6] If the party has the capacity to understand what is needed to pursue or defend a

---

[4]   *Folks* v. *Faizey* [2006] EWCA Civ 381.

[5]   See *Masterman-Lister* v. *Jewell; Masterman-Lister v Brutton & Co* [2002] EWHC 417 (QB); and *Masterman-Lister* v. *Brutton & Co; Masterman-Lister* v. *Jewell* [2002] EWCA Civ 1889; [2003] 1 WLR 1511.

[6]   The person must also be able to make a decision based on that understanding, when qualities such as stability, impulsiveness and volatility may be relevant: see *Mitchell* v. *Alasia* [2005] EWHC 11 (QB).

claim, there is no reason why the law, whether substantive or procedural, should require the interposition of a litigation friend.

3. Capacity depends on time and context. Accordingly, a decision in one court as to capacity does not bind another court, which has to consider the same issue in a different context. Any medical witness asked to assist in relation to capacity therefore needs to know the particular decision and test of capacity in relation to which his advice is sought.

8.2.2 The Mental Capacity Act 2005

The CPR, the FPR and the FP(A)R now provide the same definition for lack of capacity to conduct proceedings as applies under MCA 2005.[7] The test that is to be applied is therefore the statutory test under MCA 2005 (see **Chapter 3**). However, in *Dunhill* v. *Burgin*,[8] the Supreme Court – applying the test now contained in the CPR – endorsed the approach adopted by the Court of Appeal in *Masterman-Lister* to determining capacity to conduct proceedings. It is therefore clear that the principles that evolved under the common law set out above will continue to be of assistance in applying the statutory test in the context of capacity to conduct legal proceedings.

8.2.3 Insolvency proceedings

A broader definition of an 'incapacitated person' is provided for in insolvency proceedings which takes into account incapacity due to both mental disorder and physical affliction or disability. From 1 October 2007, following implementation of MCA 2005, this is now:

> Where … it appears to the court that a person affected by the proceedings is one who lacks capacity within the meaning of the Mental Capacity Act 2005 to manage and administer his property and affairs either:
>
> 1. by reason of lacking capacity within the meaning of the Mental Capacity Act 2005; or
> 2. due to physical affliction or disability,
>
> special rules apply.

Where a finding of incapacity is made, the court may appoint such person as it thinks fit to appear for, represent or act for the incapacitated person. The appointment may be made either generally or for the purpose of any particular application

---

[7] The High Court confirmed in *Saulle* v. *Nouvet* [2007] EWHC 2902 (QB); [2008] WTLR 729 that the statutory test as set out in MCA 2005 applies in civil proceedings, by virtue of the wording of CPR Part 21. The Court of Appeal confirmed in *Re D (Children)* [2015] EWCA Civ 749 that MCA 2005 applies in family proceedings by the wording of FPR rule 23(1).

[8] *Dunhill* v. *Burgin* [2014] UKSC 18; [2014] 1 WLR 933 at para.13.

or proceeding, or for the exercise of particular rights or powers which the incapacitated person might have exercised but for their incapacity.[9]

In *De Louville De Toucy* v. *Bonhams 1793 Ltd*,[10] Vos J held that the CPR sit alongside the IR, with the latter supplementing the provisions of the CPR for purposes of insolvency proceedings. Vos J therefore held that consideration of the appointment of a person to represent somebody who lacks capacity should take in both a consideration of whether a person should be appointed under the IR and a consideration of whether a litigation friend should be appointed under CPR Part 21. Vos J observed that it would obviously be wasteful and unnecessary in any normal case for both to be appointed but the court must consider all the powers available to it in any particular case. Where the incapacity arises from a physical affliction or disability,[11] then only the powers available under the IR would be available.

8.3 APPLYING THE TEST

As there is a presumption of capacity, the burden of proof rests on those asserting lack of capacity. If there is clear evidence that the person has been incapacitated for a considerable period (for example, following a road accident) then the burden of proof may be more easily discharged, but it remains on whoever asserts lack of capacity to make the decision which now needs to be made in the context of conducting legal proceedings. The test is applied on the balance of probabilities, so it is not necessary to be satisfied beyond reasonable doubt that the person lacks litigation capacity. (See **Chapter 4** for an explanation of these legal principles.)

While the statutory test to be applied is that contained in MCA 2005 (see **Chapter 3**), the question to be asked is:

> whether the party to legal proceedings is capable of understanding, with the assistance of such proper explanation from legal advisors and experts in other disciplines as the case may require, the issues on which his consent or decision is likely to be necessary in the course of those proceedings.[12]

The Supreme Court has put a gloss on this test (at least for purposes of civil proceedings), by emphasising that the focus must be on the individual's capacity to understand the claim or cause of action they in fact have, rather than to conduct the claim as formulated by their lawyers.[13]

---

[9]   Insolvency Rules 1986, rule 7.43(1)–(2).

[10]   *De Louville De Toucy* v. *Bonhams 1793 Ltd* [2011] EWHC 3809 (Ch); [2012] BPIR 793.

[11]   An example being *Hunt* v. *Fylde Borough Council* [2008] BPIR 1368 (where the individual in question had Huntingdon's disease).

[12]   *Masterman-Lister* v. *Brutton & Co; Masterman-Lister* v. *Jewell* [2002] EWCA Civ 1889; [2003] 1 WLR 1511 at para.75, per Chadwick LJ.

[13]   *Dunhill* v. *Burgin* [2014] UKSC 18; [2014] 1 WLR 933 at para.18.

All practicable steps must first be taken to help the person make the necessary decisions for themselves.[14] The person should not be held unable to understand information relevant to a decision if they can understand an explanation given in broad terms or simple language, and with the assistance of such proper explanation from legal advisers and other experts as the case may require.[15]

When a person is treated as lacking capacity he is deprived of important rights, yet there is no requirement under the various rules (listed in **8.1**) for a judicial determination of capacity. The final decision as to capacity in respect of the particular legal proceedings rests with the court.[16] The court should investigate the question at the earliest possible opportunity.[17] If a party does not have capacity to litigate (whether or not anyone, including the party themselves, are aware of that fact), all steps taken in the litigation will be without effect, unless the court can properly validate those steps in retrospect.[18]

Where a party is legally represented, the expectation would be that the legal representatives (if they had doubts as to their client's capacity to conduct the litigation) would take steps to obtain a medical opinion and then to put the issue before the court.[19]

The court may, however, take steps of its own motion – and may be required to do so where a litigant before it is acting in person. In such a case, the court must proceed with caution because of the seriousness of the implications of the decision for the rights of the protected party, and should ordinarily seek to ensure that medical evidence is obtained.[20]

---

[14] That MCA 2005, s.1 and the principles therein (discussed in **Chapter 3**) apply for purposes of determining whether a party lacks capacity to conduct proceedings for purposes of the CPR was confirmed in *Baker Tilly (A Firm)* v. *Makar* [2013] EWHC 759 (QB); [2013] COPLR 245.

[15] MCA 2005, s.3(2); *Masterman-Lister* v. *Brutton & Co; Masterman-Lister* v. *Jewell* [2002] EWCA Civ 1889; [2003] 1 WLR 1511 and *A, B and C* v. *X and Z* [2012] EWHC 2400 (COP), [2013] COPLR 1 at para.42.

[16] *Carmarthenshire CC* v. *Lewis* [2010] EWCA Civ 1567 at para.8, per Rimer LJ.

[17] See *Re D (Children)* [2015] EWCA Civ 749 at para.56 (in the context of care proceedings and whether the mother had capacity to conduct the litigation): 'This case does ... perhaps provide a cautionary tale and a reminder that issues of capacity are of fundamental importance. The rules providing for the identification of a person, who lacks capacity, reflect society's proper understanding of the impact on both parent and child of the making of an order which will separate them permanently. It is therefore essential that the evidence which informs the issue of capacity complies with the test found in the Mental Capacity Act 2005 and that any conflict of evidence is brought to the attention of the court and resolved prior to the case progressing further.'

[18] In *Dunhill* v. *Burgin* [2014] UKSC 18; [2014] 1 WLR 933, a compromise agreement in personal injury proceedings was set aside over a decade later by the Supreme Court where it had been entered into without it being recognised at the time that the claimant lacked litigation capacity (so that she did not have the benefit of a litigation friend and the settlement was not approved by the court as required by the CPR).

[19] *Masterman-Lister* v. *Brutton & Co* [2002] EWCA Civ 1889; [2003] 1 WLR 1511 at para.30.

[20] *Baker Tilly (A Firm)* v. *Makar* [2013] EWHC 759 (QB); [2013] COPLR 245. It would, in some circumstances, be possible to invite the Official Solicitor to conduct a so-called *Harbin* v. *Masterman* investigation as to a party's capacity to conduct litigation (see [1896] 1 Ch 351). See **Appendix E** and *Bradbury* v. *Paterson* [2014] EWHC 3992 (QB).

When applying the test of capacity to litigate, expert evidence will normally be required, which could be from a doctor or psychologist, depending on the type of case and the circumstances of the person alleged to lack capacity.

Obtaining medical evidence can, on occasion, present real difficulties, especially if the person being assessed refuses to cooperate (see **2.4**). Where there are practical difficulties in obtaining medical evidence the Official Solicitor may be consulted and will try to assist (see **Appendix E**). A doctor who is asked to express an opinion as to whether a person is incapable of bringing or defending court proceedings should be provided with sufficient information as to the extent and nature of those proceedings, as well as the medical background.

The judge may be assisted by seeing the individual but this may not always be appropriate (see in this regard **4.2**).

In assessing capacity to conduct litigation, it will be particularly important to have regard to the statutory requirement to take all practicable steps to help the individual make a decision, and to provide information in an appropriate manner. If an individual's family, medical advisers and legal advisers can provide clear and straightforward information about the proposed proceedings, it may be possible for the individual to be treated as having litigation capacity, even if, for example, they would not have capacity to manage large sums of money (and would therefore be a 'protected beneficiary' despite not being a 'protected party').[21]

Finally, it is extremely important to remember that capacity is both issue-specific and time-specific. The former has three consequences:

1. The question of capacity has to be considered in relation to the specific litigation in issue. As Munby J put it in *Sheffield City Council* v. *E (An Alleged Patient)*:[22]

   > Someone may have the capacity to litigate in a case where the nature of the dispute and the issues are simple, whilst at the same time lacking the capacity to litigate in a case where either the nature of the dispute or the issues are more complex. In this sense litigation is analogous to medical treatment. Some litigation, like some medical treatment, is relatively simple and risk free. Some litigation, on the other hand, like some medical treatment, is highly complex and more or less risky. Someone may have the capacity to consent to a simple operation whilst lacking the capacity to consent to a more complicated – perhaps controversial – form of treatment. In the same way, someone may have the capacity to litigate in a simple case whilst lacking the capacity to litigate in a highly complex case. Just as medical procedures vary very considerably, so too does litigation.

2. It is necessary to analyse independently whether the person has capacity to make the decision in question and whether they have the capacity to litigate about that decision ('subject-matter capacity'). Although only in 'unusual

---

[21] Although the CPR in fact fail to provide for such a situation.

[22] *Sheffield City Council* v. *E* [2004] EWHC 2808 (Fam) at para.39. The case was decided before MCA 2005 came into force, but the approach suggested would remain applicable today.

circumstances will it be possible to conclude that someone who lacks subject-matter capacity can nonetheless have litigation capacity',[23] the possibility cannot be ruled out, particularly in the case of a person whose impairment is such that they are on the cusp of having subject-matter capacity.[24]

3.   A person may lack capacity to conduct the proceedings but nonetheless be competent to give evidence as to factual matters arising in those proceedings.[25] In *Milroy* v. *British Telecommunications plc*,[26] for instance, the claimant did not have capacity to conduct complex personal injury proceedings, but was held to be competent, with support, to give evidence as to the working practices at the company at which he worked, the training he received and (insofar as he could remember them) the circumstances in which he came to be injured.

Both the issue-specific and time-specific nature of capacity were given further consideration in *Saulle* v. *Nouvet*, when Mr Andrew Edis QC, sitting as a Deputy Judge of the High Court, made the following observations:[27]

> the Court must focus on the matters which arise for decision now, and on the Claimant's capacity to deal with them now. I am required not to attempt to foretell the future and provide for situations which may arise when he may have to take some other decision at some other time when his mental state may be different ... I consider that [Dr X] may well be right when he suggests that there may be times in the future when the Claimant will lack capacity to make particular decisions, and note his concern that if that happens when he does not have the support of his family for any reason, he may not come to the attention of the Court of Protection until it is too late. This is a risk against which the old test for capacity used by the Court of Protection under Part VII of the 1983 [Mental Health] Act used to guard. The modern law is different.

That having been said, once a court has determined that a party does not have capacity to conduct the particular proceedings in issue, it is unlikely to revisit that question unless there is evidence of material change in the party's circumstances.[28]

---

[23]   *Sheffield City Council* v. *E (An Alleged Patient)* [2004] EWHC 2808 (Fam); [2005] Fam 326 at para.49; see also *NHS Trust* v. *T (Adult Patient: Refusal of Medical Treatment)* [2004] EWHC 1279 (Fam); [2005] 1 All ER 387.

[24]   See in the context of Court of Protection proceedings: *CC* v. *KK and STCC* [2012] EWHC 2136 (COP); [2012] COPLR 627 and *Re SB (A Patient: Capacity to Consent to Termination)* [2013] EWHC 1417 (COP); [2013] COPLR 445, for examples of cases in which the person concerned was considered to have capacity to conduct proceedings which were (in part) required to determine whether they had subject-matter capacity.

[25]   The law talks in terms of 'competence' to give evidence, rather than 'capacity' to give evidence. Different courts have different provisions relating to the admissibility of information from those who are not competent to give evidence.

[26]   *Milroy* v. *British Telecommunications PLC* [2015] EWHC 532 (QB).

[27]   *Saulle* v. *Nouvet* [2007] EWHC 2902 (QB); [2008] WTLR 729 at paras.51 and 54.

[28]   See (in the context of the CPR), *Dunhill* v. *Burgin* [2014] UKSC 18; [2014] 1 WLR 933 at para.54.

8.4 LITIGATION FRIENDS

If a person lacks capacity to conduct proceedings, someone else must be appointed to act on their behalf. In civil and family proceedings, this person is known as the litigation friend.

The main function of the litigation friend has been said to carry on the litigation on behalf of the protected party and in his best interests.[29] Traditionally, a litigation friend had to act via a solicitor, but it now appears that this is no longer the case.[30]

In civil proceedings, the criteria for appointment as litigation friend (other than the Official Solicitor or person authorised by the Court of Protection) are that the person:

- can fairly and competently conduct proceedings on behalf of the child or protected party;
- has no interest adverse to that of the child or protected party;
- (where the child or protected party is a claimant) undertakes to pay any costs which the child or protected party may be ordered to pay in relation to the proceedings, subject to any right to be repaid from the assets of the child or protected party.[31]

The same criteria apply in family proceedings, although the requirement to give an undertaking as to costs is not contingent upon the child or protected party being the claimant, and does not apply where the proposed litigation friend is the Official Solicitor or (in the case of a child), an officer of the Children and Family Court Advisory and Support Service (CAFCASS) or the Welsh family proceedings officer.[32]

A certificate of suitability must be filed in the civil and family courts (in the latter where the person wishes to become a litigation friend without a court order).[33]

8.5 IMPLICATIONS OF INCAPACITY

If significant damages or compensation are to be awarded (for example, in a personal injury claim or the distribution of assets on a divorce) then an application should be made to the Court of Protection for the appointment of a deputy if the litigant is a protected beneficiary who lacks capacity to manage these funds. Where

---

[29] See *Re E (Mental Health Patient)* [1984] 1 WLR 320 at 324; *RP* v. *United Kingdom* [2013] 1 FLR 744.

[30] *Gregory* v. *Turner* [2003] EWCA Civ 183; [2003] 1 WLR 1149, and what must be considered to be *obiter* observations in *Re X (Deprivation of Liberty) (No. 2)* [2014] EWCOP 37; [2015] 2 All ER 1165 (given that the Court of Appeal held that the President had not given a binding judgment in the case (*Re X (Court of Protection Practice)* [2015] EWCA Civ 599)).

[31] CPR rule 21.4(3).

[32] FPR rule 15.4 (where the proposed litigation friend is to act for an adult protected party); FPR rule 16.9(2)(c).

[33] CPR rule 21.5; FPR rule 15.5 (where the proposed litigation friend is to act for an adult protected party) and rule 16.10 (where the proposed litigation friend is to act for a child).

there is doubt as to whether an individual is both a protected beneficiary and a protected party, especially where the potential sums that the individual may stand to recover are large, it may be appropriate for the Court of Protection to be asked to determine both questions, because it is likely that the Court of Protection will be required to approve arrangements made for the management of the sums received.[34]

8.6 THE COURT OF PROTECTION

In almost all cases before the Court of Protection, the question of whether the subject of the application – 'P' – has the capacity to take the decision(s) in question is a matter that the court will have to determine (frequently summarily, if there is no contest). This question will fall to be considered by reference to the application of the statutory test in MCA 2005, s.2 (as discussed in particular contexts elsewhere in **Part III**).

The question of whether P has capacity to conduct the proceedings will not necessarily arise for consideration because P may well not be joined to the proceedings. Indeed, the vast majority of the Court of Protection's work by volume consists of uncontested applications relating to the management of property and affairs of those lacking the requisite capacity. In such cases, P will almost invariably not be joined (but will be bound by the decision as if they were[35]).

Following a substantial reform of the proceedings of the Court of Protection in 2015, a decision is now required at the outset as to whether the court should make one or more directions from a 'menu' of directions relating to P's participation.[36] Those directions include steps short of making P a party (including, for instance, the appointment of a representative whose primary function is to give P a 'voice' by relaying information as to P's wishes and feelings).

Where P is joined as a party then, unless they have capacity to conduct the proceedings (which will be assessed by reference to the statutory test and the principles set out at **8.3**), they will require:

1. A litigation friend, who can only be appointed by court order, the criteria for appointment being the same as those applying in the civil and family courts set out at **8.4**, although without the requirement for any undertaking to be given as to costs.[37]

2. (Subject to the development of a suitable panel) an 'accredited legal representative' appointed to act on their behalf.[38] Such a representative would – it is anticipated – be a solicitor or other legally qualified individual who would act without requiring a litigation friend to give them instructions on P's behalf.

---

[34] See *Re GS* CoP Case 11582024, Preston County Court, 10 July 2008.
[35] COPR rule 74(2)(a).
[36] COPR rule 3A.
[37] COPR rule 143.
[38] COPR rule 3A(4).

An adult party to Court of Protection proceedings other than P or a child who lacks capacity to conduct those proceedings (whether because of their age or because of a material impairment or disturbance of their mind or brain) will require a litigation friend;[39] the other options discussed in relation to P above do not apply.

---

[39] COPR rule 142(3). Unless the proposed litigation friend is either the Official Solicitor or a court appointed and authorised deputy, the proposed litigation friend must file a certificate of suitability if they are seeking to be appointed without a court order: COPR rule 142(3). The court may make an order dispensing with the requirement for a child to act by a litigation friend: COPR rule 141(4).

CHAPTER 9

Capacity to enter into a contract

9.1   Introduction
9.2   General rules
9.3   Voidable contracts
9.4   Necessaries

9.5   Contractual capacity: impact of the Mental Capacity Act 2005
9.6   Deputies and attorneys
9.7   Checklist

9.1 INTRODUCTION

It is difficult to generalise about an individual's contractual capacity. Without really being aware of it, most people enter into some sort of contract every day, such as purchasing groceries, buying a bus ticket or train ticket, or depositing clothes at the dry-cleaners. Some general rules apply to each of these contracts, as well as to more complicated written agreements with several pages of small print.

9.2 GENERAL RULES

Prior to the introduction of MCA 2005, the law relating to contractual capacity was a complex combination of common law and statutory rules from which some general rules have emerged.

Contractual capacity relates to the specific contract at the time that contract is entered into, rather than to contracts in general. This means, for example that a person could have capacity to buy a cinema ticket but not the capacity required to enter into a credit agreement with a mail order firm. The person must be capable of understanding the nature and effects of the specific contract that they are entering into and of agreeing to it.[1] The degree of understanding varies according to the type of agreement or transaction involved.[2] Some contracts require a relatively low degree of understanding (buying a bus ticket), whereas others demand a much higher level of understanding (a complex hire purchase agreement).

---

[1]   *Boughton v. Knight* (1873) LR 3 P&D 64 at 72.
[2]   *Re Beaney (Deceased)* [1978] 1 WLR 770.

The law of contract also requires that the parties must have intended to enter into a contract that is legally binding. In the case of social and domestic arrangements (for example, financial arrangements within the family) there is a presumption that there is no such intention. However, this presumption may be rebutted by evidence to the contrary.

9.3 VOIDABLE CONTRACTS

In dealing with contracts made by people whose mental capacity is in doubt, the courts have had to counterbalance two important policy considerations:

- a duty to protect those who are incapable of looking after themselves; and
- a duty to ensure that other people are not prejudiced by the actions of persons who lack capacity to contract but who appear to have full capacity.

So, people without contractual capacity are bound by the terms of a contract they have entered into, even if it was unfair, unless it can be shown that the other party to the contract was aware of their lack of capacity or should have been aware of this.[3] For example, at some stage a person with hypomania may go on a reckless shopping spree. If the shopkeeper has no reason to suspect that the customer is hypomanic, the customer is bound by the contract. But if the shopkeeper was or should have been aware of the customer's mental state, the contract is voidable, and therefore cannot be enforced.

9.4 NECESSARIES

9.4.1 The Sale of Goods Act 1979

The Sale of Goods Act 1979 imposes a special rule to apply to contracts for 'necessaries'. A person without mental capacity who agrees to pay for goods or services which are necessaries is legally obliged to pay a reasonable price for them. Although the 1979 Act applies to goods, the rule regarding necessaries would also govern the provision of essential services.

9.4.2 The Mental Capacity Act 2005

These rules are now brought together and given statutory force by MCA 2005.[4] This clarifies that the obligation to pay a reasonable price applies to both the supply of necessary goods and the provision of necessary services to a person lacking capacity to contract for them. Necessaries are defined in MCA 2005 as goods or

---

[3] *Imperial Loan Company* v. *Stone* [1892] 1 QB 599; see also *Dunhill* v. *Burgin* [2014] UKSC 18 at para.25.
[4] MCA 2005, s.7.

services which are suitable to the person's condition in life (that is, to their place in society, rather than any mental or physical condition) and their actual requirements at the time of sale and delivery (for example, ordinary drink, food and clothing).[5] The MCA Code of Practice states that the aim of this provision is to make sure that people can enjoy a similar standard of living and way of life to those they had before lacking capacity. For example, the Code suggests that if a person who now lacks capacity previously chose to buy expensive designer clothes, these are still necessary goods, as long as they can still afford them. But they would not be necessary for a person who always wore cheap clothes, no matter how wealthy they were.[6]

Whether something is necessary or not is established in two stages by asking the following questions:

1.   Are the goods or services capable of being necessaries as a matter of law?
2.   If so, were the goods or services necessaries, given the particular circumstances of the incapacitated person who ordered them?

Case law has established that goods are not necessaries if the person's existing supply is sufficient. So, for instance, a person who buys a pair of shoes would probably be bound to pay for them, but if the same person purchased a dozen pairs, the contract might be voidable at the person's option.

A contract for necessaries cannot be enforced against a person who lacks mental capacity if it contains harsh or onerous terms. The requirement that only a reasonable price is to be paid is an extension of this principle because a reasonable price need not be the same as the agreed or sale price.[7]

Where a contract provides for services to be given to a mentally incapacitated person by one party, and paid for by another party, there is no basis for pursuing the incapacitated person if the costs are not paid. This reflects basic common law principles which are not affected by the provisions about necessaries in MCA 2005, s.7.[8]

9.5 CONTRACTUAL CAPACITY: IMPACT OF THE MENTAL CAPACITY ACT 2005

In relation to contracts for necessary goods and services as provided for under MCA 2005, the test for capacity to enter into a contract is the standard statutory test as set out in the Act,[9] since the statutory test applies 'for the purposes of this Act'.

---

[5] MCA 2005, s.7(2), based on the definition in the Sale of Goods Act 1979, s.3(3). Necessaries could also include the provision of care home accommodation (*Aster Healthcare Ltd* v. *Estate of Shafi* [2014] EWHC 77 (QB); [2014] 3 All ER 283).

[6] Office of the Public Guardian (2007) Mental Capacity Act 2005 Code of Practice, para.6.58, available at **www.gov.uk/government/publications/mental-capacity-act-code-of-practice**.

[7] MCA 2005, s.7(1), based on Sale of Goods Act 1979, s.8(3).

[8] *Aster Healthcare Ltd* v. *Estate of Shafi* [2014] EWHC 77 (QB); [2014] 3 All ER 283.

[9] The statutory test of capacity in MCA 2005, ss.2 and 3, taking account of the principles in s.1. (See also **Chapter 3**.)

Strictly, as noted above, the MCA 2005 test does not apply to other forms of contracts unrelated to necessaries. As discussed in **Chapter 3**, judges may choose to adopt the statutory test if they consider it to be appropriate[10] (see **3.8**), but the application of the Act to contractual capacity outside the scope of necessaries has not yet been considered by the courts.

Elements of the previous common law approach are present in the new statutory definition, particularly that capacity must be assessed in relation to the specific contract at issue at the time it is entered into. Not least because there would otherwise be a disparity between the position in relation to necessaries and the position in relation to other forms of contract, it is suggested that is now very likely the common law test would now be interpreted in light of MCA 2005. In practice, this means that a court would be likely to need to consider not just whether the individual was capable of understanding the information relating to the specific contract (including its nature and effects), but also whether they could (1) retain, and (2) use and weigh that information.

9.6 DEPUTIES AND ATTORNEYS

A person whose financial affairs are managed by an attorney acting under a registered EPA or LPA (see **Chapter 5**), or by a deputy appointed by the Court of Protection (see **Appendix C**) cannot generally enter into any contract which is inconsistent with the attorney's powers under the EPA or LPA, or the deputy's powers as determined by the court. Any such contracts are void, unless the person had contractual capacity at the time when entering into it.[11]

A deputy is not permitted to enter into any agreement for the person if the deputy believes that the person does in fact have capacity to make the decision for themselves. Further, deputies are not permitted to carry out contracts and to seek court approval retrospectively – they can only operate within the powers given to them by the Court of Protection. However, the Court of Protection has the power to make orders or give directions or authorities for the carrying out of any contract entered into by a person subject to its jurisdiction.

9.7 CHECKLIST

Solicitors may wish to seek an opinion from a doctor about a client's contractual capacity, either before a contract is agreed, or retrospectively if the validity of a

---

[10]   Office of the Public Guardian (2007) *Mental Capacity Act 2005 Code of Practice*, paras.4.32 and 4.33, available at **www.gov.uk/government/publications/mental-capacity-act-code-of-practice**.
[11]   Before MCA 2005 came into effect, any such contracts were automatically voidable, regardless of whether the person has contractual capacity and regardless of whether the other party was aware of the Court of Protection's involvement: *Re Walker* [1905] 1 Ch 160; and *Re Marshall* [1920] 1 Ch 284. However, since MCA 2005 became law, it is no longer clear whether this line of case law is still applicable.

contract is being challenged. The solicitor should identify the specific contract to which the assessment of capacity relates. Different information is required according to the type and complexity of the contract, for example fewer details may be required concerning a contract to purchase double-glazing than for a complex agreement to enter into a home income plan. The solicitor needs to provide such details as:

- the identity of the other party to the contract;
- how much the client has to pay or is being paid;
- when the payment will be made or received;
- what is being given or received in exchange;
- any important terms and conditions which affect the client's rights and liabilities;
- the circumstances in which the contract was entered into (place and time of day);
- the method of communication between the parties;
- any opportunity afforded to the client to reconsider the contract.

As noted above, MCA 2005 does not, strictly, apply to considerations of contractual capacity. It would, however, be prudent to proceed on the basis that it does, such that the doctor should be asked whether the client has an impairment of, or disturbance in the functioning of, their mind or brain which may affect their understanding of information relevant to the contract. This includes information about the nature and effect of that contract at the time a decision is (or was) required. The doctor will also need to consider whether the person is (or was) able to retain that information, and use or weigh it as part of the process of reaching the decision. If the person is not able to understand, or retain, or use or weigh relevant information, the doctor will need to explain whether that is as a result of the client's mental impairment. Where it is considered that the client was not capable of understanding a contract made previously, which is now being challenged, the doctor should also be asked whether in their opinion, the client's lack of capacity should have been obvious to the other party when the contract was made.

Solicitors should also be aware of the possibility that a vulnerable client has been pressured into entering into a contract by way of coercion or undue influence. Steps can be taken to set aside contracts on this basis, which are beyond the scope of this work.[12]

---

[12] See, generally, Law Society Practice Note: Meeting the Needs of Vulnerable Clients (2 July 2015), available at **www.lawsociety.org.uk/support-services/advice/practice-notes/meeting-the-needs-of-vulnerable-clients-july-2015/**.

CHAPTER 10

Capacity to vote

10.1   'Capacity to vote'
10.2   Entitlement to vote
10.3   Legal incapacity to vote
10.4   Registration

10.5   At the polling station
10.6   Postal and proxy voting
10.7   Conclusion

10.1   'CAPACITY TO VOTE'

This chapter addresses questions of capacity relating to voting. The concept of 'capacity to vote' is, however, highly misleading because it conflates two different matters:

1.   legal incapacity to vote, which is a technical concept having nothing (per se) to do with mental incapacity; and
2.   mental capacity to cast a vote, a test that may once have had relevance, but would appear now very unlikely to be a test that can ever properly be applied.

Because misconceptions as to the law are rife in this area, the chapter therefore breaks the issues relating to voting down into stages, from entitlement to vote, to registration, to attending at the polling station. It then addresses questions of postal and proxy voting.

10.2   ENTITLEMENT TO VOTE

It is commonly believed that any degree of learning disability or mental health problem renders a person ineligible to vote. The truth is in fact quite the reverse. The majority of people with mental health problems or learning disabilities do indeed have the right to vote in parliamentary and local elections.

   Those entitled to vote as electors in parliamentary elections in any constituency, or in local government elections are defined by statute as those who, on the date of the relevant poll:

- have their name on the electoral register for the constituency;
- are not subject to any legal incapacity to vote (apart from by virtue of their age);
- are either Commonwealth citizens or citizens of the Republic of Ireland;
- are of voting age (aged 18 or over).[1]

The main factors which determine whether a person with a learning disability or a mental disorder can vote are whether the person is:

(a) subject to any *legal* incapacity to vote; and

(b) has an address for registration purposes.

As far as voting is concerned, the main limiting factor on those suffering from learning disabilities or mental health problems is misconception regarding the law. Wrongful beliefs as to their eligibility can prevent people from registering to vote; a failure to register will mean they are certainly ineligible to vote. This is fundamentally discriminatory, and the importance of ensuring that those with learning disabilities or mental health problems are enabled to participate in the political process has been emphasised both by the European Court of Human Rights,[2] and also in the Convention on the Rights of Persons with Disabilities (see **3.9**).[3]

10.3 LEGAL INCAPACITY TO VOTE

Legal incapacity to vote was defined in *Stowe* v. *Joliffe* as applying to individuals who 'from some inherent or for the time irremovable quality in themselves have not, either by prohibition of statutes or at common law, the status of parliamentary electors'.[4] This definition still applies today. It cannot be emphasised enough that legal incapacity in this context is *not* the same as mental incapacity.

There are various categories of people who are subject to a legal incapacity to vote; that is, are disqualified from voting by law. They are:

- members of the House of Lords;[5]
- detained convicted prisoners;[6]

---

[1] RPA 1983, ss.1–2 (as amended by RPA 2000, s.1(1)).

[2] See *Kiss* v. *Hungary* (2013) 56 EHRR 38.

[3] See art.29 of the Convention, by which states guarantee to persons with disabilities political rights and the opportunity to enjoy them on an equal basis with others. The Committee on the Rights of Persons with Disabilities have emphasised that mental incapacity does not serve as a proper basis upon which to restrict voting rights: see *Zsolt Bujdosó and five others* v. *Hungary*: Views Adopted by the UN Committee for the Rights of Persons with Disabilities at its 10th session, 2 to 13 September 2013, on Communication No. 4/2011 (CRPD/C/10/D/4/2011).

[4] *Stowe* v. *Joliffe* (1874) LR 9 CP 734.

[5] The House of Lords Act 1999 removed the incapacity to be a parliamentary elector from hereditary peers unless they continue to sit in the House of Lords. The incapacity relating to sitting members does not extend to local elections, where members of the House of Lords are entitled to vote.

[6] RPA 1983, s.3(1).

- offenders detained in a mental hospital;[7]
- persons found guilty of certain corrupt or illegal practices.[8]

It was previously the case at common law that a person suffering from severe mental illness (an 'idiot') was considered to lack capacity to vote at elections;[9] save for periods of lucidity – a *'lucidum intervallum'* – during which the incapacity might be lifted.[10]

However, since the coming into force of the Electoral Administration Act 2006, s.73, a person's mental health problems or learning disabilities *cannot*, by themselves, constitute a ground to disqualify them from voting. In other words, even if – in practice – the person is not capable because of those difficulties of deciding for whom to cast their vote, that functional inability does not constitute a ground to prevent them from casting their vote. It is in this regard important to note what Lord Rix, who introduced what became s.73 of the 2006 Act, said in moving the relevant amendment to the (then) Electoral Administration Bill:

> Amendment No. 188 would abolish any common law rule which links a person's incapacity to vote to his mental state. That is what currently ties the language of 'idiots' and 'lunatics' to electoral law, and has led to disabled people being denied the right to vote as the result of unjustified assumptions about their mental capacity being made by election officials and members of the public. Abolishing the common law rule would make disabled people subject to exactly the same eligibility criteria as everyone else.
>
> The other amendments clarify the language used about disabled people in election law by replacing 'incapacity' with 'disability.' Incapacity is an important concept in the law around disabled people's decision making ... Yet it has a different meaning in electoral law, for it means legal disqualification from voting, rather than a physical or mental condition which makes voting difficult. For the purposes of this Bill, it seems best to avoid suggestions that disabled people have any kind of incapacity.[11]

10.4 REGISTRATION

10.4.1 Individual registration

In order to exercise the right to vote in an election, the voter must first be registered on the relevant electoral roll. Since the coming into force in June 2014 of the Electoral Registration and Administration Act 2013, it is necessary for each voter *themselves* to apply to be registered.[12]

The effect of the introduction of the new regime has – it would appear inadvertently – been to introduce a hurdle to enabling those with mental health or learning

---

[7] RPA 1983, s.3A.
[8] RPA 1983, s.160(4)(a)(i).
[9] *Bedford (County) Case, Burgess' Case* (1785) 2 Lud EC 381.
[10] *Okehampton Case, Robin's Case* (1791) 1 Fras 29, 162.
[11] *Hansard* HL Deb 15 May 2006, vol 692, col 123.
[12] Replacing the old 'head of every household' system under which one individual had been able to take control of who was registered to vote in a particular property.

disabilities to enjoy the right to vote that had been secured by the passage of s.73 of the Electoral Administration Act 2006. That hurdle takes the form of a requirement that the relevant Electoral Registration Officer (ERO) be satisfied that the individual applicant has made the declaration of truth that must accompany the application for registration.[13] As interpreted by the Electoral Commission,[14] this means that the declaration of truth must be completed either by:

- The applicant, even though it may in some cases be necessary to provide them with substantial assistance to enable them to do so.[15]
- If the applicant does not have the capacity to make the declaration of truth (the test for which is not specified), an attorney under a power of attorney with powers wide enough to cover making an application for registration.[16] It is not entirely clear what forms of powers of attorney the Electoral Commission has in mind, but it is suggested that is likely that the Commission has in mind powers of attorney for property and financial affairs (see **Chapter 5**). It is important to note that an attorney cannot cast a vote on behalf of the donor.[17]

As noted above, precisely what is required to have capacity to make the required declaration of truth is not clear. It is also unclear why the Electoral Commission did not in its guidance provide for the ability of a deputy appointed by the Court of Protection to make the application and complete the declaration of truth, and it is suggested that there is no proper reason why such a deputy should not also be able to do so if the scope of their powers extended sufficiently wide.

It is likely that, in due course, a challenge will be brought to the legislative scheme in this regard because of the hurdle that it places in the way of individuals with mental health problems or learning disabilities securing their place upon the electoral registers in order to be able to exercise their right to vote.

10.4.2 Place of residence

The Representation of the People Act 2000 (RPA 2000), which came into effect in September 2001, introduced changes in electoral procedures and registration intended to make it easier for disabled people to register and to vote. Under previous electoral legislation, people were only able to register if they could establish their

---

[13] The requirement for a declaration of truth arises from the Representation of the People (England and Wales) Regulations 2001, SI 2001/341, reg.26(1)(j), as amended by the Representation of the People (England and Wales) (Description of Electoral Registers and Amendment) Regulations 2013, SI 2013/3198, reg.10.
[14] See the Electoral Commission (2014) *Guidance on Assisted Applications in England and Wales*, available at **www.electoralcommission.org.uk/__data/assets/pdf_file/0011/176168/IER-Guidance-on-assisted-applications-in-England-and-Wales.pdf**.
[15] See paras.1.19–1.12.
[16] See paras.1.13–1.18.
[17] Because of the bar in MCA 2005, s.29(1). The Electoral Commission distinguishes between a decision on voting at an election and registration, the guidance at para.1.15 noting that: 'registration is an administrative step that enables a person to exercise their voting right; it is not a decision on voting.'

place of residence on a specific qualifying date each year. There were special rules relating to the voting rights of patients in 'mental hospitals' (see below) as such hospitals could not be used as a place of residence for the purpose of electoral registration. RPA 2000 removed the annual qualifying date, and introduced 'rolling' electoral registration to enable people to be added to (or deleted from) the electoral register at any time of the year.[18] This means that registration is tracked from the date of an application for registration, rather than on an annual basis.

Both voluntary (informal) and detained patients in mental hospitals (with the exception of those detained as a consequence of criminal activity) may continue to be registered for electoral purposes at their home address. However, if their stay in hospital is so long that they have lost their residence, they may still register as electors by making a 'declaration of local connection' providing a local contact address. This could be:

- the address of the hospital;
- an address where they would be resident if they were not in hospital; or
- an address in the UK where they have lived at any time in the past.[19]

Registration by declaration of local connection is also available to homeless people who can register by reference to the place where they commonly spend a substantial part of their time, whether it is a park bench, a bus shelter, or a doorway.[20]

Registration by declaration of local connection does not extend to detained patients who have been sentenced by the courts or transferred to hospital from prison under MHA 1983, Part III. These people, along with all sentenced prisoners, are disqualified from voting.[21] The European Court of Human Rights has held that a blanket ban on voting rights for prisoners violates the European Convention on Human Rights.[22] The Supreme Court has confirmed, however, that despite censure from Strasbourg, the ban on prisoners' right to vote remains.[23]

The definition of 'mental hospital' includes any establishment or unit, the purpose or main purpose of which is the reception and treatment of people suffering from any form of mental disorder.[24] Mental disorder has the same meaning as under MHA 1983. This definition does not include hostels or care homes where the treatment of residents is not the primary purpose; it also excludes psychiatric wards of district general hospitals and homes for older people.

---

[18] RPA 1983, s.4(6) (as amended by RPA 2000, s.1(2)).
[19] RPA 1983, s.7 (as amended by RPA 2000, s.4).
[20] RPA 1983, s.7B(4)(b).
[21] Offenders in prison are incapable of voting during the time that they are detained in prison pursuant to RPA 1983, s.3; offenders detained in mental hospitals are deemed legally incapable of voting pursuant to s.3A (as inserted by RPA 2000, s.2).
[22] *Hirst v. United Kingdom (No. 2)* Application 74025/01, (2006) 42 EHRR 41.
[23] *R (on the application of Chester) v. Secretary of State for Justice* [2013] UKSC 63; [2014] AC 271.
[24] RPA 1983, s.7(6) (as amended by RPA 2000, s.4).

It is for EROs to decide which hostels or care homes for older people, for people with mental health problems, or those with learning disabilities, come within the definition of a 'mental hospital'.

Hostels or homes which are not 'mental hospitals' should be treated, for electoral purposes, in the same way as any other qualifying address.[25] The Electoral Commission suggests that EROs liaise with local authority social services departments to obtain provide lists of residential and care homes, as well as shelters and hostels, noting that the wardens of these types of accommodation may be helpful in providing information on changes of residents.[26] The Electoral Commission has also issued specific advice to care staff on assisting those in their care with registering to vote and absent voting.[27]

10.5 AT THE POLLING STATION

A decision as to whether and how to vote must be made by the elector themselves and cannot be made by any other person on their behalf, and MCA 2005 makes clear that nothing in that Act provides for such decisions to be made on behalf of another person.[28]

However, if the person who is registered as an elector presents themselves at the polling station, they cannot be refused a ballot paper, or in other words be excluded from voting, on the grounds of mental incapacity.[29] The presiding officer is entitled to ask limited questions of a putative voter to establish that they the person they say they are, and whether they have already voted.[30] The presiding officer is *not* entitled to seek to question whether the person has the capacity to vote.

In practice, therefore, the most relevant factor in whether a registered voter with disabilities is able actually to exercise their right to vote is likely to be the prohibition on anyone accompanying an elector into the polling booth or giving any other assistance in marking the ballot paper, save for the limited statutory exceptions that apply to:

---

[25] Electoral Commission (2008) *Managing Electoral Registration in Great Britain: Guidance for Electoral Registration Officers*, available at **www.electoralcommission.org.uk**, Part B, para.5.9.

[26] Electoral Commission (2015) *Individual Electoral Registration Guidance, Part 4: Maintaining Registration Throughout the Year*, available at **www.electoralcommission.org.uk/i-am-a/electoral-administrator/running-electoral-registration**.

[27] Electoral Commission (2013) *Supporting Care Home Residents in England and Wales to Register to Vote*, available at **www.electoralcommission.org.uk**.

[28] MCA 2005, s.29.

[29] Electoral Administration Act 2006, s.73, reflected in the Electoral Commission (2014) *Polling Station Handbook*, available at **www.electoralcommission.org.uk/__data/assets/pdf_file/0004/175621/Polling-station-handbook-UKPGE.pdf**, at p.21.

[30] RPA 1983, Sched.1 – Parliamentary Election Rules, rule 35; Local Elections (Principal Areas) (England and Wales) Rules 2006, SI 2006/3304. The questions are: (1) 'are you the person whose name appears on the register as [...]'?; and (2) 'have you already voted?'

- some voters who, because of blindness or other physical incapacity or inability to read, are entitled to assistance from a companion;[31]
- electors who are unable to read, who can ask the presiding officer to help them by marking their votes on the ballot paper, but must be capable of giving directions to the presiding officer as to how they wish to vote.

10.6 POSTAL AND PROXY VOTING

RPA 2000 extended the provisions for permitting an elector to vote by post or by appointing a proxy to vote on their behalf.[32] These methods of voting are now available either at the time of registration for the period of the register, or before a particular election. EROs are able to explain the procedures and provide the relevant application forms. Anyone on the electoral register can vote by post; there is no need to give a reason for doing so. It follows that no check is made on the capacity of those who have voted by postal vote.

As regards proxy votes, the position is not entirely clear. The Electoral Commission considers that a person can only appoint a proxy to vote on their behalf if they have the capacity to vote (a test the components of which are not identified).[33] It is, however, suggested that there are grounds to doubt the accuracy of this proposition and, in practice, it is unclear what, if any, steps are taken by registration officers to check whether a person making an application for the appointment of a proxy has the requisite capacity.

In particular, MCA 2005 simply provides that nothing in the Act permits a decision on voting at an election to be made on behalf of a person (i.e. for instance, a deputy cannot decide upon a person's behalf for whom to vote). It could therefore be argued that appointing a proxy to vote is not caught by this restriction. Alternatively, if questions of capacity are relevant, it could properly be argued that they are only relevant in terms of the question of whether the person has the capacity to make a declaration of truth to register as a voter. If they do, then it might properly be said they should be considered then to have the capacity (and the right) to appoint a proxy to act on their behalf to exercise that right.

It may be that future Electoral Commission guidance addresses this issue in more detail or that a court case puts the question beyond doubt.

10.7 CONCLUSION

It is important that patients in hospital and residents in hostels and care homes are aware of their voting rights, and staff should assist them by providing information,

---

[31] RPA 2000, s.13. The presiding officer may also be entitled to give assistance to the voter.
[32] RPA 2000, s.12.
[33] Electoral Commission (2008) *Managing Electoral Registration in Great Britain: Guidance for Electoral Registration Officers*, available at **www.electoralcommission.org.uk**, Part B, para.5.10.

declaration forms and absent voting forms. People with mental health problems or disabilities living in the community may require help from their relatives, carers and sometimes their doctors to ensure they are not deprived unnecessarily of this most basic of civil rights. It is perhaps not a coincidence that the Care Quality Commission are increasingly checking whether care homes and hospitals have taken appropriate steps to ensure that those within their care are registered to vote.

CHAPTER 11

Capacity and personal relationships

11.1   Right to form relationships
11.2   Family relationships
11.3   Sexual relationships
11.4   Capacity to consent to marriage or
       to enter into a civil partnership

11.5   Capacity to separate, divorce or
       dissolve a civil partnership
11.6   Conclusion

11.1   RIGHT TO FORM RELATIONSHIPS

Every person has fundamental rights which may not be infringed unless there are special and widely agreed grounds justifying such an infringement. Respect for individual rights in those matters which people can decide for themselves is embodied in national and international agreements. For example, the United Nations Declaration on Human Rights of 1948 articulates the rights of adults to freedom and equal treatment. Also, the European Convention on Human Rights (ECHR), incorporated into UK law under the Human Rights Act 1998, states:

> Everyone has the right to respect for his private and family life, his home and his correspondence ...[1]

and

> Men and women of marriageable age have the right to marry and to found a family, according to the national laws governing the exercise of this right.[2]

More recently, the Convention on the Rights of Persons with Disabilities (see **3.9**) requires states to take effective and appropriate measures to eliminate discrimination against persons with disabilities in all matters relating to marriage, family, parenthood and relationships.[3]

---

[1]   ECHR, art.8.
[2]   ECHR, art.12.
[3]   CRPD, art.23.

A balance must be maintained between respecting individual rights to family relationships, friendships, sexual relationships, marriage, and parenthood, and the duty of society (the state, parents, carers and others) to protect adults at risk of abuse or neglect. These two facets (respect for rights and protection from abuse and exploitation) have traditionally been reflected in the differences between the civil and the criminal law, which have taken different approaches in relation to the capacity of people to embark on intimate relationships.

Whereas the civil law has provided for the private rights of all citizens to enjoy family contact and personal or sexual relationships, the criminal law has concentrated on providing an effective deterrent aimed at protecting people at risk from abuse, including sexual abuse. The provisions of the criminal law relating to sexual relations are discussed in **Chapter 12**. In this chapter, by contrast, the focus is on the civil law.

In the context of family relationships, questions of influence very often arise, and in the case of an individual who has an impairment, difficult questions may arise as to whether their apparent inability to make decisions stems from that impairment or from the influence of a family member of family members. In this context, the dividing line between those whom the law considers to lack capacity, and those whom the law considers to have capacity but to be vulnerable, becomes very important (see further **3.5**).

11.2 FAMILY RELATIONSHIPS

For most people it is important to maintain family relationships (which of course vary in degree and intensity) at least with close relatives. In the context of family proceedings where children are minors, there is a general presumption of a right to a relationship between a parent and child, which should be protected so long as this is in the child's best interests. The welfare of the child is always the paramount consideration in such cases.[4] Where there is a disagreement between the parents, the right to a relationship with a child can be enforced through a contact order under the provisions of the Children Act 1989.[5]

Once children reach the age of 18 the right to a relationship with their parents, or with other family members, extends for only so far as the people involved consent to it. There are no means, in legal proceedings or otherwise, of enforcing a relationship between adult family members who have capacity to decide they no longer wish the relationship to continue. Nevertheless, the courts have been asked to intervene in cases where disputes have arisen between family members about contact with adult relatives who lack capacity to make their own decisions, or to resolve disagreements about where such individuals should live. Questions of residence or contact are clearly important in enabling a relationship to continue.

---

[4]   Children Act 1989, s.1.
[5]   Children Act 1989, s.8.

131

Under MCA 2005, the Court of Protection has the power to make declarations and make decisions in respect of the personal welfare of those lacking capacity[6] (for further discussion of the role and powers of the Court of Protection see **Appendix C**). However, the Court of Protection cannot make decisions on behalf of a person lacking capacity on any of the following matters:

- consenting to marriage or a civil partnership;
- consenting to have sexual relations;
- consenting to a decree of divorce on the basis of two years' separation;
- consenting to the dissolution of a civil partnership;
- consenting to a child being placed for adoption or the making of an adoption order;
- discharging parental responsibility for a child in matters not relating to the child's property; or
- giving consent under the Human Fertilisation and Embryology Act 1990.[7]

11.2.1 Capacity to make decisions about family or personal relationships

When the Court of Protection is considering capacity to make decisions about family or personal relationships, it must apply the test set down in MCA 2005 (discussed further in **Chapter 3**).

Capacity is issue-specific, so if the question before the court is a multifaceted one (for instance, as to both residence and contact with particular family members), the question of capacity must be approached in a similarly multifaceted way, addressing each question separately. Of course, there will be some decisions which overlap – for example, a decision whether to reside in a particular place may also involve a decision whether to live with or apart from a particular person.

The most obvious overlap is, perhaps, the overlap between decisions as to contact and decisions as to sexual relations. As set out at **11.3**, the courts have determined that decisions about sexual relations are not person-specific. In other words, a person's capacity to consent to sexual relations in general should be assessed, not their capacity to consent to sexual relations with a particular individual. The capacity assessment is a general evaluation of a person's ability to make a decision whether to consent to sexual relations. This approach is driven by considerations of public policy and pragmatism.[8] It would not be practical or appropriate to assess capacity at the time of a particular sexual encounter, nor should the state be concluding that a person has capacity to consent with only some sexual partners and not others, since that would be akin to making a best interests decision about their sexual contact.

---

[6] MCA 2005, ss.15 and 16.
[7] MCA 2005, s.27.
[8] *IM* v. *LM* [2014] EWCA Civ 37; [2015] Fam 61 at para.77: '[o]n a pragmatic basis, if for no other reason, capacity to consent to future sexual relations can only be assessed on a general and non-specific basis.'

In contrast, decisions about contact with another person may well be person-specific, since without taking into account information about the other person and any particular risks they pose, the assessment of capacity will have nothing to bite on.[9]

This means that it may be the case that a person has capacity to consent to sexual relations in general, but lacks capacity to decide whether to have contact with a particular person. In such cases, difficult questions arise about what support or restrictions can be imposed, and legal advice should be taken about facilitating a sexual relationship between the two individuals even though it may not be in the incapacitated person's best interests to spend unsupervised time with the other person.

It is likely that the courts will have to consider in due course the question of precisely what it means to lack capacity to consent to sexual relations where a person has capacity to make decisions about sexual relations in general, but who is prevented by reason of mental impairment from:

- acting on those decisions; or
- taking them at the time they fall to be taken.

It is possible that when a court looks in detail at either or both of these situations, it will find that, in fact, the person in question lacks the capacity to consent to sexual relations. It is important, therefore, for both lawyers and doctors to keep abreast of the case law in this area (see **Appendix J** for useful resources).

11.3   SEXUAL RELATIONSHIPS

Deciding to enter into a sexual relationship with another individual is a personal decision which does not generally require any formal contract or test of capacity. Men and women can give legal consent to either opposite or same sex relationships at the age of 16.[10] Relationships can be of any duration and of varying degrees of intensity and commitment. Sexual relationships are personal in nature, which means that it is entirely for the individuals involved to decide whether or not to embark upon them. The courts cannot consent to sexual relations on behalf of incapacitated people who are over 16 but society has obligations to ensure that their choice is voluntary.

11.3.1   Capacity to consent to sexual relationships

The courts have in recent years had cause to consider the question of capacity to consent to sexual relationships in the civil context in a number of cases. The courts have said that capacity to consent to sexual relationships must be assessed in general

---

[9]   *City of York Council* v. *C* [2013] EWCA Civ 478; [2014] Fam 10.
[10]   Sexual Offences (Amendment) Act 2000, s.1.

terms, not in relation to specific individuals, and have identified the following information as that relevant to the decision:

- their understanding of the mechanics of sexual intercourse, in basic terms;
- their understanding of the reasonably foreseeable consequences of sexual intercourse (including their knowledge, even if at a basic level) of the risks of pregnancy (in relation to heterosexual intercourse involving a woman of child-bearing age) and sexually transmitted diseases; and
- their understanding that they have a choice whether to agree to or to refuse intercourse.[11]

Factors which the courts have said are *not* relevant include the particular relationship or sexual partner, and the ability of the individual to exercise their capacity to give consent in real-life situations. This can pose particular concerns where an individual is able to understand information relevant to sexual relations, but is vulnerable to exploitation in the community. As noted above, this area of the law may be subject to revision in the future. Capacity to make decisions about contraception must be assessed separately to capacity to consent to sexual relations.[12] It may be that a person lacks capacity to make decisions about contraception, but has capacity to consent to sexual relations.

Relatives or carers may try to stop a relationship involving people with a learning disability because of concerns about pregnancy, risks of infection, moral objections to the existence of a sexual relationship, or opposition to possible future marriage and parenthood. Doctors may be asked to give a view about the appropriateness of two people embarking on a close relationship and there may be concern about the ability of one or both parties to give valid consent to sexual intercourse. It is important that each party is seen privately and assessed individually before doctors advise on their capacity. Every attempt must be made to provide individuals with the information they require to be able to make a decision as to whether or not to have a sexual relationship. It is particularly important also here to recall the principle enshrined in MCA 2005[13] that all practicable steps must be taken to support a person to take their own decisions: it may very well be that a number of sessions of one to one work with an appropriately trained specialist can enable an individual to achieve the relatively limited understanding required in order to consent to sexual relations.[14]

---

[11] See, in particular, *IM* v. *LM* [2014] EWCA Civ 37; [2015] Fam 61 and *London Borough of Tower Hamlets* v. *TB & SA* [2014] EWCOP 53; [2015] COPLR 87.

[12] See *Re A (Capacity: Refusal of Contraception)* [2010] EWHC 1549 (Fam); [2011] Fam 61.

[13] MCA, s.1(3).

[14] In *An NHS Trust* v. *DE* [2013] EWHC 2562 (Fam); [2013] COPLR 531 for instance, 14 sessions of work done by a clinical psychologist with a man with learning disabilities put the question of whether he had capacity to consent to sexual relations beyond doubt.

11.4 CAPACITY TO CONSENT TO MARRIAGE OR TO ENTER INTO A CIVIL PARTNERSHIP

The pre-MCA 2005 case of *Sheffield City Council* v. *E (An Alleged Patient)*[15] continues to set down the test to determine whether a person has capacity under English law to marry or to enter into a civil partnership (in the interests of space, references in this and the following sections are, where relevant, to marriage alone).

The court concluded that:

- As with sexual relations, the question is not whether a person has capacity to marry X rather than Y.[16] The relevant question is whether the person has capacity to marry. If the person does, it is not necessary to show that they also have capacity to take care of their own person and property.
- The question of whether a person has capacity to marry is quite distinct from the question of whether the person is wise to marry: either wise to marry at all, or wise to marry X rather than Y, or wise to marry X.
- In relation to a proposed marriage the only question for the court is whether the person has capacity to marry. The court has no jurisdiction to consider whether it is in the person's best interests to marry or to marry X.
- In relation to the question of whether the person has capacity to marry the law remains as it was set out by Singleton LJ in *Park's Estate, Re; Park* v. *Park*:[17]

  > [… was the person] capable of understanding the nature of the contract into which he was entering, or was his mental condition such that he was incapable of understanding it? To ascertain the nature of the contract of marriage a man must be mentally capable of appreciating that it involves the responsibilities normally attaching to marriage. Without that degree of mentality, it cannot be said that he understands the nature of the contract.

- It is not enough that someone appreciates that they are taking part in a marriage ceremony or understands its words. They must understand the nature of the marriage contract. This means that they must be mentally capable of understanding the duties and responsibilities that normally attach to marriage.

There are thus, in essence, two aspects to the inquiry whether someone has capacity to marry:

- Does the person understand the nature of the marriage contract (which is, in essence, a simple one, which does not require a high degree of intelligence to comprehend)?[18]

---

[15] *Sheffield City Council* v. *E (An Alleged Patient)* [2004] EWHC 2808 (Fam); [2005] Fam 326. This decision has been applied subsequent to the coming into force of MCA 2005 in *A Local Authority* v. *AK (Capacity to Marry)* [2013] COPLR 163.

[16] In contrast, a decision whether to cohabit may be person-specific: *City of York Council* v. *C* [2013] EWCA Civ 478; [2014] Fam 10.

[17] *Park's Estate, Re; Park* v. *Park* [1954] P 112 at 127.

[18] *Sheffield City Council* v. *E (An Alleged Patient)* [2004] EWHC 2808 (Fam); [2005] Fam 326 at para.141(viii), quoting Sir James Hannen in *Durham* v. *Durham* (1885) 10 PD 80 at 81.

- Do they understand the duties and responsibilities that normally attach to marriage?

The duties and responsibilities that normally attach to marriage were summarised in the *E* case as follows:

> Marriage, whether civil or religious, is a contract, formally entered into. It confers on the parties the status of husband and wife, the essence of the contract being an agreement between a man and a woman to live together, and to love one another as husband and wife, to the exclusion of all others. It creates a relationship of mutual and reciprocal obligations, typically involving the sharing of a common home and a common domestic life and the right to enjoy each other's society, comfort and assistance.[19]

In addition to the points that arise from the *E* judgment, four further points should be noted:

- Given the nature of marriage, capacity to consent to marriage will normally require the capacity to consent to sexual intercourse.[20]
- The question of capacity arises in a somewhat different context in respect of marriages contracted under Sharia law, where the capacity to consent of the spouses is not relevant, and a marriage can therefore validly be contracted even if one or both would lack capacity under the tests set out above. However, such a marriage may not be recognised as such under the English civil law.[21]
- As set out above (see **11.2**), the Court of Protection is expressly precluded from consenting on behalf of an incapacitated person to marriage or sexual relations.[22]
- The courts have not determined whether a person needs to understand the implications of marriage for their property and assets in order to have capacity to consent to marriage. If a person is thought to lack capacity solely in relation to this issue, legal advice should be sought.

11.4.1 The effect of mental disorder

Under the Matrimonial Causes Act 1973, a marriage is voidable (that is, it can be annulled at the request of one of the parties) if at the time of marriage either party, although capable of giving valid consent, was suffering (whether continuously or intermittently) from mental disorder of such a kind or to such an extent as to be unfitted to marriage.[23] The mental disorder (now defined under MHA 1983, s.1(2),

---

[19] *Sheffield City Council* v. *E (An Alleged Patient)* [2004] EWHC 2808 (Fam); [2005] Fam 326 at para.132.

[20] *City of Westminster Social and Community Services Dept* v. *C* [2008] EWCA Civ 198; [2009] Fam 11 at para.32, per Thorpe LJ: 'physical intimacy is an ordinary consequence of a celebration of a marriage.'

[21] *City of Westminster Social and Community Services Dept* v. *C* [2008] EWCA Civ 198; [2009] Fam 11.

[22] MCA 2005, s.27(1)(a).

[23] Matrimonial Causes Act 1973, ss.11–13.

as amended, as 'any disorder or disability of the mind') may be of the petitioner or the respondent. There is no other way under English law for a marriage to be declared void except by bringing a petition under the 1973 Act.[24]

To succeed in proving that a marriage is voidable on a petition under the 1973 Act, the petitioner must show that the person's mental disorder made them incapable of living in a married state and carrying out the duties and obligations of marriage. Merely being difficult to live with will not make a person unfitted to marriage.[25] This provision of the 1973 Act is not strictly a 'capacity test'.

Proceedings must be started within three years of the marriage, although the court may give leave for proceedings to be instituted at a later date. The court may not grant a decree in the case of a voidable marriage if the petitioner, knowing it was open to them to have the marriage avoided, had acted in such a way that the respondent reasonably believed an annulment would not be sought and it would be unjust to grant a decree (for example, in a marriage for companionship only). A doctor asked to give an opinion about such an application should consult with those who know the party who is alleged to be mentally disordered and who have professional experience of the mental disorder.

Although the Court of Protection cannot, itself, declare a marriage a nullity, it can, however, authorise a person (most often the Official Solicitor) to bring proceedings in the name of the person lacking capacity for the annulment of a marriage under the provisions of the Matrimonial Causes Act 1973.[26] The High Court can also grant a declaration that a marriage contracted abroad where one party lacked capacity to consent to that marriage (applying the provisions of MCA 2005) shall not be recognised as a marriage under the law of England and Wales.[27]

It should, finally, be noted that a marriage to which one party cannot give consent[28] is a forced marriage, which means that:

(a)   a person who takes any steps to cause that person to enter into the marriage is committing a criminal offence;[29]

(b)   the person lacking capacity can be made the subject of a Forced Marriage Protection Order; and

---

[24] *City of Westminster Social and Community Services Dept* v. *C* [2008] EWCA Civ 198; [2009] Fam 11 at para.21.

[25] *Bennett* v. *Bennett* [1969] 1 WLR 430.

[26] *A Local Authority* v. *AK* [2013] COPLR 163.

[27] *XCC* v. *AA* [2012] EWHC 2183 (COP); [2012] COPLR 730. Parker J confirmed in that case that such a 'non-recognition' declaration has to be granted by the High Court under its inherent jurisdiction even in relation to an adult lacking the relevant decision-making capacity, because the Court of Protection does not have the power to grant such a declaration. She also held that, in deciding whether to grant such a declaration, the High Court is not bound by the provisions of MCA 2005, s.4 and can take into account public policy issues such as the importance of maintaining immigration control.

[28] Applying the statutory test in MCA 2005, s.2(1): see Anti-social Behaviour, Crime and Policing Act 2014, s.121(5).

[29] Anti-social Behaviour, Crime and Policing Act 2014, s.121(2).

(c)   other people can be the subject of criminal prosecution for breaching that order.[30]

11.4.2   What objections can be raised to a proposed marriage?

Sometimes a relative or carer of a person whose capacity to consent to marriage may be in doubt is concerned about a proposed marriage. There are a number of ways in which an objection to a pending marriage can be made. A person can:

- dissent from the publication of banns in the case of a church wedding;
- enter a caveat against the granting of a special or common licence;
- enter a caveat with a superintendent registrar or the Registrar General (in the case of register office or other civil weddings).

If a caveat is entered, this puts the registrar or clergyman on notice and creates a requirement to investigate and enquire into the capacity of both parties to marry. The burden of proof of lack of capacity falls on the person seeking to oppose the marriage. The registrar may ask for a doctor's report or a report from a social worker, a psychologist, or other person who can give information about the ability of the parties to understand the contract of marriage. The tests to be applied are those stated above and it is important that a full consultation with all relevant people takes place. Any opinion should be based on a sound knowledge of the person, their way of life and any relevant religious or cultural facts. It is not necessary for the person to appreciate or consider every aspect of a marital relationship.

When one or both parties proposing to marry has a learning disability it may be important to suggest counselling and advice about the practical aspects of marriage including financial, housing and legal matters. Information and advice about sexuality and sexual relations, including contraception, may be useful and should be made available. A judgment about the person's capacity to understand the responsibilities of parenthood may also be relevant here. For example, additional support may be needed to avoid the possibility of future proceedings under the Children Act 1989 resulting in a child being removed from the person's care.

The courts have also expressed their views as to the obligations upon statutory bodies in relation to potential marriages involving those who may lack the material capacity. In *XCC* v. *AA*,[31] Parker J[32] expressed the view that it was the duty of a doctor or other health or social work professional who becomes aware that an incapacitated person may undergo a marriage abroad, to notify the learning disabilities team of Social Services and/or the Forced Marriage Unit if information comes to light that there are plans for an overseas marriage of a patient who has or may lack capacity.

---

[30]   Family Law Act 1996, Part IVA.
[31]   *XCC* v. *AA* [2012] EWHC 2183 (COP); [2012] COPLR 730.
[32]   Drawing on Forced Marriage Unit (2010) *Forced Marriage and Learning Disabilities: Multi-agency Practice Guidelines*.

In *A Local Authority* v. *AK (Capacity to Marry)*,[33] Bodey J expressed his concerns in relation to the role of registrars and of the registration service when a borderline-incapacitated individual presents wanting to marry. Bodey J noted that it was not the registrar's job to assess mental capacity 'and plainly he or she would be wholly unqualified to do so'. He was, however, critical of the absence of the guidance in the Registrar's Handbook as to the key components of MCA 2005, and also emphasised the need for aspiring spouses to be seen separately (especially in cases of any doubt that one party had the requisite capacity).

The February 2015 version of the General Register Office *Guide for Authorised Persons* contains the following guidance on the issue of mental capacity:[34]

3.12 Both parties to the marriage must have the mental capacity to understand the nature of the marriage that they are about to contract. A person should understand:

    (i)   that they are taking part in a marriage ceremony and understands the words used;

    (ii)   the nature of the marriage contract. This means the person must be capable of understanding the duties and responsibilities which normally attach to marriage.

3.13 A person's mental capacity will have been assessed and considered at the time they gave their notice of marriage. However, if at pre-marriage questioning you have any concerns, you should immediately discuss the matter with your local superintendent registrar or GRO. A marriage cannot proceed if a person does not have the mental capacity to marry.

3.14 A key principle of the Mental Capacity Act 2005 is that a person must be assumed to have capacity unless it is established that he/she lacks capacity. It should never be assumed that because a person has a learning disability, that they lack the capacity to marry.

11.4.3 Implications of marriage

As discussed above, the level of understanding required for marriage is less than that required for some other decisions or transactions. Since the status of marriage affects other matters, such as financial affairs and rights to property, subsequent arrangements may need to be made for a person who lacks capacity to manage these affairs (see **Chapter 5**). In particular, marriage revokes any existing will made by either of the parties. If one person lacks testamentary capacity (see **6.2**) an application may need to be made to the Court of Protection for a statutory will to be made on the person's behalf (see **6.9**).[35]

---

[33]   *A Local Authority* v. *AK (Capacity to Marry)* [2013] COPLR 163.
[34]   General Register Office (2015) *A Guide for Authorised Persons*, available at **www.gov.uk/government/publications/a-guide-for-authorised-persons**.
[35]   *Re Davey (Deceased)* [1980] 3 All ER 342.

11.5 CAPACITY TO SEPARATE, DIVORCE OR DISSOLVE A CIVIL PARTNERSHIP

The Court of Appeal has stated that just as a decision to marry is act-specific, rather than person-specific, so is a decision to divorce.[36] Apart from this simple statement, there is little guidance in the case law in England and Wales as to the assessment of capacity to end a legally recognised relationship.

There are no reported court decisions in which the matter being specifically considered by the court was the capacity required to separate, divorce or dissolve a civil partnership except *Calvert (Litigation Guardian)* v. *Calvert* in the Ontario Court[37] (such decisions are regarded as persuasive but not binding on UK courts). In this case, Mr and Mrs Calvert married in 1979, having signed a pre-marriage contract which said that any property owned by one of the parties at the date of the agreement would not be a family asset. Mrs Calvert managed a clothes shop and Mr Calvert owned a substantial farm in Ontario. Each of them had a grown-up child from a previous marriage. Nine years later Mr Calvert sold the farm for a small fortune. Despite his enormous wealth, he paid his wife a minimal allowance and begrudged the small gifts she sent to her daughter and grandchildren. In 1993, Mrs Calvert began to show signs of the early stages of Alzheimer's disease. A few months later, however, she made her own arrangements to visit her daughter in Calgary and travelled alone. She never returned to her husband and instructed a lawyer to start divorce proceedings. Mr Calvert contended that his wife did not have capacity to form the intention to separate from him and thus was not entitled to any financial settlement. Relying on *Re Park's Estate; Park* v. *Park*[38] (see **11.4**) the Ontario Court recognised the varying levels of capacity required to make different decisions and gave separate consideration to the three levels of capacity relevant to that case: capacity to separate, capacity to divorce, and capacity to instruct counsel in connection with the divorce. The judge held as follows:[39]

> Separation is the simplest act requiring the lowest level of understanding. A person has to know with whom he or she does or does not want to live. Divorce, while still simple, requires a bit more understanding. It requires the desire to remain separate and to be no longer married to one's spouse. It is the undoing of the contract of marriage ... If marriage is simple, divorce must be equally simple ... the mental capacity required for divorce is the same as required for entering into a marriage ... The capacity to instruct counsel involves the ability to understand financial and legal issues. This puts it significantly higher on the competence hierarchy ... While Mrs Calvert may have lacked the ability to instruct counsel, that did not mean she could not make the basic personal decision to separate and divorce.

Chapter 8 provides further details on capacity to litigate and on the appointment of a 'litigation friend' or 'next friend' to act on behalf of people involved in legal

---

[36] *City of York Council* v. *C* [2013] EWCA Civ 478; [2014] Fam 10.
[37] *Calvert (Litigation Guardian)* v. *Calvert* (1997) 32 OR (3d) 281.
[38] *Park's Estate, Re; Park* v. *Park* [1954] P 112; [1953] 3 WLR 1012.
[39] *Calvert (Litigation Guardian)* v. *Calvert* (1997) 32 OR (3d) 281 at 293f, 294g and 298e–g.

proceedings (such as divorce proceedings) who lack capacity to instruct a legal representative. Further advice about capacity to instruct a solicitor is given in **2.1**.

Finally, it should be noted that the Court of Protection is expressly precluded from consenting on behalf of an incapacitated person to either a decree of divorce being granted (or a dissolution order being made in relation to a civil partnership) on the basis of two years' separation.[40]

11.6 CONCLUSION

It is important to remember the rights of people with a disability or illness when considering their ability to make their own decisions. As noted above, the United Nations Declaration of Human Rights states that all adults are of equal value and have a right to the same freedoms. One of these rights for adults is the right to express their sexuality and to participate in family life.

---

[40] MCA 2005, s.27(1)(c)–(d).

CHAPTER 12

Capacity to consent: the criminal law and sexual offences

12.1	Introduction	12.3	Giving evidence in court
12.2	The Sexual Offences Act 2003	12.4	Conclusion

12.1 INTRODUCTION

This chapter deals with the approach of the criminal law towards sexual behaviour and people who are at risk of abuse because of mental health problems or learning disability. The primary focus of the criminal law is upon non-consensual conduct. It is recognised that people with mental health problems or learning disabilities have an equal right to express their sexuality and to form relationships commensurate with their ability to give consent[1] (see **Chapter 11**). The role of the law is to police the line between the legitimate right of all adult persons to engage in sexual relationships and the need to protect adults at risk of exploitation and abuse.

The law in this area underwent significant changes following the passage of the Sexual Offences Act 2003, which clarified a previously confused and overlapping series of provisions.

12.2 THE SEXUAL OFFENCES ACT 2003

12.2.1 Consent and mental capacity

A person consents to engaging in sexual activity if they agree by choice and have the freedom and capacity to make that choice.[2] There is no definition of capacity in the Sexual Offences Act 2003, but the Court of Appeal has made clear that the tests of capacity to consent to sexual activity should be similar whether the tests are applied

---

[1] The right to respect for private life, of which intimate sexual activity forms a part, is protected by ECHR, art.8.
[2] Sexual Offences Act 2003, s.74.

in the context of the criminal law or for purposes of MCA 2005.[3] Reference should therefore also be made to **11.3** where the approach under MCA 2005 is discussed, although it should be noted that the *way* in which the test will apply will differ according to the context:

- the test is applied retrospectively under the criminal law, to examine whether the person consented to *that* particular activity at *that* particular time with *that* particular defendant;
- the test is applied prospectively under MCA 2005, and the question is whether the person in question has the capacity to consent to a sexual activity or category of sexual activities, not whether they have the capacity to consent to sexual activity with a particular person.[4]

In addition, the 2003 Act states that a person may lack capacity to consent not just on the common law grounds, but 'for any other reason'.[5] In an appeal to the House of Lords, Baroness Hale of Richmond has held that these words:

> are clearly capable of encompassing a wide range of circumstances in which a person's mental disorder may rob them of the ability to make an autonomous choice, even though they may have sufficient understanding of the information relevant to making it.[6]

The 2003 Act made clear that, where the defendant intentionally deceived the victim as to the nature or purpose of the sexual act, or intentionally induced the complainant to consent to it by impersonating someone known personally to the complainant, consent will conclusively be presumed to be absent.[7] A series of situations are also set out in the Act where it will be presumed that no consent exists unless there is evidence to the contrary. These include situations of violence, fear of violence, or unlawful detention, and where the complainant had been asleep or unconscious or unable to communicate whether or not they consented, due to physical disability.[8]

12.2.2 Rape

In respect of those complainants aged 13 and above, rape is the intentional penetration with the penis of the vagina, anus or mouth of a complainant without their consent.[9] To be guilty of rape, the perpetrator must lack a reasonable belief that

---

[3] *IM v. LM, AB and Liverpool City Council (Capacity to Consent to Sexual Relations)* [2014] EWCA Civ 37; [2015] Fam 61.
[4] *IM v. LM, AB and Liverpool City Council (Capacity to Consent to Sexual Relations)* [2014] EWCA Civ 37; [2015] Fam 61 at paras.48 and 75–79. See also *R v. A (G)* [2014] EWCA Crim 299; [2014] 1 WLR 2469, where it was held that the standard of proof for lack of capacity under the 2003 Act is the criminal standard.
[5] Sexual Offences Act 2003, s.30(2)(a).
[6] *R v. C* [2009] UKHL 42; [2009] 1 WLR 1786 at para.25.
[7] Sexual Offences Act 2003, s.76.
[8] Sexual Offences Act 2003, s.75.
[9] Sexual Offences Act 2003, s.1(1).

there is consent. There can in any event be no defence of consent where sexual activity is alleged in relation to a child aged under 13 years.

The burden of proving the absence of consent lies upon the prosecution. It is important to bear in mind the following general principles, which apply in all cases where rape is alleged and whatever the capacity of the complainant:

- The vital ingredients of the offence are penetration (including partial penetration) and lack of consent.
- The use of force is not required.
- The victim's consent may be vitiated by threat, duress, or inculcation of fear.
- Mere submission does not equate to consent although the dividing line may on occasion be difficult to draw.[10]

Where a complainant is able to give evidence, the jury will accordingly have to decide whether they did in fact consent. A particular problem may arise where the complainant has difficulties giving a lucid or coherent account of events. Expert evidence of limited mental functioning, social functioning or intellectual impairment will not necessarily prove lack of consent apart from in the most extreme cases.

In such cases where it may be difficult to provide conclusive evidence of rape, the prosecution may have to grasp the nettle and seek a conviction for an alternative lesser offence (see below).[11] The consequence may be that on conviction, a perpetrator faces a markedly lower sentence than his behaviour might otherwise justify.

12.2.3 Other sexual offences: general

The previous offence of indecent assault has been replaced by several different offences:

- assault by penetration[12] (with a separate offence relating to child victims[13]);
- sexual assault[14] (or sexual assault on a child under 13[15]); and
- causing a person to engage in sexual activity without consent[16] (or causing or inciting a child under 13 to engage in sexual activity[17]).

---

[10] See *R* v. *Olugboja* [1981] 3 WLR 585 at 585–93 and *R* v. *NW* [2015] EWCA Crim 559 at paras.33–34.

[11] For instance, an offence under the Sexual Offences Act 2003, s.30(1), which makes it an offence to undertake sexual activity with a person with a mental disorder impeding capacity to make a choice, or an alternative charge under s.34(1) that agreement was obtained by means of inducement, threat or deception of a person with a mental disorder. The House of Lords has commented that alternative charges would enable the judge to explain the various concepts and relate them to the evidence: *R* v. *C* [2009] UKHL 42; [2009] 1 WLR 1786 at para.32.

[12] Sexual Offences Act 2003, s.2(1).

[13] Sexual Offences Act 2003, s.6(1).

[14] Sexual Offences Act 2003, s.3(1).

[15] Sexual Offences Act 2003, s.7(1).

[16] Sexual Offences Act 2003, s.4(1).

[17] Sexual Offences Act 2003, s.8(1).

The Sexual Offences Act 2003 deals with the question of consent in the same way as consent for rape (see above).

12.2.4 Sexual offences against people with mental disorders or learning disabilities

The Sexual Offences Act 2003 introduced a range of offences specific to victims with a 'mental disorder' or 'learning disability'. The offences are committed by sexual activity with,[18] or in the presence or view of,[19] someone who is unable to refuse because they are suffering from mental disorder or learning disability, or by intentionally causing or inciting such a person to engage in sexual activity.[20] It must be the case that the defendant knows, or could reasonably be expected to know, of the victim's condition and that this is likely to make them unable to refuse. A separate group of sections in the Sexual Offences Act 2003 created offences where the same situations are brought about by inducement, threat or deception.[21]

Where some capacity to consent exists there may still be the potential for exploitation. Even where a person with mental health problems or a learning disability fully understands and consents to a sexual relationship there may be grounds for the criminal law to intervene for public policy reasons should that person be under the professional care of the other person involved.

To provide for such circumstances, the 2003 Act created a final group of offences which can be committed only by 'care workers'.[22] This term is defined to include workers in NHS bodies, independent medical agencies, care homes, community homes, voluntary homes, and children's homes, independent clinics, and independent hospitals, who have had or are likely to have regular face-to-face contact with the victim in the course of their employment.[23] It also includes those who, whether or not in the course of employment, provide care, assistance, or services to the victim in connection with the victim's learning disability or mental disorder, where they have regular face-to-face contact with the victim.

12.3 GIVING EVIDENCE IN COURT

12.3.1 Assisting the vulnerable witness

Even if a person with mental health problems or a learning disability is able to provide an account of an assault to the police, giving evidence to a court may be more difficult for them than for other witnesses. The legal process can be intimidating or confusing enough to any witness but for those with a learning disability or

---

[18]   Sexual Offences Act 2003, s.30(1).
[19]   Sexual Offences Act 2003, ss.32(1) and 33(1).
[20]   Sexual Offences Act 2003, s.31(1).
[21]   Sexual Offences Act 2003, ss.34–37.
[22]   Sexual Offences Act 2003, ss.38–41.
[23]   Sexual Offences Act 2003, s.42.

mental disorder it may seem to be practically impossible. Lawyers may use confusing terms and jargon; complex questions and court procedures may cause bewilderment and justice may be difficult to achieve.

The need to offer effective support and assistance in giving evidence to those who may be particularly vulnerable was addressed in Part II of the Youth Justice and Criminal Evidence Act 1999. A lack of ability to understand and communicate may in due course be met by the judge making a 'special measures direction'. This might include the witness receiving assistance from an intermediary explaining questions and communicating answers 'so far as is necessary to enable them to be understood by the witness or person in question'.[24]

Witnesses are eligible for this assistance[25] if they suffer from a mental disorder within the meaning of mental health legislation (MHA 1983)[26] or otherwise have 'significant impairment of intelligence and social functioning'. The purpose of providing the assistance is to preserve the 'quality' of the witness's evidence in terms of its 'completeness, coherence and accuracy'.[27]

The presence in court of the alleged abuser may provide a powerful disincentive for a witness to give an account of what took place. Legislation now permits the giving of evidence by pre-recorded video tape and cross-examination via a video link, thereby avoiding the need for direct confrontation of complainant and accused.[28] The Ministry of Justice has provided detailed guidance in relation to the use of such special measures.[29] In addition, where required, judges should set 'ground rules', aimed at ensuring the fair treatment of the witness, which the cross-examiner must abide by.[30]

12.3.2 The absent witness

If a witness is unable to give evidence, consideration may be given to having their witness statement read to the court instead,[31] subject to strict rules. For present purposes, the most relevant rules are:

1. The witness is 'unfit to be a witness' by reason of 'bodily or mental condition'.[32]

2. The witness, through fear, does not give (or continue to give) oral evidence in the proceedings, either at all or in connection with the subject-matter of the

---

[24] Youth Justice and Criminal Evidence Act 1999, s.29(2).
[25] Youth Justice and Criminal Evidence Act 1999, s.16(2).
[26] Defined as 'any disorder or disability of the mind' in MHA 1983, s.1(2), as amended by MHA 2007.
[27] Youth Justice and Criminal Evidence Act 1999, s.16(1)(b) and (5).
[28] Youth Justice and Criminal Evidence Act 1999, ss.24 and 27.
[29] Ministry of Justice (2011) *Achieving Best Evidence in Criminal Proceedings: Guidance on Interviewing Victims and Witnesses, and Guidance on Using Special Measures*, available at **www.cps.gov.uk/publications/docs/best_evidence_in_criminal_proceedings.pdf**.
[30] CPR rule 3.9(7)
[31] Criminal Justice Act 2003, s.116(1).
[32] Criminal Justice Act 2003, s.116(2)(b).

statement.[33] If an application is made to introduce evidence under this rule, the application will only be granted if it is considered by the trial judge to be in the interests of justice so to do.[34]

Whatever the difficulties, a prosecution may in certain circumstances proceed in the absence of the complainant's evidence provided that 'consent' is not the primary issue. In those circumstances it may be practically impossible to secure a conviction. Where a complainant's consent is not material (as in the offences against people with mental disorders or learning disabilities discussed at **12.2**) then the essential requirement will be evidence to prove that sexual touching or interference took place combined with proof of the condition of the complainant.

12.4 CONCLUSION

The rights of those with mental health problems or learning disabilities to make their own decisions, to express their sexuality and to participate as fully as possible in family life remain profoundly important. Whether the criminal law appears to strike the correct balance between the protection of people at risk of abuse on the one hand, and an unduly paternalistic and authoritarian stance upon the other, will doubtless depend upon the circumstances of each individual case.

---

[33] Criminal Justice Act 2003, s.116(2)(e).
[34] Criminal Justice Act 2003, s.116(4).

CHAPTER 13

Capacity and medical treatment

13.1   Introduction
13.2   The need for patient consent
13.3   Treatment without consent
13.4   Capacity to consent to medical
       procedures

13.5   Care and treatment for adults who
       lack capacity to consent
13.6   Attorneys and deputies
13.7   Advance statements and decisions
13.8   Confidentiality and disclosure

13.1   INTRODUCTION

The House of Lords Select Committee established in 2013 to scrutinise how MCA 2005 was working in practice found there to be widespread ignorance of its provisions.[1] The Committee found that healthcare professionals, in particular, were not aware of MCA 2005, and were failing to implement the provisions of the Act. The report served, and should still serve, as a 'wake-up' call for healthcare professionals, and a stimulus for greater focus upon the need to consider questions of capacity carefully in all aspects of the delivery of medical treatment.

This chapter describes the provisions of MCA 2005 as they apply to decisions about medical treatment and procedures (see also **Chapter 3**, where the key concepts of MCA 2005 are explained). It is important for healthcare professionals to be aware that the provision of any treatment to incapacitated adults that does not comply with the provisions of MCA 2005 may be unlawful. 'Adult' in this context means those aged 18 and over, since special considerations apply to young people aged 16–17 (see **3.8**). 'Treatment' in this chapter includes a diagnostic or other procedure, for example examination, and medical or nursing interventions (including treatment) aimed at alleviating a medical condition or preventing its deterioration. Therapies designed to rehabilitate patients are also included in this definition. Medical research and innovative treatments are considered in **Chapter 14**.

---

[1] House of Lords Select Committee on the Mental Capacity Act 2005 (2014) *Mental Capacity Act 2005: Post-legislative Scrutiny*, HL Paper 139, available at **www.publications.parliament.uk/pa/ld201314/ldselect/ldmentalcap/139/139.pdf**, paras.103–110.

The chapter, finally, considers the issues that arise when a healthcare professional may have to disclose confidential information relating to a patient who cannot give the requisite consent.

13.2 THE NEED FOR PATIENT CONSENT

It has long been established at common law that touching a patient without valid consent may constitute the criminal offence of battery or the tort of trespass and, except in cases where the law permits otherwise, any treatment given to a competent person without their consent will be unlawful.[2] A healthcare professional who does not respect this principle may be liable both to legal action by the patient and to action by their professional body. Employing bodies may also be liable for the actions of their staff. Further, if healthcare professionals fail to obtain proper consent and the patient subsequently suffers harm as a result of treatment, this may be a factor in a claim of negligence against the healthcare professional involved.[3]

Consent may be given verbally, for example by a patient agreeing to have an X-ray or scan, or in writing, for example by signing a consent form prior to a surgical procedure. Patients may allow treatment to take place – for example by holding out an arm to show they are happy to have a blood test. This is usually referred to (including in guidance from the General Medical Council[4]) as 'implied consent'. However, reliance upon such implied consent is appropriate only in the case of minor or routine investigations or treatments, if the doctor is satisfied that the patient understands what they propose to do and why. In the case of any doubt as to the patient's capacity in this regard, reliance upon implied consent is unlikely to be appropriate, and it may be necessary to take steps formally to assess the patient's capacity.

For consent to be valid, it must be given voluntarily by an appropriately informed patient who has the capacity to consent to the intervention in question. If the patient lacks capacity to consent to the intervention consent may be given by a person authorised to do so under an LPA or someone who has the authority to make treatment decisions as a court appointed deputy. Acquiescence where the person does not know what the intervention entails is not 'consent'.

In almost all cases where a patient has the capacity to make a decision as to whether they wish to be treated or examined, legally and ethically, their informed consent is required before the treatment or examination can proceed.

Some people, however, may consent to treatment while choosing not to be given the full details of their diagnosis or treatment. This is nevertheless valid so long as

---

[2]   See, e.g., *Re F (Mental Patient: Sterilisation)* [1990] 2 AC 1; and *Re B (Adult: Refusal of Medical Treatment)* [2002] EWHC 429 (Fam); [2002] 2 All ER 449.

[3]   Department of Health (2009) *Reference Guide to Consent for Examination or Treatment* (2nd edn), para.2, available at **www.gov.uk/government/publications/reference-guide-to-consent-for-examination-or-treatment-second-edition**.

[4]   *Consent Guidance: Expressions of Consent*, available at **www.gmc-uk.org/guidance/ethical_guidance/consent_guidance_expressions_of_consent.asp**.

they had the option of receiving more information. People who refuse information must still be provided with some basic information, since without this they cannot make a valid choice to delegate responsibility for treatment decisions to the doctor. The amount of basic information depends upon the individual circumstances, the severity of the condition, and the risks associated with the treatment. Doctors must seek to strike a balance between giving the patient sufficient information for a valid decision, and respecting the patient's wish not to know.

13.3 TREATMENT WITHOUT CONSENT

In some circumstances the law permits healthcare professionals to treat the patient without consent, for example certain treatment under the mental health legislation (see **Chapter 16**) and in circumstances where the patient needs treatment urgently but is unconscious or is otherwise unable to make a decision either himself or by a proxy decision-maker. In an emergency, where consent cannot be obtained, health-care professionals should provide medical treatment that is in the patient's best interests and is immediately necessary to save life or avoid significant deterioration in the patient's health. Treatment may also be given during an operation, if it becomes obvious that the patient immediately requires an additional procedure to treat a life-threatening problem that was not included in their original consent, and is not capable of giving consent to that further procedure.[5]

Wherever a person lacks capacity to make a decision, MCA 2005 provides the legal framework for acting and making decisions on behalf of the patient and those decisions must be made in the patient's best interests[6] (see further **3.3**).

If a patient has appointed an attorney with authority to make decisions relating to their medical treatment, or there is a court appointed deputy with this authority then that attorney or deputy is the decision-maker, and treatment should not be given without their consent unless in the event of an emergency where it is not possible to contact the decision-maker (see further **13.6**).

If the patient is an adult and has made a valid and applicable advance refusal of a particular treatment (such as a refusal of blood by a Jehovah's Witness) that treatment should not be given if the treating team are (or ought reasonably to be aware) of that advance refusal (see further **13.7**, including as to the circumstances when treatment may be given in cases of doubt as to the validity or applicability of the refusal).

---

5   *Connolly v. Croydon Health Services NHS Trust* [2015] EWHC 1339 (QB).
6   MCA 2005, s.4.

13.4   CAPACITY TO CONSENT TO MEDICAL PROCEDURES

13.4.1   Application of the MCA principles to capacity to consent to or refuse treatment

The assessment of an adult patient's capacity to make a decision about their own healthcare or medical treatment is a matter for the professional judgment of the doctor or the healthcare professional proposing the intervention, applying the statutory test of capacity set out in MCA 2005 (see **13.4.2**).

The assessment of capacity relates to the particular healthcare decision at the time the decision needs to be made. The starting point is the presumption that every adult has capacity to make their own healthcare decisions unless there is evidence to the contrary.[7] It is a fundamental principle of MCA 2005 that: '[a] person is not to be treated as unable to make a decision unless all practicable steps to help him to do so have been taken without success.'[8] Therefore, every effort must be made to explain all relevant information relating to the proposed treatment in terms the patient can understand, offering appropriate support and other aids to communication, and not 'by bombarding the patient with technical information which the patient cannot reasonably be expected to grasp'.[9]

Even where there is a welfare attorney or deputy with authority to make healthcare decisions, every effort should be made to help the patient make the decision for themselves since the patient's capacitous decision takes priority. If the patient does not accept the doctor's advice, and therefore makes what the doctor considers to be an unwise decision, it should not automatically be assumed that the patient lacks capacity to make that decision (see **13.4.3**).

13.4.2   The test of capacity

All people aged 16 and over are presumed, in law, to have the capacity to consent to treatment unless there is evidence to the contrary. The test of capacity of an adult patient to give consent to medical treatment is the test of capacity set out in MCA 2005 (see also **3.4**).[10] The test in MCA 2005 enshrines, with some modifications, the common law tests established in the judgments of *Re C (Adult: Refusal of Medical Treatment*[11] and *Re MB (Medical Treatment),*[12] which continue to provide assistance in applying the MCA test of capacity in relation to decisions about medical procedures.

In order to give a valid consent to treatment a patient should be able to understand the nature, purpose and effects of the proposed treatment, the last of these entailing

---

[7]   MCA 2005, s.1(2).

[8]   MCA 2005, s.1(3).

[9]   *Montgomery* v. *Lanarkshire Health Board* [2015] UKSC 11 at para.90.

[10]   The statutory test of capacity in MCA 2005, ss.2 and 3, taking account of the principles in MCA 2005, s.1.

[11]   *Re C (Adult: Refusal of Medical Treatment)* [1994] 1 WLR 290; [1994] 1 All ER 819.

[12]   *Re MB (Medical Treatment)* [1997] 2 FLR 426.

an understanding of the benefits and risks of deciding to have or not to have the proposed treatment, or of not making a decision at all.[13] The patient is required to have a broad, general understanding of the kind that is expected from the population at large and is not required to understand every last piece of information about their situation and their options.[14]

The Supreme Court in *Montgomery* v. *Lanarkshire Health Board*[15] made clear in 2015 that the doctrine of informed consent is now part of English law (reflecting what had been good clinical practice for some considerable period of time). A doctor is now under a *legal* duty to make sure that the patient is aware of the material risks associated with a medical procedure. The test of materiality is:

> whether, in the circumstances of the particular case, a reasonable person in the patient's position would be likely to attach significance to the risk, or the doctor is or should reasonably be aware that the particular patient would be likely to attach significance to it.[16]

Information as to material risks can only be withheld on the basis of therapeutic necessity, not on the basis of value judgments on the part of the treating doctor.[17] In other words, information can only be withheld if the giving of that information would, itself, cause harm to the patient.

There may be situations in which considerable clinical judgment and – above all – communication skills must be deployed in order to ensure that a patient with mental health problems and/or learning disabilities is put in a position whereby they are given the information material to the procedure without being overloaded with unnecessary information. The Supreme Court emphasised in *Montgomery* the importance of ensuring that a proper dialogue takes place between doctor and patient prior to any procedure being carried out: this is one aspect of that dialogue.

If there is any doubt about a patient's capacity the reasons why capacity is in doubt should be recorded in the patient's medical record, as should details of the key elements of discussion with the patient. This should include the information discussed, any specific requests by the patient, any written, visual or audio information given to the patient, and details of any assessments, findings and decisions that were made.[18] The more serious the decision, the more formal the assessment of capacity may need to be. In cases of doubt or in relation to complex or major

---

[13]   *Heart of England NHS Foundation Trust* v. *JB* [2014] EWHC 342 (COP); (2014) 137 BMLR 232 at para.25.

[14]   *Heart of England NHS Foundation Trust* v. *JB* [2014] EWHC 342 (COP); (2014) 137 BMLR 232 at para.26.

[15]   *Montgomery* v. *Lanarkshire Health Board* [2015] UKSC 11; [2015] 2 WLR 768.

[16]   *Montgomery* v. *Lanarkshire Health Board* [2015] UKSC 11; [2015] 2 WLR 768 at para.87.

[17]   The limits to the ability to withhold information also applies in relation to DNA CPR notices: see *R (Tracey)* v. *Cambridge University Hospitals NHS Foundation Trust* [2014] EWCA Civ 822; [2014] 3 WLR 822 and guidance from the BMA, the Resuscitation Council (UK) and the Royal College of Nursing (2014) *Decisions Relating to Cardiopulmonary Resuscitation* (3rd edn), available at **www.resus.org.uk/dnacpr/decisions-relating-to-cpr/**.

[18]   General Medical Council (2013) *Good Medical Practice*, available at **www.gmc-uk.org/guidance/good_medical_practice.asp**, para.51

decisions, it might also be advisable to refer to another professional with experience of assessing mental capacity in relation to the needs of the specific individual, such as a psychiatrist, psychologist, speech and language therapist or social worker. Situations where a professional opinion may be required are set out in the MCA Code of Practice.[19] However, it would be inappropriate and impractical for professional experts to be routinely called upon in situations where assessments using the statutory test of capacity can be carried out by other decision-makers. Responsibility rests with the person intending to make the decision on behalf of the incapacitated adult or to carry out the proposed medical procedure, not with the professional advising about capacity (see further **3.6**).

Practical aspects of assessment of capacity are discussed in more detail in **Part IV** of this book.

13.4.3 Capacity to refuse medical procedures

At common law competent adults have long been held to have a right to refuse medical diagnostic procedures or treatment, except where compulsory treatment is authorised under the mental health legislation. They can do so for reasons which are 'rational, irrational or for no reason'. This principle was established in the case of *Sidaway* v. *Board of Governors of the Bethlem Royal Hospital and Maudsley Hospital*[20] and upheld in subsequent cases. It is irrelevant whether refusal is contrary to the views of most other people. The principle that an adult patient has the right to refuse treatment as long as they have been properly informed of the implications and can make a free choice was affirmed by the Court of Appeal in the case of *Re T (Adult: Refusal of Treatment)*.[21] The Master of the Rolls in the same case emphasised the need for doctors faced with a refusal of consent to give very careful and detailed consideration to the patient's capacity to decide at the time when the decision was made.[22]

The propositions set out above hold just as true now that the governing framework is MCA 2005. In other regards, some of the pre-MCA case law should be approached with caution now that a body of cases decided under MCA 2005 has been built up. In particular, the pre-MCA case law emphasised that a refusal of consent which carries with it serious consequences required a greater level of capacity than a refusal of consent with lesser consequences.[23] This proposition has not been tested since the passage of MCA 2005, but judges of the Court of Protection have repeatedly warned against both the 'protective impulse' (i.e. the natural tendency of treating professionals to conflate apparently unwise decisions with a lack of capacity) and the discrimination inherent in asking 'more of people

---

[19] Office of the Public Guardian (2007) *Mental Capacity Act 2005 Code of Practice*, paras.4.51–4.54, available at **www.gov.uk/government/publications/mental-capacity-act-code-of-practice**.
[20] *Sidaway* v. *Board of Governors of the Bethlem Royal Hospital and Maudsley Hospital* [1985] AC 871.
[21] *Re T (Adult: Refusal of Treatment)* [1992] 4 All ER 649.
[22] *Re T (Adult: Refusal of Treatment)* [1992] 4 All ER 649 at 661h.
[23] See both *Re T* and also *Re MB (Medical Treatment)* [1997] EWCA Civ 3093 at 30.

whose capacity is questioned than those of whose capacity is undoubted'.[24] It is undoubtedly appropriate in the case of a refusal of treatment to investigate with rigour whether the person concerned can retain, understand, use and weigh the relevant information, but that investigation must remain governed by the principles of MCA 2005.

The courts have recommended that, in cases of uncertainty about the capacity of the patient to consent to or refuse treatment, doubt should be resolved as soon as possible by doctors within the hospital or NHS body or by other normal medical procedures, for example seeking a second opinion from an appropriately qualified independent healthcare professional. Under MCA 2005, in cases of doubt that cannot be resolved locally, application should be made to the Court of Protection for a declaration as to the patient's capacity to consent to or to refuse treatment and, if the court determines that the patient lacks capacity, whether the proposed treatment is in the patient's best interests (see **Appendix C**). It is possible to obtain relief very quickly from the Court of Protection (a Court of Protection judge is available 24 hours a day, 365 days a year).

13.4.4 Duress and undue influence

For a patient's consent to be valid it must be given voluntarily. There may be patients who are unable to take their own decisions because of influence exercised over them by others (for example, family members) rather than from an impairment of, or disturbance in the functioning of their mind or brain.

In these circumstances it is possible for any person or body concerned as to whether the individual is under duress or subject to undue influence to seek the assistance of the High Court to provide its protection under its inherent jurisdiction.[25] The High Court has the power to grant injunctive or other relief with the aim of putting in place a framework to enable the individual to make their own decision (for a fuller discussion see **3.5**).

It is possible for relief to be sought and granted very quickly from the High Court (which is available 24 hours a day, 365 days a year), and the pre-MCA case of *Re T (Adult: Refusal of Treatment)*[26] remains a good example of how quickly it is possible for the courts to react in such cases.

---

[24]   *Heart of England NHS Foundation Trust* v. *JB* [2014] EWHC 342 (COP); (2014) 137 BMLR 232 at para.25. In the same case, Peter Jackson J also pointed out that none of the following statements (which routinely appear in assessments of capacity in the medical context) 'sit easily with the burden or standard of proof contained in the [MCA]:' (1) the person was 'unable to clearly show that she had considered the option' of amputation; (2) 'one needs to be certain of her capacity;' and (3) the person 'is unable to fully understand, retain and weigh information ...'

[25]   See *Re L (Vulnerable Adults with Capacity: Court's Jurisdiction)* [2012] EWCA Civ 253; [2013] Fam. 1.

[26]   *Re T (Adult: Refusal of Treatment)* [1993] Fam 35. It is more likely than not that this would be viewed, now, as a case relating to a vulnerable adult whose will was overborne rather than a person who lacked capacity within the meaning of MCA 2005.

13.5 CARE AND TREATMENT FOR ADULTS WHO LACK CAPACITY TO CONSENT

13.5.1 Best interests

If it has been established that an adult lacks the capacity to consent to a treatment or intervention it is a fundamental principle of MCA 2005 that any act done or decision made for or on behalf of that person, must be done, or made, in his best interests (see **3.7**).[27] This requirement had been established for some time at common law prior to the Act.[28]

The only exceptions to this principle are where the person has previously made an advance decision refusing medical treatment which is both valid and applicable in the current circumstances (see **13.7**) and in some situations where the incapacitated person is involved in research (see **Chapter 14**).

An assessment of a patient's best interests involves more than just an assessment of what would be best clinically and includes consideration of the patient's welfare in the wider sense:

> In considering the best interests of a particular patient at a particular time the decision-makers must look at the patient's welfare in the widest sense, not just medical but social and psychological; they must consider the nature of the medical treatment in question, what it involves and its prospects of success; they must consider what the outcome of that treatment for the patient is likely to be; they must try and put themselves in the place of the individual patient and ask what his attitude to the treatment is or would be likely to be; and they must consult others who are looking after him or interested in his welfare, in particular for their view of what his attitude would be.[29]

Whenever possible, reasonable efforts should be made to encourage the patient to participate in the decision and ascertain their wishes and values if they can be ascertained. A crucial part of any best interests assessment will involve a discussion with those close to the person lacking capacity as they will often have important information about what would be in the person's best interests. MCA 2005 provides a list of those who should be consulted, where it is practical or appropriate to do so, including:

- anyone previously named by the person as someone they wish to be consulted;
- anyone engaged in caring for the person or interested in their welfare; and
- any donee or deputy appointed for the person.[30]

There may be circumstances where consultation might not be possible, for example in an emergency, or circumstances where consultation might not be practicable and appropriate, for example where healthcare professionals are providing routine care,

---

[27] MCA 2005, s.1(5).
[28] *Re F (Mental Patient: Sterilisation)* [1990] 2 AC 1.
[29] *Aintree University Hospitals NHS Foundation Trust* v. *James* [2013] UKSC 67; [2014] AC 591 at para.39.
[30] MCA 2005, s.4(7).

such as taking a patient's temperature, which is manifestly both necessary and in the patient's best interests.

It is important, however, not to take short cuts when making an assessment of best interests. Health professionals involved in making best interests determinations should ensure that a record is kept of the process by which the person's best interests were worked out.[31]

Where decisions need to be made about serious medical treatment (described further below) or where a healthcare decision may involve a decision about where the person should live in the longer term (such as a placement in a care home or hospital), and there is no one available who fits into the above categories who it is appropriate to consult in an assessment of best interests, an Independent Mental Capacity Advocate (IMCA) must be appointed to represent and support the incapacitated person.[32]

13.5.2   Acts in connection with care and treatment

If an adult patient temporarily or permanently lacks capacity to consent to medical treatment, no other person can consent on the patient's behalf unless they are acting under the authority of a registered health and welfare LPA or under a deputyship authorised by the Court of Protection (see **13.6**).

However, MCA 2005 allows carers (both informal and paid carers) and health professionals to carry out certain acts in connection with the personal care, healthcare or treatment for a person lacking capacity to consent to those acts without incurring liability.[33] In a healthcare setting, this allows actions to be taken to ensure a person who lacks capacity to consent to treatment receives necessary medical care and treatment. Such actions can be carried out, provided that:

- the decision-maker has a reasonable belief that the individual lacks capacity; and
- the act, decision or treatment is in the best interests of the incapacitated person.[34]

In these circumstances, it is not necessary to obtain any formal powers or authority to act. However, if practical, anyone involved in the person's care or interested in their welfare, should be consulted in determining whether the proposed treatment is in their best interests. Attempts should also be made to confirm whether the individual has either made a health and welfare LPA or has a court appointed health

---

[31]   General Medical Council (2013) *Good Medical Practice*, available at **www.gmc-uk.org/ guidance/good_medical_practice.asp**, para.51.

[32]   MCA, ss.35–41 established the Independent Mental Capacity Advocate (IMCA) service, to provide a statutory right to advocacy services for particularly vulnerable people who lack capacity to make certain serious decisions. See the SCIE Mental Capacity Act Directory at **www.scie.org.uk/ mca-directory/keygovernmentdocuments.asp**.

[33]   MCA 2005, s.5.

[34]   MCA 2005, s.5(1).

and welfare deputy, as both an attorney and a deputy will have an elevated status in decision-making (see **13.6**).

This legal protection applies not only to an episode of treatment itself, but also to those ancillary procedures that are necessary, such as conveying a person to hospital (so long as those procedures do not, themselves, amount to a deprivation of the person's liberty: see further **13.5.3** and **Chapter 15**). All interventions under these provisions must be in accord with the principles of MCA 2005 (see **Chapter 3**). MCA 2005 also makes clear that anyone acting unreasonably, negligently or not in the person's best interests could forfeit protection from liability.

This protection given to healthcare professionals acting in connection with care or treatment does not permit them to give a treatment contrary to a person's valid and applicable advance decision to refuse treatment[35] (see **13.7**). Similarly, they cannot act contrary to any decision taken by an attorney acting under a registered health and welfare LPA or a court appointed deputy (see **13.6**), so long as that attorney or deputy has the authority to make the decision in question.

13.5.3 Restraint

MCA 2005 sets out the limits of the protection offered to decision-makers carrying out acts in connection with a person's care or treatment.[36] In particular, it places conditions on the protection offered to healthcare professionals under MCA 2005, s.5 when they perform an act which 'restrains' a person who lacks capacity.[37] Restraint is defined by MCA 2005 as the use or threat of force to secure the doing of an act which the person resists, or restriction of the person's liberty of movement, whether or not they resist.[38]

As a general rule, any act that is intended to restrain a person lacking capacity will not attract protection from liability, unless the following conditions are met:

- the person using restraint must reasonably believe that it is necessary to do the act in order to prevent harm to the person lacking capacity; and
- the restraint is proportionate to the likelihood of the person suffering harm and to the seriousness of that harm.

In such circumstances, only the minimum necessary force or intervention may be used and for the shortest possible duration. Careful records must be kept of the reasons justifying any use of restraint. The point at which restraint may become a deprivation of liberty is discussed further in **Chapter 15**. A person can only be deprived of their liberty pursuant to MCA 2005 where this is authorised by the Court of Protection, or under MCA 2005, Sched.A1 or under the provisions of MHA 1983, as appropriate. See further in this regard **Chapter 15**.

---

[35] MCA 2005, s.5(4).
[36] MCA 2005, s.6.
[37] MCA 2005, s.6(1)–(3).
[38] MCA 2005, s.6(4).

13.5.4 Serious medical treatment

MCA 2005 provides additional safeguards where 'serious medical treatment' may be required for someone who lacks capacity to consent to it. Serious medical treatment includes the provision, withholding or withdrawal of treatment in circumstances where:

- if a single treatment is proposed, there is a fine balance between the likely benefits and the burdens to the patient and the risks involved; or
- a decision between a choice of treatments is finely balanced; or
- the proposed treatment is likely to have serious consequences for the patient.[39]

Where a serious medical treatment decision is contemplated for a person lacking capacity to consent, and there is no one available to consult as to the person's best interests other than those engaged in providing professional or paid care or treatment for that person, the NHS body responsible for the patient's treatment must ensure that advice is sought from an IMCA.

Before MCA 2005 came into force, the courts had decided that some medical treatment decisions were so serious that each case should be taken to court so that a declaration of lawfulness could be made. This procedure has continued under MCA 2005. Practice Direction 9E (reproduced at **Appendix D**) issued under COPR 2007 as amended describes the procedures to be followed and sets out the types of cases which should be brought before the court.[40] For purposes of PD 9E, 'serious medical treatment' means treatment which involves providing, withdrawing or withholding treatment in circumstances where:

- in a case where a single treatment is being proposed, there is a fine balance between its benefits to the person and the burdens and risks it is likely to entail for him;
- in a case where there is a choice of treatments, a decision as to which one to use is finely balanced; or
- the treatment, procedure or investigation proposed would be likely to involve serious consequences for the person.

Certain types of serious medical treatment cases *have* to go to court, including:

---

[39] For the meaning of 'serious medical treatment', see Mental Capacity Act (Independent Mental Capacity Advocates) (General) Regulations 2006, SI 2006/1832, reg.4. A similar definition is used in Court of Protection Practice Direction 9E, reproduced in **Appendix D**.

[40] Court of Protection Practice Direction 9E: Applications relating to serious medical treatment, paras.5–6. This practice direction was under review as at summer 2015, and is reproduced in **Appendix D**.

- decisions about the proposed withholding or withdrawal of artificial nutrition and hydration from a person in a permanent vegetative state or a minimally conscious state;[41]
- cases involving organ or bone marrow donation by a person who lacks capacity to consent; and
- cases involving non-therapeutic sterilisation of a person who lacks capacity to consent.[42]

Practice Direction 9E also gives a non-exhaustive list of examples of other decisions which should be considered serious medical treatment. It does not state that decisions other than those listed above should be brought to court. However, case law makes clear that at least two categories of case must come to court:

- In respect of a proposed termination of a pregnancy in relation to a person who lacks capacity to consent to such a procedure, an application must be made where:
  - (a) there is dispute over capacity;
  - (b) the patient may regain capacity during her pregnancy;
  - (c) there is any lack of unanimity;
  - (d) the procedures under the Abortion Act 1967, s.1 have not been followed;
  - (e) the patient or members of her immediate family have opposed a termination;
  - (f) there are other exceptional circumstances, including that this may be the patient's last chance to bear a child;[43]

- Certain types of obstetric cases, in particular those involving the use of force. Guidance as to the types of obstetric case that should be brought to court by NHS Trusts has been given by Keehan J in *NHS Trust 1 and NHS Trust 2* v. *FG*.[44]

13.6 ATTORNEYS AND DEPUTIES

13.6.1 Lasting power of attorney

One of the innovations introduced by MCA 2005 is the creation of a power of attorney enabling competent adults to nominate another individual or individuals to make health and welfare decisions on their own behalf when they lack the capacity

---

[41] NB, in all such cases, reference must now be made to the guidelines issued by the Royal College of Physicians in December 2013 on *Prolonged Disorders of Consciousness*, available at **www.rcplondon.ac.uk/resources/prolonged-disorders-consciousness-national-clinical-guidelines**.

[42] See also in this regard *A Local Authority* v. *K* [2013] EWHC 242 (COP); [2013] COPLR 194.

[43] *D* v. *An NHS Trust (Medical Treatment: Consent)* [2003] EWHC 2793 (Fam); [2004] 1 FLR 1110; see also *Re P (Abortion)* [2013] EWHC 50 (COP); [2013] COPLR 405.

[44] *NHS Trust 1 and NHS Trust 2* v. *FG* [2014] EWCOP 30; [2015] 1 WLR 1984.

to make those decisions. This power, known as a lasting power of attorney (LPA), replaces the enduring power of attorney (EPA), which relates only to property and affairs. There is a common misunderstanding among patients and their families (and indeed among healthcare professionals) that an attorney acting under an EPA has the same power as an attorney acting under a health and welfare LPA. They do not, and it is frequently necessary for a sensitive conversation to take place in the hospital setting to explain that an attorney under an EPA does not have any specific decision-making role (although it is very likely that such an attorney should be consulted for purposes of making any best interests decision on behalf of the patient).[45]

There are two types of LPA:

- one relating to a person's property and affairs;
- the other for decisions relating to a person's health and welfare.

An LPA relating to health and welfare decisions can only be used when the individual lacks the capacity to make a relevant decision covered by the LPA. This chapter offers a further explanation of the health and welfare LPA as it affects decisions relating to medical treatment.

Chapter 5 considers the property and affairs LPA and also includes further details (at **5.3**) about capacity to create an LPA and the procedures for creating and registering an LPA, which apply to both property and affairs LPAs and health and welfare LPAs.

13.6.2   Creating and registering a health and welfare LPA

In order to create an LPA an individual must be aged 18 or over and have the necessary mental capacity in accordance with the statutory test of capacity set out in MCA 2005.[46] An LPA has to be created by completing a form prescribed by regulations and it must state that it applies to health and welfare decisions at such a time as the individual creating the LPA lacks the capacity to make those decisions. An LPA must also contain a certificate, signed by an independent person chosen by the donor (either someone who has known the donor for at least two years or a professional), stating that in their opinion, at the time the LPA is created, the donor understands what is involved in making an LPA and has not been put under any undue pressure to do so (see **5.3** for further details). A health and welfare LPA does not give the attorney authority to refuse life-sustaining treatment unless it is

---

[45]   As a person interested in their welfare (MCA 2005, s.4(7)(c)).

[46]   The statutory test of capacity in MCA 2005, ss.2 and 3, taking account of the principles in s.1. (See also **Chapter 3**.)

explicitly stated on the LPA form.[47] There is an online service for making, registering or ending an LPA.[48]

The donor creating the LPA can also set a variety of conditions and limits on the exercise of the powers given to the attorney.

An LPA cannot be used until it has been registered with the Public Guardian. It can be registered before or after the individual lacks capacity. An application to register can be made either by the donor, or by the attorney(s) and can now be made online. Registration can take some time; therefore early registration is advisable to ensure the LPA is valid at the time it needs to be used. Health professionals should check that a health and welfare LPA has been registered before accepting the attorney's authority to make healthcare decisions.

13.6.3 Scope of a health and welfare LPA

Where an individual requires medical treatment, and has been assessed as lacking capacity to consent, an attorney (also called a donee) nominated to act on their behalf under a health and welfare LPA can consent or refuse medical treatment on behalf of the person lacking capacity provided it is within the scope of his authority. An attorney with relevant powers to make health care decisions must be consulted, unless an emergency makes consultation impossible. There are, however, a number of restrictions imposed on the attorney:

- The scope of the attorney's authority to make health and/or welfare decisions must be specified in the LPA. In particular, it is important to check whether the LPA authorises the attorney to make decisions about life-sustaining treatment.
- Any act or decision made under the LPA must be in the incapacitated person's best interests and be in keeping with the other guiding principles of MCA 2005.
- An attorney cannot consent to treatment if the donor has capacity at the time to make the decision for themselves.
- If the donor has previously made a valid advance decision refusing the specified treatment (see **13.7**), the advance decision takes priority unless the LPA was made after the advance decision and gives the attorney the right to consent to or refuse the proposed treatment.
- While LPAs can relate to treatment for a mental disorder, the attorney's decision can be overridden if the individual is subject to compulsory treatment under MHA 1983.

When a health professional has a significant concern relating to decisions taken under the authority of an LPA about serious medical treatment, or believes that an

[47] Available from the Office of the Public Guardian (**www.publicguardian.gov.uk**). The LPA forms were revised in 2009, and these revised forms prescribed in the Schedule to the Lasting Powers of Attorney, Enduring Powers of Attorney and Public Guardian (Amendment) Regulations 2009, SI 2009/1884 must be used after 1 October 2009.
[48] *Make, Register or End a Lasting Power of Attorney* at **www.gov.uk/power-of-attorney/make-lasting-power**. See also the Lasting Powers of Attorney, Enduring Powers of Attorney and Public Guardian (Amendment) Regulations 2013, SI 2013/506.

attorney is not acting in the best interests of the person lacking capacity, the matter should be placed as a matter of urgency before the Court of Protection. Healthcare professionals may properly provide such immediately necessary treatment as is required to secure the patient's interests in the meantime.

13.6.4 Deputies appointed by the Court of Protection

In circumstances where on-going healthcare decisions may need to be made on behalf of a person lacking capacity to consent, the Court of Protection may make an order appointing a welfare deputy to make those specific decisions on the person's behalf (see **Appendix C**). The deputy could be a family member or a professional, as decided by the court. The court must be satisfied that appointing a deputy is in the person's best interests and the court order will set out the extent of the deputy's powers (which should be as limited in scope and duration as is practicable in the circumstances). The deputy can only make decisions that the person lacks capacity to make, and must always act in the person's best interests. MCA 2005, s.20(5) makes clear that a welfare deputy has no power to make decisions about life-sustaining treatment and that such matters must be referred to the court.

Health and welfare deputies are not often appointed; the most common situation is where a parent of a learning disabled child is appointed to act as their deputy upon their turning 18 so as to secure them the same status vis-à-vis health and social care professionals as they enjoyed prior to their child's majority.

13.7 ADVANCE STATEMENTS AND DECISIONS

Adults who are capable of making decisions about their medical treatment can make anticipatory decisions about their preferences for medical treatment, intending them to apply at a later stage when they lose capacity to make such decisions for themselves. The legal enforceability of one type of anticipatory decision, known as 'an advance decision to refuse medical treatment' has been established by the common law and given statutory authority by MCA 2005.[49] Advance decisions cannot be used to *request* specific medical treatment; any such requests (or advance statements of wishes relating to matters other than medical treatment) will be treated as a statement of the person's previous wishes and taken into account when considering the person's best interests in accordance with MCA 2005, s.4 (see **3.7**).

13.7.1 Advance statements

An advance statement is a statement made at a time when the patient has capacity to make decisions about his care and treatment that sets out his preferences, wishes, beliefs and values regarding future care. Under MCA 2005, such wishes and

---

[49] MCA 2005, ss.24–26.

preferences set out in an advance statement are treated as indicative of the person's past wishes and feelings, and in written form as relevant written statements, which must be considered when determining whether any proposed treatment is in the incapacitated person's best interests[50] (see **3.7**). The BMA has published a detailed guidance note on aspects of drafting, storage and implementation of advance statements.[51]

Advance statements can take a variety of forms ranging from general lists of values and preferences, to specific requests for or refusals of treatment. They can be in a written document, a clear oral statement or a note of a discussion recorded in the patient's file. Individuals who are aware of a terminal illness or a progressive condition which may affect their capacity often seek to discuss with their doctors how they wish to be treated. Advance statements enable a structured discussion and recording of the person's views to take place. They can also be very useful in ensuring that matters of importance to the patient that are not strictly medical in nature can be taken into account: a very good example being the advance statement made by the patient in *RGB* v. *Cwm Taf Health Board*.[52] In that case, the statement concerned, in particular, the patient's desire not to have contact with her husband in hospital, and the statement was given effectively determinative weight by the Court of Protection in refusing the husband's application to be allowed contact with her after the Health Board staff had – properly – refused him access on the basis of the statement.

A person is presumed to have capacity to make an advance statement (including about medical treatment) unless it is proven otherwise. The patient should be aware that if the statement concerns a positive consent or request for certain treatments, doctors are not legally bound by such a consent or request, and cannot be compelled to carry out treatments which are contrary to their clinical judgment or to guidance given by the National Institute for Health and Clinical Excellence.[53]

13.7.2 Advance decisions to refuse medical treatment

An advance decision to refuse medical treatment enables adults aged 18 or over to refuse specified medical treatment at a future time when they lack capacity to give or refuse consent to that treatment.[54] An advance decision cannot be used to give effect to an unlawful act, such as euthanasia or assisted suicide or any intervention with the express aim of ending life.[55]

---

[50] MCA 2005, s.4(6)(a).
[51] BMA (2007) *Advance Decisions and Proxy Decision-making in Medical Treatment and Research*, available at **http://bma.org.uk/support-at-work/ethics/mental-capacity**.
[52] *RGB* v. *Cwm Taf Health Board* [2013] EWHC B23 (COP); [2014] COPLR 83.
[53] *Aintree University Hospitals NHS Foundation Trust* v. *James* [2013] UKSC 67; [2014] AC 591 at para.18.
[54] MCA 2005, s.24(1).
[55] MCA 2005, s.62.

13.7.3 Making an advance decision to refuse treatment

Except for decisions relating to life-sustaining treatment (see below), MCA 2005 does not impose any particular formalities concerning the making of advance decisions to refuse treatment. For other types of treatment, both written and oral decisions are acceptable and legally valid, so long as they are supported by appropriate evidence to confirm their existence, validity and applicability (see below). Although there is no prescribed form for making an advance decision, the MCA Code of Practice recommends that it is helpful to include:[56]

- Full details of the person making the advance decision, including date of birth, home address and any distinguishing features (in case healthcare professionals need to identify an unconscious person, for example).
- The name and address of the person's GP and whether they have a copy of the document.
- A statement that the document should be used if the person ever lacks capacity to make treatment decisions.
- A clear statement of the decision, the treatment to be refused and the circumstances in which the decision will apply.
- The date the document was written (or reviewed).
- The person's signature (or the signature of someone the person has asked to sign on their behalf and in their presence).
- The signature of the person witnessing the signature, if there is one (or a statement directing somebody to sign on the person's behalf).

Where an advance decision is made verbally, health professionals should make a record in the patient's notes, which should include:

- a note that the decision should apply if the person lacks capacity to make treatment decisions in the future;
- a clear note of the decision, the treatment to be refused and the circumstances in which the decision will apply;
- details of someone who was present when the oral advance decision was recorded and the role in which they were present (for example, healthcare professional or family member); and
- whether they heard the decision, took part in it or are just aware that it exists.[57]

Where an advance decision is made in writing the onus is on patients to make arrangements for it to be known, for example by giving a copy to their GP, and people close to the patient should be aware of its existence. For chronically ill patients, who are treated by a specialist team over a prolonged period, a copy of the advance decision should be in both relevant hospital files and the GP record. Some

---

[56] Office of the Public Guardian (2007) *Mental Capacity Act 2005 Code of Practice*, para.9.19, available at **www.gov.uk/government/publications/mental-capacity-act-code-of-practice**.
[57] Office of the Public Guardian (2007) *Mental Capacity Act 2005 Code of Practice*, para.9.23, available at **www.gov.uk/government/publications/mental-capacity-act-code-of-practice**.

people also carry a card, bracelet or other measure indicating the existence of an advance decision. Health professionals, once alerted to the existence of a relevant decision, should make reasonable efforts to find it. In an emergency, however, this may not be possible unless it is very promptly made available or registered on a system such as the electronic patient record.[58]

13.7.4 Advance decision refusing life-sustaining treatment

MCA 2005 imposes additional safeguards in relation to advance decisions refusing life-sustaining treatment.[59] Life-sustaining treatment is defined by MCA 2005 as treatment which a person providing healthcare regards as necessary to sustain life.[60] It is for the doctor to assess whether a treatment is life-sustaining in each particular situation and this will depend not only on the type of treatment, but also on the particular circumstances in which it may be prescribed. An advance decision to refuse life-sustaining treatment must meet the following requirements:[61]

- It must be made in writing. If the person is unable to write, someone must write it down for them.
- The person must sign it in the presence of a witness, or if unable to sign it, the person must direct someone to sign it on their behalf, in their presence and in the presence of a witness.
- The witness must sign it, or acknowledge his signature, in the person's presence.
- The document must include a clear, specific written statement from the person making the advance decision that the advance decision is to apply to the specific treatment even if life is at risk.

MCA 2005 distinguishes between 'treatment' and 'care', so it would seem that 'basic care' is not categorised as treatment and can therefore not be refused in an advance decision (but it is important to note that this proposition has yet to be tested in court). 'Basic care' includes warmth, shelter, hygiene measures to maintain body cleanliness, and the offer of food and water by mouth. Under MCA 2005, s.5 this basic and essential care can be carried out in the best interests of the person lacking capacity to consent. However, an advance decision may apply to the refusal of clinically assisted nutrition and hydration which has been recognised as medical treatment[62] (as opposed to feeding which is not clinically assisted).

Although it is not compulsory, it is advisable that anyone drawing up an advance decision discusses it with a health professional such as a GP. It is generally recognised that one of the difficulties with advance decisions is ensuring that they

---

[58] BMA (2007) *Advance Decisions and Proxy Decision-making in Medical Treatment and Research*, available at **http://bma.org.uk/support-at-work/ethics/mental-capacity**.
[59] MCA 2005, s.25(5)–(6).
[60] MCA 2005, s.4(10).
[61] MCA 2005, s.25(5)–(6).
[62] *Airedale NHS Trust* v. *Bland* [1993] AC 789.

will apply to the particular circumstances that may arise. Discussion with individuals with experience of the progress of certain diseases can help to ensure greater compatibility between the terms of an advance decision and the circumstances that are likely to arise.

It may also be prudent (especially if the person in question has fluctuating capacity) to ensure that the decision is accompanied by a contemporaneous assessment of their capacity to make the decision.[63] Precisely what the components of the test of capacity to make an advance decision are has not been be identified by the courts, but the relevant information is likely to include information both as to the medical treatment(s) in question and also the consequences of refusing such treatment(s).

Legal aid is not generally available for making an advance decision.[64]

13.7.5 Safeguards relating to advance decisions

MCA 2005 also provides important statutory safeguards concerning the making and implementation of advance decisions to refuse treatment.[65] It must first be shown that an advance decision to refuse medical treatment as provided for by MCA 2005[66] actually exists. This includes meeting the following requirements:

- The advance decision must be made by a person of 18 years or older with the mental capacity to make it, in accordance with the MCA test of capacity (see above and **Chapter 3**).
- It must specify, in lay terms if necessary, the specific treatment to be refused and the particular circumstances in which the refusal is to apply.

In order for the refusal to be legally effective at the time when it is proposed to carry out or continue treatment, an advance decision to refuse it must also be both valid and applicable to the proposed treatment. A healthcare professional who provides treatment to a patient who has made an advance decision refusing it will not be legally liable unless the advance decision is both valid and applicable to that treatment at the material time.

13.7.6 Validity

Events or circumstances that would make an advance decision invalid are:

- that the person lacked capacity to make the advance decision at the time it was made;
- that the person has withdrawn the decision while they still had capacity to do so;

---

[63] *A Local Authority* v. *E* [2012] EWHC 1639 (COP); [2012] COPLR 441.
[64] Legal Aid, Sentencing and Punishment of Offenders Act 2012, Sch.1, Part 1, para.5(3).
[65] MCA 2005, ss.24–25.
[66] MCA 2005, s.24.

- that, after making the advance decision, the person has created a lasting power of attorney conferring authority on the attorney to give or refuse consent to the treatment specified in the advance decision; or
- that the person has done something which is clearly inconsistent with the advance decision remaining their fixed decision (for example, before MCA 2005 came into force, an advance decision made by a former Jehovah's Witness refusing blood products was held to be invalid after she became betrothed to a Muslim and had indicated she would live by the principles of that faith[67]).

13.7.7 Applicability

An advance decision to refuse treatment is not applicable if:

- the maker still has capacity to give or refuse consent to the treatment in question at the time the treatment is proposed;
- the proposed treatment is not the treatment specified in the advance decision;
- the circumstances are different from those set out in the advance decision; or
- there are reasonable grounds for believing that circumstances have now arisen (such as the development of new treatments or changes in personal circumstances) which were not anticipated by the person when making the advance decision and which would have affected the advance decision had they anticipated them at the time.

How long ago the advance decision was made and whether it has been regularly reviewed and updated to take account of changed circumstances will be key factors in determining its applicability. For example, an advance decision made by a woman who later becomes pregnant may not be applicable during her pregnancy unless the implications for her unborn child have been specifically addressed in the advance decision.

Anyone considering making an advance decision to refuse treatment should also consider either regularly updating it or otherwise indicating that it is still an expression of that person's considered wishes. However, although it is prudent to include a review date, caution should be exercised before including any form of termination date unless there is a very specific reason to do so.[68]

13.7.8 Effect of an advance decision

An advance decision to refuse treatment, which is both valid and applicable to the treatment in question, is as effective as a contemporaneous refusal of a person with capacity to make that decision.[69] Any health professionals who knowingly provide treatment contrary to the terms of a valid and applicable advance decision may be

---

[67] *HE* v. *A Hospital NHS Trust* [2003] EWHC 1017 (Fam); [2003] 2 FLR 408.
[68] *X Primary Care Trust* v. *XB* [2012] EWHC 1390 (Fam); [2012] COPLR 577.
[69] MCA 2005, s.26(1).

liable to a claim for damages for battery or possibly to criminal liability for assault. However, treatment providers would be protected from liability if they:

- were unaware of the existence of an advance decision; or
- were not satisfied that an advance decision existed which was both valid and applicable to the particular treatment.

In an emergency or where there is doubt about the existence, validity or applicability of an advance decision, doctors can provide treatment that is immediately necessary to stabilise or to prevent a deterioration in the patient until the legality of the advance directive can be established. The MCA Code of Practice gives some further guidance on this subject:[70]

> Healthcare professionals should not delay emergency treatment to look for an advance decision if there is no clear indication that one exists. But if it is clear that a person has made an advance decision that is likely to be relevant, healthcare professionals should assess its validity and applicability as soon as possible. Sometimes the urgency of treatment decisions will make this difficult.

Where there are genuine doubts (i.e. if health professionals are not 'satisfied') about the existence, validity or applicability of the advance decision, treatment can be provided without incurring liability, so long as that treatment is in the person's best interests.

Conversely, health professionals who follow the terms of what they believe to be a valid and applicable advance decision to refuse treatment would not be liable for the consequences of withholding or withdrawing treatment specified in the advance decision, so long as they can demonstrate that their belief was reasonable.[71] Having a 'reasonable belief' requires less certainty than being 'satisfied' that a valid and applicable advance decision exists and can only be based on the information and evidence available at the time.

Where a patient is subject to detention and compulsory treatment under MHA 1983, an advance refusal relating to treatment provided for the mental disorder for which compulsory powers have been invoked will not be binding, although the treating professional should take the advance decision into account when deciding whether the proposed treatment is in the person's best interests.[72] In accordance with the MCA principles, they must also consider whether there are any other treatment options available that are less restrictive. An agreed advance treatment plan for mental health conditions can be helpful and would represent a kind of advance statement, although it would not be binding if the person was subject to

---

[70] Office of the Public Guardian (2007) *Mental Capacity Act 2005 Code of Practice*, para.9.56, available at **www.gov.uk/government/publications/mental-capacity-act-code-of-practice**.

[71] MCA 2005, s.26(3).

[72] See *Nottinghamshire Healthcare NHS Trust* v. *RC* [2014] EWCOP 1317; [2014] COPLR 468 and also (in England) Chapter 13 of Department of Health (2015) *Mental Health Act 1983 Code of Practice*, available at **www.gov.uk/government/publications/code-of-practice-mental-health-act-1983**. At the time of publication, the Welsh government was consulting upon a further iteration of the Code of Practice issued in Wales to accompany MHA 1983.

compulsory powers. However, if the person is being treated on a voluntary basis for a mental disorder, a valid and applicable advance decision refusing specific types of treatment for that disorder should be respected in the same way as any other advance decision, so long as it is valid and applicable to the treatment in question. For further detail on the interaction between MCA 2005 and MHA 1983, see **Chapter 16**.

If there is disagreement about an advance decision relating, for example, to its validity or applicability, an application can be made to the Court of Protection for clarification. While a decision is being sought from the court, health professionals are entitled to provide any necessary treatment required either to sustain life, or to prevent a serious deterioration in the patient's health, until such time as the court makes a decision.

13.8 CONFIDENTIALITY AND DISCLOSURE

A duty of confidence arises when a patient discloses information to a healthcare professional in circumstances where it is reasonable to expect that the information will be held in confidence. This is a legal obligation that is derived from case law, and is a requirement established within professional codes of conduct and must be included within NHS employment contracts as a specific requirement linked to disciplinary procedures.

Confidentiality is central to the trust between patients and healthcare professionals. Confidentiality, however, is not absolute and personal information can be disclosed if:

- disclosure is required by law;
- the patient consents – either implicitly or expressly;
- it is justified in the public interest;
- the patient lacks capacity to consent or refuse to consent, and disclosure can be justified in the patient's best interests.

13.8.1 Disclosure required by law

Health professionals are required by law to disclose certain information, regardless of the patients' consent. Where such a statutory requirement exists, the patient's consent to disclosure is not necessary. Patients have no right to refuse but they should be generally aware of the disclosure and that it is to a secure authority. For example:

- In England, a person must supply information requested by a Safeguarding Adults Board under the Care Act 2014.[73] This section would potentially

---

[73] Care Act 2014, s.45. The safeguarding provisions in Wales contained in the Social Services and Wellbeing (Wales) Act 2014 are not yet in force. When they come into force, the equivalent duty will be contained in s.137 of that Act. There will also be a positive duty in s.128, including on Local Health Boards, to report concerns as to adults at risk to local authorities.

encompass, for instance, a GP who provided medical advice or treatment to an adult in respect of whom a Safeguarding Adult Board was carrying out a serious case review.[74]

- Under the Abortion Regulations 1991,[75] a doctor carrying out a termination of pregnancy must notify the Chief Medical Officer of the date of birth and postcode of the woman concerned.
- Under public health legislation a health professional must notify local authorities of the identity, sex and address of any person suspected of having a notifiable disease.[76]

The courts, some tribunals and bodies appointed to hold inquiries such as the General Medical Council, have legal powers to require disclosure, without the patient's consent, of information that may be relevant to matters within their jurisdiction.[77]

13.8.2 Patients who lack capacity to consent to disclosure

Patients with mental disorders or learning disabilities should not automatically be regarded as lacking the capacity to give or withhold their consent to disclosure of confidential information. Patients can authorise or prohibit the sharing of information about themselves if they broadly understand the implication of doing so. All practicable steps should be taken to help and support the patient to make their own decision. A careful assessment of the patient's capacity to consent or withhold consent to disclosure of confidential information must be made and the results of the assessment recorded in the patient's records[78] (for assessments of capacity more generally see also **Chapter 3**).

A patient who lacks capacity to consent to disclosure is still owed a duty of confidentiality and consideration should be given to whether the proposed sharing of information would be in their best interests. MCA 2005 requires healthcare professionals to consult relevant people when considering the patient's best interests. It may therefore be necessary to share personal information with a relevant person (for example, the patient's relatives, friends or carers) or authority to enable the healthcare professional to assess the patient's best interests, even if the patient

---

[74] See Chapter 14 of Department of Health (2014) *Care and Support Statutory Guidance* accompanying Part 1 of the Care Act 2014 (**www.gov.uk/government/publications/care-act-2014-statutory-guidance-for-implementation**), and in particular paras.14.150–14.161.

[75] Abortion Regulations 1991, SI 1999/499, reg.4.

[76] For further information see BMA (2008) *Confidentiality and Disclosure of Health Records Tool Kit* (**http://bma.org.uk/practical-support-at-work/ethics/confidentiality-and-health-records**), Card 9.

[77] BMA (2008) *Confidentiality and Disclosure of Health Records Tool Kit* (**http://bma.org.uk/practical-support-at-work/ethics/confidentiality-and-health-records**).

[78] In BMA (2008) *Confidentiality and Disclosure of Health Records Tool Kit* (**http://bma.org.uk/practical-support-at-work/ethics/confidentiality-and-health-records**), Card 7 para.1.

asks the healthcare professional not to disclose the information.[79] Disclosure should only be made of such information as is relevant to the decision being made. Relevant personal information should also be shared with anyone who is authorised to make decisions on the patient's behalf, such as a deputy appointed by the Court of Protection or an attorney acting under a welfare LPA (see **13.6**), or a person who is appointed to support and represent the patient, such as an advocate or an IMCA.[80]

13.8.3   Disclosure justified in the public interest

Confidential information can be disclosed without consent to prevent serious harm or death to others. Such disclosure is likely to be defensible in common law in the public interest on the grounds that it is both necessary and proportionate.[81] The bar as to what constitutes serious harm is set high and disclosure of a patient's confidential information to a third party without consent or other lawful authority is rarely justified in the public interest.[82]

In exceptional cases, there may be justification for the disclosure of information to other people to whom an incapacitated person may represent a potential health hazard, having first informed the patient of the intention to disclose. An example might be of an incapacitated person who has HIV embarking upon an intimate relationship. There can be no justification, however, for routine disclosure of a person's HIV status to people whose contact with the HIV-infected person contains no element of risk of infection.

13.8.4   Disclosure justified in the patient's best interests

Where the patient lacks capacity to consent, disclosure can be justified if it is in the patient's best interests in order to prevent the patient from being harmed. Information can be disclosed to an appropriate responsible person or authority if, for example, a healthcare professional believes that a patient may be a victim of neglect or physical, sexual or emotional abuse. A decision not to disclose information and the reason for non-disclosure should be noted in the patient's records

13.8.5   Disclosure under the Data Protection Act 1998

The Data Protection Act 1998 (DPA 1998) provides individuals with a number of important rights to ensure that personal information and, in particular, sensitive personal information such as health information is processed fairly and lawfully. Processing includes holding, recording, using and disclosing information. The Act

---

[79]   General Medical Council (2009) *Confidentiality: Guidance for Doctors*, available at **www.gmc-uk.org/guidance/ethical_guidance/confidentiality.asp**, para.61.

[80]   **www.gmc-uk.org/guidance/ethical_guidance/confidentiality.asp**, para.62.

[81]   Department of Health (2010) *Confidentiality: NHS Code of Practice – Supplementary Guidance: Public Interest Disclosures*, available at **www.gov.uk/government/publications/confidentiality-nhs-code-of-practice-supplementary-guidance-public-interest-disclosures**.

[82]   *ABC* v. *St George's Healthcare NHS Trust* [2015] EWHC 1394 (QB); [2015] Med LR 307.

applies to all forms of media, including paper and images. The requirement in DPA 1998 that all data processing must be 'fair' and 'lawful' means that all patients including those who lack capacity must know when and what information about them is being processed. The processing itself must be lawful: this includes meeting common law confidentiality obligations, which are likely to require patient or nominated proxy consent to be obtained. DPA 1998 also requires organisations that wish to process identifying information to use the minimum of information necessary and to retain it only for as long as it is needed for the purpose for which it was originally collected.

Further information and guidance on confidentiality and disclosure of health information is available from the BMA[83] and from the Department of Health.[84]

---

[83] BMA (2008) *Confidentiality and Disclosure of Health Records Tool Kit*, available at **http://bma.org.uk/practical-support-at-work/ethics/confidentiality-and-health-records**.
[84] Department of Health (2010) *Confidentiality: NHS Code of Practice – Supplementary Guidance: Public Interest Disclosures*, available at **www.gov.uk/government/publications/confidentiality-nhs-code-of-practice-supplementary-guidance-public-interest-disclosures**.

CHAPTER 14

Capacity to consent to research and innovative treatment

14.1 Introduction	14.4 Research involving adults who lack capacity
14.2 Capacity to consent to research	
14.3 Research governance: the ethical framework	14.5 Innovative treatment

14.1 INTRODUCTION

A person's capacity to consent to research is assessed in the same way as capacity to consent to medical treatment (see **Chapter 13**); that is, in accordance with the statutory test in MCA 2005 (see **Chapter 3**).[1] Pursuant to MCA 2005, it is presumed that people have capacity. Where a person's capacity to consent is in doubt it must be assessed.

This chapter considers the capacity of adults to agree to participate in research. It also considers the safeguards that apply to research involving adults who lack the capacity to give such consent. There are two significant pieces of legislation that apply in this context:

1. The Medicines for Human Use (Clinical Trials) Regulations 2004 (the 2004 Regulations),[2] which regulate clinical trials relating to medicinal products for human use, and implement EU Directive 2001/20/EC.
2. MCA 2005, which regulates all other forms of research involving incapacitated adults.

In April 2014, the EU adopted a new regulation (Regulation 536/2014) on clinical trials on medicinal products for human use (the Clinical Trials Regulations 2014) repealing the earlier EU Directive. The stated aim of the Clinical Trials Regulations

---

[1] The statutory test of capacity in MCA 2005, ss.2 and 3, taking account of the principles in MCA 2005, s.1.

[2] Medicines for Human Use (Clinical Trials) Regulations 2004, SI 2004/1031, as amended by the Human Medicines Regulations 2012, SI 2012/1916.

2014 is to create an environment that is favourable to conducting clinical trials while maintaining the highest standards of patient safety. It allows for a streamlined application procedure via an EU portal and database, single authorisation for all clinical trials, the extension of the 'tacit agreement' principle to the whole authorisation process and strengthened transparency for clinical trials data. It is unlikely that the Regulations will come into force prior to May 2017 at the earliest; prior to that point, the 2004 Regulations will have to have been substantially amended or replaced in their entirety to bring them into line with the EU Regulation.

14.2 CAPACITY TO CONSENT TO RESEARCH

Consent is a key principle to the lawful conduct of any research involving human subjects. Generally speaking, an individual's ability to give valid consent to participate in research will depend on their ability to understand what the research entails. This in turn will require that the individual has been given sufficient information to make a properly considered decision: consent must be informed.

The degree of detail required will vary according to the needs of the individual patient and the complexity of the procedures involved. Where a patient has capacity, it is for the patient to decide whether to participate in research and take the associated risks, having been given the fullest possible information. Where a patient lacks capacity, their involvement in medical trials is permissible only in closely regulated and clearly defined circumstances.[3]

An adult is deemed to lack capacity to give valid consent to research if at the material time that person is unable, because of an impairment of, or disturbance in the functioning of, the mind or brain:

- to understand the information relevant to the decision to consent to the research in question;
- to retain that information;
- to use or weigh that information as part of the process of making the decision; or
- to communicate their decision (whether by talking, using sign language or any other means).[4]

For further information about the statutory test for capacity under MCA 2005, see **Chapter 3**.

---

[3]   See Medicines for Human Use (Clinical Trials) Regulations 2004, SI 2004/1031, Part 3.
[4]   MCA 2005, ss.2–3.

14.3 RESEARCH GOVERNANCE: THE ETHICAL FRAMEWORK

The World Medical Association's Declaration of Helsinki[5] sets internationally recognised standards for ethical governance of research, which are reflected in both legal instruments.[6] In summary, the basic principles in the Declaration of Helsinki in relation to the involvement of incapacitated adults are as follows:

- Adults who lack the capacity to give informed consent should not be included in research which is unlikely to benefit them personally, unless that research:

  - is necessary to promote the health of the population represented by the potential research subjects;
  - cannot instead be performed on legally competent persons; and
  - involves only minimal risk and minimal burden to participants.

- Where an adult is incapable of giving informed consent, the responsible researcher must obtain informed consent from a legally authorised representative.
- Where an adult who lacks the capacity to give informed consent is nonetheless capable of assenting to decisions about participation in research, this assent must be obtained, in addition to the consent of the legally authorised representative. Any dissent by the person should be respected.
- The research must be intended to provide knowledge relating to the condition or conditions that have contributed to the impairment of the individual's incapacity.

These principles are also reflected in the Clinical Trials Regulations 2014. These regulations refine the definition of clinical trials contained in the previous EU Directive, defining 'clinical trials' more precisely as a category of the broader concept of 'clinical study' (see art.2).

14.4 RESEARCH INVOLVING ADULTS WHO LACK CAPACITY

All research subjects should give informed and considered consent to participation in any form of trial. In practice, however, there will be occasions where trials need to include those unable to give consent. Research into various causes of mental incapacity, for example, may need to be conducted on subjects who share a specific incapacity. To prevent the involvement of subjects lacking capacity would therefore be to deny them the chance to participate in the development of a therapy which could be to their benefit. There are, therefore, mechanisms subject to strict controls to allow those who lack capacity to consent to participate in such research. The presence of a mental disorder or disability does not itself mean that an individual

---

[5] World Medical Association (1964) *Declaration of Helsinki*, World Medical Association (as subsequently amended: see **www.wma.net/en/30publications/10policies/b3/**).
[6] Medicines for Human Use (Clinical Trials) Regulations 2004, Sch.1, Part 2, para.6.

lacks the capacity to consent. As with all other areas where an individual's capacity may be in doubt, it is important to enhance as far as possible their decision-making capacity. Care must be taken in in order to explain in clear language the procedures and risks involved. Capacity must be presumed until proven otherwise, and individuals must be given all appropriate opportunities in order to demonstrate their ability to make a decision on their own behalf.

14.4.1 The legal framework

The framework in England and Wales within which incapacitated adults can be involved in innovative research is set out in the 2004 Regulations and MCA 2005. The 2004 Regulations reflect the goals set out in the EU legislation: human dignity and the right to the integrity of the person are fundamental. As noted above, the 2004 Regulations will either be amended substantially or replaced in their entirety in due course prior to the entry into force of the 2014 Clinical Trials Regulations; the core legal framework will, however, remain similar.

The aim of regulation in the context of those who lack capacity to consent is to balance the need to undertake research to ensure that innovative therapies can be developed which will benefit incapacitated individuals, and the need to protect those incapacitated individuals from potential abuse.[7]

Research on anonymised medical information or tissue is regulated separately by either the Data Protection Act 1998 or the Human Tissue Act 2004.

14.4.2 The Mental Capacity Act 2005

With the exception of clinical trials and research on anonymised data, MCA 2005 covers all research that is 'intrusive'.[8] Intrusive research is defined as research that would be unlawful if carried out on an individual with capacity without their consent.[9] Although MCA 2005 does not define research, the MCA Code of Practice[10] refers to the definition given by the Department of Health and National Assembly for Wales,[11] that is:

---

[7] A useful resource is the sub-site of the NHS Health Research Authority's website dedicated to adults unable to consent for themselves: **www.hra.nhs.uk/resources/before-you-apply/consent-and-participation/adults-unable-to-consent-for-themselves/**.

[8] MCA 2005, ss.30–34.

[9] MCA 2005, s.30(2)

[10] Office of the Public Guardian (2007) *Mental Capacity Act 2005 Code of Practice*, para.11.2, available at **www.gov.uk/government/publications/mental-capacity-act-code-of-practice**.

[11] Department of Health (2005) *Research Governance Framework for Health and Social Care* (2nd edn), available at **www.gov.uk/government/publications/research-governance-framework-for-health-and-social-care-second-edition**. A new UK-wide Research Policy Framework for Health and Social Care Research will be issued in due course by the NHS Health Research Authority: see **www.hra.nhs.uk**. In the draft framework issued for consultation, research was defined as: 'the attempt to derive generalisable and/or transferrable new knowledge by addressing clearly defined questions with systematic, rigorous and repeatable methods.'

research can be defined as the attempt to derive generalisable new knowledge by addressing clearly defined questions with systematic and rigorous methods.

Under MCA 2005, research cannot include incapacitated adults unless it has first received the authorisation of an 'appropriate body'.[12] As of January 2015, the appropriate body is:

- in England, a research ethics committee recognised or established by or on behalf of the Health Research Authority under the Care Act 2014;[13]
- in Wales, a group of persons which assesses the ethics of research involving individuals and which is recognised for that purpose by or on behalf of the Welsh Ministers.[14]

Further information about research ethics committees can be obtained from the Health Research Authority.[15]

A research ethics committee can only approve a research project that involves a person who lacks the capacity to consent to involvement (P) if the following requirements of MCA 2005 are met:[16]

1. The research must be connected to an impairing condition affecting P or its treatment.[17]
2. There must be reasonable grounds for believing that research of comparable effectiveness cannot be carried out if the project has to be confined to, or only relate to, people who have capacity to consent to taking part.
3. The research must:

   (a) have the potential to benefit P without imposing a burden that is disproportionate to the benefit; or
   (b) be intended to provide knowledge about the causes of the impairing condition, its treatment or about the care of people affected by the same or a similar condition as P.

Where research meets the requirement of 3(b) (i.e. it is intended to provide knowledge about the causes of the impairing condition) but not 3(a) (i.e. it does not have a potential benefit to P without imposing a burden disproportionate to their benefit), MCA 2005 imposes a number of additional requirements. These are that there must be reasonable grounds for believing that:[18]

- the risk to P from taking part in the project is likely to be negligible;

---

[12] MCA 2005, s.30(1).
[13] Mental Capacity Act 2005 (Appropriate Body) (England) Regulations, 2006/2810, reg.2.
[14] Mental Capacity Act 2005 (Appropriate Body) (Wales) Regulations, 2007/833, reg.2.
[15] See **www.hra.nhs.uk/news/research-summaries/**.
[16] MCA 2005, s.31(2)–(5).
[17] An impairing condition is a condition which is or is attributable to or causes or contributes or may cause or contribute to the impairment of or disturbance of the functioning of the mind or brain.
[18] MCA 2005, s.31(6).

- anything done to, or in relation to P will not interfere with their freedom of action or privacy in a significant way;
- anything done to, or in relation to P will not be unduly invasive or restrictive.

The explanatory notes accompanying the Act give some guidance as to what this form of research is likely to be. Research that does not interfere with a person's freedom of action or privacy and is not likely to be unduly invasive or restrictive is likely to include indirect research on medical notes or on tissue already taken; or interviews or questionnaires with carers about health or social care services. It could also include taking samples such as blood samples for a research project.[19]

An appropriate body may not approve a research project involving the participation of a person lacking capacity until reasonable arrangements are in place for ensuring the safeguards in MCA 2005 will be met.[20]

MCA 2005 imposes a number of conditions that must be met to ensure the incapacitated person's interests are protected.[21] First, the researcher must make reasonable efforts to identify an individual (who is not acting in a professional capacity), who has been involved in the research subject's care or is interested in their welfare, and is prepared to act as a 'consultee'. This will ordinarily be a family member or someone close to the person. It could also be someone acting under an LPA, or a court appointed deputy. If the researcher cannot identify a suitable person to act as a consultee, then the researcher must nominate someone independent of the research project, in accordance with the guidance jointly issued by the Secretary of State and the Welsh Ministers.[22] This is likely to be a professional such as a GP or a specialist providing care to the individual.

The researcher must provide the consultee with information about the project and ask for the consultee's opinion of:[23]

- whether P should take part in the research; and
- what P's wishes and feelings would be likely to be, if they had capacity to decide whether to take part in the project.

If at any time the consultee advises that the incapacitated person would not want to be involved, or to continue to be involved in the research then the researcher must ensure that the incapacitated person is withdrawn from the research project. The individual may continue to receive any treatment they received as part of the research if the researcher has reasonable grounds for believing there would be a significant risk to the person's health if that treatment were withdrawn.[24]

---

[19] MCA 2005, Explanatory Notes, para.101.
[20] MCA 2005, ss.32 and 33.
[21] MCA 2005, s.32.
[22] Department of Health and Welsh Assembly Government (February 2008) *Guidance on Nominating a Consultee for Research Involving Adults who Lack Capacity to Consent*, available at **www.scie-socialcareonline.org.uk**.
[23] MCA 2005, s.32(4).
[24] MCA 2005, s.32(6).

MCA 2005 also provides additional safeguards in an emergency when urgent treatment is required in circumstances where it is not possible to carry out the necessary consultations.[25] The agreement of a registered medical practitioner not involved in the organisation or conduct of the research is required before any treatment can be undertaken. The need for such treatment should be anticipated and set out in the research proposal; any researcher relying on the exceptions under MCA 2005, s.32 must do so having previously gained approval for the same at the time when the initial research project was approved.

Even where a consultee has agreed that an incapacitated person can take part in a research project, MCA 2005 imposes a number of additional safeguards once the research has started. These are given below:[26]

(a)   Nothing may be done to, or in relation to P in the course of the research:

   (i)   to which the person appears to object (except if what is being done is intended to protect them from harm or to reduce or prevent pain or discomfort); or

   (ii)   which would be contrary to any valid and applicable advance decision refusing relevant treatment or contrary to any other statement of wishes or preferences previously made by the person and not subsequently withdrawn of which the researcher involved is aware.

(b)   The interests of the research subject must be assumed to outweigh the interests of medical science and society.

(c)   If the person lacking capacity indicates in any way that they wish to be withdrawn from the research, or if the researcher has reasonable grounds to believe that the requirements for approval[27] of the research are no longer met, the incapacitated adult must be removed from the research without delay.

(d)   If the person lacking capacity is withdrawn for either reason in (c) above, they may continue to receive any treatment that they were receiving as part of the research if the researcher believes on reasonable grounds that withdrawal from that treatment would pose a significant risk to the person's health.

14.4.3   Medicines for Human Use (Clinical Trials) Regulations 2004

The Medicines for Human Use (Clinical Trials) Regulations 2004 (2004 Regulations)[28] govern clinical trials in relation to medicinal products for human use. As noted above (see **14.1**), they will be either replaced or amended very substantially in due course to reflect the entry into force of the European Clinical Trial Regulations 2014.[29] It is important to note that the arrangements for adults who cannot give the

---

[25]   MCA 2005, s.32(9).
[26]   MCA 2005, s.33.
[27]   The requirements are set out in MCA 2005, s.31(2)–(7).
[28]   Medicines for Human Use (Clinical Trials) Regulations 2004, SI 2004/1031.
[29]   EU Regulation 536/2014.

requisite consent to participate in such trials are governed by the 2004 Regulations themselves, rather than by MCA 2005.

'Clinical trials' are defined as investigations in human subjects intended to discover or verify the clinical, pharmacological or other pharmacodynamic effects of one or more medicinal products, to identify any adverse reactions in any such products or to study the absorption, distribution, metabolism and excretion of any such products with the object of ascertaining their safety or efficacy.[30] They govern research involving both those who have capacity to consent and those who do not. They also extend to research involving children. In addition to the principles set out at **14.3**, the 2004 Regulations set out a number of principles that must apply to all clinical trials involving human participants, and a number of these are set out below:[31]

- Before the trial is initiated, foreseeable risks and inconveniences must have been weighed against the anticipated benefit for the individual trial subject and other present and future patients. A trial should be initiated and continued only if the anticipated benefits justify the risks.
- The rights, safety and well-being of the trial subjects shall prevail over the interests of science and society.
- Clinical trials shall be scientifically sound and guided by ethical principles in all their aspects.
- A trial shall be initiated only if an ethics committee and the licensing authority comes to the conclusion that the anticipated therapeutic and public health benefits justify the risks and may be continued only if compliance with this requirement is permanently monitored.
- The medical care given to, and medical decisions made on behalf of, subjects shall always be the responsibility of an appropriately qualified doctor or, when appropriate, qualified dentist.

If a person lacking capacity is to participate in a clinical trial covered by these regulations, the consent of that person's 'legal representative' must first be given. The regulations define a legal representative[32] as:

- a person unconnected with the conduct of the trial who by virtue of their relationship with the patient is suitable to act as their legal representative and willing and able to do so; or
- (if there is no one available who has such a relationship with the patient) the doctor primarily responsible for the provision of treatment to them; or
- a person nominated by the relevant healthcare provider.

---

[30]   2004 Regulations, reg.2.
[31]   2004 Regulations, Sched.1, Part 2, as amended by Medicines for Human Use (Clinical Trials) (Amendment) Regulations 2006, SI 2006/1928, para.27.
[32]   2004 Regulations, Sched.1, Part 1, para.2.

14.4.4 Clinical trials for medicinal products in emergency situations

The 2004 regulations were amended in December 2006 by the Medicines for Human Use (Clinical Trials) (Amendment) (No. 2) Regulations 2006.[33] The amended regulations permit patients in urgent situations to be enrolled in clinical trials without prior consent, provided the research has been approved by an appropriate research ethics committee. Where the clinical trials do not relate to medicinal products, the research would be regulated by MCA 2005.

14.5 INNOVATIVE TREATMENT

Although MCA 2005 covers the involvement of incapacitated adults in research, it does not make specific mention of innovative treatments. These are often an extension of usual treatments but they may expose the patient to a greater degree of risk than established procedures. Efforts should be made to inform patients, so far as they are able to understand, of how and why the proposed treatment differs from the usual measures and the known or likely risks attached. They should also be given any relevant information about the success rate of the treating clinician.

Innovative treatments are usually a standard feature of medical practice and the fact that useful information may be gained in the process is seen as largely incidental, rather than part of medical research. However, any test by 'trial and error' obviously leaves patients in a vulnerable situation unless carefully monitored and will require high standards of informed consent.

If carried out on someone lacking capacity to consent, any such intervention must be governed by the underlying principles of MCA 2005, including the requirement that it must be in the incapacitated person's best interests (see **Chapter 3**). Great care must be taken, as exposing incapacitated patients to innovative therapies is likely to give rise to legal and ethical uncertainty. Where a doctor proposes a procedure which diverges substantially from accepted practice, involving an unknown or increased risk, it would be advisable to obtain in advance both expert scrutiny and legal advice as to the ethics and legality of the procedure. In some circumstances, it may be necessary to apply to a court for authorisation to carry out the procedure.

Although decided before the passage of MCA 2005, a case decided in the context of the search for effective treatment of Creutzfeldt Jakob disease (CJD) provides an example of when court intervention may be appropriate. In *Simms* v. *Simms*,[34] the court was asked to decide whether it would be lawful to provide treatment that had not been tested on human beings to two young patients who were thought to be suffering from variant CJD. Both patients, JS (aged 18) and JA (aged 16), lacked the capacity to make treatment decisions but their parents argued that it would be in

---

[33] Medicines for Human Use (Clinical Trials) (Amendment) (No. 2) Regulations 2006, SI 2006/2984.
[34] *Simms* v. *Simms; PA* v. *JA; sub nom A* v. *A* [2002] EWHC 2734 (Fam); [2003] 1 All ER 669.

their best interests to have the new therapy. Although not expected to provide a cure, it was hoped that the treatment could improve the patients' lives. The judge said that although the patients would not recover, the concept of 'benefit' to a patient suffering from variant CJD would encompass:

> an improvement from the present state of illness, or a continuation of the existing state of illness without deterioration for a longer period than might otherwise have occurred, or the prolongation of life for a longer period than might otherwise have occurred.[35]

Given the possibility of some benefit being derived and the lack of any other alternative, it was held that this treatment would be in the best interests of both JS and JA and so could lawfully be provided.[36] As Dame Elizabeth Butler-Sloss, then President of the Family Division said:

> Where there is no alternative treatment available and the disease is progressive and fatal, it seems to me to be reasonable to consider experimental treatment with unknown benefits and risks, but without significant risks of increased suffering to the patient, in cases where there is some chance of benefit to the patient. A patient who is not able to consent to pioneering treatment ought not to be deprived of the chance in circumstances where he would be likely to consent if he had been competent.[37]

Although this decision was made before MCA 2005 came into force, it is likely that the Court of Protection would reach a similar decision. The statutory framework of MCA 2005 effectively mirrors the judgment, providing for circumstances where innovative treatment and/or research may be carried out when specified safeguards are in place and where the benefits clearly outweigh any disadvantages to the proposed patient.

---

[35] *Simms* v. *Simms* [2002] EWHC 2734 (Fam); [2003] 1 All ER 669 at para.57.
[36] *Simms* v. *Simms* [2002] EWHC 2734 (Fam); [2003] 1 All ER 669 at para.73.
[37] *Simms* v. *Simms* [2002] EWHC 2734 (Fam); [2003] 1 All ER 669 at para.57.

CHAPTER 15

Capacity and deprivation of liberty

15.1   Introduction
15.2   Deprivation of liberty: an overview
15.3   Authorising a deprivation of liberty

15.4   Capacity and the deprivation of liberty

15.1   INTRODUCTION

It might appear odd to have a chapter dedicated to the assessment of capacity to consent to arrangements which may mean that someone is deprived of liberty, but the question of such consent arises regularly in respect of people accommodated in care homes, nursing homes and in hospitals where they may be compliant but appear unable to consent to remaining there.

Depending on the circumstances under which they are accommodated, difficult questions may arise as to whether such people are deprived of their liberty within the meaning of art.5 of the European Convention on Human Rights (ECHR). If they are deprived of their liberty, and if this is not authorised, the deprivation of liberty may be unlawful under art.5. A complex regime – known as the Deprivation of Liberty Safeguards (DoLS)[1] – was introduced in 2009 designed to plug the so-called 'Bournewood gap,' named after the decision of the European Court of Human Rights in 2004,[2] in which the absence of proper safeguards was identified.

The law in this area is widely recognised as being unsatisfactory[3] and is the subject of a wide-ranging review by the Law Commission, a report and draft

---

[1]   MCA 2005, Sched.A1. The term does not actually appear in Sched.A1, but it is a very commonly used shorthand.

[2]   *HL* v. *United Kingdom* Case 45508/99, [2004] 40 EHRR 761; (2004) 81 BMLR 131, Mr L being an informal patient at Bournewood psychiatric hospital.

[3]   In its post-legislative scrutiny report on MCA 2005, the House of Lords Select Committee convened for the purpose was strongly critical of Sched.A1 and recommended a comprehensive review of Sched.A1 with a view to replacing the regime contained there with provisions 'that are compatible in style and ethos to the rest of the Mental Capacity Act': House of Lords Select Committee on the Mental Capacity Act 2005 (2014) *Mental Capacity Act 2005: Post-legislative scrutiny,* HL Paper 139, available at **www.publications.parliament.uk/pa/ld201314/ldselect/ldmentalcap/139/139.pdf**, summary.

legislation being anticipated by the end of 2016.[4] In the interim, it is important for both legal and clinical professionals to keep abreast of developments in the case law: resources to do so can be found in Chapter 11 of the Law Society's *Deprivation of Liberty: A Practical Guide*.[5]

15.2 DEPRIVATION OF LIBERTY: AN OVERVIEW

MCA 2005 provides protection from liability for professionals and carers who carry out acts in connection with the care or treatment of a person lacking capacity to consent (see **Chapter 13**), including the use of restraint, so long as certain conditions are met.[6] The definition of 'restraint' and the circumstances when it may be used are described at **13.5**. However, restraint is different in law to deprivation of liberty, and MCA 2005 itself does not set out where the dividing line is to be drawn. Rather, it provides that, for purposes of MCA 2005, a deprivation of liberty has the same meaning as in ECHR, art.5.[7] The same definition will also be applied by courts considering (for instance) whether an individual is deprived of their liberty under MHA 1983 (see further in this regard **Chapter 16**).

As interpreted by the European Court of Human Rights and by the courts in this country, art.5(1) has been identified as having three elements, all of which need to be satisfied before a particular set of circumstances will amount to a deprivation of liberty falling within the scope of the article:

1. **The objective element.** I.e. that the person is confined to a particular restricted place for a non-negligible period of time.
2. **The subjective element.** I.e. that the person does not consent (or cannot, because they do not have the capacity to do so) to that confinement.
3. **State imputability.** I.e. that the deprivation of liberty can be said to be one for which the state is responsible.

Deciding when a person is confined is not always straightforward. The Deprivation of Liberty Safeguards Code of Practice (DoLS Code of Practice)[8] published to accompany the new regime provides some useful assistance with the question of whether a person is deprived of their liberty. However, this must now be read subject

---

[4] At the time of publication, the Law Commission had published a consultation paper suggesting wide-ranging reforms to the area: see **www.lawcom.gov.uk/wp-content/uploads/2015/07/cp222_mental_capacity.pdf**.

[5] Available at **lawsociety.org.uk/support-services/advice/articles/deprivation-of-liberty/**. The Law Society was commissioned by the Department of Health to produce this guidance for front-line health and social care professionals to assist them identify when a deprivation of liberty may be occurring. Parts of this chapter draw upon that guidance, with the permission of the Law Society.

[6] MCA 2005, ss.5 and 6. The conditions are described in more detail in **Chapter 13**.

[7] MCA 2005, s.64(5).

[8] Ministry of Justice (2008) *Mental Capacity Act 2005: Deprivation of Liberty Safeguards – Code of Practice to Supplement the Main Mental Capacity Act 2005 Code of Practice*, available at **www.scie.org.uk/mca-directory/keygovernmentdocuments.asp**.

to the decision of the Supreme Court in *Surrey County Council* v. *P; Cheshire West and Chester Council* v. *P*,[9] commonly known as *Cheshire West.*

In *Cheshire West*, the Supreme Court decided that when an individual lacking capacity was under continuous (or complete) supervision and control *and* was not free to leave, they should be considered to be confined. This is now commonly called the 'acid test'.[10]

Precisely how the 'acid test' applies in practice is not always straightforward: detailed guidance can be found for different settings in the Law Society's *Deprivation of Liberty: A Practical Guide.*[11] It is extremely important to remember two overarching points:

1. In this context, a deprivation of liberty is neither 'good' nor 'bad'. It is simply a description of a factual state of affairs. Whether it is *justified* is a separate question.

2. The starting point should always be consideration of where the individual's best interests lie. If, but only if, their best interests dictate that the arrangements made for them amount necessarily to a deprivation of their liberty, then authorisation should be sought. In other words, deprivation of liberty forms part of a much bigger picture, and an unduly narrow focus upon the minutiae of authorisation can lead to sight being lost of whether the steps being taken in respect of the individual are really in their interests, as opposed to for the convenience of those around for them.[12]

15.3   AUTHORISING A DEPRIVATION OF LIBERTY

It is possible for the deprivation of liberty of a person lacking capacity to consent to be admitted to a hospital or a care home for their care and treatment to be authorised under MCA 2005 in one of three ways:

*   by the Court of Protection exercising its powers to make personal welfare decisions under MCA 2005;[13]

*   in accordance with the authorisation scheme known as the DoLS set out in MCA 2005[14] (see below);

---

9   *Surrey County Council* v. *P; Cheshire West and Chester Council* v. *P* [2014] UKSC 19; [2014] AC 896.
10   Because Lady Hale, at para.48 of the judgment, started her analysis by asking: '[s]o is there an acid test for the deprivation of liberty in these cases?'
11   Available at **www.lawsociety.org.uk/support-services/advice/articles/deprivation-of-liberty/**. The Law Society was commissioned by the Department of Health to produce this guidance for front-line health and social care professionals to assist them identify when a deprivation of liberty may be occurring. Parts of this chapter draw upon that guidance, with the permission of the Law Society.
12   See in this regard, in particular, the decision of Peter Jackson J in *Hillingdon London Borough Council* v. *Neary* [2011] EWHC 1377 (COP); [2011] COPLR Con Vol 632.
13   MCA 2005, s.16(2).
14   MCA 2005, Sched.A1.

- where it is necessary in order to give life-sustaining treatment or do any 'vital act'[15] while a decision is sought from the Court of Protection;[16]

Space precludes a full discussion of DoLS,[17] but in very broad terms the authorisation scheme provides a regime whereby a local authority[18] (known as the 'supervisory body') can authorise the deprivation of liberty of an adult in a hospital or care home, subject to the satisfaction of certain requirements (see below). Once authorisation has been granted, a representative is appointed for the person deprived of their liberty and a regular review process is carried out. Either the person being deprived of their liberty (if able to do so) or their representative may request a review at any time and both have the right to apply to the Court of Protection to challenge the authorisation or seek to vary it.[19]

An order of the Court of Protection will be required in order to give authority to deprive a person of their liberty in a setting outside a hospital or a care home, such as a foster placement or in supported living.[20]

It also continues to be possible to authorise a deprivation of liberty where a person falls under the provisions of MHA 1983 and meets the criteria for detention under that Act (see further **Chapter 16**), as well as under the inherent jurisdiction of the High Court.[21]

15.4 CAPACITY AND THE DEPRIVATION OF LIBERTY

15.4.1 Personal welfare orders of the Court of Protection

If the question as to whether a person is being, or should be deprived of their liberty, arises in the context of an application to the Court of Protection for a personal welfare order,[22] then the court will need to be satisfied that the person lacks capacity to consent to the arrangements giving rise to the deprivation of liberty. This will be linked to the question of whether the individual can make decisions as to where they

---

[15] MCA 2005, s.4B, where a vital act is defined as 'any act which the person doing it reasonably believes to be necessary to prevent a serious deterioration in P's condition'.

[16] Although s.4B only refers to 'the court,' it is clear that this means the Court of Protection: see s.64(1).

[17] For more detail see, e.g., G Ashton (ed.) (2015) *Mental Capacity: Law and Practice* (3rd edn), Jordan Publishing, Chapter 7.

[18] Alternatively in relation to deprivation of liberty in a hospital, the National Assembly for Wales if: (1) the hospital is in England, the individual is not ordinarily resident in England and their care or treatment is commissioned by the National Assembly for Wales or a Local Health Board (Sched.A1, para.180); or (2) the hospital is in Wales and the individual is not ordinarily resident in England (para.181).

[19] MCA 2005, s.21A. The importance of the role of the representative in securing the rights of the person deprived of their liberty was emphasised in *Re AJ (Deprivation of Liberty Safeguards)* [2015] EWCOP 5; [2015] COPLR 167.

[20] As in the case of all three individuals whose circumstances were considered by the Supreme Court in *Surrey County Council* v. *P; Cheshire West and Chester Council* v. *P* [2014] UKSC 19; [2014] AC 896.

[21] As to the latter, see *NHS Trust* v. *Dr A* [2013] EWHC 2442 (COP); [2013] COPLR 605.

[22] I.e. an order under MCA 2005, s.16(2).

should live and whether to consent to care or treatment arrangements made for them.[23] However, it goes further, and the court will need to consider whether the person has capacity to understand, retain, use and weigh information about the restrictions to which they are subject which amount to a confinement. Evidence as to the person's capacity does not need to be given by a medical professional but could, for instance, be given by a social worker (see further **4.2**).

Importantly, the court will *also* need to be satisfied that the person is 'of unsound mind'. In the vast majority of cases this will equate to them suffering a mental disorder within the meaning of MHA 1983 (disregarding the exclusion there for persons with learning disability).[24] Professional medical opinion will be needed to establish unsoundness of mind, but where the facts are clear this need not involve expert psychiatric opinion (there will be cases where a GP's evidence will suffice).[25]

If both of these conditions are satisfied, the court must be satisfied that it is in the person's best interests to be accommodated and cared for in conditions which amount to a deprivation of their liberty, after considering whether any less restrictive alternative might meet the person's needs.

15.4.2 Deprivation of liberty safeguards

If the question of deprivation of liberty arises in the context of a care home or a hospital, an application for authorisation should be made under the DoLS procedures, when additional considerations arise. The supervisory body must arrange for assessments to be carried out to determine whether the following six qualifying requirements are met:[26]

1. **Age.** The person must be aged 18 or over.
2. **Mental health.** The person must be suffering from mental disorder within the meaning of MHA 1983 which is 'any disorder or disability of the mind', including for these purposes, a learning disability, whether or not associated with abnormally aggressive or seriously irresponsible conduct. This test is distinct from, and narrower than, the broad 'diagnostic' element of the MCA test of capacity (see **3.4**). The assessment must be carried out by a doctor

---

[23]   See *A Primary Care Trust* v. *LDV* [2013] EWHC 272 (Fam); [2013] COPLR 204.

[24]   This requirement arises from ECHR, art.5(1)(e), as interpreted by the European Court of Human Rights in *Winterwerp* v. *Netherlands* Application 6301/73 (1979) 2 EHRR 387. It is suggested that to the extent that the Court of Appeal suggested otherwise in *G* v. *E (By His Litigation Friend The Official Solicitor)* [2010] EWCA Civ 822; [2010] COPLR Con Vol 431, this cannot be correct, and would not be followed now in light of the confirmation in *Cheshire West* that art.5(1)(e) is directly engaged in the context of care outside psychiatric hospitals: see *Surrey County Council* v. *P; Cheshire West and Chester Council* v. *P* [2014] UKSC 19; [2014] AC 896 at para.25.

[25]   The President of the Court of Protection suggested that this was the case in *Re X (Deprivation of Liberty)* [2014] EWCOP 25; [2014] COPLR 674 at para.14. The Court of Appeal subsequently held that his purported 'judgments' in this case were not in fact binding decisions (*Re X (Court of Protection Practice)* [2015] EWCA Civ 599); however, no party to the appeal nor the Court of Appeal cast any doubt upon what must now be seen as an *obiter* observation.

[26]   MCA 2005, Sched.A1, para.10.

approved under MHA 1983, s.12 or who has special experience in the diagnosis and treatment of mental disorder.

3.   **Mental capacity.** The person must lack capacity to decide whether or not they should be accommodated in the particular hospital or care home for the purpose of being given the care or treatment concerned.[27] This test must be determined in accordance with the statutory test of capacity in MCA 2005, s.2.[28] It is suggested that *information* relevant to the question must include the core information relating to the confinement (i.e. analogous to the position considered immediately above in relation to the Court of Protection).[29]

4.   **Best interests.** It must be in the person's best interests to be detained in the hospital or care home and the deprivation of liberty must be necessary to prevent harm to the person and must be a proportionate response to the likelihood and seriousness of that harm. The assessor must apply the best interests checklist in MCA 2005[30] having consulted with all relevant people (see **3.7**).

5.   **Eligibility.** A person is ineligible if already subject, or could be subject, to compulsory powers under MHA 1983).[31]

6.   **'No refusals'.** There must be no valid and applicable advance decision made previously by the detained person refusing the treatment that will be provided in the place where they are to be deprived of their liberty (see **13.7**), nor a valid refusal by a deputy or donee of a health and welfare LPA acting within the scope of their authority.

15.4.3   Admission under the Mental Health Act 1983

As set out in **16.3**, the question of whether a patient has capacity to consent to their admission to hospital for purposes of assessment or treatment for mental disorder is an important one (and will almost invariably arise in the context that such admission will lead to the 'acid test' being met). It is suggested that the test to apply is the statutory test under MCA 2005, s.2, and that it is to be applied in a similar fashion that applied under DoLS – i.e. with a particular focus on individual's ability to understand, retain, use and weigh the information relating to the circumstances of

---

[27]   MCA 2005, Sched.A1, para.15.

[28]   This is expressly provided for in Ministry of Justice (2008) *Mental Capacity Act 2005: Deprivation of Liberty Safeguards – Code of Practice to Supplement the Main Mental Capacity Act 2005 Code of Practice*, at **www.scie.org.uk/mca-directory/keygovernmentdocuments.asp**, para.4.30.

[29]   In *A Primary Care Trust v. LDV* [2013] EWHC 272 (Fam); [2013] COPLR 204, Baker J proceeded in his consideration of the questions to ask relevant to capacity to consent on the basis that he should follow the capacity requirement set down in MCA 2005, Sched.A1, para.15. It is therefore suggested that the conclusions he reached as to the information relevant to the question of capacity apply equally to those applying Sched.A1 outside the court setting.

[30]   MCA 2005, s.4.

[31]   MCA 2005, Sched.1A sets out detailed provisions for determining whether or not a person meets the eligibility requirement. See also Chapter 13 of Department of Health (2015) *Mental Health Act 1983 Code of Practice*, available at **www.gov.uk/government/publications/code-of-practice-mental-health-act-1983**.

their admission and treatment, and the core elements of the confinement to which they were to be subjected.[32]

---

[32] The decision in *A Primary Care Trust* v. *LDV* [2013] EWHC 272 (Fam); [2013] COPLR 204 related to the question of whether the individual had the capacity to consent to admission to a private psychiatric hospital.

CHAPTER 16

Capacity and the Mental Health Act 1983

16.1   Introduction
16.2   Treatment for mental disorder: MCA
        2005 or MHA 1983?
16.3   Admission under MHA 1983
16.4   Mental health treatment under MHA
        1983: patients who are not
        detained in hospital

16.5   Mental health treatment under MHA
        1983: patients detained in hospital
16.6   Patients detained under MHA
        1983: other decisions

16.1 INTRODUCTION

Mental health legislation and mental capacity legislation have traditionally been seen as having very different aims. The Mental Health Act 1983 (MHA 1983) provides powers for the detention and treatment of a person with a mental disorder, if necessary without that person's consent. It is primarily concerned with the reduction of risk both to the patient and to others, using compulsion where necessary. By contrast, mental capacity legislation seeks to enable and support people to make their own decisions wherever possible. The principles of MCA 2005 ensure that decisions made on behalf of someone lacking capacity must reflect that person's best interests and should restrict that person as little as possible. In practice there are circumstances where mental health and mental capacity legislation may be applicable to the same person and sometimes choices must be made as to which legal framework should be used.

This chapter looks briefly at the situations in which questions of mental capacity will be relevant in the context of decisions as to admission and/or treatment under MHA 1983. A detailed discussion of the detail of mental health legislation, including certain specific provisions that apply only in Wales, is beyond the scope of this book. Guidance on the use and operation of MHA 1983 can be found in the

Code of Practice[1] accompanying that Act (the MHA Code of Practice), and the 2015 version of that Code contains in Chapter 13 a useful guide to a number of the areas in which MCA 2005 and MHA 1983 overlap.[2] At the time of publication, the Welsh government was consulting on a replacement for the Code of Practice that applies to MHA 1983 in Wales, which is likely to be published in the early part of 2017. In light of that fact, references are given in this chapter to the English Code alone. This chapter only covers the position in relation to those aged 18 and above. Different rules apply in some contexts in relation to those aged 16 and 17, and then again for those aged 15 and under.[3]

It is particularly important to remember in the context of those who may require treatment for mental disorder that capacity is decision-specific (see **3.4**). A person may be profoundly mentally unwell, and require detention under MHA 1983 for purposes of treatment of that disorder, but nonetheless retain capacity to make significant decisions in their life. A very clear example of this is the case of *Re SB*,[4] in which a woman with bipolar disorder who was detained under MHA 1983 was nonetheless found to have capacity to make a decision to undergo a termination.

16.2 TREATMENT FOR MENTAL DISORDER: MCA 2005 OR MHA 1983?

Where an individual lacks capacity to consent to treatment for mental disorder, and it is reasonable and possible to do so, professionals should generally apply the provisions of MCA 2005, since it is likely to be less restrictive of a person's human rights and freedom of action. However, there may be circumstances when the more formal safeguards provided under MHA 1983 may be more appropriate. The Code of Practice accompanying MCA 2005[5] suggests that consideration may need to be given to using mental health legislation where, for example:

- It is not possible to give the person the care or treatment they require without doing something that will deprive them of their liberty. The DoLS procedure under MCA 2005, Sched.1A will usually apply to those for whom mental health legislation is not appropriate, such as those living in a care home (see **Chapter 15**);

---

[1] Department of Health (2015) *Mental Health Act 1983 Code of Practice*, available at **www.gov.uk/ government/publications/code-of-practice-mental-health-act-1983**. See also R. Jones (2015) *Mental Health Act Manual* (18th edn), Sweet & Maxwell, a new edition of which is produced roughly annually.
[2] See also para.24.54 and fig. 12 of the Department of Health (2015) *Mental Health Act 1983 Code of Practice*, which provides further details as to the interface between MCA 2005 and MHA 1983 as regards treatment of patients lacking the material decision-making capacity
[3] The position of those under 18 is covered in Chapter 19 of the MHA Code of Practice.
[4] *Re SB (A Patient: Capacity to Consent to Termination)* [2013] EWHC 1417 (COP); [2013] COPLR 445.
[5] Office of the Public Guardian (2007) *Mental Capacity Act 2005 Code of Practice* and Ministry of Justice (2008) *Mental Capacity Act 2005: Deprivation of Liberty Safeguards – Code of Practice to Supplement the Main Mental Capacity Act 2005 Code of Practice*, both available at **www.scie.org.uk/mca-directory/keygovernmentdocuments.asp**.

- The person needs treatment that cannot be given under MCA 2005, such as where the person has made a valid and applicable advance decision to refuse the proposed treatment or part of it (see **Chapter 13**), although see further **16.5**.
- The person may need to be restrained in a way that is not permitted under MCA 2005 (see **Chapter 13**).
- It is not possible to assess or treat the person safely or effectively without using compulsory powers.
- The person may lack capacity in some areas but retains the capacity to refuse a vital part of the treatment and has done so.

16.3 ADMISSION UNDER MHA 1983

A person can be compulsorily admitted to hospital for assessment and/or treatment for mental disorder under the provisions of MHA 1983.[6] They can also be admitted as an informal patient.[7] There are important differences between the two classes of patient, not least that an informal patient cannot be prevented from leaving the hospital unless the 'holding powers' in MHA 1983, s.5 are invoked or the patient is subjected to compulsory treatment under the provisions of MHA 1983, Part IV).

'Informality' only applies to the patient's status under the provisions of MHA 1983. Therefore informal patients can include people with and without the capacity to consent to an informal admission. The former are admitted through their own consent; the latter are admitted in their best interests.

Whether a patient has the capacity to consent to their admission is particularly important following the decision of the Supreme Court in *Cheshire West*[8] (discussed at **15.2**), because it is clear that the conditions in the majority of psychiatric wards will satisfy the 'acid test' for deprivation of liberty identified in that case. In other words, the majority of patients in a psychiatric ward will – in their own interests – (1) be under continuous supervision and control; and (2) not be free to leave as and when they wish. If they cannot give their capacitous (and valid – i.e. non-coerced) consent to such confinement, they will be considered to be deprived of their liberty for purpose of ECHR, art.5(1),[9] and authority will be required for that deprivation. As a consequence, a patient lacking the ability to give such capacity cannot be admitted informally if they are likely to be deprived of their liberty in the hospital.[10]

---

[6] Most usually under the provisions of MHA 1983, s.2 (assessment) or s.3 (treatment).

[7] Under MHA 1983, s.131.

[8] *Surrey County Council* v. *P; Cheshire West and Chester Council* v. *P* [2014] UKSC 19; [2014] AC 896.

[9] For purposes of the law relating to deprivation of liberty, the deprivation of liberty of patients in all psychiatric settings will be considered to be the responsibility of the state – the third element required for circumstances to amount to a deprivation of liberty requiring the obtaining of statutory or judicial authority.

[10] See para.13.53 of the MHA Code of Practice.

Since compulsory admission under MHA 1983 can only be justified if detention is necessary, and alternative means of admission to hospital must be considered, the question of whether a patient has the capacity to consent to an informal admission will therefore always be of importance in deciding whether it is necessary to invoke the procedures for compulsory admission.

It is suggested that the test to apply to whether the patient has capacity to consent to an informal admission is the statutory test under MCA 2005, s.2. It is further suggested that the test should be applied in a similar fashion that applies under DoLS – i.e. with a particular focus on an individual's ability to understand, retain, use and weigh the information relating to the circumstances of their admission and treatment, and the core elements of the confinement to which they were to be subjected (see further **15.4**).

Where a patient does not have capacity to consent to admission to hospital for treatment for mental disorder in circumstances amounting to a deprivation of their liberty, complex questions will arise as to whether the compulsory provisions of MHA 1983 must be invoked, or whether the deprivation of liberty can be authorised under the provisions of DoLS (see further **Chapter 15**). Chapter 13 of the MHA Code of Practice contains detailed guidance, and helpful flow-charts, identifying which regime can (or in some cases must) be used. It should be noted that it is very likely that the law in this area is will be substantially reformed in due course, as it is recognised that the interface between DoLS and MHA 1983 is (unintentionally) unduly complex and unhelpful.

16.4   MENTAL HEALTH TREATMENT UNDER MHA 1983: PATIENTS WHO ARE NOT DETAINED IN HOSPITAL

A number of powers under the 1983 Act that can be exercised where a patient is not detained in hospital depend on the patient's mental capacity to make the relevant decision. Patients who are subject to Community Treatment Orders (CTOs)[11] and who have capacity to consent or withhold consent to treatment can only be given treatment in the community with their consent and those who refuse must be recalled to hospital in order to be given treatment without their consent.[12]

Community patients without capacity to consent or to withhold consent to treatment (who have not been recalled) can be given treatment if an attorney with the requisite authority under a health and welfare LPA or a Court of Protection

---

[11]   I.e. under the provisions of MHA 1983, ss.17A–17G.
[12]   Subject to the (complex) provisions of MHA 1983, s.62A. A patient on a CTO can also agree to being admitted informally to hospital without the recall procedure being used, in which case the treatment of their mental disorder is governed by MCA 1983, Part 4A.

appointed deputy consents on their behalf.[13] They can also be given such treatment by or under the direction of the approved clinician in charge of the treatment unless:[14]

- the treatment would be contrary to a valid and applicable advance decision made by the patient or the treatment would be against the decision of someone with the authority under MCA 2005 to refuse it on the patient's behalf (i.e. a health and welfare attorney, a deputy or the Court of Protection); or
- in the case of a patient aged 16 or over, the patient objects to the treatment and physical force needs to be used in order to administer the treatment.[15]

There are also emergency provisions which apply in certain strictly defined circumstances so as to give authority to treat a community patient who has not been recalled and who lacks the material decision-making capacity.[16]

The test of whether a patient has capacity to consent to medical treatment for mental disorder (or withhold that consent) to treatment is that set down in MCA 2005.[17] As the MHA Code of Practice emphasises, the questions of whether a patient (a) has capacity to consent to or refuse a particular treatment; and (b) has, in fact, consented are questions that are to be answered in exactly the same way for patients within the scope of MHA 1983 as in relation to any other patient. For further detail on the test for capacity to consent to (and to withhold consent to) medical treatment, see **Chapter 13**.

16.5 MENTAL HEALTH TREATMENT UNDER MHA 1983: PATIENTS DETAINED IN HOSPITAL

With the exception of 'short-term' patients (i.e. those brought into hospital as a place of safety under MHA 1983, s.136 in respect of whom an emergency application has been made under MHA 1983, s.4, or detained using the holding powers under MHA 1983, s.5), to whom MHA 1983, Part 4 does not apply, the vast majority of detained patients unable or refusing to consent to treatment will be treated under the provisions of that Part.

General authority to give medical treatment for mental disorder without consent is provided by MHA 1983, s.63, which provides that the consent of the patient is not required to give medical treatment for mental disorder. This is subject to the following four exceptions, most of which depend upon consideration of whether the patient has the capacity to consent to or refuse the specific treatment:

---

[13]   MHA 1983, s.64C(2)(b).
[14]   See MHA 1983, s.64D. See also MHA Code of Practice, paras.24.14–24.23.
[15]   MHA 1983, s.64D(4). See also MHA Code of Practice, paras.24.24–24.28.
[16]   MHA 1983, s.64G.
[17]   See MHA Code of Practice, paras.24.30–23.32.

- Serious treatment for mental disorder, currently limited solely to neurosurgery and surgical implantation of hormones to reduce male sex drive. A patient who does not have capacity to consent to such treatment can never be administered this treatment.[18]
- Specified forms of treatment that can be given after three months of being liable to detention under the Act either with the patient's capacitous consent or, where the capacitous patient refuses or is not capable of consent, only subject to a second opinion (an example is treatment with antipsychotic medication).[19]
- Treatment (currently limited to electro-convulsive therapy (ECT)) that can only be administered to a patient capable of (and in fact) consenting or to an incapable patient subject to a second opinion, so long as the delivery of such treatment does not conflict with:

  (1) a valid and applicable advance decision to refuse ECT (see further **13.7** for advance decisions);
  (2) the decision of a donee or court appointed deputy (see further **13.6**); or
  (3) a decision of the Court of Protection.[20]

- Treatment in an emergency. This will primarily be of relevance in the case of ECT, which can be administered without the protections set out above where it is immediately necessary to save the patient's life or prevent serious deterioration of their condition.[21]

MHA 1983, Part 4 does not specifically refer to the patient's capacity to consent or withhold consent to treatment (the test in MHA 1983, ss.58 and 58A being whether the patient is 'capable of understanding the nature, purpose and likely effects of the treatment'). However, it is clear that, for all practical purposes, this test is the same as the statutory test that applies under MCA 2005, s.2 in relation to all those aged above 16.[22] For further detail on the test for capacity to consent to (and to withhold consent to) medical treatment, see **Chapter 13**.

It is important to note that where the provisions of MHA 1983, Part 4 are invoked, as they will be almost invariably be in relation to any patient detained under that Act, nothing in MCA 2005 authorises anyone to:

- give the person treatment for mental disorder; or
- consent to the person being given treatment for mental disorder.[23]

---

[18] The combined effect of MHA 1983, s.57 and s.28; see also MHA Code of Practice, fig. 12.
[19] MHA 1983, s.58.
[20] MHA 1983, s.58.
[21] MHA 1983, s.62. Treatments falling within MHA 1983, ss.57 and 58 could, theoretically, also be delivered on the same emergency basis, but by the nature of the treatments in question, it is very unlikely in practice that s.62 could ever properly be invoked in relation to such treatments. In relation to neuro-surgery, it is also difficult to see how this could be said to be anything other than irreversible, a further reason why s.62 would not apply.
[22] See MHA Code of Practice, paras.24.30–23.32.
[23] MHA 1983, s.28.

This suggests, therefore, that there is a bright line between MCA 2005 and MHA 1983 in terms of the psychiatric treatment of those detained in hospital. However, the courts have made clear that the presence of an advance decision to refuse medical treatment (see **13.7**) should weigh very heavily in the balance where consideration is given to whether to use the compulsory treatment provisions of MHA 1983 to administer treatment contrary to that directive.[24] Therefore, even if a valid and applicable advance decision to refuse the treatment in question cannot serve to prevent treatment being administered under MHA 1983, Part 4, the treating team should nonetheless proceed with caution before overriding that decision. Where the advance decision is one to refuse life-sustaining treatment, the treating team would also be 'well advised'[25] to consider putting the matter before a court to determine whether the use of compulsory powers is appropriate.

16.6 PATIENTS DETAINED UNDER MHA 1983: OTHER DECISIONS

It is very important to remember that MHA 1983 does not provide authority to:

- treat a patient for physical disorders unrelated to the mental disorder (or disorders) underpinning the detention;
- make decisions about other aspects of the patient's life – for instance as to the management of their finances or as to contact.

There may in some cases be a need to consider carefully whether the physical disorder which is being addressed is or is not connected with the patient's mental disorder.[26] If it is, then the medical treatment for that disorder can properly be said to be 'treatment for mental disorder' and can be given using the power given by MHA 1983, s.63, whether or not the patient has the capacity to consent to that treatment. A good example would be the taking of bloods for purposes of addressing the deterioration of a patient's physical health which has arisen in consequence of their mental disorder: the taking of that blood, and the associated restraint[27] would be authorised under MHA 1983.

However, if the physical disorder is *not* related to the mental disorder, it will always be necessary to consider – applying the MCA test (see **13.4**) – whether the patient has or lacks the capacity to consent to that treatment. Where the patient lacks that capacity, it will be possible to rely upon the general defence in MCA 2005, s.5 if

---

[24] *Nottinghamshire Healthcare NHS Trust* v. *RC* [2014] EWCOP 1317; [2014] COPLR 468. See also the MHA Code of Practice at para.24.6.
[25] *Nottinghamshire Healthcare NHS Trust* v. *RC* [2014] EWCOP 1317; [2014] COPLR 468 at para.21.
[26] The leading case remaining *B* v. *Croydon Health Authority* [1995] 1 All ER 683.
[27] Following *Tameside* v. *Glossop Acute Services Health Trust* v. *CH* [1996] 1 FLR 762, it is clear that restraint may lawfully be used, so long as reasonably required and clinically necessary, to administer treatment under s.63. Where the use of such restraint is doubtful, or will go beyond restraint into force, an application should be made to the court for a declaration that the treatment would be lawful. See R Jones (2015) *Mental Health Act Manual* (18th edn), Sweet & Maxwell, para.1–787.

the treatment falls within the scope of routine acts of care and treatment and is reasonably believed to be in the patient's best interests. It will also be possible to restrain that patient for purposes of providing that treatment if the conditions in MCA 2005, s.6 are met (see further **13.5**).[28]

It may, in some cases, be necessary to obtain the authority of the court, if:

- the treatment amounts to serious medical treatment as defined in Practice Direction 9E; or
- the patient will need to be deprived of their liberty for purposes of administering that treatment.

In the case of a patient detained under MHA 1983, it will be necessary in such a case to invoke the inherent jurisdiction of the High Court.[29] It is important to note that the High Court will decide whether the patient lacks the relevant capacity and whether the treatment (and associated deprivation of liberty) is in their best interests *as if* it was applying the tests provided for under MCA 2005.[30]

---

[28] I.e. (in the hospital context) that: (1) the person carrying it out reasonably believes it is in the patient's best interests and it is necessary to do it in order to prevent harm to the patient; and (2) the act is a proportionate response to the likelihood of the patient suffering harm and the seriousness of that harm.

[29] See, e.g., *NHS Trust* v. *Dr A* [2013] EWHC 2442 (COP); [2013] COPLR 605.

[30] See *NHS Trust* v. *Dr A* [2013] EWHC 2442 (COP); [2013] COPLR 605 at paras.47 and 53–4.

PART IV

Practical aspects of the assessment of mental capacity

CHAPTER 17

Practical guidance for doctors

17.1   Introduction
17.2   Balancing empowerment with protection
17.3   Mental capacity – a legal concept
17.4   Preparing for an assessment of capacity
17.5   The duty to 'enhance' mental capacity

17.6   Recording the assessment
17.7   A systematic approach to assessing capacity
17.8   The mental state in relation to capacity
17.9   Assessment tools
17.10 Retrospective assessment

17.1   INTRODUCTION

Doctors and other health professionals can be involved in assessing capacity in a variety of contexts. In the majority of cases they will be assessing the ability of their patients to consent to medical interventions. Doctors present relevant treatment options, and information about their likely benefits and side effects. Patients weigh up the options – including the option of no treatment – and make decisions accordingly. Adult patients are presumed to be the final arbiters of their own interests. (The legal issues regarding capacity to consent to medical interventions are discussed in **Chapter 13**.) Where adults lack, or may lack, the capacity to consent, they are less likely to be in a position to protect and promote their own interests. In these circumstances, it may be necessary for other people, including doctors, to make decisions on their behalf.

In addition to decisions about medical interventions for their patients, doctors can also be asked to offer independent medical advice about a person's capacity. They can be asked to:

- provide a medical 'certificate' or opinion at a solicitor's request as to a person's capacity to do something unrelated to medical treatment (such as making a will);
- witness or otherwise certify a legal document signed by a patient, including an advance decision refusing treatment;

- give an opinion as to a particular capacity which is relevant to other legal proceedings.

Another matter on which a doctor's opinion is frequently sought is whether someone with cognitive impairment is able to continue to live in their own home or whether a move to sheltered housing or a care home is advisable.

This section provides practical guidance for doctors when called upon to assess capacity in a variety of circumstances.

17.2 BALANCING EMPOWERMENT WITH PROTECTION

Doctors clearly have great powers to benefit adults who lack capacity. They can provide them with necessary treatment. They may also be able to help safeguard patients from exploitation and abuse or promote their best interests. Doctors can also identify medical conditions which may cause them to lack capacity to protect themselves or make autonomous choices. However, they also risk doing harm to patients, particularly if their assessments of capacity result in patients being inappropriately deprived of the right to make their own decisions.

MCA 2005 has a focus on empowerment. It is designed to enable adults to make as many of their own decisions as possible, and ensure they are as involved as possible in those decisions they cannot make. In 2014, the House of Lords Select Committee on the Mental Capacity Act[1] identified a significant and worrying lack of awareness of the requirements of MCA 2005 among health professionals. In practice, the focus on empowerment was lost. On the one hand, a culture of risk aversion meant that MCA 2005 was used restrictively for safeguarding purposes. On the other, a misunderstanding of the legal presumption that people are assumed to have the capacity to make their own decisions unless it is established that they do not, was used to justify non-intervention, thereby exposing adults at risk to unnecessary harm.

Given the range of medical involvement in assessing capacity for a variety of purposes, it is essential that all health professionals working with adults who may lack capacity are familiar with the requirements of MCA 2005. In all their work, doctors have to balance the risks of doing harm against the possible advantages of intervention, including in clinical assessments of capacity. This chapter provides practical advice for doctors and other health professionals who may be called upon to assess an individual's capacity or to provide independent medical advice about a person's capacity to a third party.

---

[1] House of Lords Select Committee on the Mental Capacity Act 2005 (2014) *Mental Capacity Act 2005: Post-legislative Scrutiny,* HL Paper 139, available at **www.publications.parliament.uk/pa/ld201314/ldselect/ldmentalcap/139/139.pdf**.

17.3 MENTAL CAPACITY – A LEGAL CONCEPT

Ultimately, mental capacity is a legal concept and the tests which are applied to determine whether a person has capacity to make specific decisions are laid out in MCA 2005 and for some decisions, by the common law. The legal framework is set out with some thoroughness in other chapters of this book. In this section we set out briefly the key legal issues relevant to an assessment of capacity. Where there is disagreement or doubt about a person's capacity that cannot be decided locally, the matter can be decided by the Court of Protection (see **Appendix C**).

17.3.1 What is decision-making capacity?

Decision-making capacity refers to the everyday ability that adults possess to make decisions or to take actions that influence their life, from simple decisions about what to have for breakfast, to far-reaching decisions about investments or serious medical treatment. In a legal context, capacity refers to a person's ability to do something, including making a decision, which may have legal consequences for the person themselves or for other people (see **Chapter 3**). Capacity is therefore pivotal in balancing the rights of people to make decisions and their right to protection from harm.

The starting point in any assessment of capacity is the presumption that a person has capacity unless it is demonstrated that they do not[2] (see **3.2**). This means that lack of cooperation or apathy with respect to an assessment of capacity should not lead to a conclusion that the person lacks capacity. If a person has capacity, they have the right to refuse to be assessed.

An assessment of capacity is based on a judgment about the mental processes a person must be able to go through in order to arrive at a decision, not the outcome or the decision itself. The question 'would a rational person make this decision?' is not directly relevant to the question of capacity. Individuals who have mental capacity may make decisions which are apparently irrational or unwise – and the law allows them to do so.[3]

An assessment of capacity must be based on a person's ability to make a specific decision at the time it needs to be made, not on whether they have the ability to make decisions in general.

17.3.2 When does a person lack capacity?

Under MCA 2005, a person lacks capacity if, at the time the decision in question needs to be made, there is a reasonable belief that the person is unable to make or communicate the decision because of an 'impairment of, or a disturbance in the

---

[2] MCA 2005, s.1(2).
[3] MCA 2005, s.1(4).

functioning of, the mind or brain' (see (**3.4**)).[4] In practice it can be helpful to approach an assessment of capacity by breaking down this single test into three questions:

- Is there an impairment of, or disturbance in the functioning of, the person's mind or brain? This is sometimes referred to as the 'diagnostic test'.
- Is the person unable to make a decision because of one or more of the four reasons given in MCA 2005? This is sometimes referred to as the 'functional test'.
- Is the person's inability to make the specific decision at the time when it needs to be made a result of the impairment of, or disturbance in the functioning of, their mind or brain? This is sometimes referred to as the 'causative nexus'.

There will be times when more emphasis will need to be placed on either the diagnostic or functional test (and sometimes, it may be more appropriate to reverse the first and second questions). In all cases, however, all three elements of the test must be satisfied. The test as set out below follows the approach which is most likely to be relevant where a doctor has cause to consider the question of capacity.

Stage 1 – The 'diagnostic test'

The legal requirement to point to an impairment or disturbance of the mind or brain means that doctors and other health professionals are frequently involved in assessing capacity. A clinical assessment of capacity will always involve identifying the presence (or absence) of a 'medical condition'. Although a specific medical diagnosis is not required, medical symptoms or signs must be present in order for a doctor to have any role in determining capacity. If there is no indication of any impairment or disturbance, the person must be presumed to have capacity and their ability to make decisions should not be questioned.

The assessment of capacity must focus on the specific decision that needs to be made at the time the decision is required. It does not matter therefore if the condition is temporary, or that the person retains the capacity to make other decisions, or if the person's capacity fluctuates. The inability to make a decision, however, must be a result of an impairment of, or disturbance in the functioning of, the person's mind or brain. This could relate to 'a range of problems, such as psychiatric illness, learning disability, dementia, brain damage or even a toxic confusional state, as long as it has the necessary effect on the functioning of the mind or brain, causing the person to be unable to make the decision'.[5] Clearly, however, if the impairment is temporary and the decision can realistically be put off until such a time as the person is likely to regain capacity, then it should be deferred.

In addition, a person cannot be assessed as lacking capacity until all reasonable steps have been taken to help them make the decision themselves (see **17.5**).

---

4   MCA 2005, s.2(1).
5   Explanatory Notes to MCA 2005, para.22.

Stage 2 – Inability to make a decision

It is equally important to identify whether the person is unable to make the decision in question. MCA 2005 uses a 'functional' test, focusing on the ability of the individual to make a particular decision at a particular time and the processes followed by the person in arriving at the decision. A person lacks the capacity to make a specific decision if they are unable:

    (a)   to understand the information relevant to the decision,
    (b)   to retain that information,
    (c)   to use or weigh that information as part of the process of making the decision, or
    (d)   to communicate his decision (whether by talking, using sign language or any other means).[6]

Where the impairment or disturbance stems from a diagnosable medical condition, it is not the diagnosis itself which determines capacity or incapacity but its impact on the individual's ability to understand, retain and use information in order to make the decision. Similarly, the ability to make different decisions can be variously affected by a particular medical disability. A person with schizophrenia may have the capacity to accept or refuse some medical treatments but not others, depending upon the extent or nature of their illness.[7] More generally, a person may have the capacity to carry out one type of legal act, such as marrying, while not having the capacity to carry out another, such as making a will.[8]

A person's capacity will largely be determined by their mental state. However, this does not mean that a particular diagnosis automatically renders a person incapable of making a decision. In addition, there may also be some physical conditions, such as severe pain or fatigue, which do not directly affect mental functioning but which can sometimes interfere with capacity. Poor eyesight, deafness and problems with speech and language may be relevant to whether a person's wishes can be ascertained and to how information relevant to the decision is given to them.

As it is a principle of MCA 2005 that a person is 'not to be treated as unable to make a decision unless all practicable steps to help him do so have been taken without success',[9] every effort must be made to overcome such problems with perception and communication (see also Chapter 3 of the MCA Code of Practice, reproduced at **Appendix B**).

Stage 3 – Is the inability to make the decision caused by the impairment or disturbance?

The third step is to establish that the individual's inability is because of the impairment or disturbance in their mind or brain. When making a decision that an

---

6   MCA 2005, s.3(1).
7   *Re C (Adult: Refusal of Medical Treatment)* [1994] 1 WLR 290, [1994] 1 All ER 819.
8   *Re Park's Estate, Park* v. *Park* [1954] P 112.
9   MCA 2005, s.1(3).

individual lacks capacity the assessor has to identify a causal link between the disturbance in question and the inability to make the decision. The important point is that the impairment or disturbance causes the individual to be unable to make the decision in question (see **3.4**).

There may be times when it is unclear whether, despite the presence of an impairment or disturbance in the individual's mind or brain, it is actually the cause of the inability to make the decision. This may be, for example, where someone has mild learning disabilities but may be subject to pressure from a coercive partner or relative. These circumstances can be challenging for health professionals. Identifying to what extent their decision-making is being enhanced or undermined by those close to them can be difficult. In these circumstances it is strongly recommended that health professionals take legal advice (see **3.5**).

Where it is not clear that a person has capacity to make a decision, doctors must balance the need to protect the person from harm against respecting their autonomy. The assessment they make could be criticised or challenged and should therefore be carefully documented and their findings recorded.

17.3.3 The medical role in assessing capacity

Although assessing any particular capacity does not require detailed legal knowledge, the doctor must understand in broad terms the relevant legal tests as set out in the preceding chapters of this book. Where the doctor is not the decision-maker, his or her role is to supply information (including expert opinion) on which an assessment of the person's capacity can be based. They need to describe the consequences of medical conditions which may compromise an individual's ability to pass the relevant legal test. If there is no medical diagnosis or medically describable symptoms or signs, there can be no medical evidence relevant to determining capacity. For example, to say that a person 'makes poor judgments' is not a medical opinion but a lay observation and one which is heavily subjective. This emphasises the importance of the doctor first of all determining that it is appropriate to give a medical opinion about capacity.

Although a doctor may be asked to give an opinion about capacity, this opinion is not necessarily the deciding factor since evidence from other people and other sources may also need to be taken into account.[10] Also, some tests of capacity make explicit or implicit reference to social functioning rather than to medical disabilities per se (see, for example, **Chapter 11** on personal relationships) and a doctor is no more expert in assessing social functioning than anyone else.

Where the relevant legal capacity is the capacity to consent to a specific medical treatment, doctors should take particular care and have regard to the professional

---

[10] For example, in *Masterman-Lister* v. *Brutton & Co.* [2002] EWCA Civ 1889 the court gave detailed consideration to diaries, letters and computer documents. In *Saulle* v. *Nouvet* [2007] EWHC 2902 (QB); [2008] WTLR 729 the court considered witness statements and oral evidence from family members as well as home videos.

and other guidance available[11] (see also **Chapter 13**). A doctor's opinion of what is the best or most appropriate form of treatment may conflict with what the patient wants. It is tempting, but ethically and legally wrong, for the doctor to underestimate the capacity of a patient in order to achieve what they believe to be in that person's best interests. In so doing, the doctor deprives the patient of autonomy and would be acting unlawfully.

17.3.4 Professional ethics – seeking consent

There are two distinct contexts in which doctors examine people. The most common is the therapeutic context aimed at ensuring that patients receive appropriate care and treatment. Patient consent can be explicit or implied. For example, permission to disclose information essential for the provision of care to other health professionals involved in the episode of treatment is usually implied. Nevertheless, the BMA maintains[12] that it is good practice to inform patients about the scope of disclosure within the therapeutic context, since care is increasingly provided by multidisciplinary teams and information may be spread more widely than patients anticipate (see **2.2** and **13.8** on confidentiality).

The second situation is where doctors act as independent examiners in order to provide a report for purposes other than medical treatment, for example for use in legal proceedings. When a doctor is carrying out this second type of assessment, it cannot be assumed that the person has given their consent to examination and to disclosure of information. It is therefore essential that the doctor's role and the purpose of the exercise are explained to the person at the outset. Where an adult lacks the capacity to consent to examination and subsequent disclosure, MCA 2005 contains specific powers, such as LPAs, that permit certain forms of delegated decision-making. Where these powers are not available (for example, because no one is nominated to act as an attorney), decisions have to be made based upon an assessment of the incapacitated adult's best interests (see **3.7**).

Particular care may be required when assessment for a report to third parties is carried out by the patient's own doctor and takes place within the context of a continuing therapeutic relationship. In such cases, the doctor must explain how the examination differs from the usual doctor–patient encounter and obtain explicit consent from the patient. Patients must also be told who will have access to the information gained and whether other material from their past records will be needed. The patient's consent to such disclosure should be recorded.

If an individual appears competent and refuses to cooperate with the assessment, the doctor must note that fact in conjunction with the other evidence available (see

---

[11] There are various sources of guidance on consent to medical treatment which are summarised in BMA (2012) *Consent Tool Kit* (5th edn), available at **http://bma.org.uk/practical-support-at-work/ethics/consent/consent-tool-kit**. See also Department of Health (2009) *Reference Guide to Consent for Examination or Treatment* (2nd edn), available at **www.gov.uk/government/publications/reference-guide-to-consent-for-examination-or-treatment-second-edition**.

[12] BMA (2008) *Confidentiality and Disclosure of Health Records Tool Kit* (**http://bma.org.uk/practical-support-at-work/ethics/confidentiality-and-health-records**), Card 2, para.4.

also **2.4** on the refusal to be assessed). If it appears likely that the person lacks capacity to consent to assessment or to disclosure, the doctor should take a decision whether or not to proceed with the assessment based on a judgment of the person's best interests. Such judgment necessarily includes, among all other relevant considerations, that appropriate weight be given to the ascertainable past and current wishes of that individual (see **3.7**).

17.3.5 Which doctor should assess the person?

Where a doctor is assessing a patient's capacity to consent or refuse the proposed treatment, legally, he or she will usually be the decision-maker and in many cases will be the one to assess capacity. In complex cases, such as where there is fluctuating capacity or significant psychiatric disorder, it may be necessary to enrol specialist advice. The role of the specialist is to advise the decision-maker.

Where third parties are seeking an expert assessment of capacity, the choice of doctor will depend on the requirements of the assessment and the medical condition of the person being assessed. Many people can be assessed by their GP, and indeed in some cases, a close, long-term acquaintance with the person being assessed may be an asset, particularly if that person is more relaxed with a familiar doctor. However on some occasions, the GP's personal knowledge of a patient, and perhaps also of the patient's family, may make an objective assessment more difficult. Alternatively, the patient may attend a practice where they see different GPs, so no single doctor may have detailed knowledge of the patient. If the nature or complexity of the person's medical disorder or disabilities suggests that a specialist would be more appropriate then it will usually be important for that doctor to obtain information from the person's GP, and take this into account in making their own assessment of the patient's capacity. Other members of the multidisciplinary team, particularly nurses, psychologists, speech and language therapists and occupational therapists may also have specific skills to assist the doctor in assessing capacity.

Whoever carries out the assessment should make efforts to create the most congenial environment to optimise the conditions for assessing the person's capacity at their highest level of functioning (see **2.3** and **17.4**).

17.4 PREPARING FOR AN ASSESSMENT OF CAPACITY

Before making an assessment of an individual's capacity, doctors should consider a number of issues in advance. Assessment of capacity is not a function which can usually be carried out in only a few minutes. Aside from situations where the patient is comatose, or otherwise so severely disabled that their lack of capacity to take the material decision(s) is obvious, assessment will usually take a substantial period of time, even if only a single area of capacity is to be explored. This is required both because of the need to be thorough and comprehensive and because of the legal importance which attaches to the assessment. The doctor should never be constrained in making an assessment by time or resources.

Each assessment of capacity must be an assessment of an individual in their own circumstances. No assumptions should be made about capacity just on the basis of the person's known diagnosis or their age or appearance.[13] What matters is how the medical condition affects that particular person's own ability to make the decision in question, not the diagnosed medical condition itself.

It is worth emphasising again that the doctor must guard against allowing a personal view of what is in the person's best interests to influence an assessment of capacity. It may be disconcerting for the doctor to determine that the patient has capacity when the doctor believes that allowing the patient to make the decision will be against their long-term interests. However, the doctor must not consider the implications for the person of being allowed to make the decision except to the extent that this is relevant in deciding whether the person has the capacity to do so.

Given that mental capacity is decision-specific, it is vital that doctors identify with as much precision as possible the specific legal test or decision for which they are being asked to assess an individual's capacity – without this an assessment of capacity is likely to be meaningless. Doctors should keep in mind that it is not necessary for an individual to understand every facet of the question, rather they need to understand, in general terms the information relevant to the decision.

17.5 THE DUTY TO 'ENHANCE' MENTAL CAPACITY

Doctors will be aware both that medical disabilities can fluctuate and that there are many factors other than a person's medical disorder which may adversely influence capacity. It is the duty of the assessing doctor, reinforced by one of the guiding principles of MCA 2005,[14] to optimise the conditions and to provide appropriate kinds of support that allow the person's capacity to be assessed at their highest level of functioning in relation to the decision in question.

Some pointers are suggested in **2.3**, and a further elaboration on the relevant pointers for doctors is set out below. Any treatable medical condition which affects capacity should, as far as possible, be treated before a final assessment is made.

Incapacity may be temporary, albeit for a prolonged period. For example, the mental capacity of an older patient with delirium caused by infection may continue to improve for some time after the infection has been eradicated. If a person's condition is likely to improve, the assessment of capacity should, if possible, be delayed. The effect of drugs, particularly hypnotics and tranquillisers should be considered carefully. If there is a treatable physical disorder present, assessment should, if possible, be delayed until the patient is as well and as comfortable as possible.

---

[13]   MCA 2005, s.2(3).
[14]   MCA 2005, s.1(3).

17.5.1 Fluctuating capacity

Some conditions, such as dementia, may give rise to fluctuating capacity. Thus, although a person with dementia may lack capacity at the time of one assessment, the result may be different if a second assessment is undertaken during a lucid interval. In cases of fluctuating capacity the medical report should detail the level of capacity during periods of maximal and minimal ability. Where possible, decisions should be made during lucid periods.

Some mental health problems may be untreatable and yet their impact can be minimised. For example, the capacity of a person with a short-term memory deficit to make a particular decision may be improved if trained in suitable techniques by an occupational therapist or psychologist. If the assessing doctor believes that capacity could be improved by such assistance then this should be stated in any opinion.

17.5.2 Improving and supporting communication

Some physical conditions which do not directly affect the mental state can appear to interfere with capacity. For example, disabilities of communication will not impair the ability to understand relevant information or make a choice, but they may prevent the person's wishes being made known. Many communication difficulties which result from physical disabilities can be helped. There should, therefore, be careful assessment of speech, language functioning, hearing and (if appropriate) sight. Any disabilities discovered should, as far as possible (and if time allows), be corrected before any conclusion is reached about capacity. MCA 2005 makes it clear, however, that where an individual lacks the ability 'to communicate his decision (whether by talking, using sign language or any other means)'[15] that person is deemed to lack capacity in relation to the matter.

17.5.3 Choosing the best time and place for the assessment

Care should be taken to choose the best location and time for the assessment. For someone who is on the borderline of having capacity, added anxiety may tip them into apparent incapacity. It may be appropriate to assess the person in their own home if it is thought that an interview at either a hospital or a GP's surgery would adversely affect the result. A relative or carer may be able to indicate the most suitable location and time for the assessment.

17.5.4 Supported decision-making

The way in which someone is approached and dealt with generally can have a significant impact upon apparent capacity and the doctor should be sensitive to this. Educating the person being assessed as to the factors relevant to the proposed

---

[15] MCA 2005, s.3(1)(d).

decision may enhance capacity. Indeed, the assessing doctor should always establish what the person understands about the decision they are being asked to undertake. It is important for the doctor to re-explain and, if necessary, write down those aspects of the decision which have not been fully grasped. The person being assessed should be allowed sufficient time to become familiar with concepts relevant to the decision. For example, people with learning disabilities may acquire the capacity to consent to a blood test after receiving appropriate information in an accessible manner.[16]

The capacity of some people may be enhanced by the presence of a friend, relative or other person at the interview. Alternatively, the presence of a third party may increase the anxiety and thus reduce the person's capacity. The person being assessed should be asked specifically whether they would feel more comfortable with another person present. A professional advocate may be able to ensure that the person's views have been adequately represented.

17.5.5 Depression and capacity

Depression is common but is often not recognised. Its presence may profoundly affect capacity and yet it is amenable to treatment. Making a diagnosis of depression in the presence of other disabilities affecting mental functioning can be particularly difficult, especially in patients with dementia. The opinion of a psychiatrist may be necessary in such cases. Some depressed patients whose capacity may be in question can be at particular risk of 'going along with' suggestions regardless of their own private views. The assessing doctor should be aware of this and structure the interview so as to avoid the use of leading questions.

17.6 RECORDING THE ASSESSMENT

Careful thought should be given to how the assessment of capacity is documented. As capacity is a legal issue, it is a good idea if the assessment is recorded in a structured manner that reflects the requirements of MCA 2005. It can be helpful therefore to record the following:

- Details of the specific decision that the individual is being asked to make or the relevant legal test as appropriate.
- The steps that have been taken to support and enhance the individual's ability to make the decision in question, including any aids to communication and understanding.
- The nature of the medical condition and/or relevant medical symptoms that give rise to the disturbance or impairment of the mind or brain – the 'diagnostic criterion'.

---

[16] JG Wong, ICH Clare, MJ Gunn and AJ Holland (1999) 'Capacity to make health care decisions: its importance in clinical practice', *Psychological Medicine* 29: 437–446.

- The reasons why the impairment or disturbance renders the individual incapable of making the specified decision.

As with all medical note-keeping, wherever possible, records should be made at the time the capacity assessment is being made – contemporaneous notes are always preferable to retrospective ones. Statements of opinion should be supported by relevant facts and doctors should avoid unwarranted speculation. In some circumstances, such as in emergencies, notes will inevitably be briefer, but wherever possible, reports should be detailed and systematic.

17.7 A SYSTEMATIC APPROACH TO ASSESSING CAPACITY

17.7.1 Background information

Once sure of the relevant legal test, the assessing doctor should become familiar with any background information about the person likely to be relevant to that particular test. The amount of information required will be determined by the complexity of the decision to be taken. For example, if the assessment relates to the capacity to make a will, the assessing doctor will need to have some idea about the extent and complexity of the person's estate and whether the person understands the claims of those who may have a call on the estate when deciding about disposal of their assets (see **Chapter 6**). The doctor must therefore have some knowledge of the number and nature of the potential claims on the individual. Although the medical assessment should be carried out with regard to the relevant legal criteria, there must be a clear distinction between the description of the disabilities and the interpretation of how they affect legal capacity. Therefore, the doctor should first define the diagnosis or any medical disabilities and then assess how these affect the person's ability to make the decision or decisions in question.

17.7.2 Medical records and reports

Prior to undertaking the assessment, if possible the doctor should have access to relevant past medical and psychiatric records. An understanding of the progression of the person's illness or condition will be relevant to prognosis, to any likely response to treatment, and thus to future potential capacity. Assessment of the permanence or transience of disabilities may be crucially important in offering a view about achievable capacity. Also, the medical records may give a picture of those disabilities in general terms which differs from the impression that the doctor gains at an individual assessment. It is important for the doctor to make an assessment on the basis of current evidence from various information sources, including examination of the person concerned, rather than relying entirely on past evaluations.

The doctor should also take full account of relevant information from other disciplines. An assessment by a psychologist may already be available, or could be sought, and this may assist in giving a detailed, validated and systematic assessment of cognitive functioning. An occupational therapist might be consulted when information about activities of daily living is of importance. Also, a report from a social worker, a nurse or a care worker may be helpful, for example where the person is living in a care home.

17.7.3 Information from others

Information from friends, relatives or carers is often important in the assessment of capacity and may reveal the person's known previous patterns of behaviour, values and goals. Such information may indicate whether their current behaviour and thinking reflects an abnormal mental state. However, great care must be taken when gaining information from third parties, particularly if they have an interest in the outcome of the assessment of capacity. Aspects of a person's current thinking may derive not from a mental impairment but from their personality, or from a particular cultural or ethnic background, and this will need to be considered carefully before any assessment of capacity is made. It may even be necessary for the doctor to seek advice from others on such cultural issues, or to suggest that the patient be examined by a doctor of a cultural or ethnic background similar to that of the person being assessed.[17]

17.7.4 Medical diagnosis

Where the person suffers from a mental disorder, it is good practice to express the diagnosis in terms of one of the accepted international classifications of mental disorders, the World Health Organization's *International Classification of Diseases* (WHO ICD-10), or the American Psychiatric Association's *Diagnostic and Statistical Manual of Mental Disorders* (DSM-5) (see further **18.3**). This will ensure greater diagnostic consistency between doctors and minimise diagnostic confusion.

17.8 THE MENTAL STATE IN RELATION TO CAPACITY

Examination of the mental state is fundamental to the assessment of capacity. Although particular diagnoses may tend to be associated with particular mental state disabilities which can affect capacity, what matters are the disabilities themselves. It is only through detailed assessment of specific aspects of mental functioning that capacity can be properly assessed.

---

[17] See, e.g., S Fernando and F Keating (2008) *Mental Health in a Multi-ethnic Society: A Multidisciplinary Handbook* (2nd edn), Routledge; and H Sewell (2008) *Working with Ethnicity, Race and Culture in Mental Health: A Handbook for Practitioners*, Jessica Kingsley Publishers.

17.8.1 Mental state examination

The doctor should consider the patient's mental functioning under the following headings when making an assessment of mental state, indicating the relevance of any findings to the specific test of capacity. It is also important to document any medical or psychometric tests or other assessment tools used in the process (see **17.9** for information about assessment tools).[18]

Appearance and behaviour

A patient may be so agitated or overactive in their behaviour that it may be impossible to impart relevant information to them. Although MCA 2005 makes it clear that a person cannot be assessed as lacking capacity on the basis of appearance alone, appearance and behaviour may suggest a mood disorder or cognitive impairment which might be relevant to the person's capacity and might therefore justify further consideration.

Speech

The rate, quantity, form or flow of speech may be such as to interfere with communication, as well as reflecting abnormality of thought processes. For example, a depressed patient may be so lacking in speech that they are unable to communicate effectively; or the speech of a person with bipolar effective disorder may be rapid with quickly changing subjects ('flight of ideas') so that communication is severely impaired. Similarly, the thought disorder of a patient with schizophrenia (moving between topics without apparent logical connections) may make communication very difficult or even impossible. Damage to the language areas of the brain following a stroke may also make direct verbal communication impossible. Once again, communication difficulties are not by themselves indicative of a lack of capacity, and in many cases, people with very restricted communication abilities can still, particularly with relevant support, communicate their decisions.

Mood

Mood may be very important in determining capacity. A depressed patient with delusions of poverty may make decisions relevant to their affairs on an entirely erroneous basis. Similarly, the grandiose approach of a patient with bipolar effective disorder may lead to rash financial or other decisions. Lability of mood,

---

[18] See, e.g., MF Folstein, SE Folstein and PR McHugh (1975) '"Mini-mental state": a practical method for grading the cognitive state of patients for the clinician', *Journal of Psychiatric Research*. 1975, 12(3): 189–198; T Grisso and PS Appelbaum (1998) *Assessing Competence to Consent to Treatment: A Guide for Physicians and Other Health Professionals*, Oxford University Press; and JS Janofsky, RJ McCarthy and MF Folstein (1992) 'The Hopkins competency assessment test', *Hospital and Community Psychiatry* 43: 132–136.

common after stroke, may render a patient unable to make consistent decisions. Anxiety may also have some effect on the assessed level of capacity.

Thought

Abnormalities of thought may have a profound effect upon decision-making. Delusions which are strongly held, and which relate specifically to the decision at hand, may substantially distort a person's ability to make the decision. For example, a delusional belief that a close relative is plotting against them might affect capacity to make a will. Similarly, a delusional belief that doctors have magical powers to cure may render the patient incapable of consenting to medical treatment. Thought abnormalities falling short of delusions, such as extreme preoccupation or obsessional thoughts, can also interfere with capacity but are less likely to do so. Overvalued ideas falling short of delusions, such as occur in anorexia nervosa, present particular difficulties in relation to the capacity of such patients to consent to treatment or to accept or refuse food.

Perception

Illusions (misinterpretation of the nature of real objects) are rarely significant enough to inhibit capacity. Hallucinations, however, may well be of direct relevance to decision-making. They are often congruent with, or reinforce, delusions and so the two should be considered together. Auditory hallucinations instructing the patient may have two distinct effects. First, by their content and authority they may directly interfere with the patient's ability to think about relevant issues as well as decision-making ability. Second, hallucinations may be so intrusive that they distract the person from thinking about the decision at all.

Cognition

Defects in cognitive functioning can have profound significance for capacity. Decision-making and all tests of legal capacity require not only consciousness but some continuity of consciousness and of recollection. Attention (the ability to focus on the matter in hand) and concentration (the ability to sustain attention) are necessary for effective thought and for capacity. Patients who are highly distracted, whether by hallucinations or because of delirium, may lack capacity. Most psychiatrists use the mini-mental state examination[19] as a convenient way of assessing different domains of cognitive function. If this test reveals areas of impairment it may be helpful to make a more detailed appraisal of the affected cognitive abilities.

---

[19]   MF Folstein, SE Folstein and PR McHugh (1975) '"Mini-mental state": a practical method for grading the cognitive state of patients for the clinician', *Journal of Psychiatric Research* 12(3): 189–198.

Orientation

Awareness of time, place and person might be seen as relevant only to set the context for decisions rather than being directly relevant to capacity. However, disorientation is usually a marker of brain dysfunction, for instance in delirium or dementia, and in these conditions capacity is commonly impaired.

Memory

Problems with long-term memory may not necessarily reduce capacity. However a person who cannot remember their relatives or the extent of financial assets could be significantly impaired in decision-making ability. A person with a severe short-term memory deficit (an inability to recall information given a few minutes earlier) which may occur as a result of chronic alcoholism, a stroke, or Alzheimer's disease, is likely to lack capacity for some, but not necessarily all, decisions.

Intellectual functioning

Low IQ level (for example, as a result of learning disability) may reduce capacity for certain decisions, although it may be possible to use aids to communication, such as pictures or videos to enhance understanding. Care should be taken not to presume incapacity just because the person has a learning disability, however severe. There should be careful investigation of the person's abilities specifically in relation to the decision in question. Acquired brain damage, whether from trauma or from disease processes affecting the brain, may also affect cognitive functioning and, therefore, capacity. However, where only certain aspects of intellectual functioning are significantly impaired it is important to be very specific in distinguishing which functions, or combination of functions, are necessary for the legal capacity which the person must have. Standardised psychometric tests may be of help in assessing the severity of cognitive impairment. Many simple tests of cognitive functioning assess only orientation and memory, but it is important also to assess other areas of mental functioning, such as calculation, reasoning, visuo-spatial functioning and sequencing. An occupational therapist or psychologist may be able to help in these areas.

Insight

People can lack insight into one aspect of their lives and retain it for others. For example, lack of insight as to the presence of illness might not deprive a person of the capacity to make decisions about treatment of the illness if the person has insight into the need for such treatment. Furthermore, insight may not be completely absent. The person with reduced insight may have specific awareness of their condition so as to have the capacity necessary for decisions about treatment. Of course, lack of insight into mental illness may not inhibit the person's capacity to decide about something else in their life. No report should read 'has insight' or 'has no insight' as either statement is valueless if left unqualified.

Personality disorders

By contrast with mental illness or organic brain syndromes, personality disorders present particular problems in relation to assessment of capacity. Such patients have disorders which affect many areas of mental and social functioning, as well as behaviour. They often experience intense states of arousal and labile mood and are frequently impulsive. Their thought processes are unusual, but they are not deluded. It is the manner in which such persons weigh information in the balance which is generally affected, not their ability to think or to understand the information.[20] Assessment of capacity in such patients is therefore extremely difficult since there are no clear-cut abnormalities in the mental state such as dementia, hallucinations or delusions and yet the doctor will often perceive that they are not making decisions in the way that an ordinary person would (see **17.9** on the use of assessment tools to aid such assessments). There should be no automatic assumption that this necessarily indicates lack of capacity.

17.9 ASSESSMENT TOOLS

To assist practitioners involved in assessing capacity, and to enhance the reliability and validity of assessments, several assessment tools have been developed and are likely to be used increasingly. One example, the FACE Mental Capacity Assessment was specifically designed for health and care practitioners applying the MCA test of capacity in situations where there is no need for detailed clinical assessment.[21] Where specific clinical assessment is needed, assessment tools are not a substitute but merely an aid to be used within such assessment.

The most commonly used tool in clinical assessments of capacity, the MacArthur Competence Assessment Tool for Treatment (MacCAT-T),[22] structures the assessment around four elements of capacity to consent to treatment, which roughly correspond to the elements in the MCA test. Three of the four elements are highly 'cognitive', and the levels of reliability and validity are highest in respect of these components, for example when assessing patients with acute or chronic brain

---

[20]   *R* v. *Collins, ex p Brady* (2000) 58 BMLR 173. In this case, it was held that severe personality disorder alone could be sufficient to have 'eschewed the weighing of information and the balancing of risks and needs to such an extent that … his decisions on food refusal and force feeding had been incapacitated'.
[21]   The FACE Mental Capacity Assessment has been adopted by some NHS Trusts and Local Authorities (see **www.face.eu.com**).
[22]   The MacArthur Competence Assessment Tool for Treatment (MacCAT-T) was developed in the USA to assess capacity to consent to medical treatment (see **www.macarthur.virginia.edu/ treatment.html**). See also T Grisso and PS Appelbaum (1998) *Assessing Competence to Consent to Treatment: A Guide for Physicians and Other Health Professionals*, Oxford University Press.

conditions or those with psychoses caused by mental (rather than physical) illness. The fourth element, referred to as the 'appreciation' test, assesses whether the person is able not just to receive and retain treatment information, and to manipulate it, but whether they can appreciate its relevance to them and their situation. Such assessment is more 'subjective' and open to variation of opinion, for example when assessing a person who is cognitively relatively intact but who may be 'distorting' the relevance to their situation. Similar concerns apply to the element of the MCA test of capacity concerning the ability to 'weigh' relevant information, which refers not only to 'manipulating' the information but also to the way in which that exercise is carried out.

17.10 RETROSPECTIVE ASSESSMENT

On occasions a doctor may be asked to advise whether a person had the capacity at some time in the past to make a decision which they made. Examples might be the capacity to make a will (see **Chapter 6**) where the person has subsequently died and the will is contested or capacity to enter into a contract (see **Chapter 9**) where the validity of the contract is subsequently challenged. Any such retrospective assessment will have to be based upon medical notes made at the time, as well as on other non-medical information which may help to suggest the nature of the person's mental functioning at the time, and whether they may have been susceptible to the exertion of undue influence or pressure. When making a retrospective assessment it is important that doctors are clear as to the relevant legal test they are applying. Clearly, the doctor will have to indicate that the assessment was retrospective and may therefore be unreliable.

CHAPTER 18

Practical guidelines for lawyers

18.1 Introduction
18.2 Who should assess the person?
18.3 Psychiatric diagnoses

18.4 Medical assessment of mental conditions
18.5 General guidance

18.1 INTRODUCTION

In cases where a client's mental capacity is in doubt, it is often desirable, or a matter of good practice, for lawyers to obtain a medical or other expert opinion. This is particularly important where the capacity in question relates to complex or serious decisions. Indeed, in some circumstances the courts have strongly advised obtaining medical evidence about a person's capacity (see the 'golden rule' discussed in **4.5** and **6.5**).

The lawyer should inform the client of any concerns they have about their capacity, the purpose of any capacity assessment, and the potential implications if they are found to lack capacity.

It is important to remember that it is the 'decision-maker' who needs to be satisfied that a person has or lacks capacity. Therefore, even when a lawyer has obtained an expert opinion on their client's capacity, it remains for the lawyer to use that report in forming (and recording) their own view on the client's capacity to instruct them and so determine whether they can accept and act on the client's instructions. (In a court, the decision-maker will be the judge.)

A summary of points for the lawyer obtaining a medical opinion is given below.

The lawyer needs to identify the most appropriate doctor or other medical practitioner to provide an expert opinion on the person's capacity to make the specific decision or decisions in question (see **18.2**). They must secure the client's written consent or otherwise confirm that the client has agreed to be assessed. (If the client is a party to proceedings it may be necessary to secure the court's permission to obtain an expert opinion.)

The lawyer then needs to provide the expert with a detailed letter of instruction, addressing the following matters:

219

- The nature of the matter or case under consideration (for example, is the person reviewing their will, planning to purchase a property, or have they been made a party to proceedings before a court?).
- Whether the report is for the purposes of the individual only, or for the court, and if the latter, whether the expert is acting for one or other party to the proceedings, or as a single joint expert.
- If the report is for the purposes of a court, any relevant protocol or practice direction the expert should be aware of (for example, CPR Part 35[1] in civil proceedings).
- The timescale for the report and the question of the expert's fee (the amount or fee scale, who will be responsible to pay the fee, and when they are likely to receive payment).
- How arrangements might be made for the expert to meet the person in order to carry out their formal assessment.
- The specific issue of capacity the lawyer wishes the expert to report upon, as individuals may retain capacity to make decisions in some areas of functioning and not in others.[2] For example, they might be able to understand the issues involved in making an LPA, appointing an attorney to deal with their finances, but lack the capacity to make specific financial decisions for themselves.
- The relevant legal tests of capacity as described in Part III. Where MCA 2005 applies, include an explanation of the statutory test of capacity and other relevant aspects of MCA 2005,[3] and signpost the expert to the MCA Code of Practice[4] and other useful guidance.[5]
- Where the particular test of capacity has been established in case law, provide the medical practitioner with a summary of the relevant judgment, and high-light the relevance of specific limbs or aspects of the common law test to the client's own situation. For example, if testamentary capacity is to be assessed it will be necessary for the expert to be given some background information about the extent of the testator's assets and those who may have a call on their estate, and perhaps a draft of the proposed will (see **Chapter 6**). This is particularly relevant where the expert is asked to witness the will in accordance with the so-called 'golden rule'.[6] If the person is a party or intended party to proceedings, it will be useful to provide the history of the proceedings to date in addition to apposite information on the client.

---

[1]   CPR 1998 Part 35 and Practice Direction 35: Experts and Assessors.

[2]   *Re Park's Estate, Park* v. *Park* [1954] P 112; *Masterman-Lister* v. *Brutton & Co; Masterman-Lister* v. *Jewell* [2002] EWCA Civ 1889; [2003] 1 WLR 1511.

[3]   The statutory test of capacity in MCA 2005, ss.2 and 3, taking account of the principles in MCA 2005, s.1. (See also **Chapter 3**.)

[4]   Office of the Public Guardian (2007) *Mental Capacity Act 2005 Code of Practice*, available at **www.gov.uk/government/publications/mental-capacity-act-code-of-practice**.

[5]   See Office of the Public Guardian (2009) *Making Decisions: A Guide for People Who Work in Health and Social Care*, available at **www.gov.uk/government/uploads/system/uploads/attachment_data/file/348440/OPG603-Health-care-workers-MCA-decisions.pdf**.

[6]   *Kenward* v. *Adams* (1975) *The Times*, 29 November 1975. The 'golden rule' about when medical evidence should be obtained is discussed in detail at **4.5** and **6.5**.

- It is important to ensure that any summary of the law is understandable to someone who is not a lawyer, but in a form which will be acceptable to the courts.
- Where a specific form must be used, such as Form COP3 for Court of Protection proceedings (see **Appendix G**) or the Certificate as to Capacity to Conduct Proceedings (see **Appendix F**) for use when a party or intended party to proceedings may lack mental capacity to conduct their own proceedings (litigation capacity), provide the expert with a copy of the relevant form and accompanying guidance. It may also be helpful to the expert if the lawyer completes relevant parts of the form in advance.
- If there is no prescribed form, set out the specific questions you are asking the expert to answer in the letter of instruction (for example: Does the person suffer from an impairment of, or disturbance in functioning of the mind or brain? If yes, what is the nature of that impairment and disturbance? What is the basis of your assessment?).
- In any situation where medical practitioners are asked to witness documents, emphasise to them that they are expected to use their professional skills and judgment in assessing and confirming the patient's competence to sign, and not merely acting as 'witnesses' (see **4.5**).

It is often helpful for there to be a discussion between lawyer and expert prior to the expert's consideration of the case, both to clarify the legal questions and to establish what documentary or other background information is available which the doctor should be aware of. It is also helpful for lawyers to have some knowledge of the basic principles which underlie medical assessment in order both to evaluate the opinion and to be sure of understanding its legal implications. A summary is set out in **18.4** and further details are given in **Chapter 16**. When deciding which particular expert to approach to request a medical assessment, lawyers must bear in mind issues of language and culture, and any sensitive matters, particular to the client.

As a matter of good practice, lawyers who visit clients in hospitals or care homes, (and experts who visit to carry out assessments) should notify the ward or home, preferably in writing, in advance of their expected visit and then introduce themselves to the duty manager to ascertain that the client is well enough to receive a professional visit. Although a client's access to their legal adviser should not be hindered, lawyers need to be sensitive to the client's condition and medical needs and consider the most appropriate time to visit, mindful of the hospital or home's protected meal-times policy. When visiting clients at home it is advisable that all professionals carry or display their official identity badges.

In some circumstances, it might also be appropriate to consult a third party as part of the assessment of the person's capacity, such as a friend or relative, carer, or other professional. They may provide valuable information or guidance on factors which may enhance or improve the person's decision-making capacity, or assist with communication of their decision. The client's permission should always be sought first (if the client has capacity to consent) before undertaking any discussion about the client with a third party. The remainder of this chapter offers basic information about different specialties and medical personnel, and about the nature of psychiatric assessment and diagnosis.

18.2 WHO SHOULD ASSESS THE PERSON?

A doctor can offer an expert opinion when the person being assessed has (or appears to have) a diagnosable medical condition. Occasionally, the lawyer may request an opinion from the doctor clarifying that the client does not have a medical or psychiatric condition. Lawyers should be wary of any assessment which appears to be 'medical' but which does not consider the impact of the symptoms the person experiences (as part of their medical condition) on their decision-making capacity, in line with the relevant test. Under MCA 2005,[7] a person can only be assessed as lacking capacity to make a particular decision if they have 'an impairment of, or disturbance in the functioning of, the mind or brain' which is the cause of their being unable to make the decision in question and this is an aspect that doctors will usually be asked to comment on. The disturbance or impairment need not necessarily stem from a mental illness; a disturbance or impairment can often be due to a physical illness, including the effects of medication used to treat one. General practitioners are able to take a full medical history, including a psychiatric history and to conduct a basic mental state examination. They are well placed to define straightforward impairments, irrespective of their diagnostic cause. Where the person's capacity to make a specific decision is uncertain and their make the application of legal tests of capacity complex or difficult, it may be appropriate to seek a specialist opinion.

18.2.1 Specialist knowledge

Medicine is divided into specialities and specialist knowledge may be required to assess how a particular illness or condition may affect the person's ability to make particular decisions. Some people may require assessment by a psychiatrist, a medical professional who is trained in the assessment, diagnosis and treatment of mental illness.

If there is a reasonable belief that the impairment affecting the individual's capacity is likely to respond to treatment, and the decision can be deferred until capacity improves, then it should be deferred. Common factors amenable to treatment are, inter alia: pain; underlying medical conditions; effects of medication; infection; dehydration; fear, etc. The requisite assessment and treatment may be best carried out by a doctor with expertise in that particular area, for example a physician might be called upon to address an underlying bladder infection, or to give an opinion on the extent to which such an infection might be affecting the

---

[7] MCA 2005, s.2(1).

person's decision-making capacity. Mental illnesses, too, are amenable to treatment, and a psychiatrist is well placed to treat any mental illness affecting capacity. In some cases, the input of more than one medical professional is required prior to a formal capacity assessment being carried out.

Medical professionals also have a significant role to play in assessing whether and to what extent symptoms may be impacting on a person's decision-making capacity. For example, a patient with a severe needle phobia may not have capacity to consent to surgical treatment requiring anaesthesia, due to the effect of his extreme fear on his ability to weigh the information and use it to make a decision. The same person may have capacity regarding other treatment decisions such as oral medication; and is likely to retain capacity regarding matters such as managing property and finance where a needle phobia would not impact on his ability to use the information.

It is important to choose a specialist who has extensive clinical experience of the particular disorder and is familiar with caring for patients with that condition, rather than having detailed research knowledge. Hence, a consultant in old-age psychiatry may be a better 'expert' on Alzheimer's disease than for example, a research neurologist. Since assessments of capacity have a practical purpose, they should be based on a practical knowledge of the condition and of its manifestations, management and prognosis.

Many patients can be appropriately assessed by their GP. A close, long-term acquaintance between the doctor and the patient may be a major asset in creating the best environment to maximise the patient's capacity (see **2.3**). However, it is important to emphasise that a GP's close and personal knowledge of a patient, even concern and affection, must not be allowed to interfere with an objective assessment of the patient's actual mental disabilities and capacity to make the decision in question. It is also desirable for the GP and any specialists involved to consult with one another in determining their individual views of the patient's capacity to make a specific decision. This offers the advantage of combining expertise in the effects and management of a complicated condition with close acquaintance with the patient, and personal knowledge of the progression or development of their condition.

18.2.2 Psychiatric sub-specialities

All psychiatrists have received training in general psychiatry and most psychiatrists are able to provide an opinion on common mental illnesses such as anxiety or depression. Most psychiatrists have chosen to specialise in a particular aspect of psychiatry or a particular patient group and there are times when specialist expertise is required.

General adult psychiatry (adults between the ages of 18 and 65)

Psychiatrists specialising in general adult psychiatry have expertise in severe and enduring mental illnesses such as schizophrenia, depression, mania, paranoid psychosis, personality disorder and bipolar affective disorder. Some general adult psychiatrists sub-specialise in areas such as addiction psychiatry or eating disorders.

Older person's mental health or old age psychiatry (adults over the age of 65)

Psychiatrists in this field address mental illness in adults over the age of 65. This encompasses all the illnesses treated by general adult psychiatrists, but also includes dementia (of whatever type).

Psychiatry of learning (or intellectual) disabilities

Such psychiatrists assess and treat adults over 18 who also have a significant impairment in functioning (the definition being that the adult's IQ falls within the lowest 3 per cent of the population). They have expertise in assessing and treating mental illness in this group, but also factors arising from the learning disability itself such as aggression and violence.

Child and adolescent psychiatry (children up until their 18th birthday)

Psychiatrists who specialise in this field will be expert in assessing and treating any mental illness or disorder affecting those under 18.

Forensic psychiatry (usually deals with adults over the age of 18)

Such psychiatrists will have expertise in assessing and treating those with a mental illness who pose a risk to the community. Children and adolescents with forensic needs are assessed and treated separately. Adults with a learning disability may be assessed and treated by forensic psychiatrists or (preferably) by learning disability psychiatrists with experience in forensic practice.

Neuropsychiatry (adults over 18)

Psychiatrists who specialise in this field will assess and treat people who have had an injury to their brain after the age of 18. This includes trauma (head injury), genetic conditions (e.g. Huntington's disease), infections (meningitis, encephalitis) or other neurological conditions causing damage to the brain such as complex epilepsy. They do not normally deal with uncomplicated dementia.

There are also psychiatrists specialising in psychotherapy, but there are very few of them and it is unlikely that they would be preparing reports for court in this regard.

18.2.3 Other disciplines

Any medical opinion should take full account of relevant information from other disciplines. An assessment by a clinical psychologist may already be available, or could be sought, and this may assist in giving a detailed, validated and systematic assessment of cognitive functioning.[8] An occupational therapist has special skills in assessing disabilities which may interfere with activities in everyday tasks. A report from a nurse or a social worker may be helpful where information about daily activities or social functioning is of importance. What is important is not the diagnosis per se, but the specific disabilities and how they may affect the person's ability to make particular decisions.

In Court of Protection proceedings, the prescribed Assessment of Capacity form COP3 must be completed by a 'practitioner'; a registered professional who might be a medical practitioner, psychiatrist, approved mental health professional, social worker, psychologist, nurse, or occupational therapist. The preamble in the COP3 advises, that '[i]n some circumstances it might be appropriate for a registered therapist, such as a speech therapist or occupational therapist, to complete the form'.

18.2.4 Medico-legal expertise

In a complex medico-legal case it may be helpful for the lawyer to choose a doctor with particular experience in medico-legal work. Experience of sifting through large volumes of medical and other information, plus knowledge of some of the potential complexities of the interface between medicine and law can greatly assist a clear presentation of the medical issues into a legal context. However, it is important that experts are chosen primarily for their medical knowledge and not simply because they 'do a lot of court work'. Medical knowledge plus medico-legal experience is often a helpful combination.

18.3 PSYCHIATRIC DIAGNOSES

18.3.1 Categories of diagnoses

The field of psychiatric diagnosis is complex and evolving, and what follows is a very brief introductory outline. Psychiatric disorders are sometimes conveniently subdivided into organic and functional disorders.

---

[8] See British Psychological Society (2010) *Audit Tool for Mental Capacity Assessments*, available at **www.bps.org.uk/sites/default/files/documents/audit-tool-mental-capacity-assessments_0.pdf**.

Psychiatric diagnoses are made on the basis of subjective symptoms (what the patient experiences) and signs (what is outwardly observable). A symptom might be that the person experiences auditory hallucinations; whereas the sign might be that the person can be observed listening to or responding to unseen stimuli. Standardised classification systems use clusters of symptoms and signs to make diagnoses, and these systems give clear guidelines as to the number of criteria required to make a diagnosis.

There are two accepted systems for classifying mental disorders:

- the World Health Organization's *International Classification of Diseases* (ICD), which is the preferred method in the UK;[9] and
- the American Psychiatric Association's *Diagnostic and Statistical Manual of Mental Disorders*, 5th edn (DSM-5).[10]

The ICD-10 is used for classification of all illnesses and disorders, and mental illness is to be found in Chapter F of the ICD-10 (so psychiatric diagnoses made using the ICD-10 will consist of the letter F followed by a number). Both manuals are being updated as at the autumn of 2015 and it is likely there will in due course be further significant changes to how some mental illnesses are diagnosed and classified in both manuals.

It is important to note that a patient may satisfy the diagnostic criteria for more than one psychiatric diagnosis and the ICD-10 recommends that doctors use as many diagnoses as are necessary to encompass the full range of pathology experienced. However, it is usual for one predominant diagnosis to be made and the other diagnoses to be considered subsidiary diagnoses. In these cases, any one of the disorders or a combination of disorders can affect capacity. For example, pervasive personality disorder, anorexia, and a needle phobia can have a profound impact on an individual's ability to make a specific decision at a specific time, but each may have a different effect on decision-making. It is also possible that one disorder will affect one type of decision-making, and another disorder may affect a different type of decision-making.

Doctors will often make a distinction between mental disorders arising out of other (physical) illness and those that can be attributed to mental illness per se. An example of a mental disorder arising out of a physical condition might be a confusional state caused by an infection. Although psychiatrists are skilled in assessing both, they specialise in the assessment and treatment of mental illness.

Aside from broad diagnostic categories, specific psychiatric diagnoses are made on the basis of particular clusters of symptoms and signs. As these tend to be largely subjective, diagnostic disputes are not uncommon. It is also possible for the same patient to receive more than one diagnosis for the same cluster of symptoms at

---

9 World Health Organization (1992–94) *International Classification of Diseases* (10th edn) (ICD-10), available at **http://apps.who.int/classifications/icd10/browse/2015/en** (11th edition due for publication in 2017).

10 American Psychiatric Association (May 2013) *Diagnostic and Statistical Manual of Mental Disorders* (5th edn) (DSM-5). See **www.dsm5.org**.

different points in time; greater knowledge of the person helps to clarify the likely diagnosis. MCA 2005 makes it clear, however, that a specific diagnosis or condition should not itself be used to determine lack of capacity.[11] It is the impact of any disorder on the individual's ability to make a specific decision at the time the decision needs to be made that must be assessed.

18.3.2 Mental and behavioural disorders caused by psychotropic substance misuse (ICD-10: F10–F19)

These relate to long-term and short-term consequences of use of psychotropic substances, including alcohol.

18.3.3 Psychotic disorders (ICD-10: F20–F29)

This encompasses schizophrenia, schizoaffective disorders, acute and transient psychosis, and delusional disorder. Although schizotypal disorders are included here, they are usually described under personality disorders. Psychosis is often understood as a total loss of contact with reality, but is best described as a belief or experience not based in normal human experience. People suffering from psychotic disorders can often function very well in areas not affected by their psychosis. People with psychosis experience delusions and/or hallucinations.

A hallucination is described as experiencing something without an external stimulus. Hallucinations can occur in any of the five senses, but psychotic disorders in this category are almost always associated with auditory hallucinations. These can be first person (also called thought broadcast, in which the person experiences their own voice); second person (experience of someone talking to the person) or third person (the experience of someone talking about the person). Auditory hallucinations in psychotic disorders are frequently third person hallucinations, and the content of the hallucination is often negative or derogatory in nature. Command hallucinations are, as the term implies, hallucinations in which the person experiences being commanded to do something. While these are not uncommon, it is rare for people actually to act on command hallucinations.

Auditory hallucinations are not always experienced as voices, and some people experience music or other sounds. It is also important to state that hallucinations are not necessary for a diagnosis of a psychotic disorder, nor does the experience of hallucinations necessarily indicate the presence of a psychotic disorder. Up to 10 per cent of people without a diagnosable mental disorder have experienced hallucinations at some point in their lives.[12]

A delusion is a fixed, false belief. Beliefs that are held with delusional intensity are unshakeable even when the person is presented with clear evidence to the

---

[11] MCA 2005, s.2(1)–(3).
[12] JJ McGrath *et al.* (2015) 'Psychotic experiences in the general population: a cross-national analysis based on 31,261 respondents from 18 countries' *JAMA Psychiatry* 72(7): 697–705, available at **http://archpsyc.jamanetwork.com/article.aspx?articleid=2298236**.

contrary. Delusions may be part of a psychotic disorder in general, or may exist on their own as a delusional disorder. For example, in delusional jealousy (Othello's syndrome), the person believes that their partner is unfaithful despite all evidence to the contrary. Their cognition and mental state remain otherwise intact and thus their capacity would not be affected, except in the very specific areas affected by their delusional belief.

Schizoaffective disorder is a condition in which the diagnostic requirements for both schizophrenia and a mood disorder are met. In this disorder, hallucinations and delusions are often in keeping with the person's mood, so someone may have delusions of grandeur when manic and delusions of persecution when depressed.

18.3.4 Mood disorders (ICD-10: F30–F39)

These are the most common psychiatric disorders, with an estimation of up to 10 per cent of the population experiencing a mood disorder during their adult lifetime (figures vary widely). While everyone experiences periods of low or elevated mood, the ICD-10 gives clear criteria for the diagnosis of a disorder. A key part of this is the extent to which functioning is impaired. While depression refers to a pathologically low mood, mania refers to a pathologically elevated mood. People with a bipolar affective disorder experience both depression and mania over the course of their lifetime; it is not required that they experience both in the same episode of illness.

18.3.5 Neurotic, stress-related and somatoform disorders (ICD-10: F40–F48)

These are best understood as mental disorders in which anxiety is the predominant component. Generalised anxiety disorders fall into this category, as well as specific anxiety disorders such as phobias. Transient reactions to stress, as well as post-traumatic stress disorder (PTSD) are also included. This category also encompasses mental illnesses that present purely with physical health symptoms (also known as medically-unexplained symptoms).

18.3.6 Behavioural syndromes associated with physiological disturbances and physical factors (ICD-10: F50–F59)

The conditions most likely to be encountered in this category are the eating disorders, predominantly anorexia and bulimia, but also other disorders such as overeating and atypical forms of anorexia and bulimia.

18.3.7 Disorders of adult personality and behaviour (ICD-10: F60–F69)

This can be a contentious diagnosis and some professionals question the existence of personality disorders, as all of us have personalities and judging a personality as being disordered has been seen as pejorative and value-laden. The spectrum of personality traits is wide, and the distinction between normal and disturbed is one of opinion rather than based in any clear diagnostic tests. While this is true for any mental illness, it remains relatively controversial in the field of personality disorders.

As for any psychiatric diagnosis, the requirement for personality traits to be diagnosed as a disorder is the extent to which it affects functioning, People with personality disorders often have severely impaired functioning as a result of their difficulties and many are significantly disabled by the levels of personal distress and social disruption experienced. A significant deviance from social norms must be present in one or more of the following areas: cognition (thoughts), affectivity (moods), impulse control and manner of relating to others. It must also manifest itself in behaviour that is 'dysfunctional across a broad range of personal and social situations'.[13]

As implied in the diagnostic category, these diagnoses can only be made in adults, as prior to 18 the personality is still developing. This is a somewhat artificial distinction, as personalities continue to develop into a person's twenties.

18.3.8 Mental retardation (ICD-10: F70–F79)

While this remains the official diagnostic category in the ICD-10, it is preferable and usual for professionals to use the term learning disability or intellectual disability. The degree of functional impairment varies and it is sometimes divided into mild, moderate, severe and profound based on level of IQ. More important in assessing capacity is the level to which functioning is impaired.

18.3.9 Disorders of psychological development (ICD-10: F80–F89)

This encompasses a broad range of disparate conditions with onset in childhood. The diagnosis that is likely to be encountered in this category is that of a pervasive developmental disorder, encompassing both autism and Asperger's (also known as high-functioning autism).

18.3.10 Behavioural and emotional disorders with onset usually occurring in childhood and adolescence (ICD-10: F90–F98)

These are predominantly childhood disorders and are unlikely to be encountered by a psychiatrist assessing capacity in an adult.

---

[13] ICD-10.

18.4 MEDICAL ASSESSMENT OF MENTAL CONDITIONS

Although capacity may be influenced by physical conditions it is crucially important for any assessing doctor to take a full psychiatric history and to carry out a
mental state examination, as well as a general medical assessment of the person. In
psychiatry, as in all medicine, 'symptoms' are what the patient tells you and 'signs'
are the doctor's objective observation of the patient. Although some signs are
clearly objective (for instance, a depressed patient may be dishevelled when their
appearance is usually kempt) many signs involve a medical interpretation of the
patient's symptom complaints. For example, is it the case that a patient's complaint
about 'voices' really amounts to auditory hallucinations? Is a strange belief held
with such conviction that it amounts to a delusion? This can introduce a degree of
ambiguity that is less common in other branches of medicine.

However, it is not the case that psychiatric assessments are inherently personal to
the individual doctor or inherently ambiguous. High levels of diagnostic reliability
should be expected. Doctors must also take into account cultural and ethnic values
and their impact on beliefs and behaviour. In some cultures, for example, belief in
witchcraft is widespread, affecting the way in which decisions are made but
unrelated to the person's mental capacity.

Psychiatric assessment includes assessment for both organic and functional
conditions. Hence the assessment should always include at least a brief physical
assessment and, when indicated by the history or by physical observation, more
detailed physical examination and investigation. The following describes briefly
the process of psychiatric assessment.

18.4.1 History

History of presenting complaint

A description by the patient of their main symptoms and their duration is important.
Acute onset of severe symptoms can, for example, imply an organic origin. The
doctor will pursue symptoms, through asking specific direct questions aimed at
elucidating the symptoms and specifically considering the possible differential
diagnosis. Where the assessment is in relation to the patient's capacity, it may also
be appropriate to pursue certain relevant symptoms in detail and to ask questions
specifically relevant to the particular decision or test of capacity concerned.

Background history

This includes a brief description of the patient's personal history, family history,
psychosexual history (including where relevant, obstetric and gynaecological
history), social history and any previous forensic history.

Pre-morbid personality

This is a description by the patient, or more appropriately by a relative or others, of the patient's usual personality (that is, when the patient is not mentally or otherwise ill). This is important as a baseline against which the patient's current symptoms and presentation at interview can be assessed.

Previous medical history

This will detail all non-psychiatric conditions and treatments, including reference to any drugs that the patient is currently taking. The history may give clues as to a physical cause of apparently psychiatric symptoms.

Previous psychiatric history

This can be of relevance to current mental state assessment. A history of previous disorder may give clues about the origins of present symptoms or signs.

Drugs and alcohol history

This may be of great relevance to the determination of the differential diagnosis of mental disorder, since alcohol and other substances can cause psychiatric presentations.

Information from others

This is important because patients may misrepresent symptoms by either hiding them or exaggerating them, or they may describe their usual personality in a way which is heavily influenced by their current illness. Depressed patients may for example describe themselves as being 'useless' and 'incapable at work', whereas the reverse is true. In assessing a person for some legal capacity, however, it is important to bear in mind that a relative or other person providing the information may have a vested interest, either social or financial, in the doctor's assessment of the person's capacity and care must be taken to allow for this possibility. Information from a number of people may be essential to sift out truth from bias, but always bearing in mind the patient's right to confidentiality (see **2.2** and **13.8**).

18.4.2   Mental state examination

This is an objective assessment of the patient's mental functioning. The purpose of such an examination is to define specific abnormalities and disabilities and to establish a diagnosis. It is only through detailed assessment of specific aspects of mental functioning that capacity can properly be assessed. The following features will be relevant in any assessment carried out by a doctor:

- appearance and behaviour;
- speech;
- mood;
- thought;
- perception;
- cognition;
- orientation;
- memory;
- level of intellectual ability;
- insight.

An explanation of the process of the mental state examination is set out in **17.8**.

18.4.3 Physical examination

Psychiatric assessment may properly include a brief physical assessment. In some cases, where indicated by the person's medical history or by physical observation, a more detailed physical examination and investigation may be required. It is important to remember that an apparent psychiatric presentation can be reflective of an organic neurological disorder and that some patients can present neurologically and yet have a primary psychiatric condition, hysterical symptoms being an obvious example. The neurology of higher cortical functions (such as memory, orientation, concentration, language) and psychiatry are often intricately intertwined, as evidenced in conditions such as dementia, which is both 'psychiatric' and 'neurological'. Many functional psychiatric conditions, such as schizophrenia, have demonstrable organic aspects and are also probably partially determined by genetic predisposition, obstetric complications, childhood infections, and perhaps other conditions affecting the brain.

18.4.4 Medical records

It is important for the assessing doctor to have access to all relevant medical and psychiatric records. In order to access these records, the assessing psychiatrist will need written permission from the person, or if the person does not have capacity to give consent, consent must be given as part of a best interests decision. Medical records give a historical picture of a known current disorder, as well as giving diagnostic clues to what might be a so far undiagnosed disorder. In assessing capacity a historical view may be of particular importance, especially in relation both to the likely response to treatment and to prognosis, since these may affect future capacity. Assessment of the likely duration of disabilities may be crucially important in offering a view about capacity. These issues are especially important in cases where the decision or the legal process relating to it can be delayed. Wherever possible, priority should be given to enabling people to regain capacity and hence to retake control over their own lives.

18.5 GENERAL GUIDANCE

The giving of effective instructions by lawyers to doctors, and the provision of reliable and focused assessments of capacity by doctors for lawyers and for the courts, depend upon each profession understanding the very different methods and ways of thinking of the other. Lawyers must be capable of giving clear questions for doctors to answer, and doctors must understand that they are providing medical information that may be used for an entirely non-medical, that is, legal, purpose. What is crucial is that each understands not only the boundaries of their own role, but also the methods and models of the other in order to negotiate the interface between the two disciplines.

APPENDIX A

Mental Capacity Act 2005, ss.1–6 (as amended by Mental Health Act 2007)

PART 1   PERSONS WHO LACK CAPACITY

The principles

1   The principles

(1)   The following principles apply for the purposes of this Act.

(2)   A person must be assumed to have capacity unless it is established that he lacks capacity.

(3)   A person is not to be treated as unable to make a decision unless all practicable steps to help him to do so have been taken without success.

(4)   A person is not to be treated as unable to make a decision merely because he makes an unwise decision.

(5)   An act done, or decision made, under this Act for or on behalf of a person who lacks capacity must be done, or made, in his best interests.

(6)   Before the act is done, or the decision is made, regard must be had to whether the purpose for which it is needed can be as effectively achieved in a way that is less restrictive of the person's rights and freedom of action.

2   People who lack capacity

(1)   For the purposes of this Act, a person lacks capacity in relation to a matter if at the material time he is unable to make a decision for himself in relation to the matter because of an impairment of, or a disturbance in the functioning of, the mind or brain.

(2)   It does not matter whether the impairment or disturbance is permanent or temporary.

(3)   A lack of capacity cannot be established merely by reference to–

   (a)   a person's age or appearance, or

   (b)   a condition of his, or an aspect of his behaviour, which might lead others to make unjustified assumptions about his capacity.

(4)   In proceedings under this Act or any other enactment, any question whether a person lacks capacity within the meaning of this Act must be decided on the balance of probabilities.

(5)   No power which a person ('D') may exercise under this Act–

   (a)   in relation to a person who lacks capacity, or

   (b)   where D reasonably thinks that a person lacks capacity, is exercisable in relation to a person under 16.

(6)   Subsection (5) is subject to section 18(3).

3   Inability to make decisions

(1)   For the purposes of section 2, a person is unable to make a decision for himself if he is unable–

    (a)   to understand the information relevant to the decision,
    (b)   to retain that information,
    (c)   to use or weigh that information as part of the process of making the decision, or
    (d)   to communicate his decision (whether by talking, using sign language or any other means).

(2)   A person is not to be regarded as unable to understand the information relevant to a decision if he is able to understand an explanation of it given to him in a way that is appropriate to his circumstances (using simple language, visual aids or any other means).

(3)   The fact that a person is able to retain the information relevant to a decision for a short period only does not prevent him from being regarded as able to make the decision.

(4)   The information relevant to a decision includes information about the reasonably foreseeable consequences of–

    (a)   deciding one way or another, or
    (b)   failing to make the decision.

4   Best interests

(1)   In determining for the purposes of this Act what is in a person's best interests, the person making the determination must not make it merely on the basis of–

    (a)   the person's age or appearance, or
    (b)   a condition of his, or an aspect of his behaviour, which might lead others to make unjustified assumptions about what might be in his best interests.

(2)   The person making the determination must consider all the relevant circumstances and, in particular, take the following steps.

(3)   He must consider–

    (a)   whether it is likely that the person will at some time have capacity in relation to the matter in question, and
    (b)   if it appears likely that he will, when that is likely to be.

(4)   He must, so far as reasonably practicable, permit and encourage the person to partici-pate, or to improve his ability to participate, as fully as possible in any act done for him and any decision affecting him.

(5)   Where the determination relates to life-sustaining treatment he must not, in considering whether the treatment is in the best interests of the person concerned, be motivated by a desire to bring about his death.

(6)   He must consider, so far as is reasonably ascertainable–

    (a)   the person's past and present wishes and feelings (and, in particular, any relevant written statement made by him when he had capacity),
    (b)   the beliefs and values that would be likely to influence his decision if he had capacity, and
    (c)   the other factors that he would be likely to consider if he were able to do so.

(7)   He must take into account, if it is practicable and appropriate to consult them, the views of–

(a)   anyone named by the person as someone to be consulted on the matter in question or on matters of that kind,
(b)   anyone engaged in caring for the person or interested in his welfare,
(c)   any donee of a lasting power of attorney granted by the person, and
(d)   any deputy appointed for the person by the court,

as to what would be in the person's best interests and, in particular, as to the matters mentioned in subsection (6).

(8)   The duties imposed by subsections (1) to (7) also apply in relation to the exercise of any powers which–

(a)   are exercisable under a lasting power of attorney, or
(b)   are exercisable by a person under this Act where he reasonably believes that another person lacks capacity.

(9)   In the case of an act done, or a decision made, by a person other than the court, there is sufficient compliance with this section if (having complied with the requirements of subsections (1) to (7)) he reasonably believes that what he does or decides is in the best interests of the person concerned.

(10)   'Life-sustaining treatment' means treatment which in the view of a person providing health care for the person concerned is necessary to sustain life.

(11)   'Relevant circumstances' are those–

(a)   of which the person making the determination is aware, and
(b)   which it would be reasonable to regard as relevant.

4A   Restriction on deprivation of liberty

(1)   This Act does not authorise any person ('D') to deprive any other person ('P') of his liberty.

(2)   But that is subject to–

(a)   the following provisions of this section, and
(b)   section 4B.

(3)   D may deprive P of his liberty if, by doing so, D is giving effect to a relevant decision of the court.

(4)   A relevant decision of the court is a decision made by an order under section 16(2)(a) in relation to a matter concerning P's personal welfare.

(5)   D may deprive P of his liberty if the deprivation is authorised by Schedule A1 (hospital and care home residents: deprivation of liberty).

4B Deprivation of liberty necessary for life-sustaining treatment etc

(1)   If the following conditions are met, D is authorised to deprive P of his liberty while a decision as respects any relevant issue is sought from the court.

(2)   The first condition is that there is a question about whether D is authorised to deprive P of his liberty under section 4A.

(3)   The second condition is that the deprivation of liberty–

(a)   is wholly or partly for the purpose of–

(i)   giving P life-sustaining treatment, or
(ii)   doing any vital act, or

(b)　consists wholly or partly of–

    (i)　giving P life-sustaining treatment, or

    (ii)　doing any vital act.

(4)　The third condition is that the deprivation of liberty is necessary in order to–

    (a)　give the life-sustaining treatment, or

    (b)　do the vital act.

(5)　A vital act is any act which the person doing it reasonably believes to be necessary to prevent a serious deterioration in P's condition.

5　Acts in connection with care or treatment

(1)　If a person ('D') does an act in connection with the care or treatment of another person ('P'), the act is one to which this section applies if–

    (a)　before doing the act, D takes reasonable steps to establish whether P lacks capacity in relation to the matter in question, and

    (b)　when doing the act, D reasonably believes–

        (i)　that P lacks capacity in relation to the matter, and

        (ii)　that it will be in P's best interests for the act to be done.

(2)　D does not incur any liability in relation to the act that he would not have incurred if P–

    (a)　had had capacity to consent in relation to the matter, and

    (b)　had consented to D's doing the act.

(3)　Nothing in this section excludes a person's civil liability for loss or damage, or his criminal liability, resulting from his negligence in doing the act.

(4)　Nothing in this section affects the operation of sections 24 to 26 (advance decisions to refuse treatment).

6　Section 5 acts: limitations

(1)　If D does an act that is intended to restrain P, it is not an act to which section 5 applies unless two further conditions are satisfied.

(2)　The first condition is that D reasonably believes that it is necessary to do the act in order to prevent harm to P.

(3)　The second is that the act is a proportionate response to–

    (a)　the likelihood of P's suffering harm, and

    (b)　the seriousness of that harm.

(4)　For the purposes of this section D restrains P if he–

    (a)　uses, or threatens to use, force to secure the doing of an act which P resists, or

    (b)　restricts P's liberty of movement, whether or not P resists.

(5)　...

(6)　Section 5 does not authorise a person to do an act which conflicts with a decision made, within the scope of his authority and in accordance with this Part, by–

    (a)　a donee of a lasting power of attorney granted by P, or

    (b)　a deputy appointed for P by the court.

(7)　But nothing in subsection (6) stops a person–

    (a)　providing life-sustaining treatment, or

(b)   doing any act which he reasonably believes to be necessary to prevent a serious deterioration in P's condition,

while a decision as respects any relevant issue is sought from the court.

Mental Capacity Act 2005 Code of Practice, Chapters 2–4

2 WHAT ARE THE STATUTORY PRINCIPLES AND HOW SHOULD THEY BE APPLIED?

Section 1 of the Act sets out the five 'statutory principles' – the values that underpin the legal requirements in the Act. The Act is intended to be enabling and supportive of people who lack capacity, not restricting or controlling of their lives. It aims to protect people who lack capacity to make particular decisions, but also to maximise their ability to make decisions, or to participate in decision-making, as far as they are able to do so.

The five statutory principles are:

1. A person must be assumed to have capacity unless it is established that they lack capacity.
2. A person is not to be treated as unable to make a decision unless all practicable steps to help him to do so have been taken without success.
3. A person is not to be treated as unable to make a decision merely because he makes an unwise decision.
4. An act done, or decision made, under this Act for or on behalf of a person who lacks capacity must be done, or made, in his best interests.
5. Before the act is done, or the decision is made, regard must be had to whether the purpose for which it is needed can be as effectively achieved in a way that is less restrictive of the person's rights and freedom of action.

This chapter provides guidance on how people should interpret and apply the statutory principles when using the Act. Following the principles and applying them to the Act's framework for decision-making will help to ensure not only that appropriate action is taken in individual cases, but also to point the way to solutions in difficult or uncertain situations.

In this chapter, as throughout the Code, a person's capacity (or lack of capacity) refers specifically to their capacity to make a particular decision at the time it needs to be made.

Quick summary

- Every adult has the right to make their own decisions if they have the capacity to do so. Family carers and healthcare or social care staff must assume that a person has the capacity to make decisions, unless it can be established that the person does not have capacity.
- People should receive support to help them make their own decisions. Before concluding that individuals lack capacity to make a particular decision, it is important to take all possible steps to try to help them reach a decision themselves.
- People have the right to make decisions that others might think are unwise. A person

who makes a decision that others think is unwise should not automatically be labelled as lacking the capacity to make a decision.

- Any act done for, or any decision made on behalf of, someone who lacks capacity must be in their best interests.
- Any act done for, or any decision made on behalf of, someone who lacks capacity should be an option that is less restrictive of their basic rights and freedoms – as long as it is still in their best interests.

What is the role of the statutory principles?

2.1   The statutory principles aim to:

- protect people who lack capacity and
- help them take part, as much as possible, in decisions that affect them.

They aim to assist and support people who may lack capacity to make particular decisions, not to restrict or control their lives.

2.2   The statutory principles apply to any act done or decision made under the Act. When followed and applied to the Act's decision-making framework, they will help people take appropriate action in individual cases. They will also help people find solutions in difficult or uncertain situations.

How should the statutory principles be applied?

Principle 1: '*A person must be assumed to have capacity unless it is established that he lacks capacity.*' (section1(2))

2.3   This principle states that every adult has the right to make their own decisions – unless there is proof that they lack the capacity to make a particular decision when it needs to be made. This has been a fundamental principle of the common law for many years and it is now set out in the Act.

2.4   It is important to balance people's right to make a decision with their right to safety and protection when they can't make decisions to protect themselves. But the starting assumption must always be that an individual has the capacity, until there is proof that they do not. Chapter 4 explains the Act's definition of 'lack of capacity' and the processes involved in assessing capacity.

Scenario: Assessing a person's capacity to make decisions

When planning for her retirement, Mrs Arnold made and registered a Lasting Power of Attorney (LPA) – a legal process that would allow her son to manage her property and financial affairs if she ever lacked capacity to manage them herself. She has now been diagnosed with dementia, and her son is worried that she is becoming confused about money.

Her son must assume that his mother has capacity to manage her affairs. Then he must consider each of Mrs Arnold's financial decisions as she makes them, giving her any help and support she needs to make these decisions herself.

Mrs Arnold's son goes shopping with her, and he sees she is quite capable of finding goods and making sure she gets the correct change. But when she needs to make decisions about her investments, Mrs Arnold gets confused – even though she has made such decisions in the past. She still doesn't understand after her son explains the different options.

Her son concludes that she has capacity to deal with everyday financial matters but not more difficult affairs at this time. Therefore, he is able to use the LPA for the difficult financial decisions his mother can't make. But Mrs Arnold can continue to deal with her other affairs for as long as she has capacity to do so.

2.5 Some people may need help to be able to make a decision or to communicate their decision. However, this does not necessarily mean that they cannot make that decision – unless there is proof that they do lack capacity to do so. Anyone who believes that a person lacks capacity should be able to prove their case. Chapter 4 explains the standard of proof required.

Principle 2: '*A person is not to be treated as unable to make a decision unless all practicable steps to help him to do so have been taken without success.*' (section 1(3))

2.6 It is important to do everything practical (the Act uses the term 'practicable') to help a person make a decision for themselves before concluding that they lack capacity to do so. People with an illness or disability affecting their ability to make a decision should receive support to help them make as many decisions as they can. This principle aims to stop people being automatically labelled as lacking capacity to make particular decisions. Because it encourages individuals to play as big a role as possible in decision-making, it also helps prevent unnecessary interventions in their lives.

2.7 The kind of support people might need to help them make a decision varies. It depends on personal circumstances, the kind of decision that has to be made and the time available to make the decision. It might include:

- using a different form of communication (for example, non-verbal communication)
- providing information in a more accessible form (for example, photographs, drawings, or tapes)
- treating a medical condition which may be affecting the person's capacity or
- having a structured programme to improve a person's capacity to make particular decisions (for example, helping a person with learning disabilities to learn new skills).

Chapter 3 gives more information on ways to help people make decisions for themselves.

Scenario: Taking steps to help people make decisions for themselves

Mr Jackson is brought into hospital following a traffic accident. He is conscious but in shock. He cannot speak and is clearly in distress, making noises and gestures.

From his behaviour, hospital staff conclude that Mr Jackson currently lacks the capacity to make decisions about treatment for his injuries, and they give him urgent treatment. They hope that after he has recovered from the shock they can use an advocate to help explain things to him.

However, one of the nurses thinks she recognises some of his gestures as sign language, and tries signing to him. Mr Jackson immediately becomes calmer, and the doctors realise that he can communicate in sign language. He can also answer some written questions about his injuries.

The hospital brings in a qualified sign-language interpreter and concludes that Mr Jackson has the capacity to make decisions about any further treatment.

2.8 Anyone supporting a person who may lack capacity should not use excessive persuasion or 'undue pressure'.[1] This might include behaving in a manner which is overbearing or dominating, or seeking to influence the person's decision, and could push a person into making a decision they might not otherwise have made. However, it is important to provide appropriate advice and information.

Scenario: Giving appropriate advice and support

Sara, a young woman with severe depression, is getting treatment from mental health services. Her psychiatrist determines that she has capacity to make decisions about treatment, if she gets advice and support.

Her mother is trying to persuade Sara to agree to electro-convulsive therapy (ECT), which helped her mother when she had clinical depression in the past. However, a friend has told Sara that ECT is 'barbaric'.

The psychiatrist provides factual information about the different types of treatment available and explains their advantages and disadvantages. She also describes how different people experience different reactions or side effects. Sara is then able to consider what treatment is right for her, based on factual information rather than the personal opinions of her mother and friend.

2.9 In some situations treatment cannot be delayed while a person gets support to make a decision. This can happen in emergency situations or when an urgent decision is required (for example, immediate medical treatment). In these situations, the only practical and appropriate steps might be to keep a person informed of what is happening and why.

Principle 3: '*A person is not to be treated as unable to make a decision merely because he makes an unwise decision.*' (section 1(4))

2.10 Everybody has their own values, beliefs, preferences and attitudes. A person should not be assumed to lack the capacity to make a decision just because other people think their decision is unwise. This applies even if family members, friends or healthcare or social care staff are unhappy with a decision.

Scenario: Allowing people to make decisions that others think are unwise

Mr Garvey is a 40-year-old man with a history of mental health problems. He sees a Community Psychiatric Nurse (CPN) regularly. Mr Garvey decides to spend £2,000 of his savings on a camper van to travel around Scotland for six months. His CPN is concerned that it will be difficult to give Mr Garvey continuous support and treatment while travelling, and that his mental health might deteriorate as a result.

However, having talked it through with his CPN, it is clear that Mr Garvey is fully aware of these concerns and has the capacity to make this particular decision. He has decided he would like to have a break and thinks this will be good for him.

Just because, in the CPN's opinion, continuity of care might be a wiser option, it should not be assumed that Mr Garvey lacks the capacity to make this decision for himself.

---

[1] Undue influence in relation to consent to medical treatment was considered in *Re T (Adult: Refusal of Treatment)* [1992] 4 All E R 649, 662 and in financial matters in *Royal Bank of Scotland v Etridge* [2001] UKHL 44.

2.11   There may be cause for concern if somebody:

- repeatedly makes unwise decisions that put them at significant risk of harm or exploitation or
- makes a particular unwise decision that is obviously irrational or out of character.

These things do not necessarily mean that somebody lacks capacity. But there might be need for further investigation, taking into account the person's past decisions and choices. For example, have they developed a medical condition or disorder that is affecting their capacity to make particular decisions? Are they easily influenced by undue pressure? Or do they need more information to help them understand the consequences of the decision they are making?

Scenario: Decisions that cause concern

Cyril, an elderly man with early signs of dementia, spends nearly £300 on fresh fish from a door-to-door salesman. He has always been fond of fish and has previously bought small amounts in this way. Before his dementia, Cyril was always very careful with his money and would never have spent so much on fish in one go.

This decision alone may not automatically mean Cyril now lacks capacity to manage all aspects of his property and affairs. But his daughter makes further enquiries and discovers Cyril has overpaid his cleaner on several occasions – something he has never done in the past. He has also made payments from his savings that he cannot account for.

His daughter decides it is time to use the registered Lasting Power of Attorney her father made in the past. This gives her the authority to manage Cyril's property and affairs whenever he lacks the capacity to manage them himself. She takes control of Cyril's chequebook to protect him from possible exploitation, but she can still ensure he has enough money to spend on his everyday needs.

Principle 4: '*An act done, or decision made, under this Act for or on behalf of a person who lacks capacity must be done, or made, in his best interests.*' (section 1(5))

2.12   The principle of acting or making a decision *in the best interests* of a person who lacks capacity to make the decision in question is a well-established principle in the common law.[2] This principle is now set out in the Act, so that a person's best interests must be the basis for all decisions made and actions carried out on their behalf in situations where they lack capacity to make those particular decisions for themselves. The only exceptions to this are around research (see chapter 11) and advance decisions to refuse treatment (see chapter 9) where other safeguards apply.

2.13   It is impossible to give a single description of what 'best interests' are, because they depend on individual circumstances. However, section 4 of the Act sets out a checklist of steps to follow in order to determine what is in the best interests of a person who lacks capacity to make the decision in question each time someone acts or makes a decision on that person's behalf. See chapter 5 for detailed guidance and examples.

Principle 5: '*Before the act is done, or the decision is made, regard must be had to whether the purpose for which it is needed can be as effectively achieved in a way that is less restrictive of the person's rights and freedom of action.*' (section 1(6))

---

[2]   See for example *Re MB (Medical Treatment)* [1997] 2 FLR 426, CA; *Re A (Male Sterilisation)* [2000] 1 FLR 549; *Re S (Sterilisation: Patient's Best Interests)* [2000] 2 FLR 389; *Re F (Adult Patient: Sterilisation)* [2001] Fam 15

2.14   Before somebody makes a decision or acts on behalf of a person who lacks capacity to make that decision or consent to the act, they must always question if they can do something else that would interfere less with the person's basic rights and freedoms. This is called finding the 'less restrictive alternative'. It includes considering whether there is a need to act or make a decision at all.

2.15   Where there is more than one option, it is important to explore ways that would be less restrictive or allow the most freedom for a person who lacks capacity to make the decision in question. However, the final decision must always allow the original purpose of the decision or act to be achieved.

2.16   Any decision or action must still be in the best interests of the person who lacks capacity. So sometimes it may be necessary to choose an option that is not the least restrictive alternative if that option is in the person's best interests. In practice, the process of choosing a less restrictive option and deciding what is in the person's best interests will be combined. But both principles must be applied each time a decision or action may be taken on behalf of a person who lacks capacity to make the relevant decision.

Scenario: Finding a less restrictive option

Sunil, a young man with severe learning disabilities, also has a very severe and unpredictable form of epilepsy that is associated with drop attacks. These can result in serious injury. A neurologist has advised that, to limit the harm that might come from these attacks, Sunil should either be under constant close observation, or wear a protective helmet.

After assessment, it is decided that Sunil lacks capacity to decide on the most appropriate course of action for himself. But through his actions and behaviour, Sunil makes it clear he doesn't like to be too closely observed – even though he likes having company.

The staff of the home where he lives consider various options, such as providing a special room for him with soft furnishings, finding ways to keep him under close observation or getting him to wear a helmet. In discussion with Sunil's parents, they agree that the option that is in his best interests, and is less restrictive, will be the helmet – as it will enable him to go out, and prevent further harm.

---

3   HOW SHOULD PEOPLE BE HELPED TO MAKE THEIR OWN DECISIONS?

Before deciding that someone lacks capacity to make a particular decision, it is important to take all practical and appropriate steps to enable them to make that decision themselves (statutory principle 2, see chapter 2). In addition, as section 3(2) of the Act underlines, these steps (such as helping individuals to communicate) must be taken in a way which reflects the person's individual circumstances and meets their particular needs. This chapter provides practical guidance on how to support people to make decisions for themselves, or play as big a role as possible in decision-making.

In this chapter, as throughout the Code, a person's capacity (or lack of capacity) refers specifically to their capacity to make a particular decision at the time it needs to be made.

Quick summary

To help someone make a decision for themselves, check the following points:

Providing relevant information

- Does the person have all the relevant information they need to make a particular decision?
- If they have a choice, have they been given information on all the alternatives?

Communicating in an appropriate way

- Could information be explained or presented in a way that is easier for the person to understand (for example, by using simple language or visual aids)?
- Have different methods of communication been explored if required, including non-verbal communication?
- Could anyone else help with communication (for example, a family member, support worker, interpreter, speech and language therapist or advocate)?

Making the person feel at ease

- Are there particular times of day when the person's understanding is better?
- Are there particular locations where they may feel more at ease?
- Could the decision be put off to see whether the person can make the decision at a later time when circumstances are right for them?

Supporting the person

- Can anyone else help or support the person to make choices or express a view?

How can someone be helped to make a decision?

3.1 There are several ways in which people can be helped and supported to enable them to make a decision for themselves. These will vary depending on the decision to be made, the time-scale for making the decision and the individual circumstances of the person making it.

3.2 The Act applies to a wide range of people with different conditions that may affect their capacity to make particular decisions. So, the appropriate steps to take will depend on:

- a person's individual circumstances (for example, somebody with learning difficulties may need a different approach to somebody with dementia)
- the decision the person has to make and
- the length of time they have to make it.

3.3 Significant, one-off decisions (such as moving house) will require different considerations from day-to-day decisions about a person's care and welfare. However, the same general processes should apply to each decision.

3.4 In most cases, only some of the steps described in this chapter will be relevant or appropriate, and the list included here is not exhaustive. It is up to the people (whether family carers, paid carers, healthcare staff or anyone else) caring for or supporting an individual to consider what is possible and appropriate in individual cases. In all cases it is extremely important to find the most effective way of communicating with the person concerned. Good communication is essential for explaining relevant information in an appropriate way and for ensuring that the steps being taken meet an individual's needs.

3.5   Providing appropriate help with decision-making should form part of care planning processes for people receiving health or social care services. Examples include:

- Person Centred Planning for people with learning disabilities
- the Care Programme Approach for people with mental disorders
- the Single Assessment Process for older people in England, and
- the Unified Assessment Process in Wales.

What happens in emergency situations?

3.6   Clearly, in emergency medical situations (for example, where a person collapses with a heart attack or for some unknown reason and is brought unconscious into a hospital), urgent decisions will have to be made and immediate action taken in the person's best interests. In these situations, it may not be practical or appropriate to delay the treatment while trying to help the person make their own decisions, or to consult with any known attorneys or deputies. However, even in emergency situations, healthcare staff should try to communicate with the person and keep them informed of what is happening.

What information should be provided to people and how should it be provided?

3.7   Providing relevant information is essential in all decision-making. For example, to make a choice about what they want for breakfast, people need to know what food is available. If the decision concerns medical treatment, the doctor must explain the purpose and effect of the course of treatment and the likely consequences of accepting or refusing treatment.

3.8   All practical and appropriate steps must be taken to help people to make a decision for themselves. Information must be tailored to an individual's needs and abilities. It must also be in the easiest and most appropriate form of communication for the person concerned.

What information is relevant?

3.9   The Act cannot state exactly what information will be relevant in each case. Anyone helping someone to make a decision for themselves should therefore follow these steps.

- Take time to explain anything that might help the person make a decision. It is important that they have access to all the information they need to make an informed decision.
- Try not to give more detail than the person needs – this might confuse them. In some cases, a simple, broad explanation will be enough. But it must not miss out important information.
- What are the risks and benefits? Describe any foreseeable consequences of making the decision, and of not making any decision at all.
- Explain the effects the decision might have on the person and those close to them – including the people involved in their care.
- If they have a choice, give them the same information in a balanced way for all the options.
- For some types of decisions, it may be important to give access to advice from

elsewhere. This may be independent or specialist advice (for example, from a medical practitioner or a financial or legal adviser). But it might simply be advice from trusted friends or relatives.

Communication – general guidance

3.10 To help someone make a decision for themselves, all possible and appropriate means of communication should be tried.

- Ask people who know the person well about the best form of communication (try speaking to family members, carers, day centre staff or support workers). They may also know somebody the person can communicate with easily, or the time when it is best to communicate with them.
- Use simple language. Where appropriate, use pictures, objects or illustrations to demonstrate ideas.
- Speak at the right volume and speed, with appropriate words and sentence structure. It may be helpful to pause to check understanding or show that a choice is available.
- Break down difficult information into smaller points that are easy to understand. Allow the person time to consider and understand each point before continuing.
- It may be necessary to repeat information or go back over a point several times.
- Is help available from people the person trusts (relatives, friends, GP, social worker, religious or community leaders)? If so, make sure the person's right to confidentiality is respected.
- Be aware of cultural, ethnic or religious factors that shape a person's way of thinking, behaviour or communication. For example, in some cultures it is important to involve the community in decision-making. Some religious beliefs (for example, those of Jehovah's Witnesses or Christian Scientists) may influence the person's approach to medical treatment and information about treatment decisions.
- If necessary, consider using a professional language interpreter. Even if a person communicated in English or Welsh in the past, they may have lost some verbal skills (for example, because of dementia). They may now prefer to communicate in their first language. It is often more appropriate to use a professional interpreter rather than to use family members.
- If using pictures to help communication, make sure they are relevant and the person can understand them easily. For example, a red bus may represent a form of transport to one person but a day trip to another.
- Would an advocate (someone who can support and represent the person) improve communication in the current situation? (See chapters 10 and 15 for more information about advocates.)

Scenario: Providing relevant information

Mrs Thomas has Alzheimer's disease and lives in a care home. She enjoys taking part in the activities provided at the home. Today there is a choice between going to a flower show, attending her usual pottery class or watching a DVD. Although she has the capacity to choose, having to decide is making her anxious.

The care assistant carefully explains the different options. She tells Mrs Thomas about the DVD she could watch, but Mrs Thomas doesn't like the sound of it. The care assistant shows her a leaflet about the flower show. She explains the plans for the day, where the show is being held and how long it will take to get there in the mini-van. She has to repeat this information several times, as Mrs Thomas keeps asking whether they will be back in time for supper. She also tells Mrs Thomas that one of her friends is going on the trip.

At first, Mrs Thomas is reluctant to disturb her usual routine. But the care assistant reassures her she will not lose her place at pottery if she misses a class. With this information, Mrs Thomas can therefore choose whether or not to go on the day trip.

Helping people with specific communication or cognitive problems

3.11   Where people have specific communication or cognitive problems, the following steps can help:

- Find out how the person is used to communicating. Do they use picture boards or Makaton (signs and symbols for people with communication or learning difficulties)? Or do they have a way of communicating that is only known to those close to them?
- If the person has hearing difficulties, use their preferred method of communication (for example, visual aids, written messages or sign language). Where possible, use a qualified interpreter.
- Are mechanical devices such as voice synthesisers, keyboards or other computer equipment available to help?
- If the person does not use verbal communication skills, allow more time to learn how to communicate effectively.
- For people who use non-verbal methods of communication, their behaviour (in particular, changes in behaviour) can provide indications of their feelings.
- Some people may prefer to use non-verbal means of communication and can communicate most effectively in written form using computers or other communication technologies. This is particularly true for those with autistic spectrum disorders.
- For people with specific communication difficulties, consider other types of professional help (for example, a speech and language therapist or an expert in clinical neuropsychology).

Scenario: Helping people with specific communication difficulties

David is a deafblind man with learning disabilities who has no formal communication. He lives in a specialist home. He begins to bang his head against the wall and repeats this behaviour throughout the day. He has not done this before.

The staff in the home are worried and discuss ways to reduce the risk of injury. They come up with a range of possible interventions, aimed at engaging him with activities and keeping him away from objects that could injure him. They assess these as less restrictive ways to ensure he is safe. But David lacks the capacity to make a decision about which would the best option.

The staff call in a specialist in challenging behaviour, who says that David's behaviour is communicative. After investigating this further, staff discover he is in pain because of tooth decay. They consult a dentist about how to resolve this, and the dentist decides it is in David's best interests to get treatment for the tooth decay. After treatment, David's head-banging stops.

What steps should be taken to put a person at ease?

3.12   To help put someone at ease and so improve their ability to make a decision, careful consideration should be given to both location and timing.

Location

3.13 In terms of location, consider the following:

- Where possible, choose a location where the person feels most at ease. For example, people are usually more comfortable in their own home than at a doctor's surgery.
- Would the person find it easier to make their decision in a relevant location? For example, could you help them decide about medical treatment by taking them to hospital to see what is involved?
- Choose a quiet location where the discussion can't be easily interrupted.
- Try to eliminate any background noise or distractions (for example, the television or radio, or people talking).
- Choose a location where the person's privacy and dignity can be properly respected.

Timing

3.14 In terms of timing, consider the following:

- Try to choose the time of day when the person is most alert – some people are better in the mornings, others are more lively in the afternoon or early evening. It may be necessary to try several times before a decision can be made.
- If the person's capacity is likely to improve in the foreseeable future, wait until it has done so – if practical and appropriate. For example, this might be the case after treatment for depression or a psychotic episode. Obviously, this may not be practical and appropriate if the decision is urgent.
- Some medication could affect a person's capacity (for example, medication which causes drowsiness or affects memory). Can the decision be delayed until side effects have subsided?
- Take one decision at a time – be careful to avoid making the person tired or confused.
- Don't rush – allow the person time to think things over or ask for clarification, where that is possible and appropriate.
- Avoid or challenge time limits that are unnecessary if the decision is not urgent. Delaying the decision may enable further steps to be taken to assist people to make the decision for themselves.

Scenario: Getting the location and timing right

Luke, a young man, was seriously injured in a road traffic accident and suffered permanent brain damage. He has been in hospital several months, and has made good progress, but he gets very frustrated at his inability to concentrate or do things for himself.

Luke now needs surgical treatment on his leg. During the early morning ward round, the surgeon tries to explain what is involved in the operation. She asks Luke to sign a consent form, but he gets angry and says he doesn't want to talk about it.

His key nurse knows that Luke becomes more alert and capable later in the day. After lunch, she asks him if he would like to discuss the operation again. She also knows that he responds better one-to-one than in a group. So she takes Luke into a private room and repeats the information that the surgeon gave him earlier. He understands why the treatment is needed, what is involved and the likely consequences. Therefore, Luke has the capacity to make a decision about the operation.

Support from other people

3.15   In some circumstances, individuals will be more comfortable making decisions when someone else is there to support them.

- ● Might the person benefit from having another person present? Sometimes having a relative or friend nearby can provide helpful support and reduce anxiety. However, some people might find this intrusive, and it could increase their anxiety or affect their ability to make a free choice. Find ways of getting the person's views on this, for example, by watching their behaviour towards other people.
- ● Always respect a person's right to confidentiality.

Scenario: Getting help from other people

Jane has a learning disability. She expresses herself using some words, facial expressions and body language. She has lived in her current community home all her life, but now needs to move to a new group home. She finds it difficult to discuss abstract ideas or things she hasn't experienced. Staff conclude that she lacks the capacity to decide for herself which new group home she should move to.

The staff involve an advocate to help Jane express her views. Jane's advocate spends time with her in different environments. The advocate uses pictures, symbols and Makaton to find out the things that are important to Jane, and speaks to people who know Jane to find out what they think she likes. She then supports Jane to show their work to her care manager, and checks that the new homes suggested for her are able to meet Jane's needs and preferences.

When the care manager has found some suitable places, Jane's advocate visits the homes with Jane. They take photos of the houses to help her distinguish between them. The advocate then uses the photos to help Jane work out which home she prefers. Jane's own feelings can now play an important part in deciding what is in her best interests – and so in the final decision about where she will live.

What other ways are there to enable decision-making?

3.16   There are other ways to help someone make a decision for themselves.

- Many people find it helpful to talk things over with people they trust – or people who have been in a similar situation or faced similar dilemmas. For example, people with learning difficulties may benefit from the help of a designated support worker or being part of a support network.
- If someone is very distressed (for example, following a death of someone close) or where there are long-standing problems that affect someone's ability to understand an issue, it may be possible to delay a decision so that the person can have psychological therapy, if needed.
- Some organisations have produced materials to help people who need support to make decisions and for those who support them. Some of this material is designed to help people with specific conditions, such as Alzheimer's disease or profound learning disability.
- It may be important to provide access to technology. For example, some people who appear not to communicate well verbally can do so very well using computers.

Scenario: Making the most of technology

Ms Patel has an autistic spectrum disorder. Her family and care staff find it difficult to communicate with her. She refuses to make eye contact, and gets very upset and angry when her carers try to encourage her to speak.

One member of staff notices that Ms Patel is interested in the computer equipment. He shows her how to use the keyboard, and they are able to have a conversation using the computer. An IT specialist works with her to make sure she can make the most of her computing skills to communicate her feelings and decisions.

4   HOW DOES THE ACT DEFINE A PERSON'S CAPACITY TO MAKE A DECISION AND HOW SHOULD CAPACITY BE ASSESSED?

This chapter explains what the Act means by 'capacity' and 'lack of capacity'. It provides guidance on how to assess whether someone has the capacity to make a decision, and suggests when professionals should be involved in the assessment.

In this chapter, as throughout the Code, a person's capacity (or lack of capacity) refers specifically to their capacity to make a particular decision at the time it needs to be made.

Quick summary

This checklist is a summary of points to consider when assessing a person's capacity to make a specific decision. Readers should also refer to the more detailed guidance in this chapter and chapters 2 and 3.

Presuming someone has capacity

- The starting assumption must always be that a person has the capacity to make a decision, unless it can be established that they lack capacity.

Understanding what is meant by capacity and lack of capacity

- A person's capacity must be assessed specifically in terms of their capacity to make a particular decision at the time it needs to be made.

Treating everyone equally

- A person's capacity must not be judged simply on the basis of their age, appearance, condition or an aspect of their behaviour.

Supporting the person to make the decision for themselves

- It is important to take all possible steps to try to help people make a decision for themselves (see chapter 2, principle 2, and chapter 3).

Assessing capacity

Anyone assessing someone's capacity to make a decision for themselves should use the two-stage test of capacity.

- Does the person have an impairment of the mind or brain, or is there some sort of disturbance affecting the way their mind or brain works? (It doesn't matter whether the impairment or disturbance is temporary or permanent.)
- If so, does that impairment or disturbance mean that the person is unable to make the decision in question at the time it needs to be made?

Assessing ability to make a decision

- Does the person have a general understanding of what decision they need to make and why they need to make it?
- Does the person have a general understanding of the likely consequences of making, or not making, this decision?
- Is the person able to understand, retain, use and weigh up the information relevant to this decision?
- Can the person communicate their decision (by talking, using sign language or any other means)? Would the services of a professional (such as a speech and language therapist) be helpful?

Assessing capacity to make more complex or serious decisions

- Is there a need for a more thorough assessment (perhaps by involving a doctor or other professional expert)?

What is mental capacity?

4.1   Mental capacity is the ability to make a decision.

- This includes the ability to make a decision that affects daily life – such as when to get up, what to wear or whether to go to the doctor when feeling ill – as well as more serious or significant decisions.
- It also refers to a person's ability to make a decision that may have legal consequences – for them or others. Examples include agreeing to have medical treatment, buying goods or making a will.

4.2   The starting point must always be to assume that a person has the capacity to make a specific decision (see chapter 2, principle 1). Some people may need help to be able to make or communicate a decision (see chapter 3). But this does not necessarily mean that they lack capacity to do so. What matters is their ability to carry out the processes involved in making the decision – and not the outcome.

What does the Act mean by 'lack of capacity'?

4.3   Section 2(1) of the Act states:

> For the purposes of this Act, a person lacks capacity in relation to a matter if at the material time he is unable to make a decision for himself in relation to the matter because of an impairment of, or a disturbance in the functioning of, the mind or brain.

This means that a person lacks capacity if:

- they have an impairment or disturbance (for example, a disability, condition or trauma) that affects the way their mind or brain works, and
- the impairment or disturbance means that they are unable to make a specific decision at the time it needs to be made.

4.4 An assessment of a person's capacity must be based on their ability to make a specific decision at the time it needs to be made, and not their ability to make decisions in general. Section 3 of the Act defines what it means to be unable to make a decision (this is explained in paragraph 4.14 below).

4.5 Section 2(2) states that the impairment or disturbance does not have to be permanent. A person can lack capacity to make a decision at the time it needs to be made even if:

- the loss of capacity is partial
- the loss of capacity is temporary
- their capacity changes over time.

A person may also lack capacity to make a decision about one issue but not about others.

4.6 The Act generally applies to people who are aged 16 or older. Chapter 12 explains how the Act affects children and young people – in particular those aged 16 and 17 years.

What safeguards does the Act provide around assessing someone's capacity?

4.7 An assessment that a person lacks capacity to make a decision must never be based simply on:

- their age
- their appearance
- assumptions about their condition, or
- any aspect of their behaviour. (section 2(3))

4.8 The Act deliberately uses the word 'appearance', because it covers all aspects of the way people look. So for example, it includes the physical characteristics of certain conditions (for example, scars, features linked to Down's syndrome or muscle spasms caused by cerebral palsy) as well as aspects of appearance like skin colour, tattoos and body piercings, or the way people dress (including religious dress).

4.9 The word 'condition' is also wide-ranging. It includes physical disabilities, learning difficulties and disabilities, illness related to age, and temporary conditions (for example, drunkenness or unconsciousness). Aspects of behaviour might include extrovert (for example, shouting or gesticulating) and withdrawn behaviour (for example, talking to yourself or avoiding eye contact).

Scenario: Treating everybody equally

Tom, a man with cerebral palsy, has slurred speech. Sometimes he also falls over for no obvious reason.

One day Tom falls in the supermarket. Staff call an ambulance, even though he says he is fine. They think he may need treatment after his fall.

When the ambulance comes, the ambulance crew know they must not make assumptions about Tom's capacity to decide about treatment, based simply on his condition and the effects of his disability. They talk to him and find that he is capable of making healthcare decisions for himself.

What proof of lack of capacity does the Act require?

4.10   Anybody who claims that an individual lacks capacity should be able to provide proof. They need to be able to show, on the balance of probabilities, that the individual lacks capacity to make a particular decision, at the time it needs to be made (section 2(4)). This means being able to show that it is more likely than not that the person lacks capacity to make the decision in question.

What is the test of capacity?

To help determine if a person lacks capacity to make particular decisions, the Act sets out a two-stage test of capacity.

Stage 1: Does the person have an impairment of, or a disturbance in the functioning of, their mind or brain?

4.11   Stage 1 requires proof that the person has an impairment of the mind or brain, or some sort of or disturbance that affects the way their mind or brain works. If a person does not have such an impairment or disturbance of the mind or brain, they will not lack capacity under the Act.

4.12   Examples of an impairment or disturbance in the functioning of the mind or brain may include the following:

- conditions associated with some forms of mental illness
- dementia
- significant learning disabilities
- the long-term effects of brain damage
- physical or medical conditions that cause confusion, drowsiness or loss of consciousness
- delirium
- concussion following a head injury, and
- the symptoms of alcohol or drug use.

Scenario: Assessing whether an impairment or disturbance is affecting someone's ability to make a decision

Mrs Collins is 82 and has had a stroke. This has weakened the left-hand side of her body. She is living in a house that has been the family home for years. Her son wants her to sell her house and live with him.

Mrs Collins likes the idea, but her daughter does not. She thinks her mother will lose independence and her condition will get worse. She talks to her mother's consultant to get information that will help stop the sale. But he says that although Mrs Collins is anxious about the physical effects the stroke has had on her body, it has not caused any mental impairment or affected her brain, so she still has capacity to make her own decision about selling her house.

Stage 2: Does the impairment or disturbance mean that the person is unable to make a specific decision when they need to?

4.13 For a person to lack capacity to make a decision, the Act says their impairment or disturbance must affect their ability to make the specific decision when they need to. But first people must be given all practical and appropriate support to help them make the decision for themselves (see chapter 2, principle 2). Stage 2 can only apply if all practical and appropriate support to help the person make the decision has failed. See chapter 3 for guidance on ways of helping people to make their own decisions.

What does the Act mean by 'inability to make a decision'?

4.14 A person is unable to make a decision if they cannot:

1. understand information about the decision to be made (the Act calls this 'relevant information')
2. retain that information in their mind
3. use or weigh that information as part of the decision-making process, or
4. communicate their decision (by talking, using sign language or any other means). See section 3(1).

4.15 These four points are explained in more detail below. The first three should be applied together. If a person cannot do any of these three things, they will be treated as unable to make the decision. The fourth only applies in situations where people cannot communicate their decision in any way.

Understanding information about the decision to be made

4.16 It is important not to assess someone's understanding before they have been given relevant information about a decision. Every effort must be made to provide information in a way that is most appropriate to help the person to understand. Quick or inadequate explanations are not acceptable unless the situation is urgent (see chapter 3 for some practical steps). Relevant information includes:

- the nature of the decision
- the reason why the decision is needed, and
- the likely effects of deciding one way or another, or making no decision at all.

4.17 Section 3(2) outlines the need to present information in a way that is appropriate to meet the individual's needs and circumstances. It also stresses the importance of explaining information using the most effective form of communication for that person (such as simple language, sign language, visual representations, computer support or any other means).

4.18 For example:

- a person with a learning disability may need somebody to read information to them.

They might also need illustrations to help them to understand what is happening. Or they might stop the reader to ask what things mean. It might also be helpful for them to discuss information with an advocate.

- a person with anxiety or depression may find it difficult to reach a decision about treatment in a group meeting with professionals. They may prefer to read the relevant documents in private. This way they can come to a conclusion alone, and ask for help if necessary.
- someone who has a brain injury might need to be given information several times. It will be necessary to check that the person understands the information. If they have difficulty understanding, it might be useful to present information in a different way (for example, different forms of words, pictures or diagrams). Written information, audio-tapes, videos and posters can help people remember important facts.

4.19 Relevant information must include what the likely consequences of a decision would be (the possible effects of deciding one way or another) – and also the likely consequences of making no decision at all (section 3(4)). In some cases, it may be enough to give a broad explanation using simple language. But a person might need more detailed information or access to advice, depending on the decision that needs to be made. If a decision could have serious or grave consequences, it is even more important that a person understands the information relevant to that decision.

Scenario: Providing relevant information in an appropriate format

Mr Leslie has learning disabilities and has developed an irregular heartbeat. He has been prescribed medication for this, but is anxious about having regular blood tests to check his medication levels. His doctor gives him a leaflet to explain:

- the reason for the tests
- what a blood test involves
- the risks in having or not having the tests, and
- that he has the right to decide whether or not to have the test.

The leaflet uses simple language and photographs to explain these things. Mr Leslie's carer helps him read the leaflet over the next few days, and checks that he understands it.

Mr Leslie goes back to tell the doctor that, even though he is scared of needles, he will agree to the blood tests so that he can get the right medication. He is able to pick out the equipment needed to do the blood test. So the doctor concludes that Mr Leslie can understand, retain and use the relevant information and therefore has the capacity to make the decision to have the test.

Retaining information

4.20 The person must be able to hold the information in their mind long enough to use it to make an effective decision. But section 3(3) states that people who can only retain information for a short while must not automatically be assumed to lack the capacity to decide – it depends on what is necessary for the decision in question. Items such as notebooks, photographs, posters, videos and voice recorders can help people record and retain information.

Scenario: Assessing a person's ability to retain information

Walter, an elderly man, is diagnosed with dementia and has problems remembering things in the short term. He can't always remember his great-grandchildren's names, but he recognises them when they come to visit. He can also pick them out on photographs.

Walter would like to buy premium bonds (a type of financial investment) for each of his great-grandchildren. He asks his solicitor to make the arrangements. After assessing his capacity to make financial decisions, the solicitor is satisfied that Walter has capacity to make this decision, despite his short-term memory problems.

Using or weighing information as part of the decision-making process

4.21 For someone to have capacity, they must have the ability to weigh up information and use it to arrive at a decision. Sometimes people can understand information but an impairment or disturbance stops them using it. In other cases, the impairment or disturbance leads to a person making a specific decision without understanding or using the information they have been given.[3]

4.22 For example, a person with the eating disorder anorexia nervosa may understand information about the consequences of not eating. But their compulsion not to eat might be too strong for them to ignore. Some people who have serious brain damage might make impulsive decisions regardless of information they have been given or their understanding of it.

Inability to communicate a decision in any way

4.23 Sometimes there is no way for a person to communicate. This will apply to very few people, but it does include:

- people who are unconscious or in a coma, or
- those with the very rare condition sometimes known as 'locked-in syndrome', who are conscious but cannot speak or move at all.

If a person cannot communicate their decision in any way at all, the Act says they should be treated as if they are unable to make that decision.

4.24 Before deciding that someone falls into this category, it is important to make all practical and appropriate efforts to help them communicate. This might call for the involvement of speech and language therapists, specialists in non-verbal communication or other professionals. Chapter 3 gives advice for communicating with people who have specific disabilities or cognitive problems.

4.25 Communication by simple muscle movements can show that somebody can communicate and may have capacity to make a decision.[4] For example, a person might blink an eye

---

[3] This issue has been considered in a number of court cases, including *Re MB* [1997] 2 FLR 426; *R v Collins and Ashworth Hospital Authority ex parte Brady* [2001] 58 BMLR 173
[4] This was demonstrated in the case *Re AK (Adult Patient) (Medical Treatment: Consent)* [2001] 1 FLR 129

or squeeze a hand to say 'yes' or 'no'. In these cases, assessment must use the first three points listed in paragraph 4.14, which are explained in more depth in paragraphs 4.16–4.22.

What other issues might affect capacity?

People with fluctuating or temporary capacity

4.26   Some people have fluctuating capacity – they have a problem or condition that gets worse occasionally and affects their ability to make decisions. For example, someone who has manic depression may have a temporary manic phase which causes them to lack capacity to make financial decisions, leading them to get into debt even though at other times they are perfectly able to manage their money. A person with a psychotic illness may have delusions that affect their capacity to make decisions at certain times but disappear at others. Temporary factors may also affect someone's ability to make decisions. Examples include acute illness, severe pain, the effect of medication, or distress after a death or shock. More guidance on how to support someone with fluctuating or temporary capacity to make a decision can be found in chapter 3, particularly paragraphs 3.12–3.16. More information about factors that may indicate that a person may regain or develop capacity in the future can be found at paragraph 5.28.

4.27   As in any other situation, an assessment must only examine a person's capacity to make a particular decision when it needs to be made. It may be possible to put off the decision until the person has the capacity to make it (see also guidance on best interests in chapter 5).

Ongoing conditions that may affect capacity

4.28   Generally, capacity assessments should be related to a specific decision. But there may be people with an ongoing condition that affects their ability to make certain decisions or that may affect other decisions in their life. One decision on its own may make sense, but may give cause for concern when considered alongside others.

4.29   Again, it is important to review capacity from time to time, as people can improve their decision-making capabilities. In particular, someone with an ongoing condition may become able to make some, if not all, decisions. Some people (for example, people with learning disabilities) will learn new skills throughout their life, improving their capacity to make certain decisions. So assessments should be reviewed from time to time. Capacity should always be reviewed:

- whenever a care plan is being developed or reviewed
- at other relevant stages of the care planning process, and
- as particular decisions need to be made.

4.30   It is important to acknowledge the difference between:

- unwise decisions, which a person has the right to make (chapter 2, principle 3), and
- decisions based on a lack of understanding of risks or inability to weigh up the information about a decision.

Information about decisions the person has made based on a lack of understanding of risks or inability to weigh up the information can form part of a capacity assessment – particularly if someone repeatedly makes decisions that put them at risk or result in harm to them or someone else.

Scenario: Ongoing conditions

Paul had an accident at work and suffered severe head injuries. He was awarded compensation to pay for care he will need throughout his life as a result of his head injury. An application was made to the Court of Protection to consider how the award of compensation should be managed, including whether to appoint a deputy to manage Paul's financial affairs. Paul objected as he believed he could manage his life and should be able to spend his money however he liked.

He wrote a list of what he intended to spend his money on. This included fully-staffed luxury properties and holiday villas, cars with chauffeurs, jewellery and various other items for himself and his family. But spending money on all these luxury items would not leave enough money to cover the costs of his care in future years.

The court judged that Paul had capacity to make day-to-day financial decisions, but he did not understand why he had received compensation and what the money was supposed to be used for. Nor did he understand how buying luxuries now could affect his future care. The court therefore decided Paul lacked capacity to manage large amounts of money and appointed a deputy to make ongoing financial decisions relating to his care. But it gave him access to enough funds to cover everyday needs and occasional treats.

What other legal tests of capacity are there?

4.31   The Act makes clear that the definition of 'lack of capacity' and the two-stage test for capacity set out in the Act are 'for the purposes of this Act'. This means that the definition and test are to be used in situations covered by this Act. Schedule 6 of the Act also amends existing laws to ensure that the definition and test are used in other areas of law not covered directly by this Act.

For example, Schedule 6, paragraph 20 allows a person to be disqualified from jury service if they lack the capacity (using this Act's definition) to carry out a juror's tasks.

4.32   There are several tests of capacity that have been produced following judgments in court cases (known as common law tests).[5] These cover:

- capacity to make a will[6]
- capacity to make a gift[7]
- capacity to enter into a contract[8]
- capacity to litigate (take part in legal cases),[9] and
- capacity to enter into marriage.[10]

4.33   The Act's new definition of capacity is in line with the existing common law tests, and the Act does not replace them. When cases come before the court on the above issues, judges

---

[5]   For details, see British Medical Association & Law Society, *Assessment of Mental Capacity: Guidance for Doctors and Lawyers* (Second edition) (London: BMJ Books, 2004)

[6]   *Banks v Goodfellow* (1870) LR 5 QB 549

[7]   *Re Beaney (deceased)* [1978] 2 All ER 595

[8]   *Boughton v Knight* (1873) LR 3 PD 64

[9]   *Masterman-Lister v Brutton & Co and Jewell & Home Counties Dairies* [2003] 3 All ER 162 (CA)

[10]   *Sheffield City Council v E & S* [2005] 1 FLR 965

can adopt the new definition if they think it is appropriate. The Act will apply to all other cases relating to financial, healthcare or welfare decisions.

When should capacity be assessed?

4.34   Assessing capacity correctly is vitally important to everyone affected by the Act. Someone who is assessed as lacking capacity may be denied their right to make a specific decision – particularly if others think that the decision would not be in their best interests or could cause harm. Also, if a person lacks capacity to make specific decisions, that person might make decisions they do not really understand. Again, this could cause harm or put the person at risk. So it is important to carry out an assessment when a person's capacity is in doubt. It is also important that the person who does an assessment can justify their conclusions. Many organisations will provide specific professional guidance for members of their profession.[11]

4.35   There are a number of reasons why people may question a person's capacity to make a specific decision:

- the person's behaviour or circumstances cause doubt as to whether they have the capacity to make a decision
- somebody else says they are concerned about the person's capacity, or
- the person has previously been diagnosed with an impairment or disturbance that affects the way their mind or brain works (see paragraphs 4.11–4.12 above), and it has already been shown they lack capacity to make other decisions in their life.

4.36   The starting assumption must be that the person has the capacity to make the specific decision. If, however, anyone thinks a person lacks capacity, it is important to then ask the following questions:

- Does the person have all the relevant information they need to make the decision?
- If they are making a decision that involves choosing between alternatives, do they have information on all the different options?
- Would the person have a better understanding if information was explained or presented in another way?
- Are there times of day when the person's understanding is better?
- Are there locations where they may feel more at ease?
- Can the decision be put off until the circumstances are different and the person concerned may be able to make the decision?
- Can anyone else help the person to make choices or express a view (for example, a family member or carer, an advocate or someone to help with communication)?

4.37   Chapter 3 describes ways to deal with these questions and suggest steps which may help people make their own decisions. If all practical and appropriate steps fail, an assessment will then be needed of the person's capacity to make the decision that now needs to be made.

---

[11]   See for example, British Medical Association & Law Society, *Assessment of Mental Capacity: Guidance for Doctors and Lawyers* (Second edition) (London: BMJ Books, 2004); the Joint Royal Colleges Ambulance Service Liaison Committee Clinical Practice Guidelines (JRCALC, available online at **www2.warwick.ac.uk/fac/med/research/hsri/emergencycare/jrcalc_2006/clinical_guidelines_2006.pdf**) and British Psychological Society, *Guidelines on assessing capacity* (BPS, 2006 available online at **www.bps.org.uk**)

WHO SHOULD ASSESS CAPACITY?

4.38   The person who assesses an individual's capacity to make a decision will usually be the person who is directly concerned with the individual at the time the decision needs to be made. This means that different people will be involved in assessing someone's capacity to make different decisions at different times.

For most day-to-day decisions, this will be the person caring for them at the time a decision must be made. For example, a care worker might need to assess if the person can agree to being bathed. Then a district nurse might assess if the person can consent to have a dressing changed.

4.39   For acts of care or treatment (see chapter 6), the assessor must have a 'reasonable belief' that the person lacks capacity to agree to the action or decision to be taken (see paragraphs 4.44–4.45 for a description of reasonable belief).

4.40   If a doctor or healthcare professional proposes treatment or an examination, they must assess the person's capacity to consent. In settings such as a hospital, this can involve the multi-disciplinary team (a team of people from different professional backgrounds who share responsibility for a patient). But ultimately, it is up to the professional responsible for the person's treatment to make sure that capacity has been assessed.

4.41   For a legal transaction (for example, making a will), a solicitor or legal practitioner must assess the client's capacity to instruct them. They must assess whether the client has the capacity to satisfy any relevant legal test. In cases of doubt, they should get an opinion from a doctor or other professional expert.

4.42   More complex decisions are likely to need more formal assessments (see paragraph 4.54 below). A professional opinion on the person's capacity might be necessary. This could be, for example, from a psychiatrist, psychologist, a speech and language therapist, occupational therapist or social worker. But the final decision about a person's capacity must be made by the person intending to make the decision or carry out the action on behalf of the person who lacks capacity – not the professional, who is there to advise.

4.43   Any assessor should have the skills and ability to communicate effectively with the person (see chapter 3). If necessary, they should get professional help to communicate with the person.

Scenario: Getting help with assessing capacity

Ms Dodd suffered brain damage in a road accident and is unable to speak. At first, her family thought she was not able to make decisions. But they soon discovered that she could choose by pointing at things, such as the clothes she wants to wear or the food she prefers. Her behaviour also indicates that she enjoys attending a day centre, but she refuses to go swimming. Her carers have assessed her as having capacity to make these decisions.

Ms Dodd needs hospital treatment but she gets distressed when away from home. Her mother feels that Ms Dodd is refusing treatment by her behaviour, but her father thinks she lacks capacity to say no to treatment that could improve her condition.

The clinician who is proposing the treatment will have to assess Ms Dodd's capacity to consent. He gets help from a member of staff at the day centre who knows Ms Dodd's communication well and also discusses things with her parents. Over several meetings the clinician explains the treatment options to Ms Dodd with the help of the staff member. The final decision about Ms Dodd's capacity rests with the clinician, but he will need to use information from the staff member and others who know Ms Dodd well to make this assessment.

What is 'reasonable belief' of lack of capacity?

4.44　Carers (whether family carers or other carers) and care workers do not have to be experts in assessing capacity. But to have protection from liability when providing care or treatment (see chapter 6), they must have a 'reasonable belief' that the person they care for lacks capacity to make relevant decisions about their care or treatment (section 5(1)). To have this reasonable belief, they must have taken 'reasonable' steps to establish that that the person lacks capacity to make a decision or consent to an act at the time the decision or consent is needed. They must also establish that the act or decision is in the person's best interests (see chapter 5).

They do not usually need to follow formal processes, such as involving a professional to make an assessment. However, if somebody challenges their assessment (see paragraph 4.63 below), they must be able to describe the steps they have taken. They must also have objective reasons for believing the person lacks capacity to make the decision in question.

4.45　The steps that are accepted as 'reasonable' will depend on individual circumstances and the urgency of the decision. Professionals, who are qualified in their particular field, are normally expected to undertake a fuller assessment, reflecting their higher degree of knowledge and experience, than family members or other carers who have no formal qualifications. See paragraph 4.36 for a list of points to consider when assessing someone's capacity. The following may also be helpful:

- Start by assuming the person has capacity to make the specific decision. Is there anything to prove otherwise?
- Does the person have a previous diagnosis of disability or mental disorder? Does that condition now affect their capacity to make this decision? If there has been no previous diagnosis, it may be best to get a medical opinion.
- Make every effort to communicate with the person to explain what is happening.
- Make every effort to try to help the person make the decision in question.
- See if there is a way to explain or present information about the decision in a way that makes it easier to understand. If the person has a choice, do they have information about all the options?
- Can the decision be delayed to take time to help the person make the decision, or to give the person time to regain the capacity to make the decision for themselves?
- Does the person understand what decision they need to make and why they need to make it?
- Can they understand information about the decision? Can they retain it, use it and weigh it to make the decision?
- Be aware that the fact that a person agrees with you or assents to what is proposed does not necessarily mean that they have capacity to make the decision.

What other factors might affect an assessment of capacity?

4.46　It is important to assess people when they are in the best state to make the decision, if possible. Whether this is possible will depend on the nature and urgency of the decision to be made. Many of the practical steps suggested in chapter 3 will help to create the best environment for assessing capacity. The assessor must then carry out the two stages of the test of capacity (see paragraphs 4.11–4.25 above).

4.47   In many cases, it may be clear that the person has an impairment or disturbance in the functioning of their mind or brain which could affect their ability to make a decision. For example, there might be a past diagnosis of a disability or mental disorder, or there may be signs that an illness is returning. Old assumptions about an illness or condition should be reviewed. Sometimes an illness develops gradually (for example, dementia), and it is hard to know when it starts to affect capacity. Anyone assessing someone's capacity may need to ask for a medical opinion as to whether a person has an illness or condition that could affect their capacity to make a decision in this specific case.

Scenario: Getting a professional opinion

Mr Elliott is 87 years old and lives alone. He has poor short-term memory, and he often forgets to eat. He also sometimes neglects his personal hygiene. His daughter talks to him about the possibility of moving into residential care. She decides that he understands the reasons for her concerns as well as the risks of continuing to live alone and, having weighed these up, he has the capacity to decide to stay at home and accept the consequences.

Two months later, Mr Elliott has a fall and breaks his leg. While being treated in hospital, he becomes confused and depressed. He says he wants to go home, but the staff think that the deterioration in his mental health has affected his capacity to make this decision at this time. They think he cannot understand the consequences or weigh up the risks he faces if he goes home. They refer him to a specialist in old age psychiatry, who assesses whether his mental health is affecting his capacity to make this decision. The staff will then use the specialist's opinion to help their assessment of Mr Elliott's capacity.

4.48   Anyone assessing someone's capacity must not assume that a person lacks capacity simply because they have a particular diagnosis or condition. There must be proof that the diagnosed illness or condition affects the ability to make a decision when it needs to be made. The person assessing capacity should ask the following questions:

- Does the person have a general understanding of what decision they need to make and why they need to make it?
- Do they understand the likely consequences of making, or not making, this decision?
- Can they understand and process information about the decision? And can they use it to help them make a decision?

In borderline cases, or where there is doubt, the assessor must be able to show that it is more likely than not that the answer to these questions is 'no'.

What practical steps should be taken when assessing capacity?

4.49   Anyone assessing someone's capacity will need to decide which of these steps are relevant to their situation.

- They should make sure that they understand the nature and effect of the decision to be made themselves. They may need access to relevant documents and background information (for example, details of the person's finances if assessing capacity to manage affairs). See chapter 16 for details on access to information.
- They may need other relevant information to support the assessment (for example, healthcare records or the views of staff involved in the person's care).

- Family members and close friends may be able to provide valuable background information (for example, the person's past behaviour and abilities and the types of decisions they can currently make). But their personal views and wishes about what they would want for the person must not influence the assessment.
- They should again explain to the person all the information relevant to the decision. The explanation must be in the most appropriate and effective form of communication for that person.
- Check the person's understanding after a few minutes. The person should be able to give a rough explanation of the information that was explained. There are different methods for people who use nonverbal means of communication (for example, observing behaviour or their ability to recognise objects or pictures).
- Avoid questions that need only a 'yes' or 'no' answer (for example, did you understand what I just said?). They are not enough to assess the person's capacity to make a decision. But there may be no alternative in cases where there are major communication difficulties. In these cases, check the response by asking questions again in a different way.
- Skills and behaviour do not necessarily reflect the person's capacity to make specific decisions. The fact that someone has good social or language skills, polite behaviour or good manners doesn't necessarily mean they understand the information or are able to weigh it up.
- Repeating these steps can help confirm the result.

4.50 For certain kinds of complex decisions (for example, making a will), there are specific legal tests (see paragraph 4.32 above) in addition to the two-stage test for capacity. In some cases, medical or psychometric tests may also be helpful tools (for example, for assessing cognitive skills) in assessing a person's capacity to make particular decisions, but the relevant legal test of capacity must still be fulfilled.

When should professionals be involved?

4.51 Anyone assessing someone's capacity may need to get a professional opinion when assessing a person's capacity to make complex or major decisions. In some cases this will simply involve contacting the person's general practitioner (GP) or family doctor. If the person has a particular condition or disorder, it may be appropriate to contact a specialist (for example, consultant psychiatrist, psychologist or other professional with experience of caring for patients with that condition). A speech and language therapist might be able to help if there are communication difficulties. In some cases, a multi-disciplinary approach is best. This means combining the skills and expertise of different professionals.

4.52 Professionals should never express an opinion without carrying out a proper examination and assessment of the person's capacity to make the decision. They must apply the appropriate test of capacity. In some cases, they will need to meet the person more than once – particularly if the person has communication difficulties. Professionals can get background information from a person's family and carers. But the personal views of these people about what they want for the person who lacks capacity must not influence the outcome of that assessment.

4.53 Professional involvement might be needed if:

- the decision that needs to be made is complicated or has serious consequences
- an assessor concludes a person lacks capacity, and the person challenges the finding
- family members, carers and/or professionals disagree about a person's capacity
- there is a conflict of interest between the assessor and the person being assessed

- the person being assessed is expressing different views to different people – they may be trying to please everyone or telling people what they think they want to hear
- somebody might challenge the person's capacity to make the decision – either at the time of the decision or later (for example, a family member might challenge a will after a person has died on the basis that the person lacked capacity when they made the will)
- somebody has been accused of abusing a vulnerable adult who may lack capacity to make decisions that protect them
- a person repeatedly makes decisions that put them at risk or could result in suffering or damage.

Scenario: Involving professional opinion

Ms Ledger is a young woman with learning disabilities and some autistic spectrum disorders. Recently she began a sexual relationship with a much older man, who is trying to persuade her to move in with him and come off the pill. There are rumours that he has been violent towards her and has taken her bankbook.

Ms Ledger boasts about the relationship to her friends. But she has admitted to her key worker that she is sometimes afraid of the man. Staff at her sheltered accommodation decide to make a referral under the local adult protection procedures. They arrange for a clinical psychologist to assess Ms Ledger's understanding of the relationship and her capacity to consent to it.

4.54 In some cases, it may be a legal requirement, or good professional practice, to undertake a formal assessment of capacity. These cases include:

- where a person's capacity to sign a legal document (for example, a will), could later be challenged, in which case an expert should be asked for an opinion[12]
- to establish whether a person who might be involved in a legal case needs the assistance of the Official Solicitor or other litigation friend (somebody to represent their views to a court and give instructions to their legal representative) and there is doubt about the person's capacity to instruct a solicitor or take part in the case[13]
- whenever the Court of Protection has to decide if a person lacks capacity in a certain matter
- if the courts are required to make a decision about a person's capacity in other legal proceedings[14]
- if there may be legal consequences of a finding of capacity (for example, deciding on financial compensation following a claim for personal injury).

Are assessment processes confidential?

4.55 People involved in assessing capacity will need to share information about a person's circumstances. But there are ethical codes and laws that require professionals to keep personal information confidential. As a general rule, professionals must ask their patients or clients if they can reveal information to somebody else – even close relatives. But sometimes

---

[12] *Kenward v Adams*, The Times, 29 November 1975
[13] Civil Procedure Rules 1998, r 21.1
[14] *Masterman-Lister v Brutton & Co and Jewell & Home Counties Dairies* [2002] EWCA Civ 1889, CA at 54

information may be disclosed without the consent of the person who the information concerns (for example, to protect the person or prevent harm to other people).[15]

4.56 Anyone assessing someone's capacity needs accurate information concerning the person being assessed that is relevant to the decision the person has to make. So professionals should, where possible, make relevant information available. They should make every effort to get the person's permission to reveal relevant information. They should give a full explanation of why this is necessary, and they should tell the person about the risks and consequences of revealing, and not revealing information. If the person is unable to give permission, the professional might still be allowed to provide information that will help make an accurate assessment of the person's capacity to make the specific decision. Chapter 16 has more detail on how to access information.

What if someone refuses to be assessed?

4.57 There may be circumstances in which a person whose capacity is in doubt refuses to undergo an assessment of capacity or refuses to be examined by a doctor or other professional. In these circumstances, it might help to explain to someone refusing an assessment why it is needed and what the consequences of refusal are. But threats or attempts to force the person to agree to an assessment are not acceptable.

4.58 If the person lacks capacity to agree or refuse, the assessment can normally go ahead, as long as the person does not object to the assessment, and it is in their best interests (see chapter 5).

4.59 Nobody can be forced to undergo an assessment of capacity. If someone refuses to open the door to their home, it cannot be forced. If there are serious worries about the person's mental health, it may be possible to get a warrant to force entry and assess the person for treatment in hospital – but the situation must meet the requirements of the Mental Health Act 1983 (section 135). But simply refusing an assessment of capacity is in no way sufficient grounds for an assessment under the Mental Health Act 1983 (see chapter 13).

Who should keep a record of assessments?

4.60 Assessments of capacity to take day-to-day decisions or consent to care require no formal assessment procedures or recorded documentation. Paragraphs 4.44–4.45 above explain the steps to take to reach a 'reasonable belief' that someone lacks capacity to make a particular decision. It is good practice for paid care workers to keep a record of the steps they take when caring for the person concerned.

Professional records

4.61 It is good practice for professionals to carry out a proper assessment of a person's capacity to make particular decisions and to record the findings in the relevant professional records.

- A doctor or healthcare professional proposing treatment should carry out an assessment of the person's capacity to consent (with a multi-disciplinary team, if appropriate) and record it in the patient's clinical notes.

---

[15] For example, in the circumstances discussed in *W v Egdell and others* [1990] 1 All ER 835 at 848; *S v Plymouth City Council and C*, [2002] EWCA Civ 388) at 49

- Solicitors should assess a client's capacity to give instructions or carry out a legal transaction (obtaining a medical or other professional opinion, if necessary) and record it on the client's file.
- An assessment of a person's capacity to consent or agree to the provision of services will be part of the care planning processes for health and social care needs, and should be recorded in the relevant documentation. This includes:
- Person Centred Planning for people with learning disabilities
- the Care Programme Approach for people with mental illness
- the Single Assessment Process for older people in England, and
- the Unified Assessment Process in Wales.

Formal reports or certificates of capacity

4.62 In some cases, a more detailed report or certificate of capacity may be required, for example,

- for use in court or other legal processes
- as required by Regulations, Rules or Orders made under the Act.

How can someone challenge a finding of lack of capacity?

4.63 There are likely to be occasions when someone may wish to challenge the results of an assessment of capacity. The first step is to raise the matter with the person who carried out the assessment. If the challenge comes from the individual who is said to lack capacity, they might need support from family, friends or an advocate. Ask the assessor to:

- give reasons why they believe the person lacks capacity to make the decision, and
- provide objective evidence to support that belief.

4.64 The assessor must show they have applied the principles of the Mental Capacity Act (see chapter 2). Attorneys, deputies and professionals will need to show that they have also followed guidance in this chapter.

4.65 It might be possible to get a second opinion from an independent professional or another expert in assessing capacity. Chapter 15 has other suggestions for dealing with disagreements. But if a disagreement cannot be resolved, the person who is challenging the assessment may be able to apply to the Court of Protection. The Court of Protection can rule on whether a person has capacity to make the decision covered by the assessment (see chapter 8).

APPENDIX C

Court of Protection

C.1 INTRODUCTION

The origins of the Court of Protection are to be found in the Middle Ages, when the Crown assumed responsibility for managing the estates of the 'mentally ill and mentally handicapped'. In the more recent past, the Court of Protection was an office of the Supreme Court, deriving its statutory powers from Part VII of the Mental Health Act 1983 and the Enduring Powers of Attorney Act 1985. Its jurisdiction was limited to matters relating to the property and affairs of a 'patient' within its jurisdiction.

As of 1 October 2007, the Mental Capacity Act 2005 established a new Court of Protection as a superior court of record,[1] having all the powers, rights and privileges of the High Court in connection with its jurisdiction. It is a specialist court which makes specific decisions or appoints other people known as deputies to make decisions on behalf of people who lack the capacity to make these decisions for themselves.[2]

Hearings are normally private, but in certain cases the media can be authorised to attend. As of autumn 2015, a pilot scheme was under preparation to trial greater public and media access.

C.2 JURISDICTION AND POWERS

The jurisdiction of the new Court of Protection is wider than its predecessor. The former court dealt exclusively with financial matters. The new court also deals with health and personal welfare. In exercising its powers under MCA 2005, the court must have regard to the provisions of the Act, in particular to s.1 (the principles) and s.4 (best interests) (see **Chapter 3**) as well as the MCA Code of Practice, the MCA Deprivation of Liberty Safeguards Code of Practice, the Court of Protection Rules and Court of Protection Practice Directions.

Test of capacity

The court must be satisfied that the person lacks capacity to make the specific decision or decisions in question, applying the statutory test of capacity set out in MCA 2005,[3] before it has jurisdiction to make any relevant decision(s) or declaration(s).

---

[1] MCA 2005, s.45(1).
[2] There are a number of practitioner handbooks relating to proceedings before the Court of Protection, including G Ashton, ed., (2015) *Court of Protection Practice* (published annually), Jordans; A Ruck Keene, *et al.* (2014) *Court of Protection Handbook: A User's Guide*, Legal Action Group; and D Rees, ed. (2015) *Heywood & Massey: Court of Protection Practice* (13th edn, looseleaf), Sweet & Maxwell.
[3] The statutory test in MCA 2005, ss.2 and 3, having regard to the principles set out in s.1. See also **Chapter 3**.

Powers

The Court of Protection can:

- decide whether a person has capacity to make a particular decision for themselves;
- make declarations, decisions or orders on financial or welfare matters affecting people who lack capacity to make these decisions;
- appoint a deputy to make ongoing decisions for people lacking capacity to make those decisions;
- decide whether a lasting power of attorney (LPA) or enduring power of attorney (EPA) is valid;
- make a declaration whether an advance decision to refuse treatment exists, is valid, and is applicable to a treatment;
- remove deputies or attorneys who fail to carry out their duties;
- hear cases concerning objections to register an LPA or EPA;
- authorise the making of a statutory will or gift on behalf of a person who lacks testamentary capacity or capacity to make a gift.

Interim orders

Where there is doubt about the person's capacity to make a relevant decision, or about the court's jurisdiction concerning the matter in question, MCA 2005 provides powers for the court to make interim orders or directions while the doubt is resolved.[4] The court has said that the 'gateway' test for using these powers is lower than that which is normally required to rebut the presumption of capacity. In such cases, the test in the first instance is whether there is evidence giving good cause for concern that the person may lack capacity in some relevant regard. Once that is raised as a serious possibility, the court then moves on to the second stage to decide what action, if any, it is in the person's best interests to take before a final determination of capacity can be made.[5]

Deputies

Where there is an ongoing need for decisions to be made on behalf of a person lacking capacity to make such decisions, the court may appoint a deputy with authority to make specific decisions. Court appointed deputies can be given wide powers by the court and, importantly, can be appointed to make decisions both in respect of property and financial affairs and also in respect of the welfare of the patient. However, the court is required where possible to make a single decision in preference to the appointment of a deputy.[6] The court has been particularly reluctant to date to appoint health and welfare deputies, preferring applications to be made each time a decision is required.

C.3 STRUCTURE OF THE COURT

The Court of Protection is based in London at First Avenue House, 42–49 High Holborn London, WC1A 9JA. It is administered by HM Courts and Tribunals Service (HMCTS). The court has four permanent district judges based at First Avenue House, whose sole remit is Court of Protection work, together with the Senior Judge, authorised officers of the court and the court's administration.

---

[4]   MCA 2005, s.48.
[5]   *Re F (Interim Declarations)* [2009] EWHC B30 (Fam); [2009] COPLR Con Vol 390.
[6]   MCA 2005 s.16(4).

The judges of the Court of Protection are divided into three tiers. The court is presided over by the President of the Court of Protection and a Vice-President who are both Tier 3 judges. Judges entitled to sit as Court of Protection judges include:

- all High Court judges (Tier 3);
- nominated circuit judges (Tier 2); and
- nominated district judges (Tier 1).

All High Court judges are nominated to sit in the Court of Protection although the only ones who do so regularly are judges of the Family Division. A total of about 125 circuit and district judges who are mainly based outside London are nominated to sit in the court.

All applications and communication are through the central registry at First Avenue House House. The vast bulk (between 92–95 per cent) of the applications made to the Court of Protection relate to property and affairs work. Ninety per cent of those applications are non-contentious and may be decided by court staff known as Authorised Court Officers (ACOs). ACOs are senior and experienced HMTCS staff, who are authorised to make decisions on straightforward, uncontested applications to the Court of Protection. The judges at First Avenue House will deal with all other aspects of the work, for example they will give directions, decide many cases on paper, decide some cases after a hearing and transfer some cases to other judges and places for a hearing.

Serious medical treatment cases will generally be referred to a Tier 3 judge, while Tier 1 and 2 judges at First Avenue House and in the regions will deal with most property and affairs and welfare cases.

Regional Hearings

The court also has a number of regional hearing venues across England and Wales. The court allocates cases to the regional centres when it is more convenient for people attending the hearing. The regional centres are not court registries, which means they cannot issue or process applications. Cases may be transferred from First Avenue House, as appropriate, to one of the regional centres (Birmingham, Bristol, Cardiff, Manchester, Newcastle and Preston). As of autumn 2015, proposals are under discussion formally to regionalise the Court of Protection.

Office of the Public Guardian

The functions given to the Public Guardian under MCA 2005 include:

- maintaining the registers of lasting powers of attorney (LPAs) and court appointed deputies;
- supervising the role of court appointed deputies;
- directing visits by a Court of Protection Visitor;
- receiving reports from donees of LPAs and deputies;
- reporting to the court on any matters as required by the court;
- dealing with representations and complaints about the conduct of both donees of LPAs and deputies.

Court of Protection Visitors

The Court of Protection Visitors provide independent advice to the court and to the Public Guardian as to how anyone given power under MCA 2005 is, or should be, carrying out their duties and responsibilities.[7] Visitors are either 'General' or 'Special', in which latter case they are registered medical practitioners with relevant expertise.

The court (or the Public Guardian) can send whichever type of visitor is most appropriate to visit and interview a person who may lack capacity. Visitors can also interview anyone who has been made an attorney or deputy and inspect any relevant healthcare or social care records. Failure to co-operate with visitors may result in the court revoking a power of attorney or discharging a deputyship.

C.4   APPLICATIONS TO THE COURT OF PROTECTION

It is important to note that the Court of Protection is intended to be a judicial forum of last resort. To this end, the MCA Code of Practice sets out a list of alternatives to recourse to the court, including the use of advocates, mediation, and formal complaints procedures.[8] However, an order of the court will usually be necessary to deal with the property and financial affairs of a person lacking capacity to make financial decisions, unless they have previously made an EPA or LPA giving a donee authority to manage those affairs (see **Chapter 5**).

Permission from the court will be needed for most applications relating to personal welfare. Permission will not generally be needed for applications relating to property and affairs. Exceptions to these rules are provided for in MCA 2005 and in the Court of Protection Rules made under the Act.

Applications to the Court of Protection must be made on specified forms (available from **www.gov.uk/courts-tribunals/court-of-protection**) together with supporting information and application and hearing fee.

Urgent or emergency applications to the court

There is an urgent application procedure that can be used if there is a serious risk that an individual may suffer serious loss or harm, for example applications about urgent medical treatment, or to execute a will or financial transaction when the individual's life expectancy is very short, or to prevent an individual from being removed from their current home (further information can be found at **www.gov.uk/emergency-court-of-protection**).

C.5   PARTIES

For cases concerning major decisions relating to medical treatment, the NHS body responsible for the patient's care will usually make the application.

Where the concern arises from non-medical social welfare issues, the relevant local authority should usually make the application. However, it is also possible for applications to be brought by persons properly concerned as to the welfare of the person, including family members.

For decisions about the property and affairs of someone who lacks capacity to manage their own affairs, the applicant will usually be the person who needs specific authority from the court to deal with the individual's money or property (for example, family carer).

In every case the court must consider whether it should make one of a range of directions to secure the participation of P in the proceedings. Where P is a party to the proceedings, a litigation friend must be appointed to represent P (for the role of the Official Solicitor as

---

[7]   MCA 2005, s.61.

[8]   Office of the Public Guardian (2007) *Mental Capacity Act 2005 Code of Practice*, Chapter 15, available at **www.gov.uk/government/publications/mental-capacity-act-code-of-practice**.

litigation friend, see **Appendix E**); if a suitable panel is set up, it may in due course also be possible for the court to appoint an accredited legal representative to act for P without a litigation friend.

C.6 THE CONDUCT OF PROCEEDINGS

The Court of Protection has its own set of procedural rules and Practice Directions, which set down in considerable detail the conduct of proceedings before it (see **www.gov.uk/courts-tribunals/court-of-protection**). The rules were the subject of substantial amendment in 2015,[9] and are likely to be further revised during the course of 2016.

Where relevant, the court will consider the question of permission, either on paper or at an oral hearing. If permission is granted (or is not needed), directions will then be made for the future conduct of the application. In every case the court is now required to consider whether it should make one of a range of directions to secure the participation of P in the proceedings.

In personal welfare applications, these directions will usually include directions for the obtaining of suitable expert reports from independent psychiatrists and/or social workers. Assuming that there is sufficient evidence of a lack of capacity to give it jurisdiction, the court can make interim declarations as to the best interests of the person to whom the application relates, and will often make such declarations relating to contact, residence and care arrangements.

Further applications can be made during the course of proceedings (and do not usually require the permission of the court). Depending on their nature, they will either be determined on the papers or at an oral hearing.

C.7 APPEALS

The Court of Protection is divided into three tiers with appeals lying from a judge in a lower tier to a judge in a higher tier. An appeal will lie to the Court of Appeal from a decision of a Tier 3 judge, or where the decision of the judge itself a decision made upon appeal. In all cases (except where the appeal is against committal to prison for contempt), an appeal requires permission.

---

[9] By the Court of Protection (Amendment) Rules 2015, SI 2015/548.

APPENDIX D

Court of Protection: Practice Direction 9E – Applications Relating to Serious Medical Treatment

[This practice direction supplements Part 9 of the Court of Protection Rules 2007]

General

1. Rule 71 enables a practice direction to make additional or different provision in relation to specified applications.

Applications to which this practice direction applies

2. This practice direction sets out the procedure to be followed where the application concerns serious medical treatment in relation to P.

Meaning of 'serious medical treatment' in relation to the Rules and this practice direction

3. Serious medical treatment means treatment which involves providing, withdrawing or withholding treatment in circumstances where:

    (a) in a case where a single treatment is being proposed, there is a fine balance between its benefits to P and the burdens and risks it is likely to entail for him;

    (b) in a case where there is a choice of treatments, a decision as to which one to use is finely balanced; or

    (c) the treatment, procedure or investigation proposed would be likely to involve serious consequences for P.

4. "Serious consequences" are those which could have a serious impact on P, either from the effects of the treatment, procedure or investigation itself or its wider implications. This may include treatments, procedures or investigations which:

    (a) cause, or may cause, serious and prolonged pain, distress or side effects;

    (b) have potentially major consequences for P; or

    (c) have a serious impact on P's future life choices.

Matters which should be brought to the court

5. Cases involving any of the following decisions should be regarded as serious medical treatment for the purpose of the Rules and this practice direction, and should be brought to the court:

    (a)   decisions about the proposed withholding or withdrawal of artificial nutrition and hydration from a person in a permanent vegetative state or a minimally conscious state;

    (b)   cases involving organ or bone marrow donation by a person who lacks capacity to consent; and

    (c)   cases involving non-therapeutic sterilisation of a person who lacks capacity to consent.

6.   Examples of serious medical treatment may include:

    (a)   certain terminations of pregnancy in relation to a person who lacks capacity to consent to such a procedure;

    (b)   a medical procedure performed on a person who lacks capacity to consent to it, where the procedure is for the purpose of a donation to another person;

    (c)   a medical procedure or treatment to be carried out on a person who lacks capacity to consent to it, where that procedure or treatment must be carried out using a degree of force to restrain the person concerned;

    (d)   an experimental or innovative treatment for the benefit of a person who lacks capacity to consent to such treatment; and

    (e)   a case involving an ethical dilemma in an untested area.

7.   There may be other procedures or treatments not contained in the list in paragraphs 5 and 6 above which can be regarded as serious medical treatment. Whether or not a procedure is regarded as serious medical treatment will depend on the circumstances and the consequences for the patient.

Consultation with the Official Solicitor

8.   Members of the Official Solicitor's staff are prepared to discuss applications in relation to serious medical treatment before an application is made. Any enquiries about adult medical and welfare cases should be addressed to a senior healthcare lawyer at the Office of the Official Solicitor, Victory House, 30 to 34 Kingsway, London WC2B 6EX, telephone 020 3681 2751, fax 020 3681 2762, email: enquiries@offsol.gsi.gov.uk.

Parties to proceedings

9.   The person bringing the application will always be a party to proceedings, as will a respondent named in the application form who files an acknowledgment of service.[1] In cases involving issues as to serious medical treatment, an organisation which is, or will be, responsible for providing clinical or caring services to P should usually be named as a respondent in the application form (where it is not already the applicant in the proceedings).

(Practice direction B accompanying Part 9 sets out the persons who are to be notified that an application form has been issued.)

10.   The court will consider whether anyone not already a party should be joined as a party to the proceedings. Other persons with sufficient interest may apply to be joined as parties to the proceedings[2] and the court has a duty to identify at as early a stage as possible who the parties to the proceedings should be.[3]

---

[1]   Rule 73(1).
[2]   Rule 75.
[3]   Rule 5(2)(b)(ii).

Allocation of the case

11. Where an application is made to the court in relation to:

    (a)   the lawfulness of withholding or withdrawing artificial nutrition and hydration from a person in a permanent vegetative state, or a minimally conscious state; or

    (b)   a case involving an ethical dilemma in an untested area,

    the proceedings (including permission, the giving of any directions, and any hearing) must be conducted by the President of the Court of Protection or by another judge nominated by the President.

12. Where an application is made to the court in relation to serious medical treatment (other than that outlined in paragraph 11) the proceedings (including permission, the giving of any directions, and any hearing) must be conducted by a judge of the court who has been nominated as such by virtue of section 46(2)(a) to (c) of the Act (i.e. the President of the Family Division, the Chancellor or a puisne judge of the High Court).

Matters to be considered at the first directions hearing

13. Unless the matter is one which needs to be disposed of urgently, the court will list it for a first directions hearing.

    (Practice direction B accompanying Part 10 sets out the procedure to be followed for urgent applications.)

14. The court may give such directions as it considers appropriate. If the court has not already done so, it should in particular consider whether to do any or all of the following at the first directions hearing:

    (a)   decide whether P should be joined as party to the proceedings, and give directions to that effect;

    (b)   if P is to be joined as a party to the proceedings, decide whether the Official Solicitor should be invited to act as a litigation friend or whether some other person should be appointed as a litigation friend;

    (c)   identify anyone else who has been notified of the proceedings and who has filed an acknowledgment and applied to be joined as a party to proceedings, and consider that application; and

    (d)   set a timetable for the proceedings including, where possible, a date for the final hearing.

15. The court should also consider whether to give any of the other directions listed in rule 85(2).

16. The court will ordinarily make an order pursuant to rule 92 that any hearing shall be held in public, with restrictions to be imposed in relation to publication of information about the proceedings.

Declarations

17. Where a declaration is needed, the order sought should be in the following or similar terms:

    •   That P lacks capacity to make a decision in relation to the (proposed medical treatment or procedure).

        E.g. 'That P lacks capacity to make a decision in relation to sterilisation by vasectomy'; and

    •   That, having regard to the best interests of P, it is lawful for the (proposed medical treatment or procedure) to be carried out by (proposed healthcare provider).

18. Where the application is for the withdrawal of life-sustaining treatment, the order sought should be in the following or similar terms:

- That P lacks capacity to consent to continued life-sustaining treatment measures (and specify what these are); and
- That, having regard to the best interests of P, it is lawful for (name of healthcare provider) to withdraw the life-sustaining treatment from P.

APPENDIX E

The Official Solicitor

The need for representation of a vulnerable person who may be unable to conduct legal proceedings for themselves has long been recognised by the state. The Office of Official Solicitor to the Senior Courts dates back to 1875. The Official Solicitor is an office holder of the Senior Court appointed by the Lord Chancellor under the Senior Courts Act 1981, s.90. The duties of the Official Solicitor are carried out pursuant to statute, rules of court, the direction of the Lord Chancellor, at common law, or in accordance with established practice.

For present purposes, the most relevant function of the Office of the Official Solicitor is to act where there is no other suitable person (such as an appropriate relative or friend) willing and able to act on behalf of someone who is vulnerable because of their age (children under 18) or because of lack of mental capacity, or where for some other reason failure to act would result in an injustice. The Official Solicitor's role in relation to children is beyond the scope of this book, apart from those cases where the Official Solicitor agrees to act for young people whose lack of capacity is likely to persist beyond their 18th birthday. In relation to adults, the work of the Office of the Official Solicitor includes:

- acting as last resort litigation friend, and in some cases solicitor, for adults who lack the mental capacity to conduct proceedings in a wide range of court proceedings (known as 'P in Court of Protection proceedings, and as 'protected parties' in proceedings in other courts) (see further **Chapter 8**);
- acting as litigation friend of a vulnerable adult where the Family Division of the High Court is being invited to exercise its inherent jurisdiction;
- acting as or appointing counsel to act as advocate to the court to provide advice and assistance to the court;
- making enquiries on behalf of the court in order to assist the court to do justice between the parties (a so-called *Harbin* v. *Masterman* enquiry);[1]
- acting as last resort administrator of estates and trustee;
- acting as last resort financial deputy.

Litigation friend of last resort

Before the Official Solicitor accepts an appointment as litigation friend, he must be satisfied that:

- there is satisfactory evidence (or the court has made a finding) that the party (or intended party) lacks capacity to conduct the proceedings (or in Court of Protection proceedings evidence or a finding with regard to P's lack of relevant decision making capacity);
- on the basis of the information available to him, there is no one else suitable and willing to act as litigation friend;
- there is satisfactory security for the costs of legal representation of the protected party or P or the case falls in one of the classes in which, exceptionally, he funds the litigation services out of, or partially out of, his budget, in accordance with long standing practice.

---

[1] After the decision in *Harbin* v. *Masterman* [1896] 1 Ch 351.

If there is a conflict in the evidence relating to an adult party's capacity to conduct the proceedings then the Official Solicitor will not accept appointment unless or until that conflict is resolved either by the experts arriving at a consensus, or by determination of the court. When the Official Solicitor acts as litigation friend, he fulfils the same role as any other person appointed to act as litigation friend.

It has always been accepted that the Official Solicitor's duty when acting as litigation friend is the same as any other litigation friend: i.e. fairly and competently to conduct the proceedings in the best interests of the protected party (or 'P' if the proceedings are taking place in the Court of Protection).

The types of court proceedings in which the Official Solicitor may be invited to act include:

- Disputes about the personal welfare of P (such as residence or contact matters).
- Cases involving decisions about serious medical treatment or disputes about health-care, examples would include the withdrawal of treatment from a person in a permanent vegetative state, or the validity of an advance decision to refuse treatment (see **Appendix D** for the Court of Protection Practice Direction 9E).
- Applications to the Court of Protection regarding P's property and affairs: examples would include applications to make gifts or a statutory will.
- Family proceedings where a party to those proceedings is a protected party. Examples of family cases would include divorce, nullity of marriage, judicial separation, dissolution or nullity of a civil partnership, care, placement or adoption proceedings, private law children proceedings, or forced marriage protection order proceedings.
- Other civil proceedings, including personal injury claims, possession actions, applications in connection with the ownership of property, claims for appropriate provision from a deceased's estate, and applications to displace a nearest relative under MHA 1983.

The Official Solicitor does not seek to recover his costs of being litigation friend. But he generally makes his involvement in proceedings conditional upon his costs of obtaining or providing legal services to the party for whom he is acting as litigation friend being secured from external sources. These may include:

- legal aid where the party is eligible for public funding;
- the party's own funds where either the party has financial capacity or the Court of Protection has given the Official Solicitor authority to recover the costs from the party;
- a conditional fee agreement (e.g. in personal injury claims);
- an undertaking from another party to pay his costs;
- the funds in dispute where the case involves a trust or estate.

There is nothing to prevent the Official Solicitor seeking his costs in the same way as any other successful litigant. In medical treatment cases, the Official Solicitor will usually ask for an order that the applicant pays half of his costs.

Provision is made as to the costs of the Official Solicitor in proceedings in respect of a person's property and affairs before the Court of Protection in Part 19 of the Court of Protection Rules 2007 and in particular rule 156, which provides that the general rule in such proceedings is that the costs of the proceedings shall be paid by the person or charged to his estate.

APPENDIX F

Certificate as to capacity to conduct proceedings (Official Solicitor)

TO THE ASSESSOR:

The attached certificate of capacity to conduct proceedings is a standard form of report for recording the assessment of the mental capacity of an adult to conduct their own proceedings ('litigation capacity') where that adult is a party or intended party to proceedings in the Family Court, the High Court, a county court or the Court of Appeal. 'Conducting one's own proceedings' includes both conducting the proceedings through solicitors and conducting them as a litigant in person ('LIP').

This assessment of capacity is being requested because there is concern that the party or intended party to the proceedings lacks litigation capacity (within the meaning of the Mental Capacity Act 2005) and is therefore a 'protected party'.

Part 15 of the Family Procedure Rules 2010 and Part 21 of the Civil Procedure Rules 1998 provide that a protected party must have a litigation friend to conduct the proceedings on that party's behalf. The litigation friend, rather than the protected party, is responsible for making the decisions about the conduct of the proceedings.

The certificate is *not* intended for any purpose other than the assessment of whether the person lacks litigation capacity in relevant proceedings.

Before you carry out your assessment and complete the certificate you should:

(1) Read the **guidance notes** attached.
(2) Read the **description of the proceedings** provided at part 3 of the certificate and/or in the accompanying letter of instruction.
(3) Consider chapter 3 of the Mental Capacity Act 2005, **Code of Practice**, issued by the Lord Chancellor in accordance with sections 42 and 43 of the Act.

The BMA/Law Society Legal Handbook, *Assessment of Mental Capacity – A Practical Guide for Doctors and Lawyers*, 3rd edition, pp 15–17 also contains useful guidance.

Your opinion:

(4) If it is your opinion that the person does lack litigation capacity please complete all 8 parts of the certificate; in such cases the certificate must identify what the impairment of, or disturbance in the functioning of the person's mind or brain is *and* why it causes the person to be unable to make the decisions necessary to conduct of those proceedings:

    (a) please note that the assessment is by reference to the proceedings as a whole not by reference to each step in the conduct of the proceedings
    (b) please consider if there are practicable steps which could be taken to enable the person to acquire capacity to conduct the proceedings.

(5) If it is your opinion that the person does have litigation capacity, there is no need for you to, and you should not, give grounds for that opinion.

Completing the certificate

Part 3 ("the information"):

(6) The description of the proceedings given to you should include the person's role in the proceedings, a summary of the issues involved (not simply the type of case), state whether the proceedings are particularly complex and what are the perceived difficulties in the person concerned making decisions about the conduct of the proceedings.

(7) If a person is represented by a solicitor, the solicitor will usually be the first to recognise or suspect that the person (their client) may lack litigation capacity. This is because the solicitor is in a unique position to make an assessment about their client's litigation capacity, as it is the solicitor who explains the information (including legal advice) relevant to the making of the decisions involved in conducting the proceedings.

(8) If a person is a LIP (that is, without legal representation), that person will often be at a disadvantage in the conduct of the proceedings but that does not of itself give rise to a lack of litigation capacity. There is a range of reasons why litigants act in person including the lack of free or affordable representation or simply that acting in person is the person's choice.

(9) Further:

  (a) the legal representative for any other party is under a professional duty to ensure that an unrepresented party is aware of what is happening during any hearing;

  (b) the judge will generally assist an unrepresented party by explaining procedural issues;

  (c) a LIP may be permitted by the court to attend a hearing with a 'McKenzie friend' who may

  - provide moral support to the LIP;
  - take notes;
  - help with case papers;
  - quietly give advice on any aspect of the conduct of the case;

  (d) the LIP may be assisted out of court by taking advice from a lawyer or from other professional advisors or from an advice organisation.

Part 7 ("the person's views")

(10) A party or intended party is entitled to dispute any opinion that they lack litigation capacity. A protected party loses their autonomy to make decisions about the conduct of the proceedings, and the decisions made by the litigation friend about conduct of the proceedings may not always accord with the party's own wishes and feelings.

(11) When completing part 7 you should therefore include any views expressed by the person themself about their litigation capacity.

PLEASE READ THESE NOTES BEFORE COMPLETING THE CERTIFICATE

GUIDANCE NOTES

Where a party or intended party lacks mental capacity (within the meaning of the Mental Capacity Act 2005) to conduct their own proceedings ('litigation capacity'), their interests must be protected by the appointment of a 'litigation friend' who will conduct the proceedings on their behalf.

The Official Solicitor is usually approached, as a last resort, in cases where there is no other suitable person who is willing to act.

Medical or psychological evidence is usually required to establish whether the person lacks mental capacity

A person who lacks litigation capacity is known as a 'protected party' within the proceedings.

The Mental Capacity Act 2005 provides

Section 2   People who lack capacity

(1)   For the purposes of this Act, a person lacks capacity in relation to a matter if at the material time he is unable to make a decision for himself in relation to the matter because of an impairment of, or a disturbance in the functioning of, the mind or brain.

(2)   It does not matter whether the impairment or disturbance is permanent or temporary.

(3)   A lack of capacity cannot be established merely by reference to –

    (a)   a person's age or appearance, or

    (b)   a condition of his, or an aspect of his behaviour, which might lead others to make unjustified assumptions about his capacity.

(4)   In proceedings under this Act or any other enactment, any question whether a person lacks capacity within the meaning of this Act must be decided on the balance of probabilities.

(5)   No power which a person ("D") may exercise under this Act –

    (a)   in relation to a person who lacks capacity, or

    (b)   where D reasonably thinks that a person lacks capacity,

is exercisable in relation to a person under 16.

(6)   Subsection (5) is subject to section 18(3).

Section 3   Inability to make decisions

(1)   For the purposes of section 2, a person is unable to make a decision for himself if he is unable –

    (a)   to understand the information relevant to the decision,

    (b)   to retain that information,

    (c)   to use or weigh that information as part of the process of making the decision, or

    (d)   to communicate his decision (whether by talking, using sign language or any other means).

(2)   A person is not to be regarded as unable to understand the information relevant to a decision if he is able to understand an explanation of it given to him in a way that is appropriate to his circumstances (using simple language, visual aids or any other means).

(3)   The fact that a person is able to retain the information relevant to a decision for a short period only does not prevent him from being regarded as able to make the decision.

(4)   The information relevant to a decision includes information about the reasonably foreseeable consequences of –

    (a)   deciding one way or another, or

    (b)   failing to make the decision.

So it can be seen that the Act contains a two-part test of capacity with diagnostic and functional elements:

(1)   Is there an impairment of, or disturbance in the functioning of, the person's mind or brain? and

(2)   Is the person is unable to make a decision for himself in relation to the matter *because of* an impairment of, or a disturbance in the functioning of, the mind or brain.

Please refer to the information set out in your instructions and/or the first box at question 3 of the certificate and any accompanying letter for details of the proceedings and relevant information about the circumstances of the person.

The assessment of capacity must be based on the party's or intended party's ability to conduct the specific proceedings and not other proceedings, or on their ability to make decisions in general. It does not matter whether the impairment or disturbance is permanent or temporary but The fact that a person is able to retain the information relevant to a decision for a short period only does not prevent him from being regarded as able to make the decision.

To have litigation capacity the party or intended party must be able to understand the information relevant to the decisions arising during the course of the proceedings, retain that information, use or weigh that information as part of the process of making the decisions, and to communicate his decision (whether by talking, using sign language or any other means).

The assessment of capacity to conduct proceedings may depend on the nature of the proceedings in train or in contemplation. The test to be applied is whether the party or intended party to legal proceedings is capable of understanding, with the assistance of such proper explanation from legal advisors and experts in other disciplines as the case may require, the issues on which their consent or decision is likely to be necessary in the course of those proceedings. Some of the matters to be considered in assessing a party's or intended party's litigation capacity are as follows:

(a)   the party or intended party would need to understand how the proceedings were to be funded;

(b)   they would need to know about the chances of not succeeding and the risk of an adverse order as to costs;

(c)   they would need to have capacity to make the sort of decisions that arise in litigation;

(d)   capacity to conduct the proceedings would include the capacity to give proper instructions for and to approve the particulars of claim, and to approve a compromise.

(e)   for a party or intended party to have capacity to approve a compromise, they would need insight into the compromise, an ability to instruct solicitors to advise them on it, and an understanding of their advice and an ability to weigh their advice.

A lack of capacity cannot be established merely because of a person's age or appearance or his condition or an aspect of his behaviour.

When assessing capacity, practitioners must have regard to the statutory principles set out in section 1(2), (3), and (4) of the Mental Capacity Act 2005 and to the Mental Capacity Act 2005 Code of Practice (see above), in particular its Chapters 2, 3 and 4.

The relevant statutory principles are that:

Section 1 . . .

(2)   A person must be assumed to have capacity unless it is established that he lacks capacity.

(3)   A person is not be treated as unable to make a decision unless all practicable steps to help him to do so have been taken without success.

(4)   A person is not to be treated as unable to make a decision merely because he makes an unwise decision.

The Code of Practice is available on line at: **www.gov.uk/government/collections/mental-capacity-act-making-decisions**.

If it is your opinion that the person does have capacity to conduct the proceedings, there is no need for you to give grounds for that opinion. However, if you are of the opinion that the person lacks capacity to conduct the proceedings, the Official Solicitor's certificate requires you to state in paragraphs 2 and 3 the grounds for that opinion.

This certificate relates only to the specific proceedings in which the party is, or intended party will be involved. A separate certificate may be required if the person is a party or intended party to any other proceedings.

Separate considerations apply to any question as to whether the person is subject to compulsory detention under the Mental Health Act 1983: in some cases the person concerned is liable to compulsory detention but may have litigation capacity, and in many cases the person concerned lacks litigation capacity but is not liable to compulsory detention.

Official Solicitor

2014

[Ref:]

CERTIFICATE AS TO CAPACITY
TO CONDUCT PROCEEDINGS

You should read the whole of this form and the attached notes for guidance before completing this form.
Please answer all questions as fully as you can.

Name of person concerned:

Date of birth:

The proceedings are .... **(and see paragraph 3 below)**

Insert your full name and address (including postcode) Give your professional Qualifications	**I** **of**
For a definition of 'a person who lacks capacity' see note 2 attached	1. Nature of your professional relationship with the person concerned: ▪ I have acted as practitioner for the person concerned since .... and last assessed him/her on .... or ▪ I assessed the person concerned on .... following a referral from .... **AND in my opinion**... ▪ **is capable** (within the meaning of the Mental Capacity Act 2005) of conducting the proceedings* or ▪ **lacks capacity** (within the meaning of the Mental Capacity Act 2005) to conduct the proceedings* (**strike through as appropriate**) **If in your opinion** .... **is a person who lacks capacity to conduct the proceedings please answer questions 2-8 below**

2. The person concerned has the following impairment of, or disturbance in the functioning of, the mind or brain (see note 2):

> [blank box]

this has lasted since:...

3. As a result, the person concerned is incapable of conducting the proceedings described below and/or in the attached letter of instructions.

> [blank box]

because (please tick as many boxes as apply)

☐   the person is unable to understand the following relevant information (please give details):

> [blank box]

and/or

☐   the person is unable to retain that information (please give details)

> [blank box]

and/or

☐ the person is unable to use or weigh the following information as part of the process of making the decisions in the conduct of the proceedings:

or

☐ for cases where the person can in fact understand, retain and use / weigh the information the person is unable to communicate their decisions by any means at all (please give details):

4. Do you consider that the person concerned might regain or develop capacity to conduct the proceedings in the future -

☐ Yes - please state why and give an indication of when this might happen

☐ No - please state why

5. Is the person concerned able to discuss the proceedings with my representative or with a solicitor instructed by me?

☐ YES ☐ NO

Please comment

6.   If so, is such discussion likely to affect the person detrimentally and if so, in what way?

☐ YES   ☐ NO

Please comment

```



```

7.   Has the person concerned made you aware of any views in relation to the proceedings and / or in relation to their capacity to conduct the proceedings?

```



```

8.   Any additional comments

```



```

Statement of Truth:

I confirm that insofar as the facts stated in this certificate are within my own knowledge I have made clear which they are and I believe them to be true and that the opinions I have expressed represent my true professional opinion.

Signed   _____

Dated   _____

COP3 Assessment of Capacity and Guidance Notes

Court of Protection

Assessment of capacity

COP
3
12.13

For office use only
Date received
Case no.

Full name of person to whom the application relates
(this is the name of the person who lacks, or is alleged to lack, capacity)

Please read first

- If you are applying to start proceedings with the court you must file this form with your COP1 application form. The assessment must contain current information.

- You must complete Part A of this form.

- You then need to provide the form with Part A completed to the practitioner who will complete Part B. The practitioner will return the form to you or your solicitor for filing with the court.

- The practitioner may be a registered:

  - medical practitioner, for example the GP of the person to whom the application relates;

  - psychiatrist

  - approved mental health professional

  - social worker

  - psychologist

  - nurse, or

  - occupational therapist

  who has examined and assessed the capacity of the person to whom the application relates. In some circumstances it might be appropriate for a registered therapist, such as a speech therapist or occupational therapist, to complete the form.

- When the form has been completed, its contents will be confidential to the court and those authorised by the court to see it, such as parties to the proceedings.

- Please continue on a separate sheet of paper if you need more space to answer a question. Write your name, the name and date of birth of the person to whom the application relates, and number of the question you are answering on each separate sheet.

- There are additional guidance notes at the end of this form.

- If you need help completing this form please check the website, www.gov.uk/court-of-protection, for further guidance or information, or contact Court Enquiry Service on 0300 456 4600 or courtofprotectionenquiries@hmcts.gsi.gov.uk

- Court of Protection staff cannot give legal advice. If you need legal advice please contact a solicitor.

- This form has been prepared in consultation with the British Medical Association, the Royal College of Physicians, Royal College of Psychiatrists and the Department of Health.

1

© Crown Copyright 2013

Part A - To be completed by the applicant

Section 1 - Your details (the applicant)

1.1 Your details ☐ Mr. ☐ Mrs. ☐ Miss ☐ Ms. ☐ Other _____

First name

Middle name(s)

Last name

1.2 Address (including postcode)

Telephone no.	Daytime	
	Evening	
	Mobile	

E-mail address

1.3 Is a solicitor representing you? ☐ Yes ☐ No

If Yes, please give the solicitor's details.

Name

Address (including postcode)

| Telephone no. | | Fax no. | |

DX no.

E-mail address

1.4 To which address should the practitioner return the form when they have completed Section 2?

☐ Your address

☐ Solicitor's address

☐ Other address (please provide details)

2

Section 2 - The person to whom the application relates (the person to be assessed by the practitioner)

2.1   ☐ Mr.   ☐ Mrs.   ☐ Miss   ☐ Ms.   ☐ Other _____

First name

Middle name(s)

Last name

Address (including postcode)

Telephone no.

Date of birth   ☐ Male   ☐ Female

Section 3 - About the application

3.1   Please state the matter you are asking the court to decide. **(see note 1)**

3.2   What order are you asking the court to make?

3.3   How would the order benefit the person to whom the application relates?

3.4   What is your relationship or connection to the person to whom the application relates?

3

Section 4 - Further information

Please provide any further information about the circumstances of the person to whom the application relates that would be useful to the practitioner in assessing his or her capacity to make any decision(s) that is the subject of your application. **(see note 2)**

Now read note 3 about what you need to do next.

Part B - To be completed by the practitioner

Section 5 - Your details (the practitioner)

5.1   ☐ Mr.   ☐ Mrs.   ☐ Miss   ☐ Ms.   ☐ Dr.   ☐ Other _____

First name

Middle name(s)

Last name

Address (including postcode)

Telephone no.

E-mail address

5.2   Nature of your professional relationship with the person to whom the application relates (For example, social worker or general practitioner (GP))

5.3   Please state your professional qualifications and practial experience with particular reference to making assessments of capacity in accordance with the Mental Capacity Act 2005 and associated Code of Practice.

5

If there is information that you do not wish to provide in this form because of its sensitive nature you can provide the information directly to the court.

6.1   Are you providing any sensitive information separately to the court?   ☐Yes   ☐No

Please provide it in writing to:
        Court of Protection
        PO Box 70185
        First Avenue House
        42-49 High Holborn
        London WC1A 9JA

        DX 160013
        Kingsway 7

Please include your name and contact details, and the name, address and date of birth of the person to whom the application relates on any information you provide separately to the court.

Section 7 - Assessment of capacity

7.1   The person to whom the application relates has the following impairment of, or disturbance in the functioning of, the mind or brain. Where this impairment or disturbance arises out of a specific diagnosis, please set out the diagnosis or diagnoses here: **(see note 4)**

This has lasted since:

As a result, the person is unable to make a decision for themselves in relation to the following matter(s) in question:

6

7.2 The person to whom the application relates is unable to make a decision in relation to the relevant matter because: **(see note 5)**

☐ he or she is unable to understand the following relevant information (please give details);

```
```

and/or

☐ he or she is unable to retain the following relevant information (please give details);

```
```

and/or

☐ he or she is unable to use or weigh the following relevant information as part of the process of making the decision(s) (please give details);

```
```

and/or

☐ is unable to communicate his or her decision(s) by any means at all (please give details).

```
```

7

7.3   My opinion is based on the following evidence of a lack of capacity:

```




```

7.4   Please answer either (a) **or** (b).

(a) I have acted as a practitioner for the person to whom the application

relates since [ ][ ][ ][ ][ ][ ][ ]   and last assessed

him or her on [ ][ ][ ][ ][ ][ ][ ]

(b) I assessed the person to whom the application

relates on [ ][ ][ ][ ][ ][ ][ ]

following a referral from:

```




```

8

7.5 Has the person to whom this application relates made you aware of any views they have in relation to the relevant matter? ☐Yes ☐No

If Yes, please give details.

7.6 Do you consider there is a prospect that the person to whom the application relates might regain or acquire capacity in the future in respect of the decision to which the application relates? **(see note 6)**

☐ Yes – please state why and give an indication of when this might happen.

☐ No – please state why.

7.7 Are you aware of anyone who holds a different view regarding the capacity of the person to whom the application relates? ☐Yes ☐No

If Yes, please give details.

9

7.8   Do you, your family or friends have any interest (financial or otherwise) in any matter concerning the person to whom the application relates?   ☐Yes   ☐No

If Yes, please give details.

7.9   Do you have any general comments or any other recommendations for future care? **(see note 7)**

Signed

Name   **Date**

Now read note 8 about what you need to do next.

10

299

Guidance notes

Note 1

About the application

These questions are repeated on the COP1 application form. Please copy your answers from the COP1 form so that the information on both forms is the same.

Note 2

Further information

Please provide any further information about the circumstances of the person to whom the application relates that would be relevant in assessing their capacity. For example, if your application relates to property and financial affairs, it would be useful for the practitioner to know the general financial circumstances of the person concerned. This information will help the practitioner evaluate the decision-making responsibility of the person to whom the application relates and may help to inform the practitioner's view on whether that person can make the decision(s) in question.

Note 3

What you need to do next

Please provide this form to the practitioner who will complete Part B.

The practitioner will return the form to you or your solicitor when they have completed Part B. You will then need to file the form with the court together with the COP1 application form and any other information the court requires. See note 8 on the COP1 form for further information.

Note 4

Assessing capacity

For the purpose of the Mental Capacity Act 2005 a person lacks capacity if, at the time a decision needs to be made, he or she is unable to make or communicate the decision because of an impairment of, or a disturbance in the functioning of, the mind or brain.

The Act contains a two-stage test of capacity:

1. Is there an impairment of, or disturbance in the functioning of, the person's mind or brain?

2. If so, is the impairment or disturbance sufficient that the person lacks the capacity to make a decision in relation to the matter in question?

Please refer to Part A of this form where the applicant has set out details of the application and relevant information about the circumstances of the person to whom the application relates. In particular, section 3.1 sets out the matter the applicant is asking the court to decide.

The assessment of capacity must be based on the person's ability to make a decision in relation to the relevant matter, and not their ability to make decisions in general. It does not matter therefore if the lack of capacity is temporary, if the person retains the capacity to make other decisions, or if the person's capacity fluctuates.

Under the Act, a person is regarded as being unable to make a decision if they cannot:

- understand information about the decision to be made;

- retain that information;

- use or weigh the information as part of the decision-making process; or

- communicate the decision (by any means).

A lack of capacity cannot be established merely by reference to a person's age or appearance or to a particular condition or an aspect of behaviour. A person is not to be treated as being unable to make a decision merely because they have made an unwise decision.

The test of capacity is not the same as the test for detention and treatment under the Mental Health Act 1983. Many people covered by the Mental Health Act have the capacity to make decisions for themselves. On the other hand, most people who lack capacity to make decisions will never be affected by the Mental Health Act.

Practitioners are required to have regard to the Mental Capacity Act 2005 Code of Practice. The Code of Practice is available online at www.gov.uk/court-of-protection Hard copies are available from The Stationery Office (TSO), for a fee, by:

- phoning 0870 600 5522;

- emailing customerservices@tso.co.uk; or

- ordering online at www.tsoshop.co.uk.

For further advice please see (for example):

- Making Decisions: A guide for people who work in health and social care (2nd edition), Mental Capacity Implementation Programme, 2007.

- Assessment of Mental Capacity: Guidance for Doctors and Lawyers (2nd edition), British Medical Association and Law Society (London: BMJ Books, 2004)

11

300

Note 5

Capacity to make the decision in question

Please give your opinion of the nature of the lack of capacity and the grounds on which this is based. This requires a diagnosis and a statement giving clear evidence that the person to whom the application relates lacks capacity to make the decision(s) relevant to the application. It is important that the evidence of lack of capacity shows how this prevents the person concerned from being able to take decision(s).

Note 6

Prospect of regaining or acquiring capacity

When reaching any decision the court must apply the principles set out in the Act and in particular must make a determination that is in the best interests of the person to whom the application relates. It would therefore assist the court if you could indicate whether the person to whom the application relates is likely to regain or acquire capacity sufficiently to be able to make decisions in relation to the relevant matter.

Note 7

General comments

The court may make any order it considers appropriate even if that order is not specified in the application form. Where possible, the court will make a one-off decision rather than appointing a deputy with on-going decision making power. If you think that an order other than the one being sought by the applicant would be in the best interests of the person to whom the application relates, please give details including your reasons.

Note 8

What you need to do next

Please return the completed form to the applicant or their solicitor, as specified in section 1.4. You are advised to keep a copy for your records.

12

GUIDANCE NOTES

Note 1   About the application

These questions are repeated on the COP1 application form. Please copy your answers from the COP1 form so that the information on both forms is the same.

Note 2   Further information

Please provide any further information about the circumstances of the person to whom the application relates that would be relevant in assessing their capacity. For example, if your application relates to property and financial affairs, it would be useful for the practitioner to know the general financial circumstances of the person concerned. This information will help the practitioner evaluate the decision-making responsibility of the person to whom the application relates and may help to inform the practitioner's view on whether that person can make the decision(s) in question.

Note 3   What you need to do next

Please provide this form to the practitioner who will complete Part B. The practitioner will return the form to you or your solicitor when they have completed Part B. You will then need to file the form with the court together with the COP1 application form and any other information the court requires. See note 8 on the COP1 form for further information.

Note 4   Assessing capacity

For the purpose of the Mental Capacity Act 2005 a person lacks capacity if, at the time a decision needs to be made, he or she is unable to make or communicate the decision because of an impairment of, or a disturbance in the functioning of, the mind or brain.

The Act contains a two-stage test of capacity:

1.   Is there an impairment of, or disturbance in the functioning of, the person's mind or brain?
2.   If so, is the impairment or disturbance sufficient that the person lacks the capacity to make a decision in relation to the matter in question?

Please refer to Part A of this form where the applicant has set out details of the application and relevant information about the circumstances of the person to whom the application relates. In particular, section 3.1 sets out the matter the applicant is asking the court to decide.

The assessment of capacity must be based on the person's ability to make a decision in relation to the relevant matter, and not their ability to make decisions in general. It does not matter therefore if the lack of capacity is temporary, if the person retains the capacity to make other decisions, or if the person's capacity fluctuates.

Under the Act, a person is regarded as being unable to make a decision if they cannot:

- understand information about the decision to be made;
- retain that information;
- use or weigh the information as part of the decision-making process; or
- communicate the decision (by any means).

A lack of capacity cannot be established merely by reference to a person's age or appearance or to a particular condition or an aspect of behaviour. A person is not to be treated as being unable to make a decision merely because they have made an unwise decision.

The test of capacity is not the same as the test for detention and treatment under the Mental Health Act 1983. Many people covered by the Mental Health Act have the capacity to make decisions for themselves. On the other hand, most people who lack capacity to make decisions will never be affected by the Mental Health Act.

Practitioners are required to have regard to the Mental Capacity Act 2005 Code of Practice. The Code of Practice is available online at www.gov.uk/court-of-protection. Hard copies are available from The Stationery Office (TSO), for a fee, by:

- phoning 0870 600 5522;
- emailing customerservices@tso.co.uk; or
- ordering online at www.tsoshop.co.uk.

For further advice please see (for example):

- Making Decisions: A guide for people who work in health and social care (2nd edition), Mental Capacity Implementation Programme, 2007.
- Assessment of Mental Capacity: Guidance for Doctors and Lawyers (2nd edition), British Medical Association and Law Society (London: BMJ Books, 2004)

Note 5   Capacity to make the decision in question

Please give your opinion of the nature of the lack of capacity and the grounds on which this is based. This requires a diagnosis and a statement giving clear evidence that the person to whom the application relates lacks capacity to make the decision(s) relevant to the application. It is important that the evidence of lack of capacity shows how this prevents the person concerned from being able to take decision(s).

Note 6   Prospect of regaining or acquiring capacity

When reaching any decision the court must apply the principles set out in the Act and in particular must make a determination that is in the best interests of the person to whom the application relates. It would therefore assist the court if you could indicate whether the person to whom the application relates is likely to regain or acquire capacity sufficiently to be able to make decisions in relation to the relevant matter.

Note 7   General comments

The court may make any order it considers appropriate even if that order is not specified in the application form. Where possible, the court will make a one-off decision rather than appointing a deputy with on-going decision making power. If you think that an order other than the one being sought by the applicant would be in the best interests of the person to whom the application relates, please give details including your reasons.

Note 8   What you need to do next

Please return the completed form to the applicant or their solicitor, as specified in section 1.4. You are advised to keep a copy for your records.

Sample letter to a GP requesting evidence of testamentary capacity

Note: The information that is relevant to the test of capacity depends on the subject area. This example uses testamentary capacity (discussed in **Chapter 6**). Please refer to the relevant chapter for details of the specific test of capacity to make other types of decisions.

SAMPLE LETTER

Dear Dr [*name*]

RE: CLIENT'S NAME [X] DATE OF BIRTH [. . .] AND SOLICITOR'S REFERENCE [. . .]

I am instructed on behalf of [X] to prepare a will on his/her behalf. As [X] is a patient of yours, he/she has agreed that I should write to ask that you provide a report on his/her mental capacity to make this will.

I attach evidence of [X]'s consent for you to disclose medical information for the purpose of this report. Please let me know the approximate cost of your report. However, if you are unable to undertake the assessment, I should be most grateful if you would let me know without delay.

Significance of a will

In the matter of a will or codicil for an elderly or infirm person the law requires that the matter is dealt with without delay. A will for an elderly person is a matter of great financial importance and dealing with this quickly provides a high degree of comfort to the testator. Undue delay can have substantial financial consequences for the testator as well as frustrating their final wishes.

The legal test for the capacity to make a will

There are four elements to the legal test for the capacity to make a valid will – known as the *Banks* v. *Goodfellow* test. This test requires that a person making a will has the ability to understand:

- The nature of the act of making a will and its effect. That is to say that he/she is giving away their estate on death to the specified beneficiaries;
- The extent of the estate. This does not involve an exact knowledge of the current value, but only a broad appreciation of the assets and their value;
- The possible claims of others. This is understanding those who, through ties of family, marriage or friendship, would normally be provided for in the will;

- When considering the ability to understand the above three elements the law requires that no disorder of the mind poisons his/her affections nor any delusions affect the terms of the will.

As you may be aware, a diagnosis of a mental disorder or illness does not necessarily mean that a person would lack the capacity to make a will. What is important is the degree to which the disorder or illness deprives them of capacity to understand on the basis of the test set out above. The law has consistently acknowledged the ability of a person to make a will, even where there might be a considerable decline in their ability, provided they retain the ability to satisfy the test set out above. You may wish to note that you need only show on the balance of probabilities whether [X] has or does not have testamentary capacity, in other words, that it is more likely than not.

For your assistance I have attached a sheet giving more material on the above test [*use the material in 6.7 to provide additional material to assist the doctor in understanding the Banks v Goodfellow test, tailored as necessary*].

Additional information

In order to assist your assessment of [X]'s understanding of the proposed will, I include:

- details of [X]'s estate
- a draft of the proposed will

both of which he/she has agreed that I may disclose to you.

[*Consider adding details of the relevant relatives as well, particularly if there is any concern that the doctor may not have knowledge of them.*]

Optional paragraphs:

I have little/no concern that [X] might not have capacity, but, because of [*other family factors and [X]'s age and health*] there is the distinct possibility of a challenge to the will after [X]'s death.

OR

My concern as to [X]'s capacity arises from the my observations which are [*list relevant information*].

The report

Your report should include:

1. Details of your professional qualifications and your experience of assessing capacity.
2. The length of time that [X] has been your patient.
3. Details of any impairment of, or disturbance in the functioning of, [X's] mind or brain and whether that has any effect on his/her ability to make decisions concerning the will. I would be grateful if you would also include reference to [X]'s physical state in so far as it may be relevant to any assessment.
4. A brief summary of any already diagnosed illness for which [X] is currently being treated together with details of any prescribed medication.
5. Where any formal tests of cognitive functions have been used, please give the score and provide a copy of the completed test score sheet.
6. Factors for and against capacity.
7. Your conclusion as to capacity to make a will, with reasons.

8. If you are unable to reach a conclusion as to capacity, you believe that the decision for or against capacity is finely balanced, or for any other reason you consider that it is essential to obtain a specialist psychiatric report, please include this in the report together with your reasons.

Please note that where comment or explanation is given by [X] of relevant points it would be helpful to cite his/her words verbatim. This will include any comments that may suggest that [X]'s reasoning process is in any way affected by the influence of family members or other third parties: it is particularly important that such comments are recorded verbatim if possible.

Optional paragraph

Given my concerns as to possible future challenges to the proposed will, it would assist considerably if you could act as one of the witnesses to the will and record and preserve your views as to [X]'s capacity at the time the will is executed (particularly with reference to any increase or decrease in capacity since your report). An additional fee will of course be payable if this is necessary.

If you require any further information or clarification on any points in this letter please do not hesitate to contact me.

Yours sincerely

[End of letter]

Addresses

British Medical Association

BMA House
Tavistock Square
London WC1H 9JP
Tel: 020 7387 4499 (switchboard)
Tel: 0300 123 1233 (BMA advisers)
http://bma.org.uk

Court Funds Office

Glasgow G58 1AB
Tel: 0300 0200 199
www.gov.uk/contact-court-funds-office

Court of Protection

PO Box 70185
First Avenue House
42–49 High Holborn
London WC1A 9JA
DX 160013 Kingsway 7
Tel: 0300 456 4600

The Law Society

113 Chancery Lane
London WC2A 1PL
DX 56 London/Chancery Lane
Tel: 020 7242 1222
Tel: 020 7320 5675 (Practice Advice Service)
www.lawsociety.org.uk

Office of the Public Guardian

PO Box 16185
Birmingham B12 2WH
Tel: 0300 456 0300

Official Solicitor and Public Trustee

Victory House
30–34 Kingsway
London WC2B 6EX
Tel: 020 3681 2751 (Health and Welfare)
Tel: 020 3681 2758 (Property and Affairs)

Royal Courts of Justice

The Strand
London WC2A 2LL
DX 44450 Strand
Tel: 020 7936 6000

The Clerk of the Rules (with responsibility for cases before judges of the Family Division sitting in the Court of Protection)
1st Mezzanine
Queen's Building
Royal Courts of Justice
London WC2A 2LL
Tel: 0207 947 6543

The Chancery Judge's Listing Officer (with responsibility for cases before judges of the Chancery Division sitting in the Court of Protection)
Room WG4
Royal Courts of Justice

London WC2A 2LL
Tel: 0207 947 7717

Solicitors Regulation Authority

The Cube
199 Wharfside Street

Birmingham B1 1RN
DX 720293 Birmingham 47
Tel: 0370 606 2555 (Contact Centre)
Tel: 0370 606 2577 (Professional Ethics help line)
www.sra.org.uk

Further reading

DRAFT LEGISLATION

- Draft Mental Incapacity Bill 2003 (Cm 5859-I), TSO.

LAW SOCIETY PRACTICE NOTES/GUIDANCE

Published online at **www.lawsociety.org.uk**:

- Lasting Powers of Attorney Practice Note (2011).
- Making Gifts of Assets Practice Note (2011).
- Wills and Inheritance Protocol (2013).
- Financial Abuse Practice Note, Law Society (2013).
- Meeting the needs of Vulnerable Clients Practice Note (2015).
- *Deprivation of Liberty: A Practical Guide* (2015).

BOOKS AND OTHER PUBLICATIONS

American Psychiatric Association (2013) *Diagnostic and Statistical Manual of Mental Disorders*, 5th edn (DSM-5), published online at **www.dsm5.org**.

Ashton, G (ed.) (2015) *Court of Protection Practice,* Jordan Publishing.

Aston, G (ed.) (2015) *Mental Capacity: Law and Practice*, 3rd edn, Jordan Publishing.

Association of Ambulance Chief Executives (2013) *UK Ambulance Services Clinical Practice Guidelines 2013*, Class Legal.

Bartlett, P (2008) *Blackstone's Guide to the Mental Capacity Act*, 2nd edn, Oxford University Press.

Bielanska, C (ed.) (2016) *Elderly Client Handbook*, 5th edn, Law Society Publishing.

Brindle, N *et al.* (2015) *A Clinician's Brief Guide to the Mental Capacity Act*, 2nd edn, RCPsych Publications.

British Medical Association (2001) *Consent, Rights and Choices in Health Care for Children and Young People*, Wiley Blackwell.

British Medical Association (2005) *Guidance for Doctors Preparing Professional Reports and Giving Evidence in Court*, British Medical Association.

British Medical Association (2007) *Expert Witness Guidance*, British Medical Association.

British Medical Association (2007) *Advance Decisions and Proxy Decision-making in Medical Treatment and Research*, British Medical Association.

British Medical Assocation (2012) *Consent Tool Kit*, 5th edn, British Medical Association.

British Medical Association (2009) *Medical Treatment for Adults with Incapacity: Guidance on Ethical and Medico-legal Issues in Scotland*, British Medical Association. See **http://bma.org.uk/practical-support-at-work/ethics/mental-capacity**.

British Medical Association (2011) *Safeguarding Vulnerable Adults – a Tool Kit for General Practitioners*, British Medical Association.

British Medical Association (2012) *Confidentiality and Disclosure of Health Information Tool Kit*, British Medical Association.

British Medical Association, Resuscitation Council (UK) and the Royal College of Nursing (2014) *Decisions Relating to Cardiopulmonary Resuscitation*, 3rd edn, Resuscitation Council, published online at **www.resus.org.uk/bold**.

British Psychological Society (2009) *Assessment of Effort in Clinical Testing of Cognitive Functioning for Adults*, British Psychological Society.

British Psychological Society (2010) *Audit Tool For Mental Capacity Assessments*, British Psychological Society.

Brown, R, Barber, P, Martin, D (2015) *The Mental Capacity Act 2005: A Guide for Practice*, Learning Matters.

Cabinet Office (2014) *The Right to Choose: Multi-agency Statutory Guidance for Dealing with Forced Marriage*, published online at **www.gov.uk/guidance/forced-marriage**.

Department of Health (2005) *Research Governance Framework for Health and Social Care*, 2nd edn, published online at **www.gov.uk**.

Department of Health and Welsh Assembly Government (February 2008) *Guidance on Nominating a Consultee for Research Involving Adults who Lack Capacity to Consent*, published online at **www.hra.nhs.net**.

Department of Health (2003) *Confidentiality: NHS Code of Practice*, Department of Health.

Department of Health (2009) *Reference Guide to Consent for Examination or Treatment*, 2nd edn, published online at **www.gov.uk**.

Department of Health (2010) *Confidentiality: NHS Code of Practice – Supplementary Guidance: Public Interest Disclosures*, published online at **www.gov.uk**.

Department of Health (2015) *Mental Health Act 1983 Code of Practice*, TSO available at **www.gov.uk**.

Department of Health (2014) *Care and Support Statutory Guidance*, issued under the Care Act 2014, available at **www.gov.uk**.

Department for Work and Pensions (2013) *Decision Makers' Guide*, published online at **www.gov.uk/government/collections/decision-makers-guide-staffguide**.

Department for Work and Pensions (2013) *Agents, Appointees, Attorneys, Deputies and Third Parties: Staff Guide*, published online at **www.gov.uk/government/publications/procedures-for-dealingwith-agents-appointees-attorneys-deputies-and-third-parties**.

Department of Health (2015) *Mental Health Act 1983 Code of Practice*, TSO, available at **www.gov.uk**.

Electoral Commission (2008) *Managing Electoral Registration in Great Britain: Guidance for Electoral Registration Officers*, published online at **www.electoralcommission.org.uk**.

Electoral Commission (2014) *Guidance on Assisted Applications in England and Wales*, published online at **www.electoralcommission.org.uk**.

Electoral Commission (2014) *Polling Station Handbook*, published online at **www.electoralcommission.org.uk**.

Electoral Commission (2015) *Individual Electoral Registration Guidance, Part 4: Maintaining Registration Throughout the Year*, published online at **www.electoralcommission.org.uk**.

Electoral Commission (2013) *Supporting Care Home Residents in England and Wales to Register to Vote*, available at **www.electoralcommission.org.uk**.

Empowerment Matters (2014) *Making Financial Decisions: Guidance for Assessing, Supporting and Empowering Specific Decision Making*, published online at **www.empowermentmatters.co.uk**.

Fennell, P, Letts, P, Wilson, J (2013) *Mental Health Tribunals: Law, Policy, and Practice*, Law Society Publishing.

Fernando, S and Keating, F (2008) *Mental Health in a Multi-ethnic Society: A Multidisciplinary Handbook*, 2nd edn, Routledge.

Frost, M, Lawson, S, Jacoby, R (2015) *Testamentary Capacity: Law, Practice and Medicine*, Oxford University Press.

General Medical Council (2008) *Consent: Patients and Doctors Making Decisions Together*, General Medical Council.

General Medical Council (2009) *Confidentiality: Guidance for Doctors*, General Medical Council.

General Medical Council (2013) *Good Medical Practice*, General Medical Council, published online at **www.gmc-uk.org.**

General Register Office (2015) *A Guide for Authorised Persons*, published online at **www-.gov.uk**.

Godefroy, S (2015) *Mental Health and Mental Capacity Law for Social Workers: An Introduction*, Learning Matters.

Gostin, L (ed.) (2010) *Principles of Mental Health Law and Policy*, Oxford University Press.

Graham, M (2015) *A Practical Guide to the Mental Capacity Act 2005: Putting the Principles of the Act into Practice*, Jessica Kingsley Publishers.

Greaney, N, Morris, F, Taylor, B (2008) *Mental Capacity Act: A Guide to the New Law*, 2nd edn, Law Society.

Grisso, T and Appelbaum, PS (1998) *Assessing Competence to Consent to Treatment: A Guide for Physicians and Other Health Professionals*, Oxford University Press.

Harper, R (2014) *Medical Treatment and the Law: Issues of Consent*, 2nd edn. Family Law.

Health and Social Care Information Centre (2013) *A Guide to Confidentiality in Health and Social Care: Treating Confidential Information with Respect*, version 1.1, Health and Social Care Information Centre.

Health and Social Care Information Centre (2014) *Code of Practice on Confidential Information*, Health and Social Care Information Centre, available at **http://systems.hscic.gov.uk/infogov/codes/cop/code.pdf**.

House of Lords Select Committee on the Mental Capacity Act 2005 (2014) *Mental Capacity Act 2005: Post-legislative Scrutiny*, HL Paper 139.

Jacob, R, Gunn, M, Holland, A (2013) *Mental Capacity Legislation: Principles and Practice*, RCPsych Publications.

Jacoby, R and Oppenheimer, C (eds) (2002) *Psychiatry in the Elderly*, 3rd edn, Oxford University Press.

Johnston, C and Francis, R (eds) (2010) *Medical Treatment: Decisions and the Law*, 2nd edn, Bloomsbury Professional.

Joint Committee on the Draft Mental Capacity Bill (2003) *Report of the Joint Committee on the Draft Mental Incapacity Bill*, Vol I (HL Paper 198-I, HC 1083-I), TSO.

Jones, R (2015) *Mental Health Act Manual*, 18th edn, Sweet & Maxwell.

Jones, R (2014) *Mental Capacity Act Manual*, 6th edn, Sweet & Maxwell.

Law Commission (1995) *Mental Incapacity* (Law Com No.231), TSO.

Law Commission (2015) *Mental Capacity and Deprivation of Liberty: A Consultation Paper* (No.222), TSO.

Law Society (2015) *Deprivation of Liberty: Collected guidance*, Law Society Publishing.

Lord Chancellor's Department (1997) *Who Decides? Making Decisions on Behalf of Mentally Incapacitated Adults* (Cm 3803), TSO.

Lord Chancellor's Department (1999) *Making Decisions: The Government's Proposals for Making Decisions on Behalf of Mentally Incapacitated Adults* (Cm 4465), TSO.

Lush, D (2015) *Cretney and Lush on Lasting Powers of Lasting and Enduring Powers of Attorney*, Jordan Publishing.

Lush, D and Rees, D (eds) (2015) *Heywood and Massey: Court of Protection Practice*, 13th edn (looseleaf), Sweet & Maxwell.

Lynch, J (2010) *Consent to Treatment*, CRC Press.

Mandelstam, M (2013) *Safeguarding Adults and the Law*, 2nd edn, Jessica Kingsley Publishers.

Ministry of Justice (2008) *Mental Capacity Act 2005: Deprivation of Liberty Safeguards – Code of Practice to Supplement the Main Mental Capacity Act 2005 Code of Practice*, TSO.

Ministry of Justice (2011) *Achieving Best Evidence in Criminal Proceedings: Guidance on Interviewing Victims and Witnesses, and Guidance on Using Special Measures*, published online at **www.cps.gov.uk**.

National Institute for Mental Health in England (2009) *The Legal Aspects of the Care and Treatment of Children and Young People with Mental Disorder: A Guide for Professionals*, National Institute for Mental Health in England .

Office of the Public Guardian et al (2009) *Making Decisions: A Guide for People Who Work in Health and Social Care*, 4th edn, The Mental Capacity Implementation Programme.

Office of the Public Guardian (2007) *Mental Capacity Act 2005 Code of Practice*, TSO.

Office of the Public Guardian (2013) *Safeguarding Policy: Protecting Vulnerable Adults*, published online at **www.gov.uk/government/publications/safeguarding-policy-protectingvulnerable-adults**.

Office of the Public Guardian (2015) *Make, Register or End a Lasting Power of Attorney*, published online at **www.gov.uk/power-of-attorney**.

Richards, S and Mughal, AF (2009) *Working with the Mental Capacity Act 2005*, 2nd edn, Matrix Training Associates.

Sewell, H (2008) *Working with Ethnicity, Race and Culture in Mental Health: A Handbook for Practitioners*, Jessica Kingsley Publishers.

Social Care Institute for Excellence (2014) *Report 70: The Mental Capacity Act (MCA) and Care Planning*, Social Care Institute for Excellence, published online at **www.scie-.org.uk**.

Taylor, C, Krish, J, Farnham, F (2009) *Advising Mentally Disordered Offenders: A Practical Guide*, 2nd edn, Law Society Publishing.

Royal College of Physicians (2013) *Prolonged Disorders of Consciousness: National Clinical Guidelines*, Royal College of Physicians.

Rucke Keene A *et al.* (2014) *Court of Protection Handbook: A User's Guide*, Legal Action Group.

World Health Organization (1992–1994) *International Classification of Diseases*, 10th edn (ICD-10), published online at **www.who.int/classifications/icd/en**.

World Medical Association (1964) *Declaration of Helsinki*, World Medical Association, published online at **www.wma.net**.

Index

absent witness 12.3.2

advance statements/decisions
see **medical treatment**

alcohol use/addiction 3.4.1,
17.8.1, 18.3.2, 18.4.1

Alzheimer's disease 17.8.1
see also **dementia**

**American Psychiatric
Association, Diagnostic and
Statistical Manual (DSM-5)**
17.7.4, 18.3.1

anorexia nervosa 17.8.1, 18.3.6

appointeeship
social security benefits 5.7.1

assessment of capacity 1.1
appearance and behaviour 17.8.1
assessors 2.8, 3.6, 17.3.5
background information 17.7.1,
18.4.1
best interests *see* **best interests**
children under 16 3.8.1, 3.8.2
cognition 17.8.1
confidentiality 2.2
consent 2.4
Court of Protection Special Visitor
2.4
cultural factors 2.3, 2.7, 3.7, 5.6.3,
11.4.2, 17.7.3, 18.1, 18.4
decision-specific/time-specific nature
of capacity 3.3, 5.6.2, 16.1, 17.4
defining capacity 17.3
depression 17.5.5
'diagnostic test' 17.3.2
disclosure of information 2.2
doctors 2.7, 18.4
assessment tools 17.9
choice of doctor 2.8, 3.6, 17.3.5
'diagnostic test' 17.3.2
enhancing mental capacity 17.5
guidance for 17.3–17.4

mental state examination 17.8.1,
18.4.2
preparing for an assessment 17.4
recording the assessment 17.6
retrospective assessment 17.10
role in assessment 17.3.3
systematic approach 17.7
enhancing capacity 2.3, 2.8, 17.5
best time and place for assessment
17.5.3
depression 17.5.5
duty to enhance 17.5
fluctuating capacity 17.5.1
improving/supporting
communication 17.5.2
supported decision-making 17.5.4
environment for 2.3, 17.5.3
ethnic factors 2.3, 2.7, 3.7, 5.6.3,
11.4.2, 17.7.3, 18.1, 18.4
FACE Mental Capacity Assessment
17.9
form COP3 5.6.2, 18.1, 18.2.3,
Appendix G
inability to make a decision 17.3.2
information from others 17.7.3,
18.4.1
insight 17.8.1
intellectual functioning 17.8.1
learning disabilities 2.7, 2.8
MacCAT-T 17.9
MCA Code of Practice 3.2
medical assessment *see* **medical
assessment of mental conditions**
medical diagnosis 17.7.4
medical records and reports 17.7.2,
18.4.4
medication, effects of 2.3
medico-legal expertise 18.2.4
memory 17.8.1
Mental Health Act 1983, under 2.4
mental state examination 17.8.1,
18.4.2

assessment of capacity – *continued*
  mood 17.8.1
  orientation 17.8.1
  perception 17.8.1
  personality disorders 17.8.1
  preparing for an assessment 17.4
  psychiatric diagnoses *see* **psychiatric diagnoses**
  recording the assessment 17.6
  refusal to be assessed 2.2.2, 2.4, 17.3.4
    influence of third party 2.4, 3.5
  religious factors 2.3, 2.7, 3.7, 5.6.3, 11.4.2, 17.7.3, 18.1, 18.4
  retrospective assessment 17.10
  review 2.7, 4.2.1
  specialist knowledge 18.2.1
  speech 17.8.1
  summary of points 2.7
  systematic approach 17.7
  thought 17.8.1
  time and place for assessment 2.3, 17.5.3
  tools 17.9
  who should assess 2.8, 3.6, 17.3.5
  young people aged 16 or 17 3.8.1, 3.8.3

assisted suicide 3.8.4

attorneys *see* **powers of attorney**

best interests 2.1.2, 2.4, 3.7
  all relevant circumstances 3.7
  care/treatment for adults lacking capacity to consent 13.5.1
  checklist 3.7
  deprivation of liberty 15.2, 15.4.1, 15.4.2
  disclosure in patient's best interests 13.8.4
  encouraging participation 3.7
  equal considerations 3.7
  life sustaining treatment 3.7
  LPAs 5.3
  Mental Capacity Act 2005 2.5.1, 2.5.2, 3.1, 3.2, 3.7, Appendix A
  non-discrimination 3.7
  permitting participation 3.7
  person's wishes, feelings, beliefs and values 3.7
  regaining capacity 3.7
  views of other people 3.7
  young people 3.8.3

brain damage 3.4.1

British Medical Association (BMA) 1.3.2
  advance statements 13.7.1
  expert evidence 4.2.7

burden of proof 4.2.1, 4.2.3
  gifts 7.4
  litigation capacity 8.3
  rape 12.2.2
  testamentary capacity 6.3

care workers
  sexual offences 12.2.4

certificate as to capacity to conduct proceedings 8.4, 18.1, Appendix F

character evidence 4.2.5

children 1.3.2, 3.8.1
  assessment of capacity 3.8.1
  behavioural/emotional disorders with childhood onset 18.3.10
  child and adolescent psychiatry 18.2.2
  Court of Protection 3.8.1, 3.8.2, 3.8.3
  family relationships 11.2
  litigation capacity 8.1
  Mental Capacity Act 2005 3.8.1
  under 16 3.8.1, 3.8.2

civil partnership
  capacity to dissolve 11.5
  capacity to enter into 11.4
  see also **marriage**

classification of mental disorders 17.7.4, 18.3.1

cognition
  mental state and 17.8.1

Committee on the Rights of Persons with Disabilities 3.9

common law test of capacity 4.1, 11.2
  gifts 7.2, 7.3
  litigation capacity 8.2.1
  property and affairs management 5.6.1
  sexual activity 12.2.1
  testamentary capacity 6.2, 6.3

communication problems 1.3.2, 2.3, 3.4.2
  improving/supporting communication 17.5.2
  speech 17.8.1

Community Treatment Orders (CTOs) 16.4

Compliance Office for Legal Practice (COLP) 2.2.1

concussion 3.4.1

confidentiality
Data Protection Act 2.2, 13.8.5
duty of 2.2, 13.8
information from others 18.4.1
professional ethics 2.2, 17.3.4
see also **disclosure**

contractual capacity 9.1
attorneys 9.6
checklist 9.7
deputies 9.6
EPAs 9.6
general rules 9.2
impact of Mental Capacity Act 2005 9.4.2, 9.5
LPAs 9.6
necessaries 9.4
Mental Capacity Act 2005 9.4.2
Sale of Goods Act 1979 9.4.1
voidable contracts 9.3

Court of Protection 3.1,
Appendix C
appointment of deputies *see* **deputies**
assessment by Special Visitor 2.4
children 3.8.1, 3.8.2, 3.8.3
declaration as to capacity 3.6
deprivation of liberty 15.3, 15.4.1
EPAs 5.3.3, 5.4.2
evidence of the person themselves 4.2.6
form COP3 5.6.2, 18.1, 18.2.3, Appendix G
litigation capacity 8.1, 8.5, 8.6
LPAs 5.3.2, 5.3.3
personal relationships 11.2
personal welfare orders 15.3, 15.4.1
property and affairs management 5.5
statutory wills 6.9
young people 3.8.3

courts
role of 4.1
see also **Court of Protection; evidence**

Creutzfeldt-Jakob Disease (CJD)
innovative treatment 14.5

criminal law 1.3.2, 11.1
see also **sexual offences**

decision-making 1.1, 1.1.1, 17.3.1
communicating decisions 1.3.2, 3.4.2
impairment or disturbance 3.4.1, 3.4.3
inability to take a decision 3.4.2, 3.4.3
Mental Capacity Act 2005 3.4
supported decision-making 17.5.4

decision-specific/time-specific nature of capacity 3.3, 5.6.2, 16.1, 17.4

Declaration of Helsinki 14.3

definition of capacity 3.3

delusions 6.2, 17.8.1, 18.3.3, 18.4

dementia 1.3.2, 3.4.1, 4.3, 17.8.1, 18.2.2
Alzheimer's disease 17.8.1
depression 17.5.5
fluctuating capacity 17.5.1
physical examination 18.4.3
testamentary capacity 6.1, 7.2

depression 15.2, 17.5.5, 18.3.4

deprivation of liberty 15.1, 15.2
advance decision to refuse medical treatment and 15.4.2
authorising 15.3
best interests 15.2, 15.4.1, 15.4.2
Bournewood gap 15.1
Court of Protection 15.3, 15.4.1
DoLS regime 15.1, 15.3, 15.4.2, 16.2, 16.3
European Convention on Human Rights 15.1, 15.2
medical treatment 13.5.2, 13.5.3
Mental Capacity Act 2005 13.5.3, 15.3, Appendix A
Mental Health Act 1983 15.3, 15.4.2, 15.4.3, 16.2, 16.3, 16.6
personal welfare orders of the Court of Protection 15.3, 15.4.1
restraint 13.5.3, 15.2, 16.2, 16.6
safeguards 15.4.2
test of capacity 15.4.2

deputies
appointment 2.1.2, 5.6, 5.7.1, 8.5
contractual capacity 9.6
gifts made by 7.7
medical treatment 13.3, 13.6.4
property and affairs deputies 5.6
welfare deputy 13.6.4

direct payments 1.3.2

disclosure 2.2, 13.8
  best interests of patient 13.8.4
  consent to 2.2
  doctors 2.2.2, 13.8
  duty of confidentiality 2.2, 13.8
  health professionals 13.8
  lawyers 2.2.1
  patients lacking capacity to consent to 2.2, 13.8.2
  personal information 2.2
  professional ethics 2.2, 17.3.4
  public interest disclosure 2.2, 2.2.2, 13.8.3
  required by law 13.8.1
  under Data Protection Act 13.8.5
divorce 11.5
doctors 1.1
  assessment of capacity 2.7, 18.4
    assessment tools 17.9
    choice of doctor 2.8, 3.6, 17.3.5
    'diagnostic test' 17.3.2
    enhancing mental capacity 17.5
    guidance for 17.3–17.4
    mental state examination 17.8.1, 18.4.2
    preparing for an assessment 17.4
    recording the assessment 17.6
    retrospective assessment 17.10
    role 17.3.3
    systematic approach 17.7
  balancing empowerment with protection 17.2
  confidentiality and disclosure 2.2.2, 13.8
  duty to enhance mental capacity 2.3, 17.5
  guidance for 2.6, 17.1–17.10
  independent medical advice 17.1, 17.2
  information for 1.3.1
  lawyers instructing 4.3
    sample letter Appendix H
  medico-legal expertise 18.2.4
  mental state examination 17.8.1, 18.4.2
  professional ethics 2.2, 17.3.4
  receiving instructions 4.4
  retrospective assessment 17.10
  witnessing documents 2.2.1, 2.7, 4.5, 4.5.1, 6.5
drug use/addiction 3.4.1, 18.4.1
duress 2.6

inherent jurisdiction of the High Court 2.4, 3.5, 13.4.4, 15.3, 16.6
  medical treatment 13.4.4
  see also **undue influence**

eating disorders 17.8.1, 18.3.6
electro-convulsive therapy (ECT) 16.5
enduring powers of attorney (EPAs) 2.1.2, 5.1, 5.4
  capacity to make 5.4.1
  capacity to revoke 5.4.2
  concurrent authority 5.4
  contractual capacity 9.6
  definition of 'mental disorder' 5.6.4
  gifts 7.6.2
  LPAs compared 5.3, 5.3.1, 5.3.3
  medical treatment 13.6.1
  notification 5.4
  objections 5.4
  property and affairs management and 5.5, 5.6.4
  registration 5.4, 5.4.2, 5.6.4
  revocation 5.4
  test of capacity 5.3.1
  see also **powers of attorney**
enhancing capacity 2.3, 2.8, 17.5
  best time and place for assessment 17.5.3
  depression 17.5.5
  duty to enhance 2.3, 17.5
  fluctuating capacity 17.5.1
  improving/supporting communication 17.5.2
  supported decision-making 17.5.4
European Convention on Human Rights (ECHR) 3.9
  deprivation of liberty 15.1, 15.2
  right to form relationships 11.1
euthanasia 3.8.4
evidence
  burden of proof 4.2.1, 4.2.3
  burden of proof *see* **burden of proof**
  character evidence 4.2.5
  expert *see* **expert evidence**
  fluctuating capacity 2.7, 2.8, 4.2.2
  litigation capacity 8.1, 8.2.1, 8.3
  lucid intervals 4.2.2
  medical evidence 4.5.1
  opinion evidence 4.2.7
  person themselves, of 4.2.6

presumption of capacity 4.2.1
presumption of continuance 4.2.1
sexual offences 12.3
  absent witness 12.3.2
  vulnerable witnesses 12.3.1
similar fact evidence 4.2.5
standard of proof *see* **standard of proof**
testamentary capacity 6.5
weight of evidence 4.2.8
wills 6.5
  'golden rule' 2.2.1, 4.5.1, 6.5, 18.1
witnesses 2.4
witnessing documents 2.7, 4.5, 6.5, 18.1
wills 2.2.1, 4.5.1, 6.5, 18.1
expert evidence 4.1, 4.2.7
  litigation capacity 8.3
  medical evidence 4.5.1
  medico-legal expertise 2.8, 18.2.4
  witnessing documents 4.5

FACE Mental Capacity Assessment 17.9
family relationships 11.2
  decisions about 11.2.1
  Mental Capacity Act 2005 3.8.4
  see also **marriage**; **personal relationships**
financial abuse
  gifts 7.8
  protection from 5.8
financial LPAs 5.3
fluctuating capacity 2.7, 3.3, 3.4, 17.5.1
  evidence 2.8, 4.2.2
  see also **lucid intervals**
forced marriage 11.4.1, 11.4.2
forensic psychiatry 18.2.2
form COP3 5.6.2, 18.1, 18.2.3, Appendix G

gifts 7.1
  attorneys 7.6
  burden of proof 7.4
  checklist 7.5
  claims to which giver ought to give effect 7.5.4
  common law test of capacity 7.2, 7.3
  deputies 7.7
  effect of transaction 7.5.2
  extent of property 7.5.3
  Mental Capacity Act 2005 7.3, 7.4

nature of transaction 7.5.1
presumption of capacity 7.4
risk of financial abuse 7.8
gifts by attorneys 7.6
  EPAs 7.6.2
  LPAs 7.6.1
'golden rule' 2.2.1, 4.5.1, 6.5, 18.1

hallucinations 17.8.1, 18.3.1, 18.3.3, 18.4
health and welfare LPA 5.3, 13.6.1
  creation 13.6.2
  EPA compared 13.6.1
  registration 13.6.2
  scope 13.6.3
  treatment without consent 13.3
  see also **lasting powers of attorney**
High Court
  inherent jurisdiction 2.4, 3.5, 13.4.4, 15.3, 16.6
hypomania 9.3

impairing capacity 2.8
incapacity 2.1.2
  consequences 2.1.2
  loss of capacity of existing client 2.1.2
  potential client 2.1.2
Independent Mental Capacity Advocate (IMCA) 3.7, 13.5.1
information from others
  assessment of capacity 17.7.3, 18.4.1
  pre-morbid personality 18.4.1
information retention 3.4.2
innovative treatment 14.5
  Creutzfeldt-Jakob Disease (CJD) 14.5
  see also **research**
insight
  mental state and 17.8.1
insolvency proceedings
  incapacitated person 8.1, 8.2.3
  litigation capacity 8.1, 8.2.3
intellectual functioning
  mental state and 17.8.1

lasting powers of attorney (LPAs) 2.1.2, 3.1, 5.1, 5.3
  best interests 5.3
  capacity to make 5.3.1
  capacity to revoke 5.3.3

lasting powers of attorney
  (LPAs) – *continued*
    certificate to confirm understanding
      5.3.1
    certificate provider 5.3, 5.3.1
    contractual capacity 9.6
    donor's decision as to assessment of
      capacity 5.3
    EPAs compared 5.3, 5.3.1, 5.3.3
    evidence of capacity 2.4
    financial LPAs 5.3
    gifts 7.6.1
    health and welfare decisions *see*
      health and welfare LPA
    legal duty of attorneys 5.3
    MCA Code of Practice 5.3
    Mental Capacity Act 2005 5.3
    notification 5.3.2
    objections 5.3.2
    property and affairs LPAs 5.3
    registration 5.1, 5.3, 5.3.2
    requirements 5.3
    revocation 5.3.3
    two or more attorneys 5.3
    see also **powers of attorney**
Law Society
  Children Law Accreditation
    Scheme 1.3.2
  Deprivation of Liberty: A Practical
    Guide 15.1, 15.2
  Practice Note on gifts of assets 7.1
  Practice Note on LPAs 5.3.1
  Vulnerable Clients Practice Note 2.6,
    5.8
lawyers 1.1, 2.8
  capacity to instruct 2.1.1
  confidentiality and disclosure 2.2.1
  guidelines 18.1
    general guidance 18.5
    medical assessment of mental
      conditions 18.4
    psychiatric diagnoses 17.3
    who should assess the person 18.2
  information for 1.3.1
  instructing doctors 4.3
    sample letter Appendix H
  loss of capacity of existing client
    2.1.2
  potential client 2.1.2
  professional ethics 2.2
learning disabilities
  assessment of capacity 2.7, 2.8
  confidentiality 2.2

  disclosure of information 13.8.2
  entitlement to vote 10.2, 10.3, 10.4.1
  giving evidence in court 12.3.1
  health and welfare deputies 13.6.4
  as impairment/disturbance 3.4.1
  as incapacity/vulnerability 3.5
  marriage 11.4.2
  mental age 2.7
  mental state examination 17.8.1
  psychiatry of learning disabilities
    18.2.2
  sexual offences against people with
    12.2.4
  sexual relationships 11.3.1
  supported decision-making 17.5.4
  vulnerable individuals 3.5
liberty *see* **deprivation of**
  liberty
life-sustaining treatment
  advance decision refusing 13.7.4
  best interests 3.7
litigation capacity 2.4, 8.1
  applying the test 8.3
  burden of proof 8.3
  certificate as to capacity to conduct
    proceedings 8.4, 18.1, Appendix F
  child 8.1
  common law test of capacity 8.2.1
  Court of Protection 8.1, 8.5, 8.6
  evidence 8.1, 8.2.1, 8.3
  expert evidence 8.3
  implications of incapacity 8.5
  incapacitated person 8.1, 8.2.3
  insolvency proceedings 8.1, 8.2.3
  issue-specific nature of test 8.2.1, 8.3
  Mental Capacity Act 2005 8.2.2
  protected beneficiary 8.1, 8.3, 8.5
  protected person 8.1, 8.2.1, 8.5
  test of capacity to litigate 8.2
litigation friend 2.1.2, 8.1, 8.2.1,
  8.4, 8.6
  certificate of suitability 8.4
  criteria for appointment 8.4
  Official Solicitor as Appendix E
lucid intervals 2.8, 17.5.1
  evidence 4.2.2
  see also **fluctuating capacity**

MacArthur Competence
  Assessment Tool for
  Treatment (MacCAT-T) 17.9
marriage
  capacity to marry 11.4

capacity to separate or divorce 11.5
effect of mental disorder 11.4.1
forced marriage 11.4.1, 11.4.2
implications 11.4.3
objections 11.4.2
revocation of will 6.8
voidable 11.4.1
see also **personal relationships**
MCA Code of Practice 2.5.2,
  3.1, Appendix B
  assessment of capacity 3.2
  capacity to manage property and
    affairs 5.6.2
  compliance/non-compliance 2.5.2
  confidentiality 2.2
  contracts for necessaries 9.4.2
  expert evidence 4.2.7
  gifts 7.3
  LPAs 5.3, 7.6.1
  people assessed as lacking capacity
    2.5.2
  review of capacity 4.2.1
  statutory duty to have regard to
    2.5.2, 2.7, 3.1
  test of capacity 3.4, 7.3
**medical assessment of mental
  conditions** 17.3.3, 18.4
  background history 18.4.1
  drugs and alcohol history 18.4.1
  history of presenting complaint
    18.4.1
  information from others 17.7.3,
    18.4.1
  medical records 18.4.4
  mental state examination 18.4.2
  physical examination 18.4.3
  pre-morbid personality 18.4.1
  previous medical history 18.4.1
  previous psychiatric history 18.4.1
  professional ethics 17.3.4
medical diagnosis 17.7.4
  see also **psychiatric diagnoses**
medical records and reports
  recording the assessment 17.6
  use in assessment 17.7.2, 18.4.4
medical treatment 13.1
  adults lacking capacity to consent
    acts in connection with 13.5.2
    best interests 13.5.1
    restraint 13.5.3
    serious medical treatment 13.5.1,
      13.5.4, 13.6.3, Appendix D

advance decision to refuse medical
  treatment 13.3, 13.7, 13.7.2, 16.2,
    16.5
  applicability 13.7.7
  deprivation of liberty safeguard
    15.4.2
  effect 13.7.8
  life-sustaining treatment 13.7.4
  making 13.7.3
  safeguards 13.7.5
  validity 13.7.6
advance statements 13.7.1
basic information 13.2
capacity to consent
  duress/undue influence 13.4.4
  Mental Capacity Act 2005 13.4.1
  test of capacity 13.4.2
deprivation of liberty 13.5.2, 13.5.3
deputy appointed by Court of
  Protection 13.3, 13.6.4
disclosure 2.2.2, 13.8
  duty of confidence 13.8
  patient's best interests 13.8.4
  patients lacking capacity to consent
    to 13.8.2
  public interest 2.2.2, 13.8.3
  required by law 13.8.1
  under Data Protection Act 13.8.5
Independent Mental Capacity
  Advocate (IMCA) 13.5.1
LPA *see* **health and welfare LPA**
Mental Capacity Act 2005 13.1,
  13.4.1, 16.2
Mental Health Act 1983 16.1–16.6
need for consent 13.2
physical disorder 16.6, 17.5
professional ethics 17.3.4
refusal
  advance decisions 13.3, 13.7, 13.7.2,
    15.4.2, 16.2, 16.5
  capacity to refuse 13.4.3
  life-sustaining treatment 13.7.4
  Mental Capacity Act 2005 13.4.1
serious medical treatment 13.5.1,
  13.5.4, 13.6.3, Appendix D
test of capacity 13.4.2
treatment without consent 13.2, 13.3
  Mental Health Act 1983 16.2,
    16.4–16.5
valid consent 13.2
medication, effects of 2.3
medico-legal expertise 2.8,
  18.2.4

memory
  mental state and 17.8.1
mental age 2.7
Mental Capacity Act 2005
  1.1.1, 1.1.2, Appendix A
  application and exclusions 3.1, 3.8
  assisted suicide 3.8.4
  balance of probabilities 4.2.4
  barriers to implementation 1.1.1
  best interests 2.5.1, 2.5.2, 3.1, 3.2, 3.7,
    Appendix A
  children under 16 3.8.1
  Code of Practice *see* **MCA Code of**
    Practice
  contracts for necessaries 9.4.2
  contractual capacity 9.5
  decision-making 3.4
    impairment or disturbance 3.4.1,
      3.4.3
    inability to take a decision 3.4.2,
      3.4.3
  decisions excluded from 3.8.4
  definition of mental capacity 3.3
  deprivation of liberty 13.5.3, 15.3,
    Appendix A
  empowering ethos 1.1.1, 17.2
  expert evidence 4.2.7
  family relationships 3.8.4
  gifts 7.3, 7.4
  inability to take a decision 3.4.2
  legal framework 3.1, 4.1
  litigation capacity 8.2.2
  LPAs 5.3
  medical treatment 13.1, 13.4.1
  Mental Health Act 1983 compared
    1.3.2, 16.2
  mental health law and 3.8.4
  powers of attorney 5.1, 5.3
  presumption of capacity 2.1.1, 2.8,
    3.2, 4.2.1, 7.4
  property and affairs management
    5.6.2
  research 3.1, 14.1, 14.2, 14.3, 14.4.2
  restraint 13.5.3, 15.2, Appendix A
  standard of proof 4.2.4
  statutory principles 3.2, 4.2.1,
    Appendix B
  test of capacity 3.4
  UN CRPD compliance 3.9
  unlawful killing 3.8.4
  voting rights 3.8.4
  vulnerable individuals 1.1.1, 3.5
  young people aged 16 or 17 3.8.1,
    3.8.3

Mental Health Act 1983 1.1.2,
  16.1
  admission under 15.4.3, 16.3
  assessment of capacity 2.4
  deprivation of liberty 15.3, 15.4.2,
    15.4.3, 16.2, 16.3, 16.6
  Mental Capacity Act 2005
    compared 1.3.2, 16.2
  restraint 16.2, 16.6
  treatment for mental disorder 16.2
    patients detained in hospital 16.5
    patients not detained in hospital
      16.4
  treatment for physical disorder 16.6
mental retardation 18.3.8
mental state 17.8
  examination 17.8.1, 18.4.2
mood
  mental state and 17.8.1
  mood disorders 18.3.4

neurological conditions 18.2.2,
  18.4.3
neuropsychiatry 18.2.2
Northern Ireland 1.3.2

Office of the Public Guardian
  (OPG) Appendix E
  capacity to make LPAs 5.3.1
  duties 5.8
  gifts 7.7
  registration of EPAs 5.4, 5.4.2, 5.6.4
  registration of LPAs 5.1, 5.3, 5.3.2
Official Solicitor
  litigation friend 8.4
opinion evidence 4.2.7
ordinary powers of attorney
  5.1, 5.2
orientation
  mental state and 17.8.1

partial incapacity 3.3
perception
  mental state and 17.8.1
personal relationships
  civil law 11.1
  Court of Protection 11.2
  decisions about 11.2.1
  right to form relationships 11.1
  see also **civil partnership; family**
    relationships; marriage; sexual
    relationships

personal welfare orders of the Court of Protection 15.3, 15.4.1

personality disorders 17.8.1

physical examination 18.4.3

physical incapacity 1.3.2

polling station 10.5

post-traumatic stress disorder (PTSD) 18.3.5

postal voting 10.6

powers of attorney
general power of attorney 5.1
nature 5.1
ordinary power of attorney 5.1, 5.2
specific power of attorney 5.1
types 5.1
see also **enduring powers of attorney; lasting powers of attorney**

pre-morbid personality 18.4.1

presumption of capacity 2.1.1, 2.8, 3.2, 4.2.1, 7.4, 8.3, 17.2

presumption of continuance 4.2.1

privacy *see* **confidentiality; disclosure**

professional ethics 2.2, 17.3.4

property and affairs deputies 5.6

property and affairs management 5.5
checklist 5.6.3
civil litigation 5.5
common law test for incapacity 5.6.1
EPAs 5.6.4
extent of property and affairs 2.2.1, 5.6.3, 5.6.4
LPAs 5.3
Mental Capacity Act 2005 5.6.2
personal information 5.6.3
protected party/protected beneficiary 5.5
test of capacity 5.5, 5.6.1, 5.6.4
vulnerability of person 5.6.3, 5.6.4
see also **Court of Protection; gifts; powers of attorney; wills**

proxy voting 10.6

psychiatric diagnoses
behavioural syndrome associated with physiological disturbances/physical factors 18.3.6
behavioural/emotional disorders with childhood/adolescent onset 18.3.10
categories of diagnoses 18.3.1
disorders of psychological development 18.3.9
medical diagnosis 17.7.4
mental retardation 18.3.8
misuse of psychotropic substances 18.3.2
mood disorders 18.3.4
neurotic disorders 18.3.5
psychiatric sub-specialities 18.2.2
psychotic disorders 18.3.3
somatoform disorders 18.3.5
stress-related disorders 18.3.5

psychological development, disorders of 18.3.9

psychotropic substances *see* **alcohol use/addiction; drug use/addiction**

Public Guardian *see* **Office of the Public Guardian**

rape 12.2.2

regaining capacity 3.7

reports *see* **medical records and reports**

research
adults lacking capacity 14.4
capacity to consent to 14.2
clinical trials
definition 14.4.3
emergency situations 14.4.4
EU Directive 14.1
Regulations 2004 14.1, 14.3, 14.4.1, 14.4.3
Regulations 2014 14.1, 14.3, 14.4.1
Declaration of Helsinki 14.3
ethical framework 14.3
governance 14.3
innovative treatment 14.5
legal framework 14.4.1
Mental Capacity Act 2005 3.1, 14.3, 14.4.2
see also **innovative treatment**

restraint
Mental Capacity Act 2005 13.5.3, 15.2, Appendix A
Mental Health Act 1983 16.2, 16.6

retrospective assessment 17.10

schizoaffective disorder 18.3.3

schizophrenia 17.3.2, 17.8.1,
18.2.2, 18.3.3
Scotland 1.3.2
serious medical treatment
13.5.1, 13.5.4, 13.6.3, Appendix D
sexual offences 1.3.2, 11.1, 12.1,
12.2.4
care workers 12.2.4
consent and mental capacity 11.1,
12.2.1
giving evidence in court 12.3
absent witnesses 12.3.2
assisting vulnerable witnesses
12.3.1
rape 12.2.2
Sexual Offences Act 2003 12.2
special measures directions 12.3.1
sexual relationships 11.3
capacity to consent 11.3.1
see also **personal relationships**
similar fact evidence 4.2.5
social security benefits
appointeeship 5.7.1
capacity to claim and receive 5.7
solicitors *see* **lawyers**
**Solicitors Regulation
Authority** 2.2.1
Code of Practice 2.6
Handbook 2.6
special measures directions
12.3.1
specialist knowledge
assessment of capacity 18.2.1
speech
mental state and 17.8.1
standard of proof 4.2.4, 4.3
balance of probabilities 4.2.4, 4.3, 8.3
beyond reasonable doubt 4.2.4, 4.3,
8.3
statutory wills 6.9
suicide, assisted 3.8.4
supervening incapacity 6.4

temporary incapacity 3.3, 17.5
test of capacity 2.1.1, 2.8, 3.4,
4.3
balance of probabilities 4.2.4, 4.3, 8.3
beyond reasonable doubt 4.2.4, 4.3,
8.3
common law *see* **common law test
of capacity**
contractual capacity 9.5
defining capacity 17.2

deprivation of liberty 15.4.2
'diagnostic test' 17.3.2
EPAs 5.3.1
family or personal relationships
11.2.1
gifts 7.2, 7.3
guidelines for lawyers 18.1
inability to make a decision 17.3.2
issue-specific nature 2.1.1, 5.6.1,
8.2.1, 8.3, 11.2.1
litigation capacity 8.2
medical treatment 13.4.2
Mental Capacity Act 2005 3.4
property and affairs management
5.5, 5.6.1, 5.6.4
testamentary capacity 6.3, 6.9
testamentary capacity 6.1, 6.2
burden of proof 6.3
checklist 6.7
claims of others 6.7.4
common law test of capacity 6.2, 6.3
dementia 6.1, 7.2
draftsman's duty to ascertain
capacity 6.5, 6.6
effects of making a will 6.7.2
evidence 6.5
sample letter to GP requesting
evidence of Appendix H
extent of property 6.7.3
'golden rule' 2.2.1, 4.5.1, 6.5, 18.1
marriage and 6.8
Mental Capacity Act 2005 6.3, 6.9
nature of act of making a will 6.7.1
revocation of will 6.8
supervening incapacity 6.4
see also **wills**
thought
mental state and 17.8.1
**time-specific/decision-specific
nature of capacity** 3.3, 5.6.2,
16.1, 17.4

undue influence 2.6
inherent jurisdiction of the High
Court 2.4, 3.5, 13.4.4, 15.3, 16.6
medical treatment 13.4.4
protection from financial abuse 5.8
SRA Code of Conduct 5.8
**United Nations Convention on
the Rights of Persons with
Disabilities (CPRD)** 1.1.2,
3.1, 3.9
entitlement to vote 10.2

equal recognition before the law 3.9
relationships 11.1
United Nations Declaration on
Human Rights 11.1, 11.6
unlawful killing 3.8.4

voidable contracts 9.3
voting
entitlement to vote 10.1
legal incapacity to vote 10.1, 10.3
Mental Capacity Act 2005 3.8.4
mental capacity to cast a vote 10.1
polling station 10.5
postal voting 10.6
proxy voting 10.6
registration 10.4, 10.7
individual registration 10.4.1
place of residence 10.4.2
vulnerable individuals 2.6
influence of third person 2.4, 3.5
Law Society Practice Note 2.6, 5.8
property and affairs management
5.6.3, 5.6.4
SRA Code of Conduct 2.6
see also **duress**; **undue influence**

weight of evidence 4.2.8
welfare LPA *see* **health and**
welfare LPA
wills 2.1.1, 6.1
capacity to make *see* **testamentary**
capacity
challenges 2.4
confidentiality 2.2.1
destruction 6.8

evidence 6.5
home-made 6.1
intestacy 6.1, 6.4
nature 6.1
revocation 6.1, 6.8
statutory wills 6.9
witnessed by medical practitioner
2.2.1, 4.5.1, 6.5, 18.1
witnessing documents
expert witnesses 4.5
medical professionals 2.2.1, 2.7, 4.5,
6.5, 18.1
wills 2.2.1, 4.5, 4.5.1, 6.5, 18.1
World Health Organization
International Classification
of Diseases (WHO ICD-10)
17.7.4, 18.3.1
World Medical Association
Declaration of Helsinki 14.3

young people 1.3.2, 3.8.1
aged 16 or 17 3.8.1, 3.8.3
assessment of capacity 3.8.1, 3.8.3
behavioural/emotional disorders with
adolescent onset 18.3.10
best interests 3.8.3
care or treatment decisions 3.8.3
child and adolescent psychiatry
18.2.2
Court of Protection 3.8.3
electro-convulsive therapy (ECT)
16.5
Mental Capacity Act 2005 3.8.3,
3.8.1